Kamisama Kiss

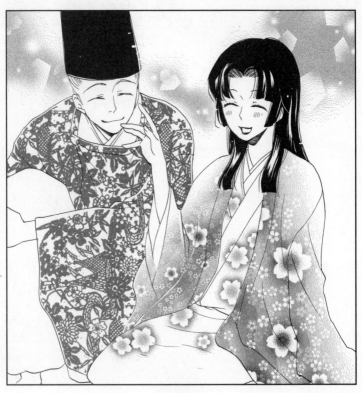

Story & Art by
Julietta Suzuki

CHARACTERS

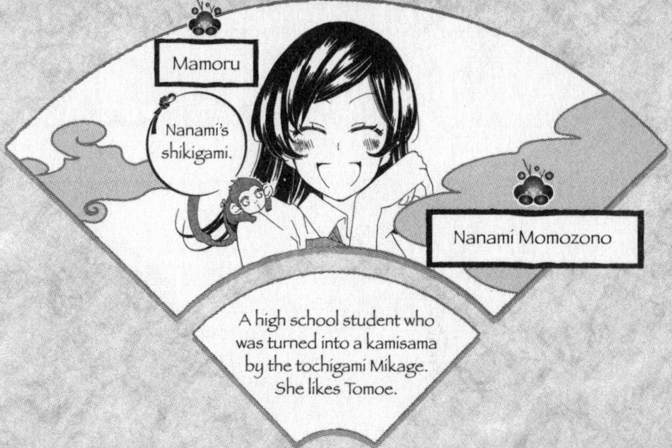
Mamoru
Nanami's shikigami.
Nanami Momozono
A high school student who was turned into a kamisama by the tochigami Mikage. She likes Tomoe.

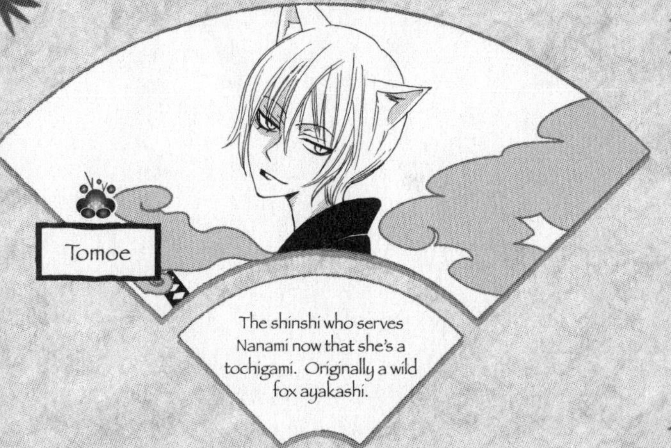
Tomoe
The shinshi who serves Nanami now that she's a tochigami. Originally a wild fox ayakashi.

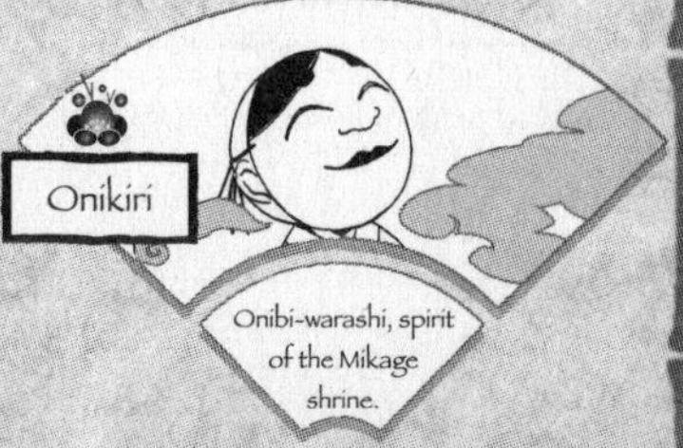
Onikiri
Onibi-warashi, spirit of the Mikage shrine.

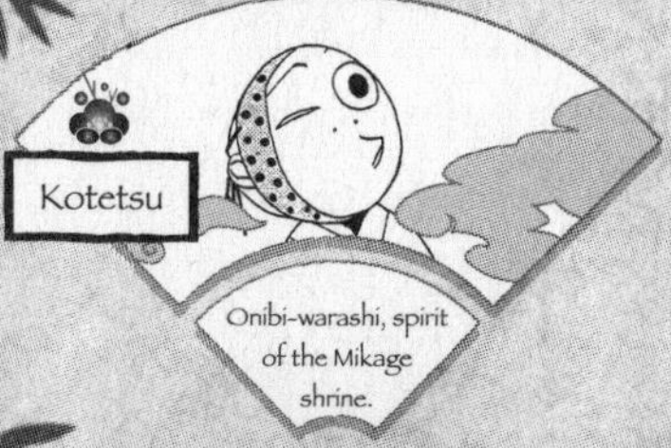
Kotetsu
Onibi-warashi, spirit of the Mikage shrine.

Yukiji

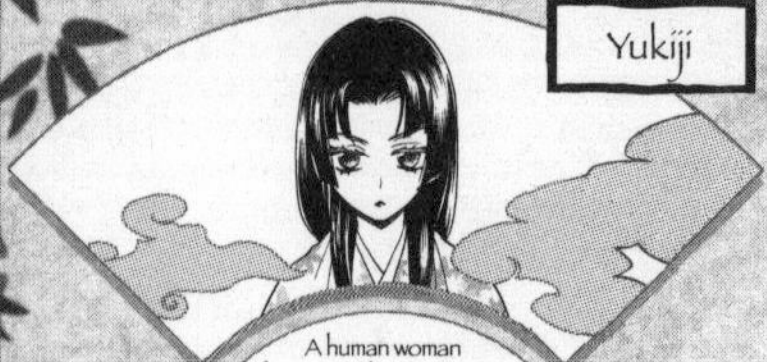

A human woman from more than 500 years ago who was somehow connected to Tomoe.

Mizuki

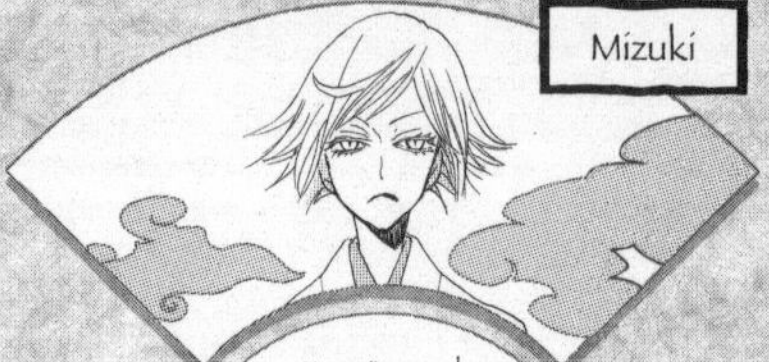

Nanami's second shinshi. The incarnation of a white snake.

Furball

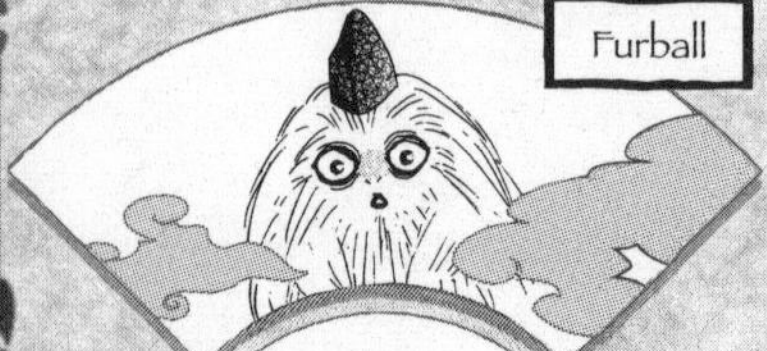

An ayakashi who serves Akura-oh. He stinks.

Akura-oh

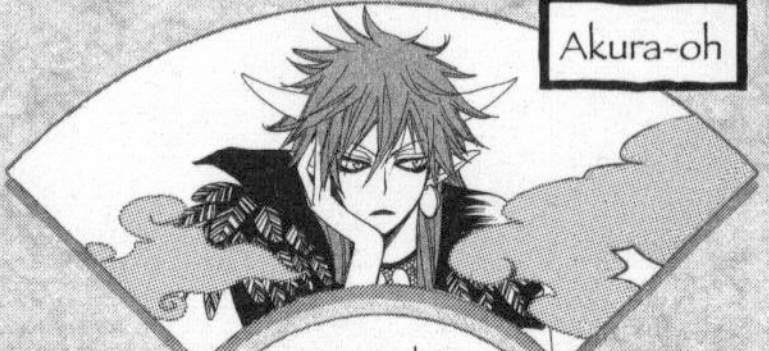

A great yokai. He committed every evil act he possible could.

Mikage

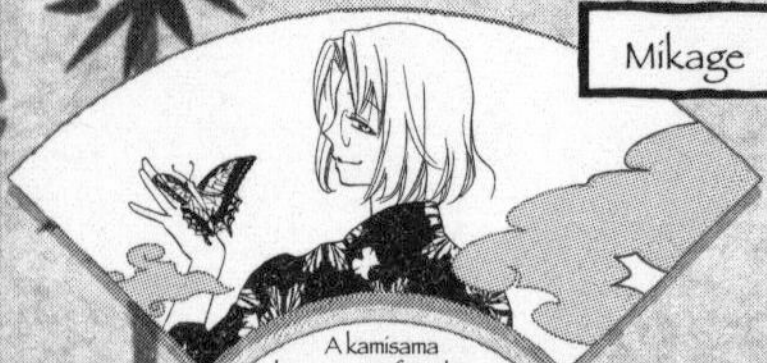

A kamisama who ran away from home. He turned Nanami into a tochigami and left his shrine in her care.

Kuromaro

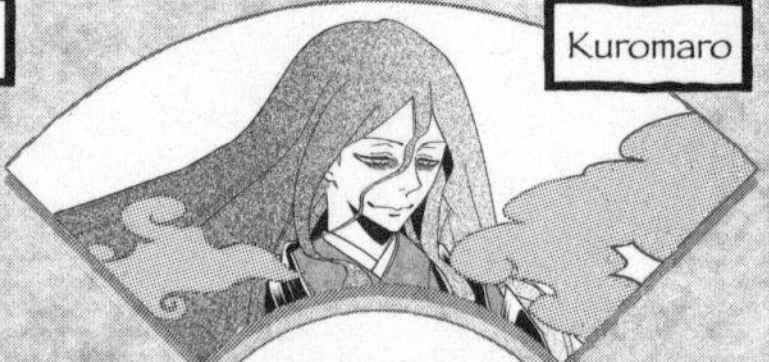

A fallen kami who lives in Mount Ontake.

Story so far

Nanami Momozono is a high school student who was evicted from her home when her dad skipped town.
She meets the tochigami Mikage in a park, and he leaves his shrine and his kami powers to her.
Now Nanami spends her days with Tomoe and Mizuki, her shinshi, and with Onikiri and Kotetsu, the onibi-warashi spirits of the shrine.
Nanami has been slowly gaining powers as a kamisama by holding a festival at her shrine, attending a big kami conference, and getting embroiled in the succession fight at the tengu village.
But mysterious marks have appeared on Tomoe's body, causing him to go into a coma. Mikage explains that the marks are part of a curse cast by a fallen kami.
So Nanami goes back in time to search for clues to break the curse. She's finally found "Kuromaro of Mount Ontake," the fallen kami who put the curse mark on Tomoe, but...

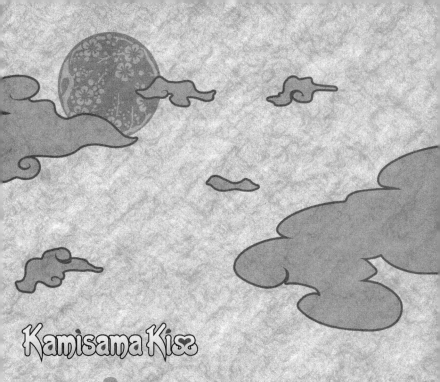

Kamisama Kiss

Volume 17
CONTENTS

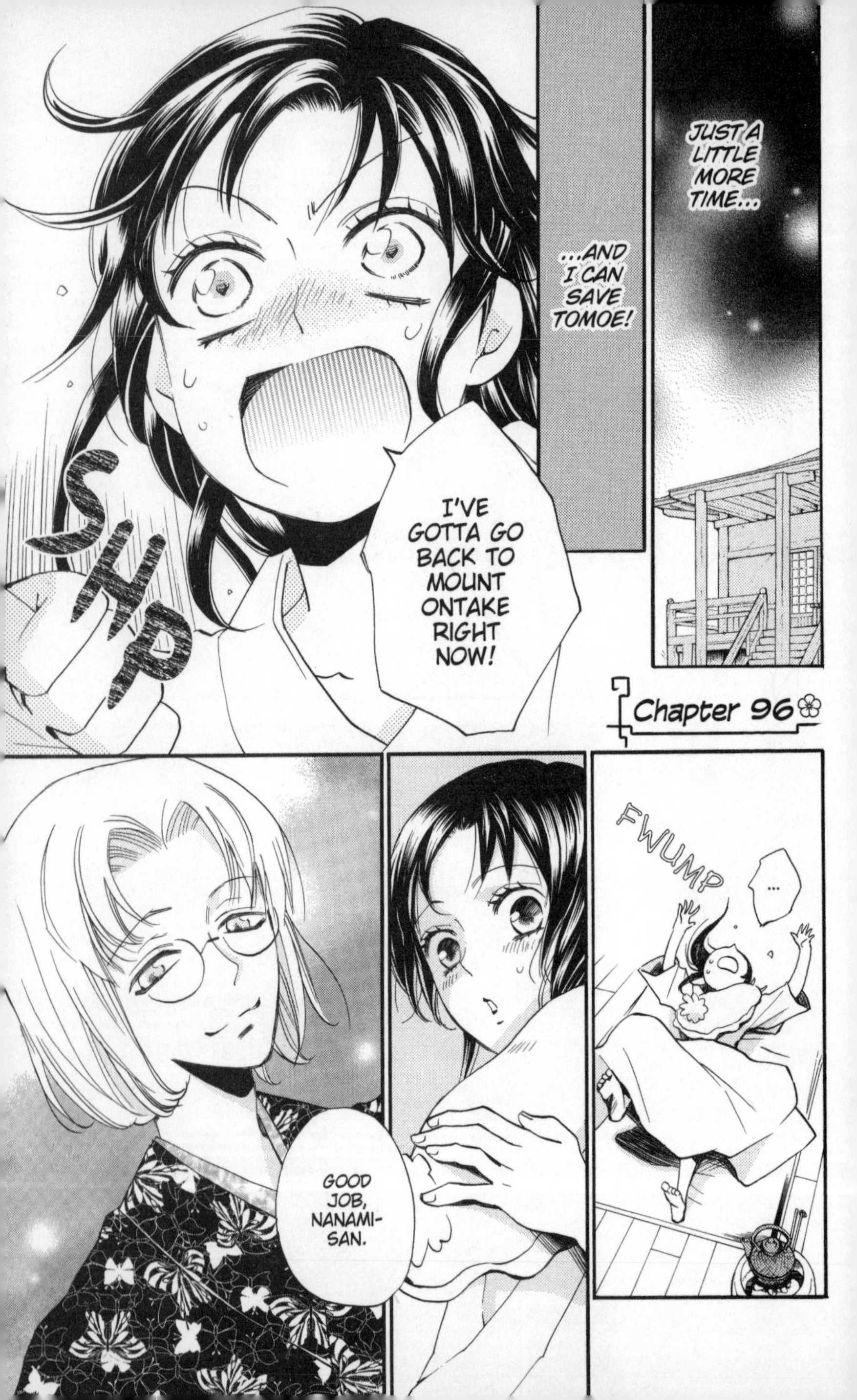
JUST A LITTLE MORE TIME...
...AND I CAN SAVE TOMOE!
I'VE GOTTA GO BACK TO MOUNT ONTAKE RIGHT NOW!
SHP
Chapter 96
FWUMP
...
GOOD JOB, NANAMI-SAN.

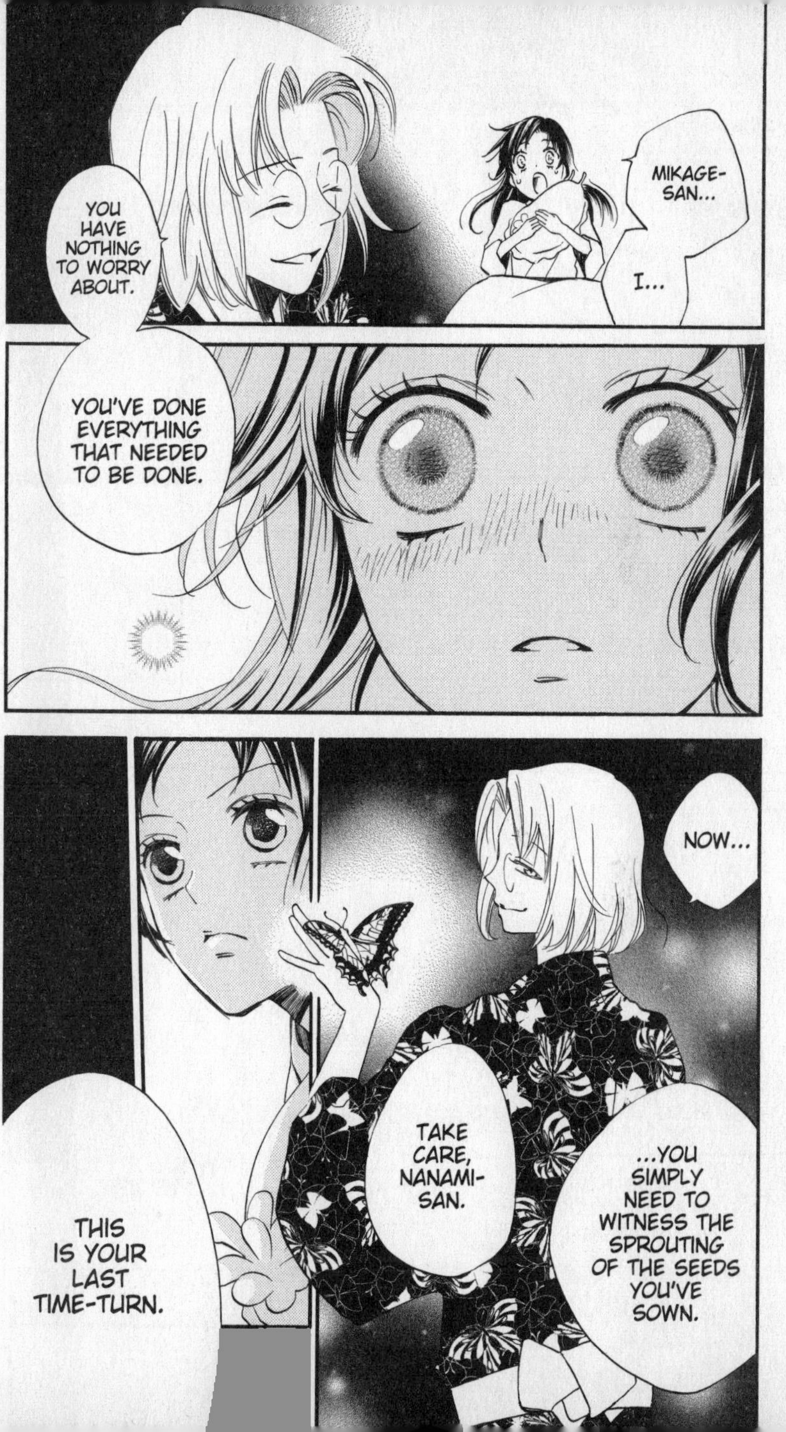
MIKAGE-SAN...
I...
YOU HAVE NOTHING TO WORRY ABOUT.
YOU'VE DONE EVERYTHING THAT NEEDED TO BE DONE.
NOW...
...YOU SIMPLY NEED TO WITNESS THE SPROUTING OF THE SEEDS YOU'VE SOWN.
TAKE CARE, NANAMI-SAN.
THIS IS YOUR LAST TIME-TURN.

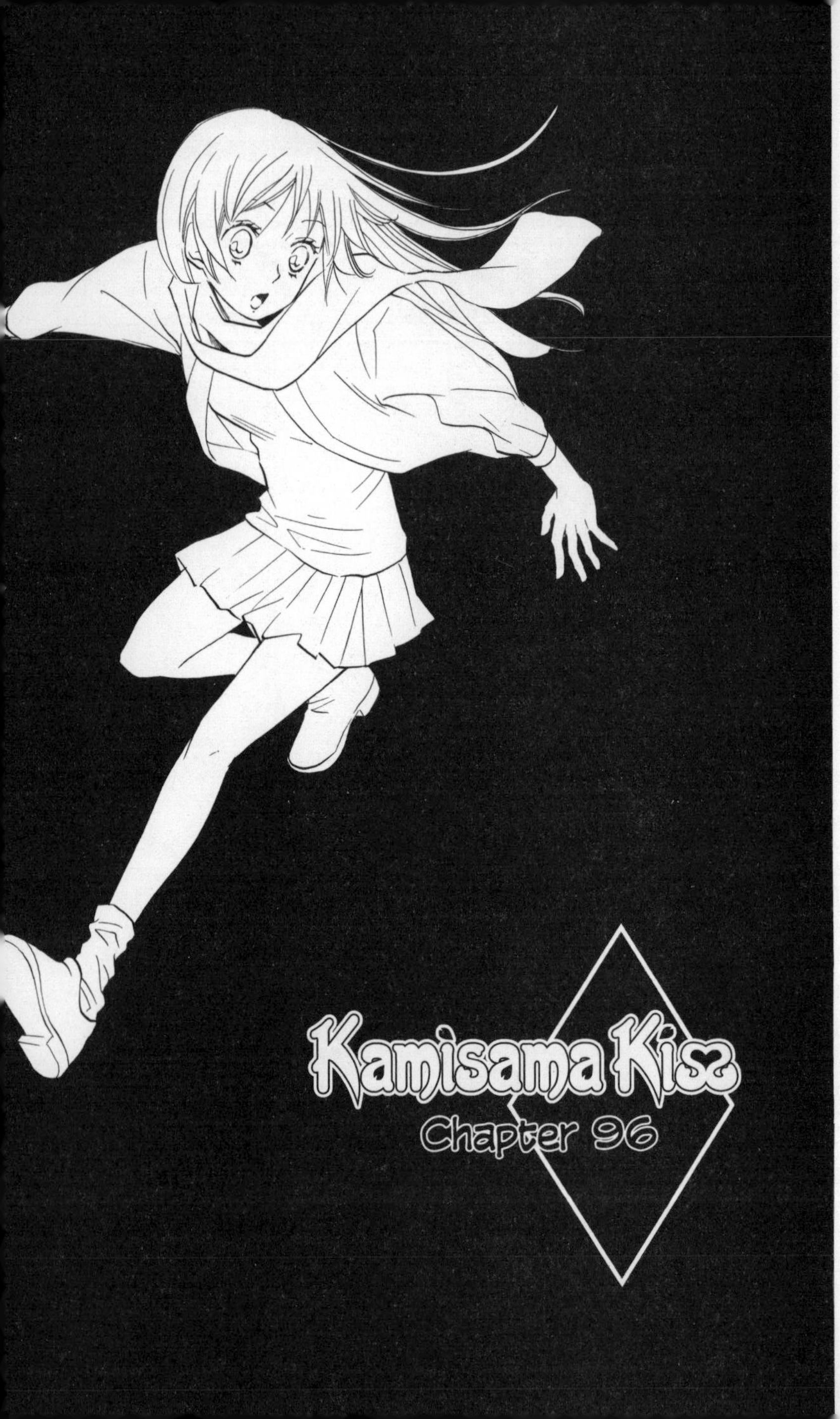
Kamisama Kiss
Chapter 96

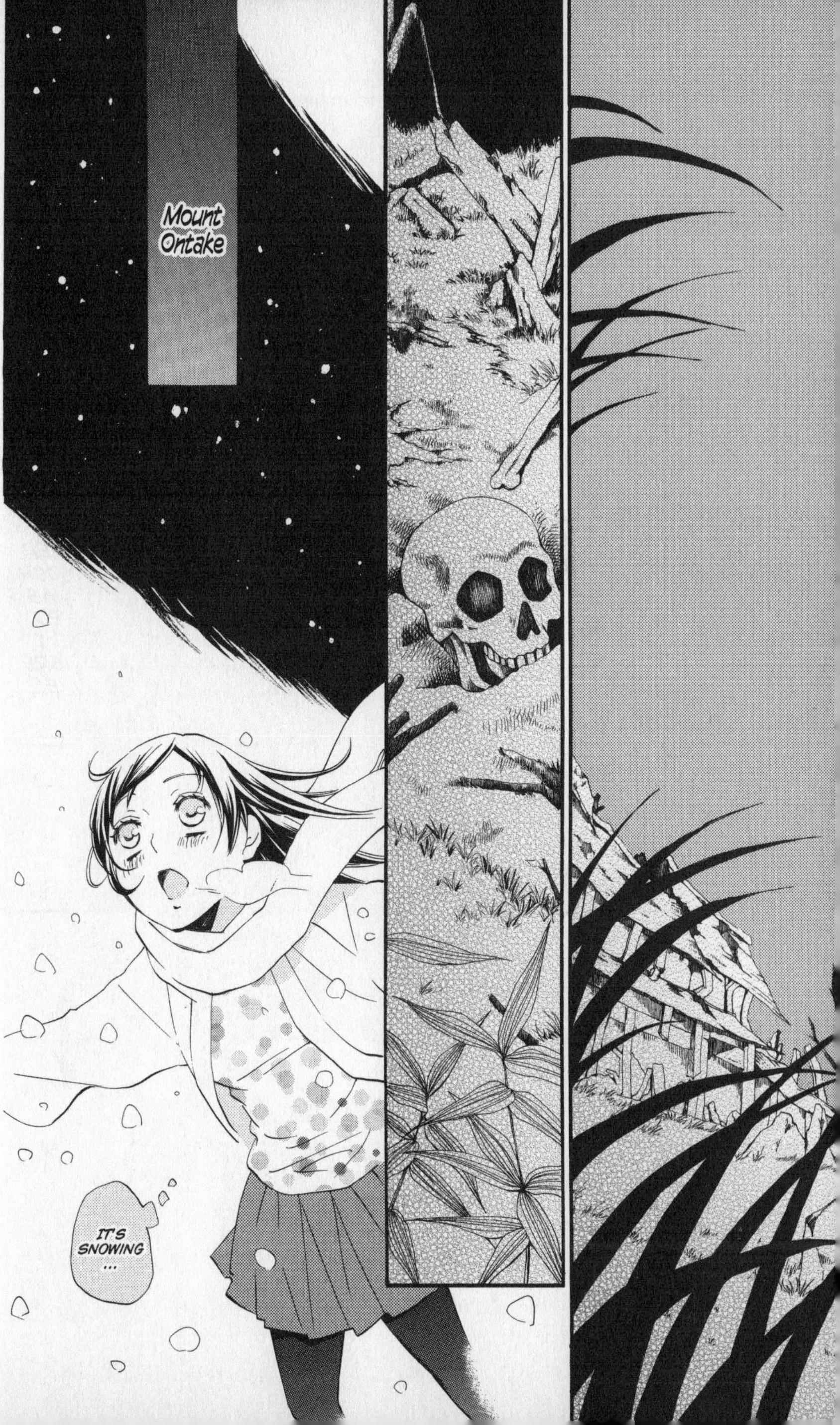
Mount Ontake
IT'S SNOWING ...

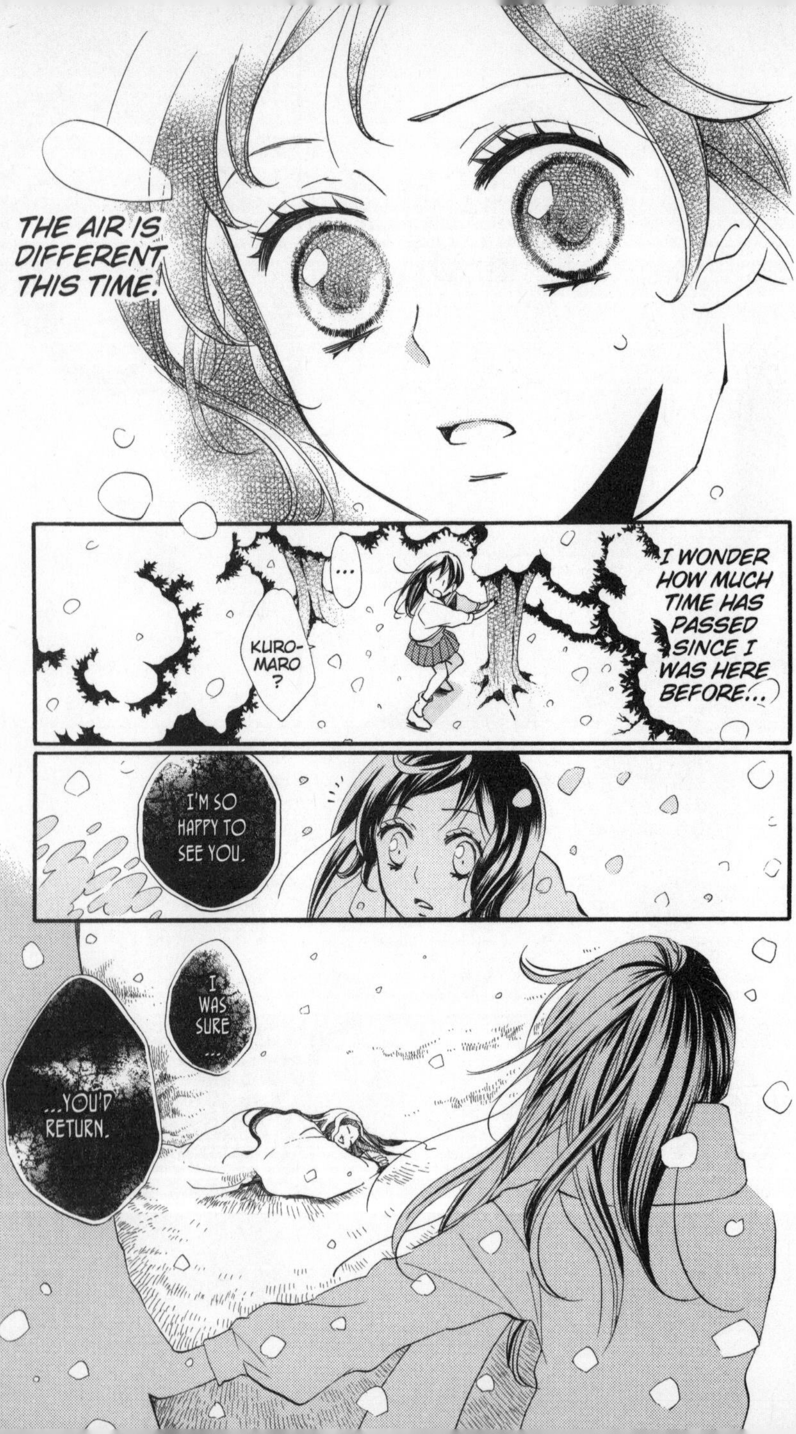
THE AIR IS DIFFERENT THIS TIME.
I WONDER HOW MUCH TIME HAS PASSED SINCE I WAS HERE BEFORE...
...
KURO-MARO?
I'M SO HAPPY TO SEE YOU.
I WAS SURE...
...YOU'D RETURN.

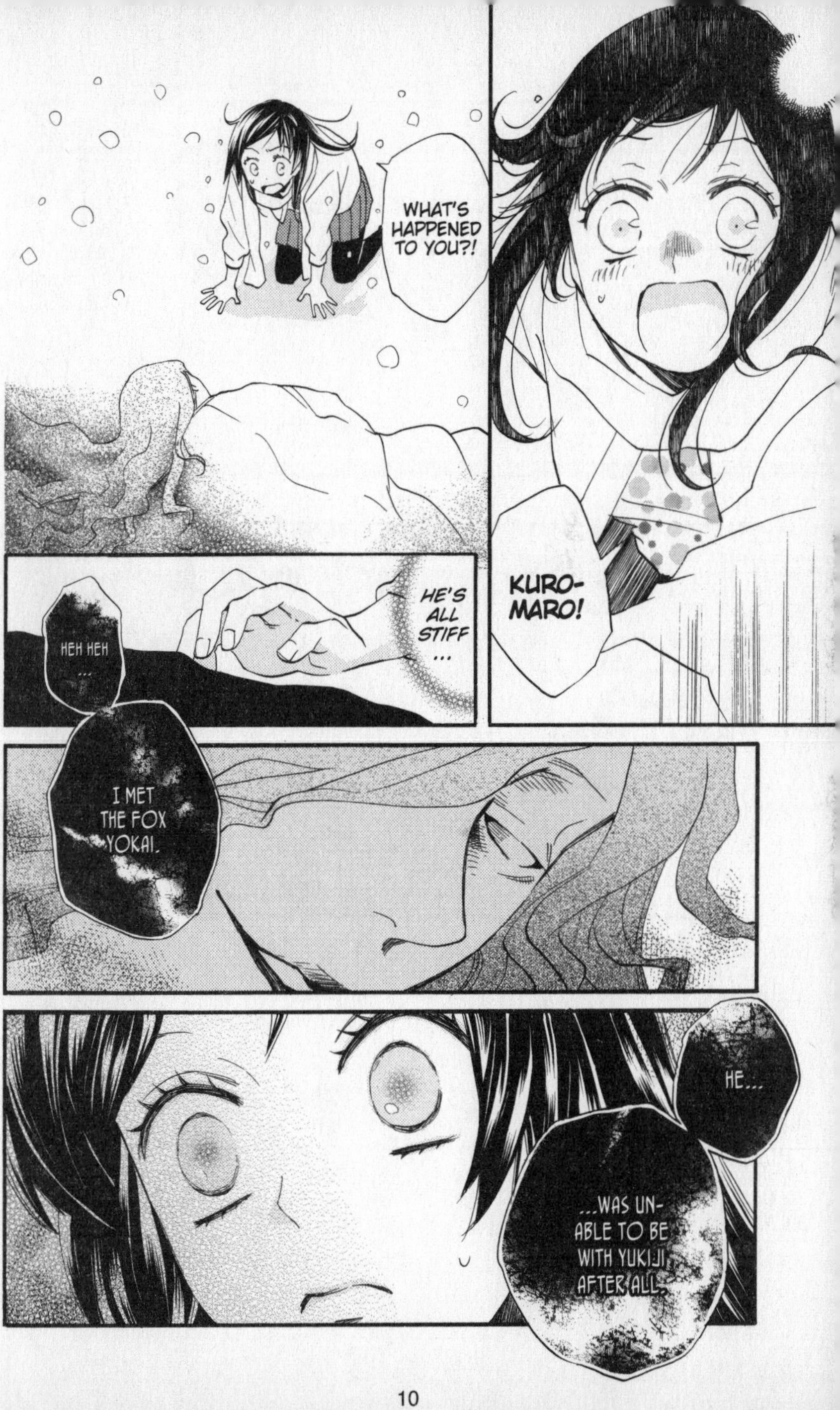
KURO-MARO!
WHAT'S HAPPENED TO YOU?!
HE'S ALL STIFF ...
HEH HEH ...
I MET THE FOX YOKAI.
HE...
...WAS UN-ABLE TO BE WITH YUKIJI AFTER ALL.

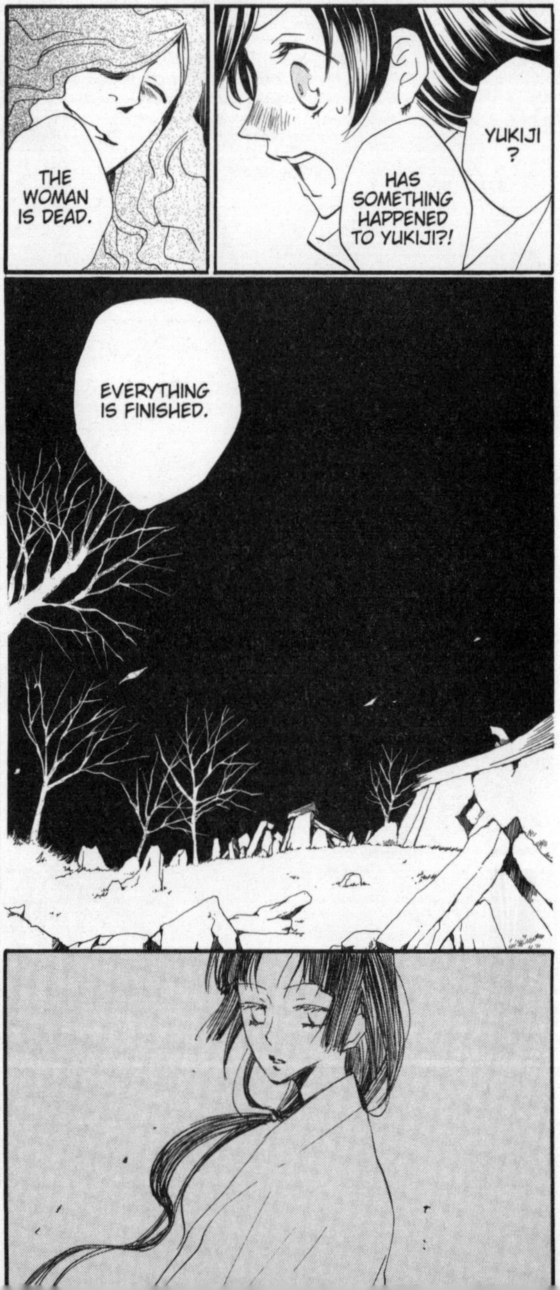
YUKIJI ?
HAS SOMETHING HAPPENED TO YUKIJI?!
THE WOMAN IS DEAD.
EVERYTHING IS FINISHED.

Hello.

Thank you for picking up volume 17 of Kamisama Kiss!

The long-running arc set in the past concludes in this volume.

I'll be happy if you follow the story to the very end. ☺

See you later.

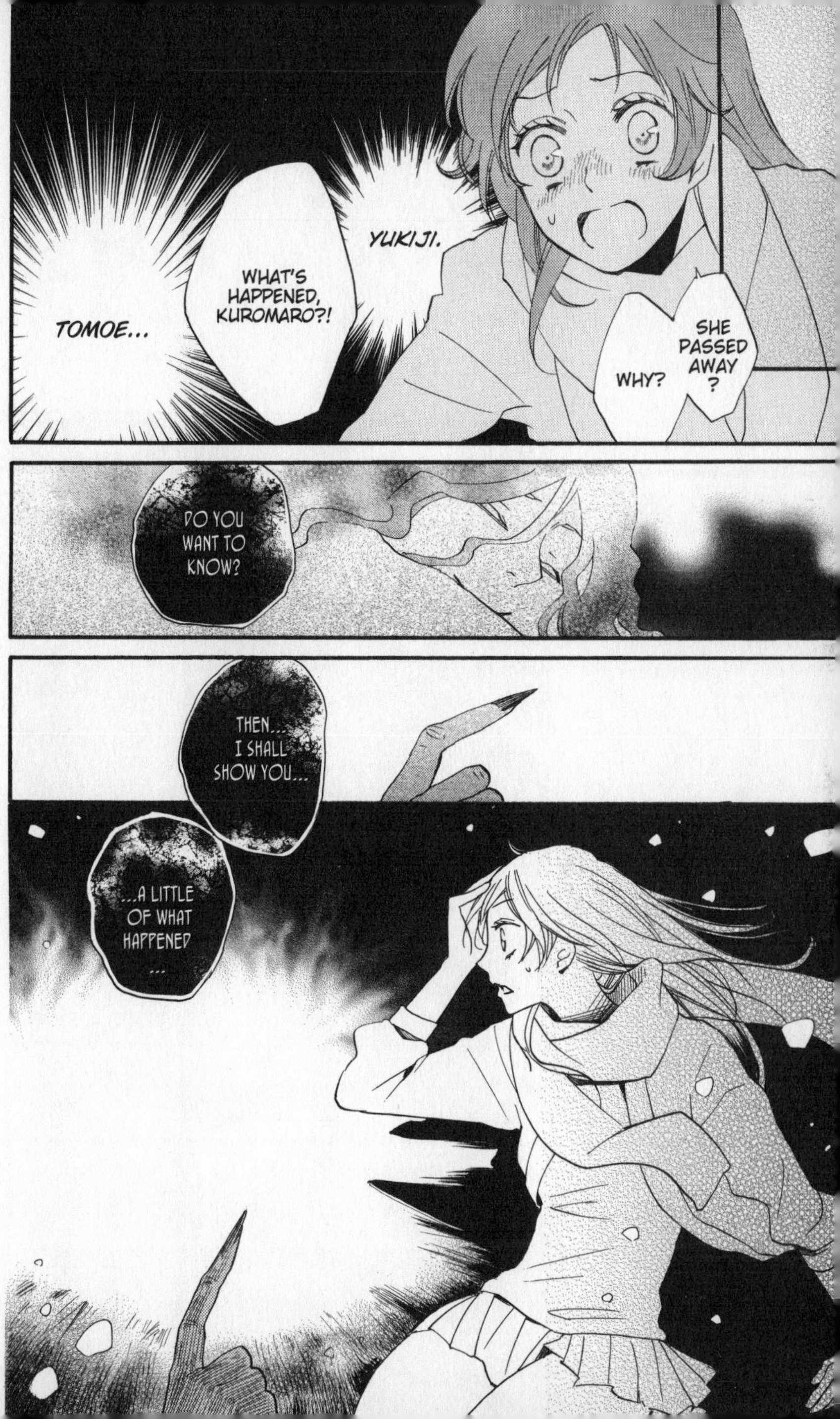
SHE PASSED AWAY?
WHY?
YUKIJI.
WHAT'S HAPPENED, KUROMARO?!
TOMOE...
DO YOU WANT TO KNOW?
THEN... I SHALL SHOW YOU...
...A LITTLE OF WHAT HAPPENED...

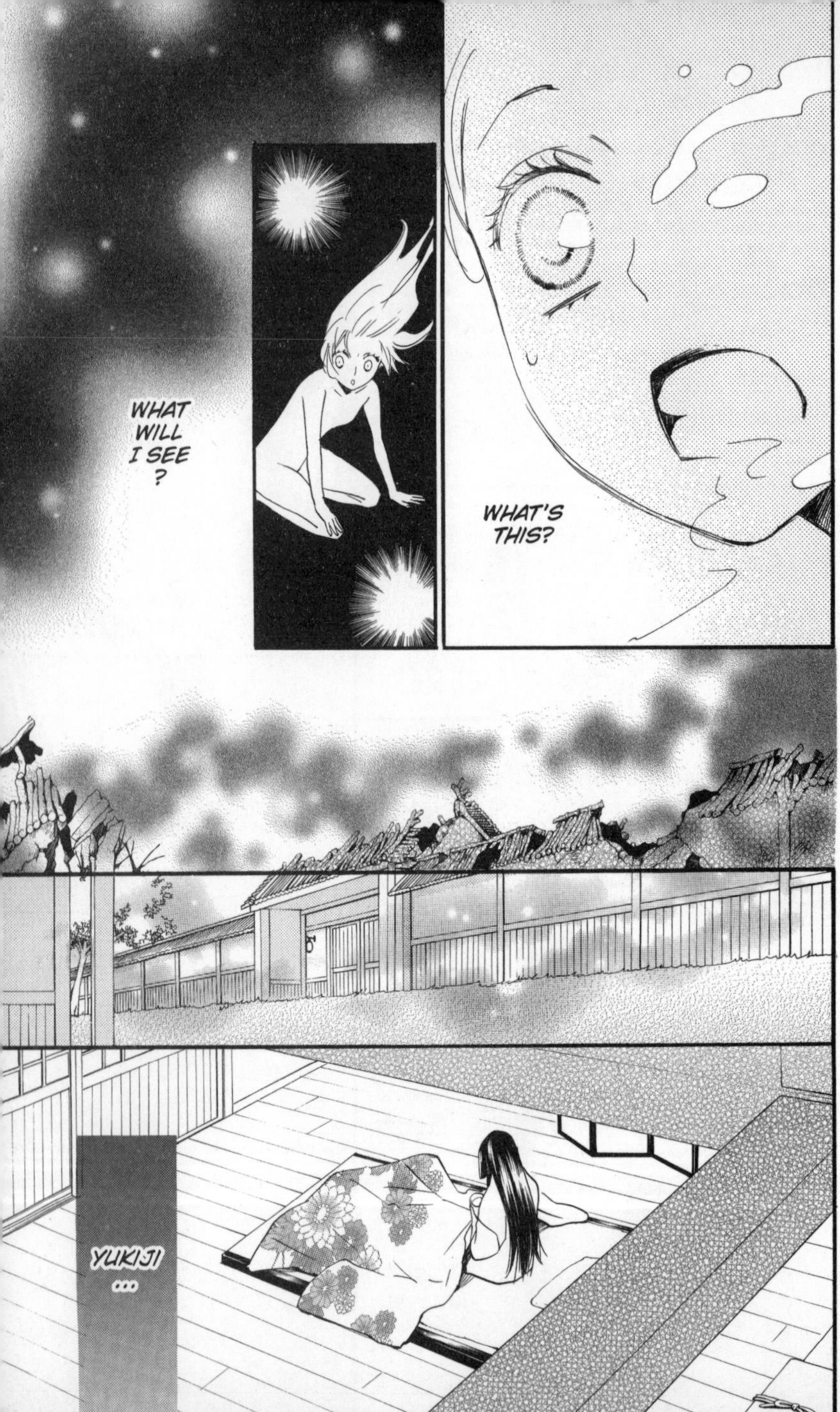
WHAT'S THIS?
WHAT WILL I SEE?
YUKIJI...

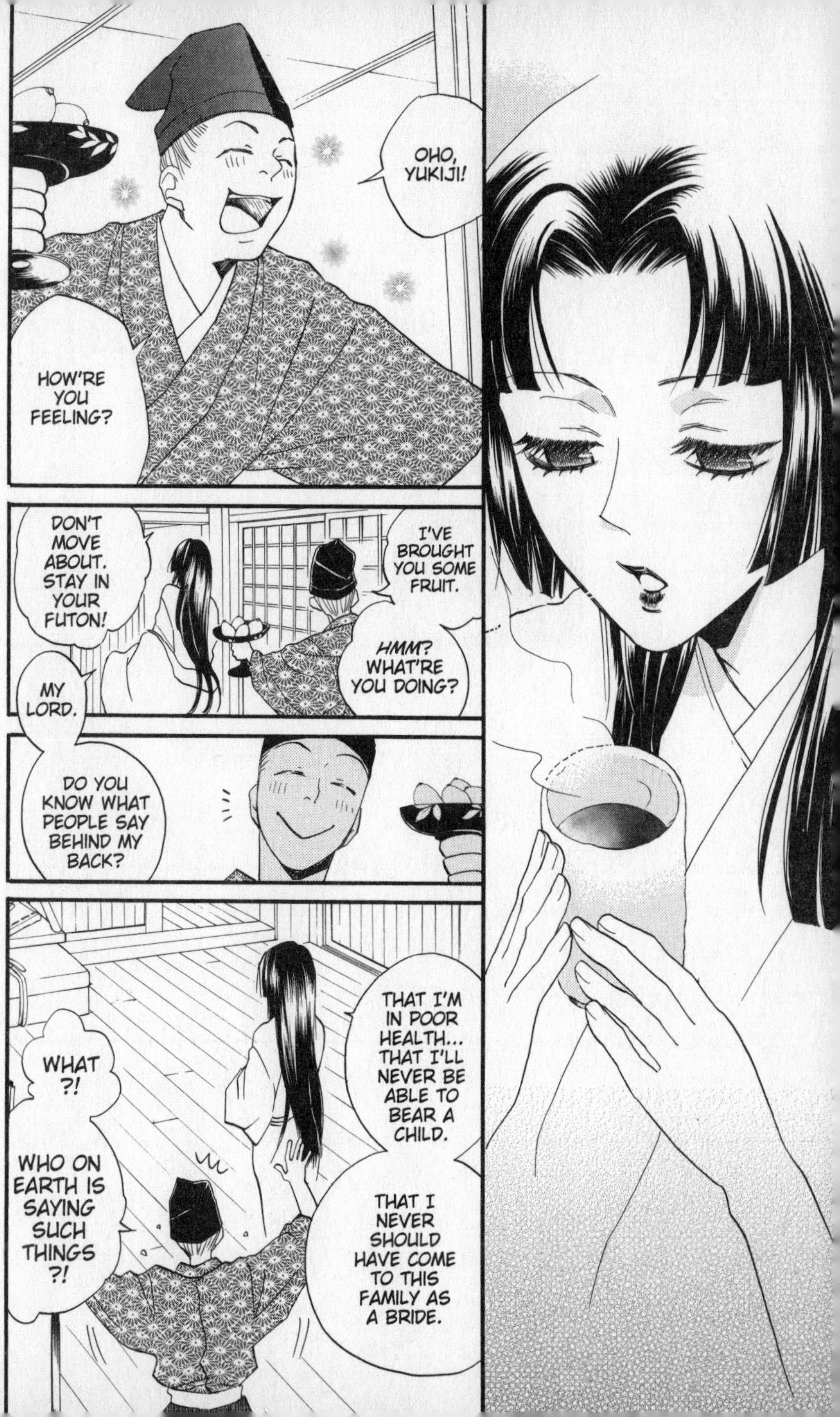
OHO, YUKIJI!
HOW'RE YOU FEELING?
I'VE BROUGHT YOU SOME FRUIT.
HMM? WHAT'RE YOU DOING?
DON'T MOVE ABOUT. STAY IN YOUR FUTON!
MY LORD.
DO YOU KNOW WHAT PEOPLE SAY BEHIND MY BACK?
THAT I'M IN POOR HEALTH... THAT I'LL NEVER BE ABLE TO BEAR A CHILD.
THAT I NEVER SHOULD HAVE COME TO THIS FAMILY AS A BRIDE.
WHAT?!
WHO ON EARTH IS SAYING SUCH THINGS?!

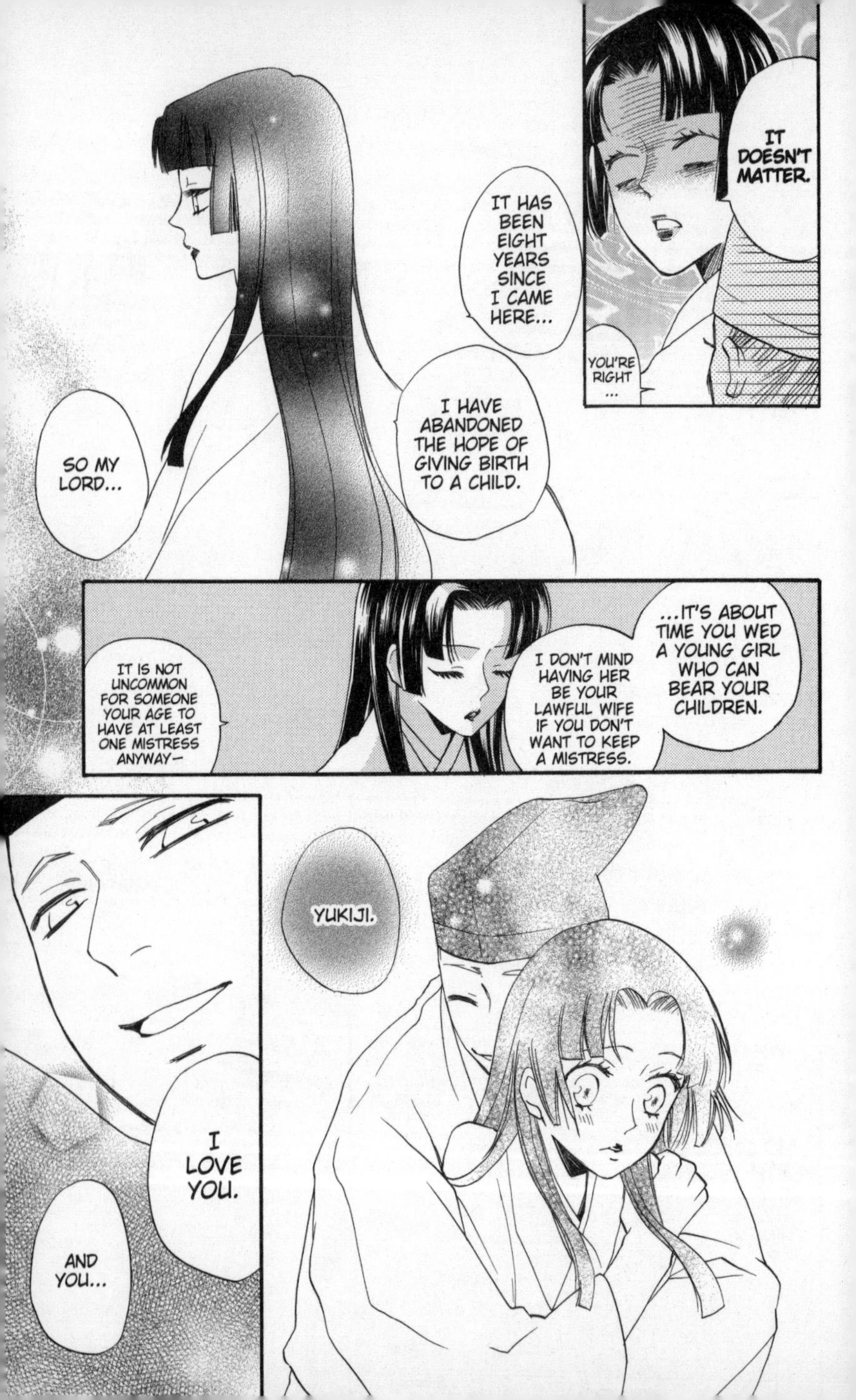
IT DOESN'T MATTER.
YOU'RE RIGHT ...
IT HAS BEEN EIGHT YEARS SINCE I CAME HERE...
I HAVE ABANDONED THE HOPE OF GIVING BIRTH TO A CHILD.
SO MY LORD...
...IT'S ABOUT TIME YOU WED A YOUNG GIRL WHO CAN BEAR YOUR CHILDREN.
I DON'T MIND HAVING HER BE YOUR LAWFUL WIFE IF YOU DON'T WANT TO KEEP A MISTRESS.
IT IS NOT UNCOMMON FOR SOMEONE YOUR AGE TO HAVE AT LEAST ONE MISTRESS ANYWAY—
YUKIJI.
I LOVE YOU.
AND YOU...

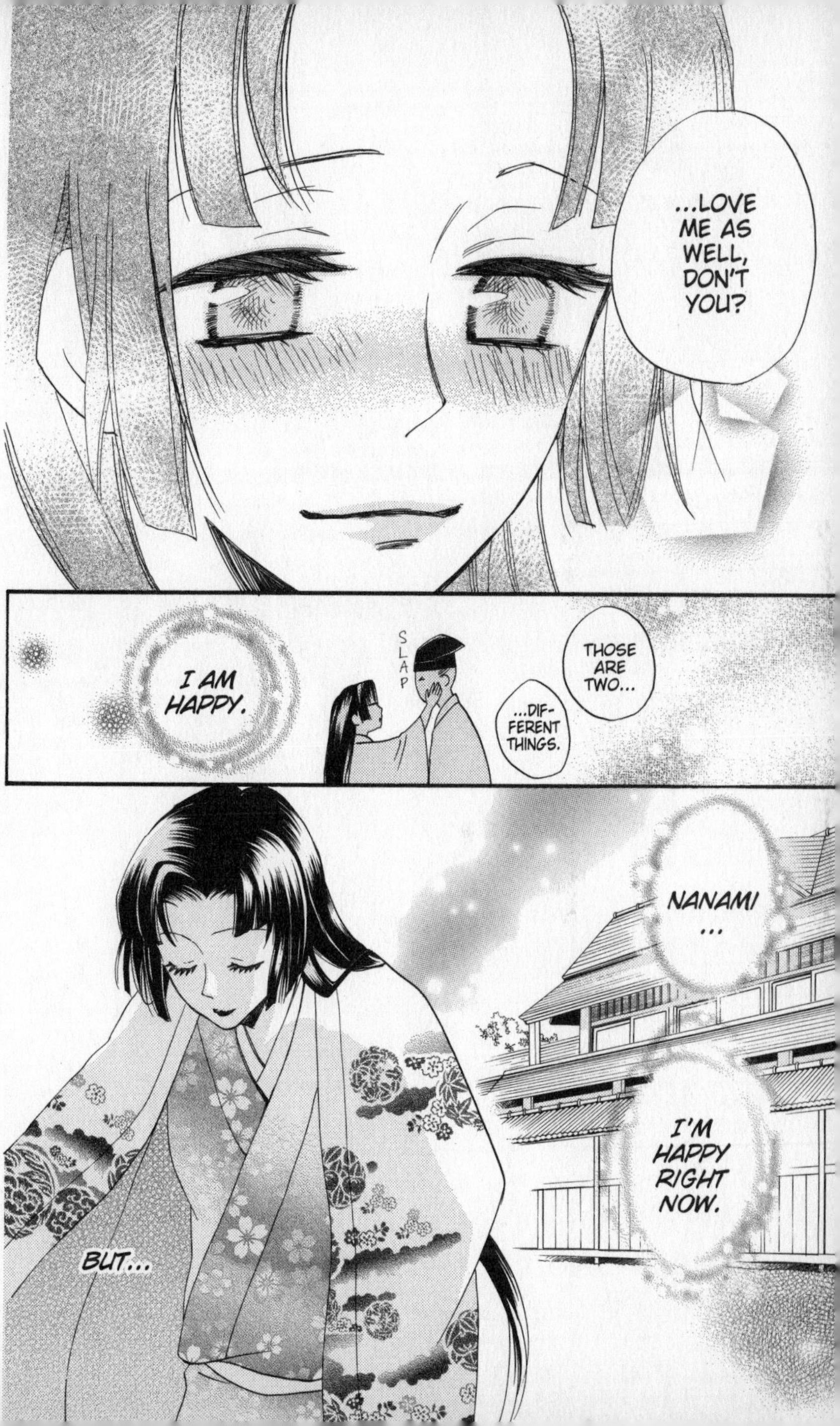
...LOVE ME AS WELL, DON'T YOU?
THOSE ARE TWO...
...DIF- FERENT THINGS.
SLAP
I AM HAPPY.
NANAMI...
I'M HAPPY RIGHT NOW.
BUT...

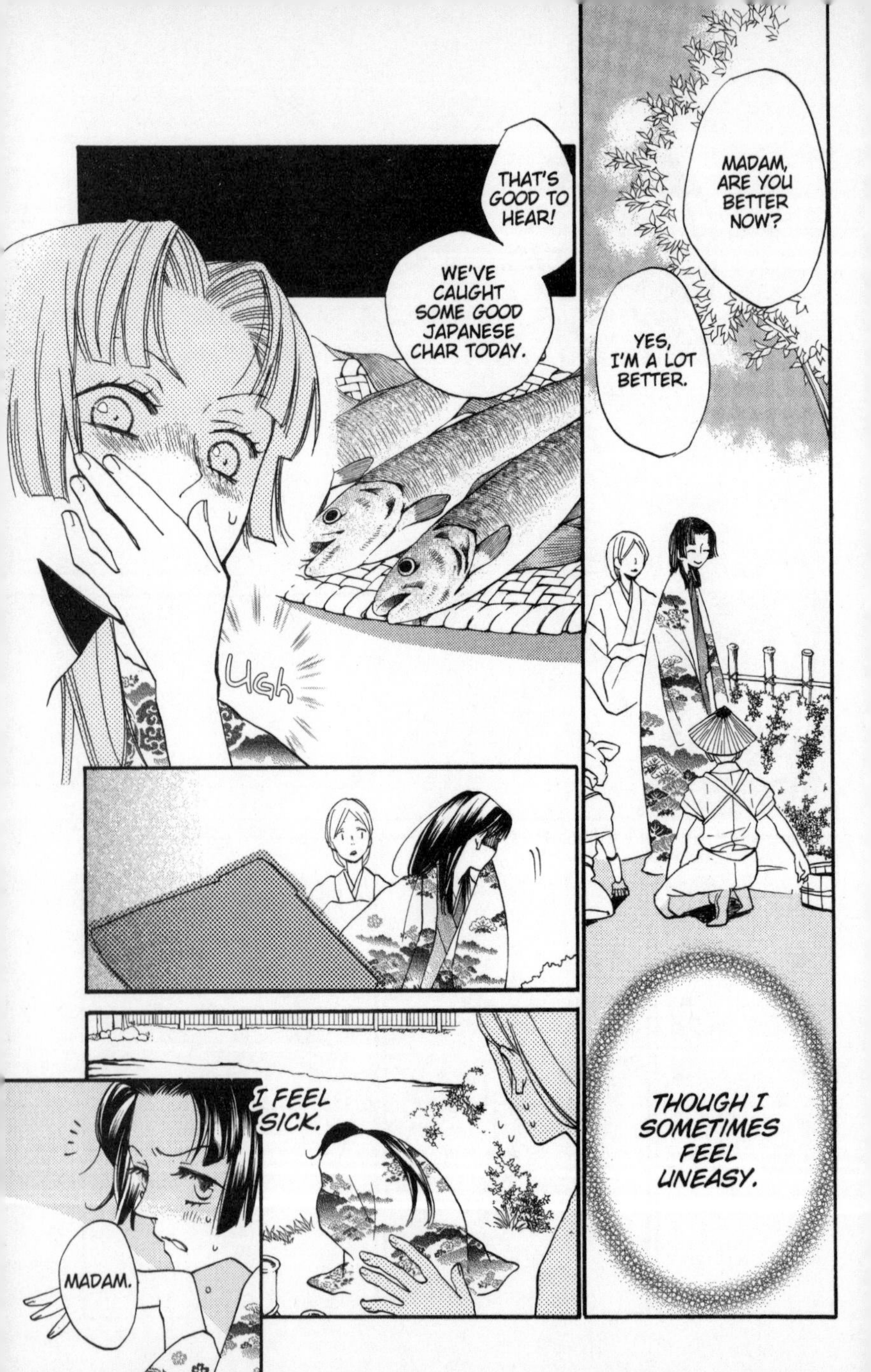
MADAM, ARE YOU BETTER NOW?
YES, I'M A LOT BETTER.
THOUGH I SOMETIMES FEEL UNEASY.
THAT'S GOOD TO HEAR!
WE'VE CAUGHT SOME GOOD JAPANESE CHAR TODAY.
Ugh
I FEEL SICK.
MADAM.

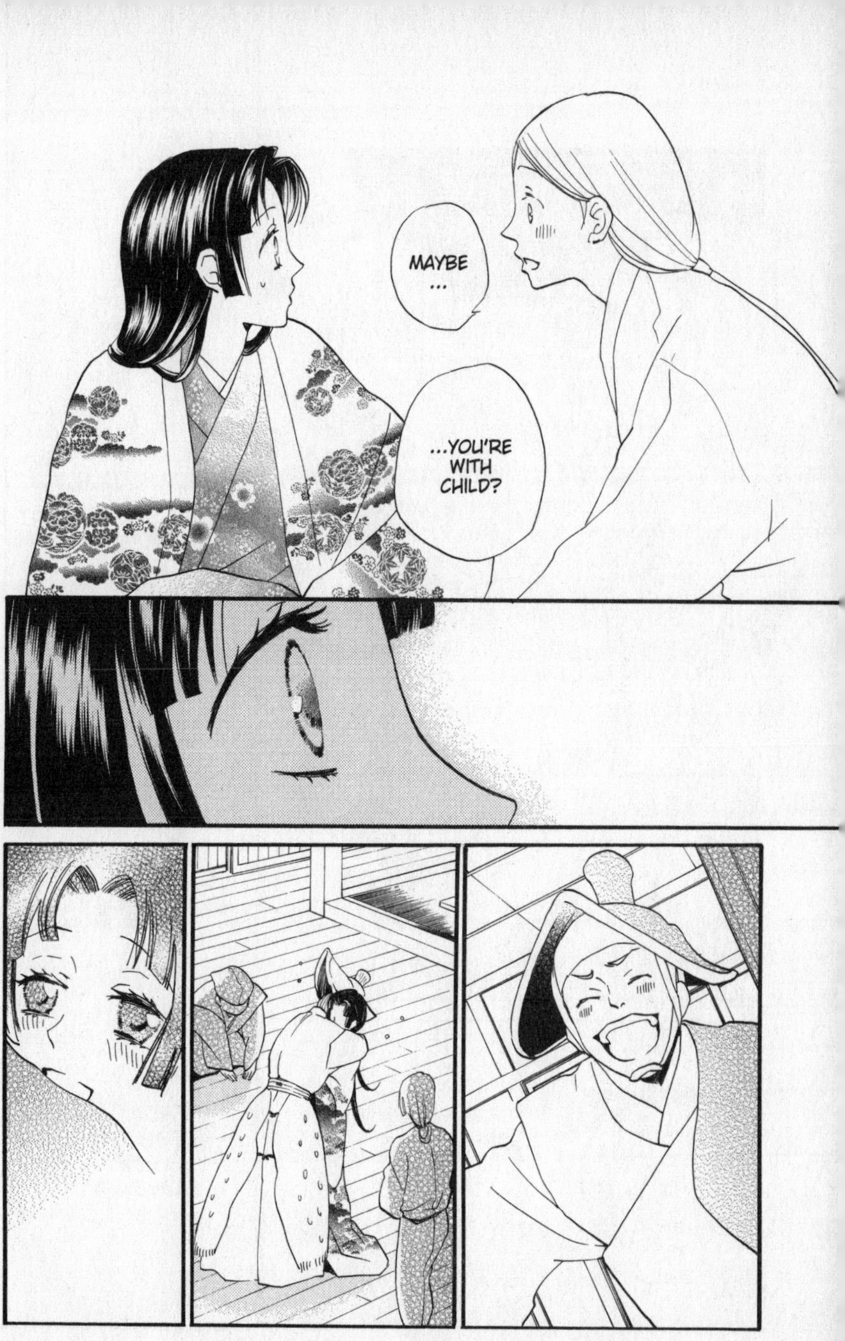
MAYBE ...
...YOU'RE WITH CHILD?

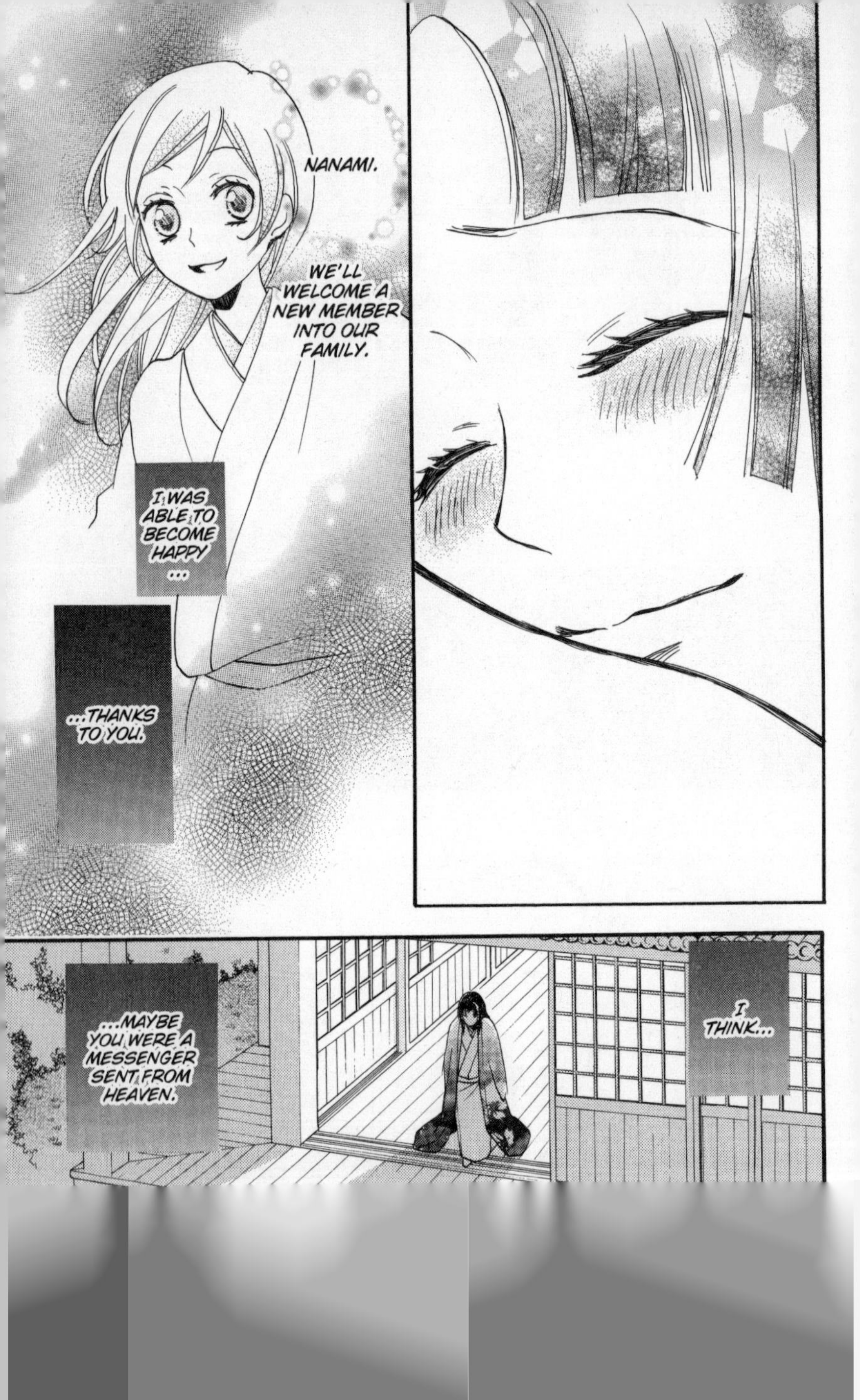
NANAMI.
WE'LL WELCOME A NEW MEMBER INTO OUR FAMILY.
I WAS ABLE TO BECOME HAPPY...
...THANKS TO YOU.
I THINK...
...MAYBE YOU WERE A MESSENGER SENT FROM HEAVEN.

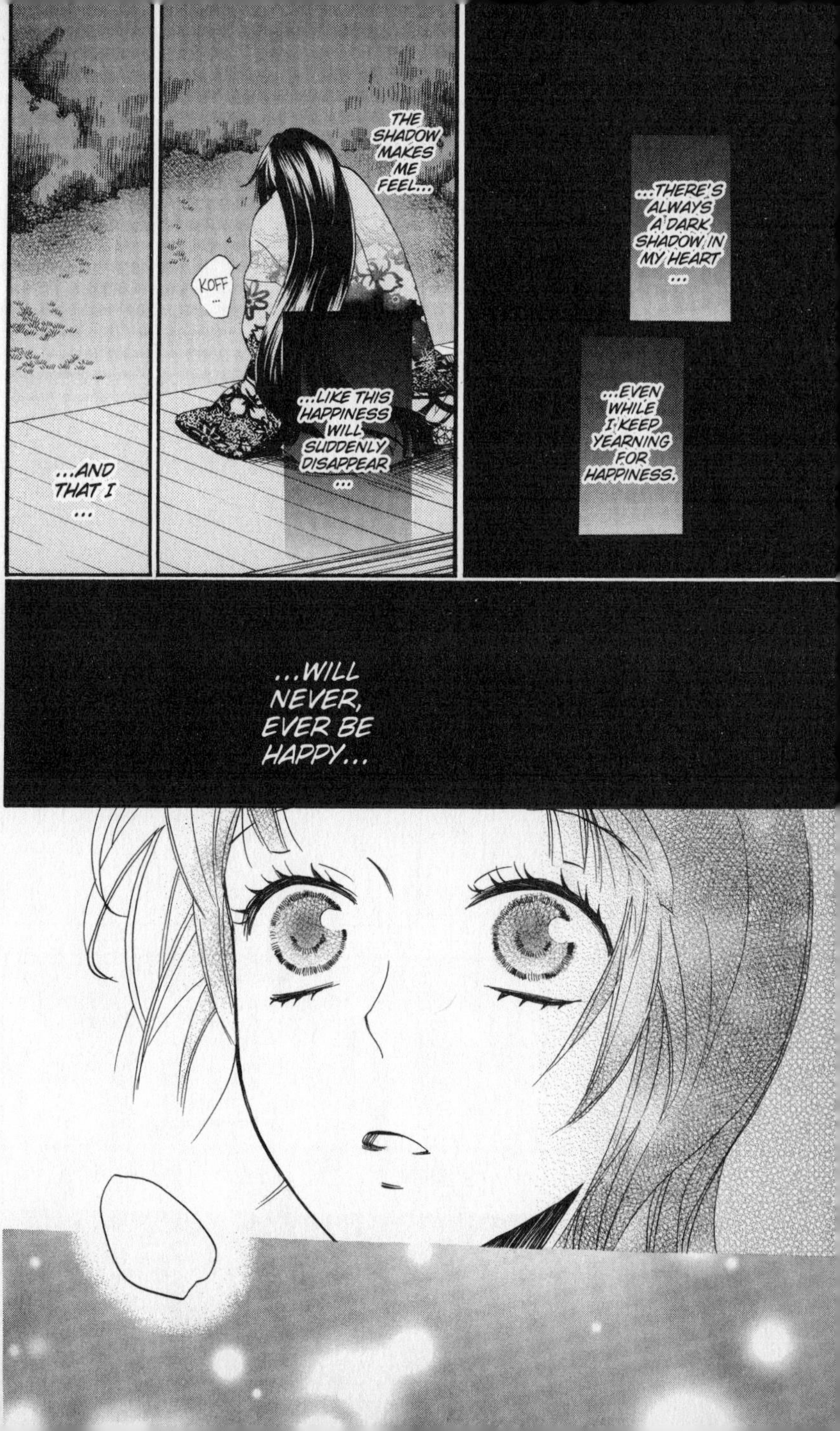
...THERE'S ALWAYS A DARK SHADOW IN MY HEART ...
...EVEN WHILE I KEEP YEARNING FOR HAPPINESS.
THE SHADOW MAKES ME FEEL...
KOFF ...
...LIKE THIS HAPPINESS WILL SUDDENLY DISAPPEAR ...
...AND THAT I ...
...WILL NEVER, EVER BE HAPPY...

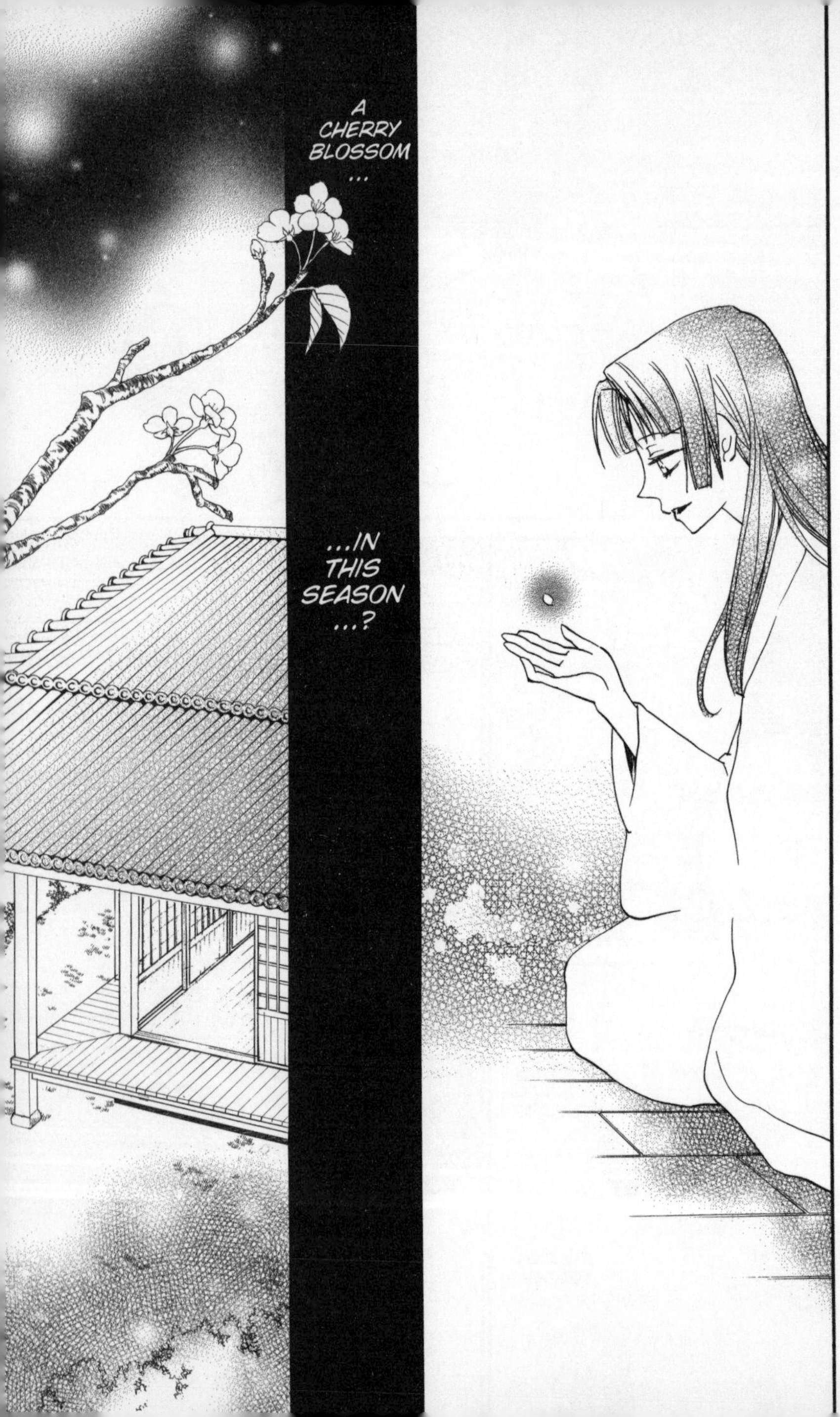
A CHERRY BLOSSOM ...
...IN THIS SEASON ...?

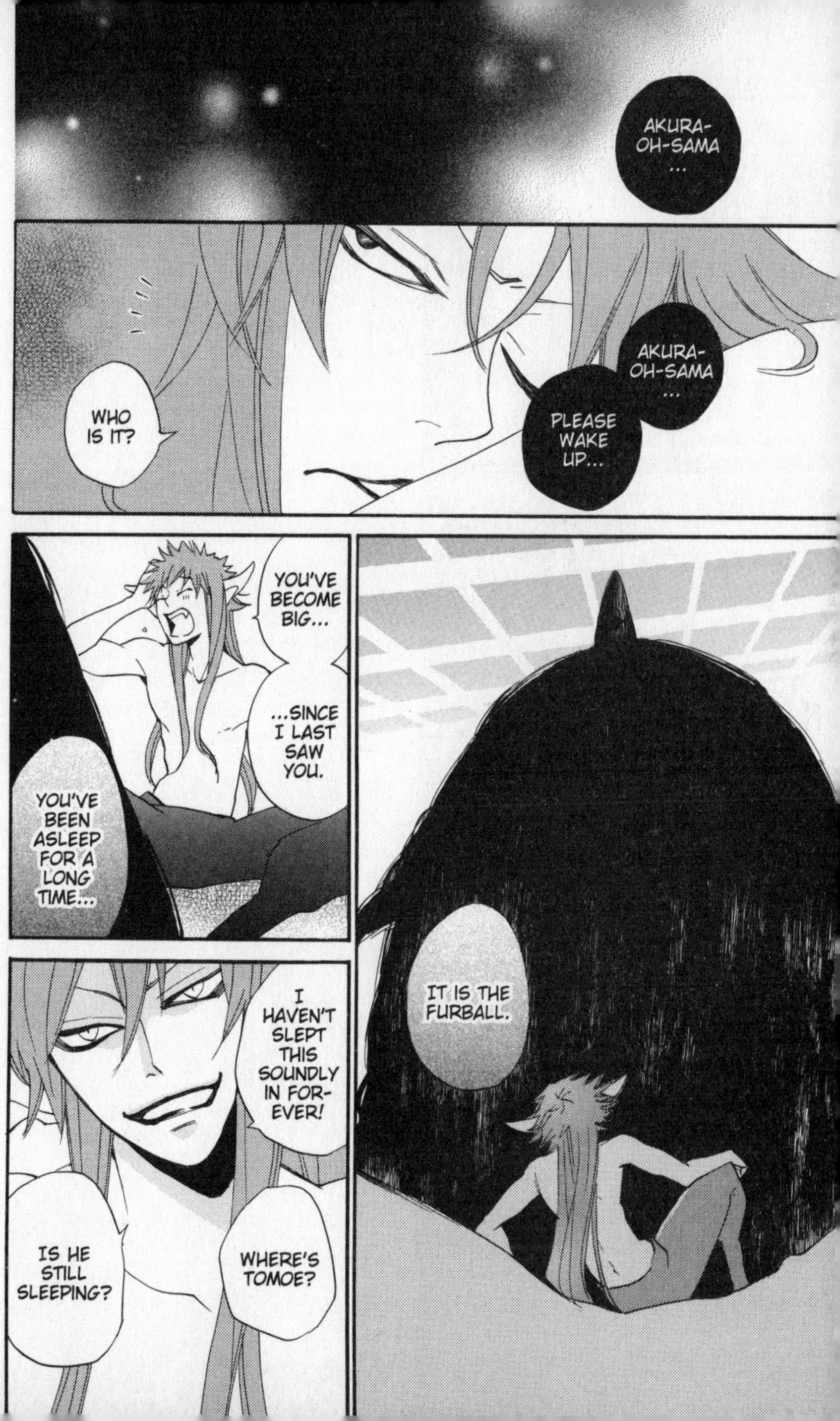
AKURA-OH-SAMA...
AKURA-OH-SAMA...
PLEASE WAKE UP...
WHO IS IT?
IT IS THE FURBALL.
YOU'VE BECOME BIG...
...SINCE I LAST SAW YOU.
YOU'VE BEEN ASLEEP FOR A LONG TIME...
I HAVEN'T SLEPT THIS SOUNDLY IN FOR-EVER!
WHERE'S TOMOE?
IS HE STILL SLEEPING?

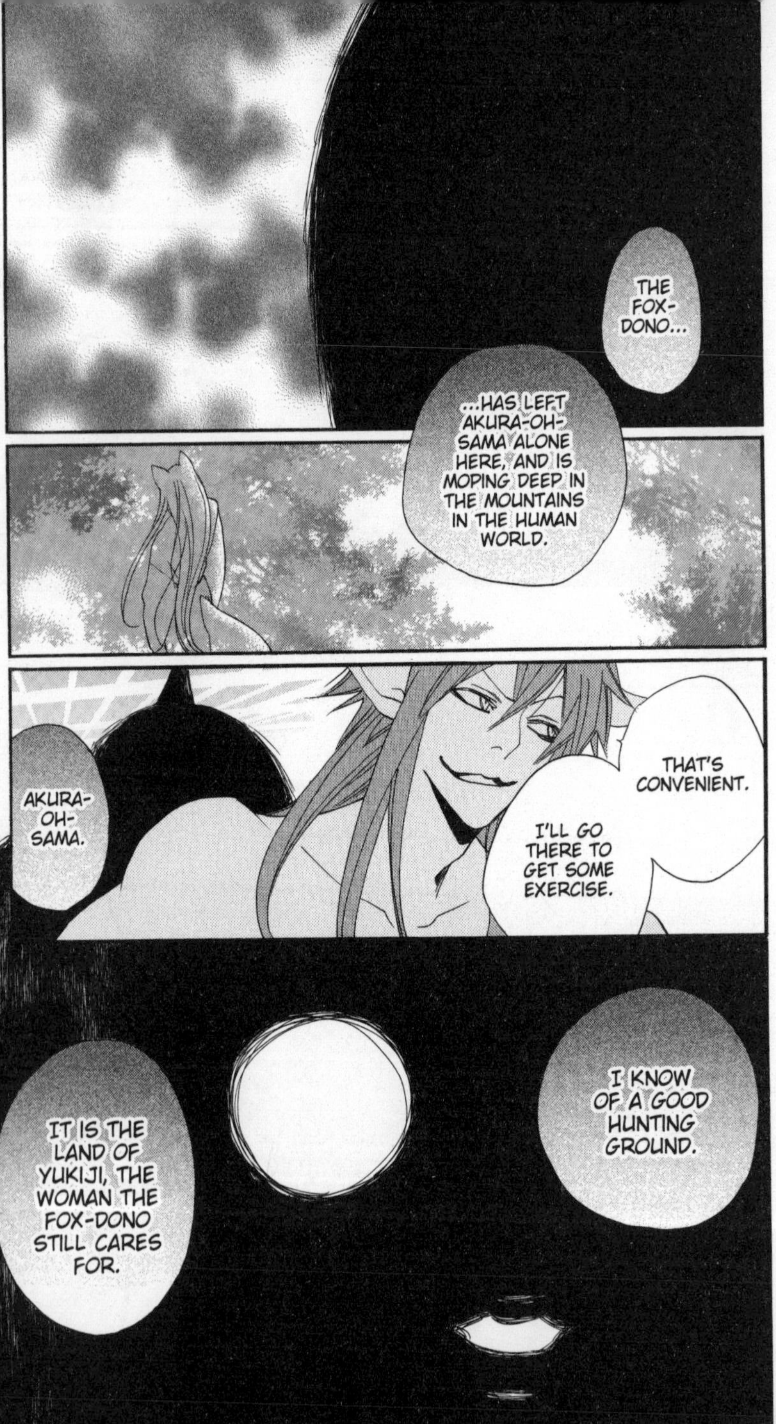
THE FOX-DONO...
...HAS LEFT AKURA-OH-SAMA ALONE HERE, AND IS MOPING DEEP IN THE MOUNTAINS IN THE HUMAN WORLD.
THAT'S CONVENIENT.
I'LL GO THERE TO GET SOME EXERCISE.
AKURA-OH-SAMA.
I KNOW OF A GOOD HUNTING GROUND.
IT IS THE LAND OF YUKIJI, THE WOMAN THE FOX-DONO STILL CARES FOR.

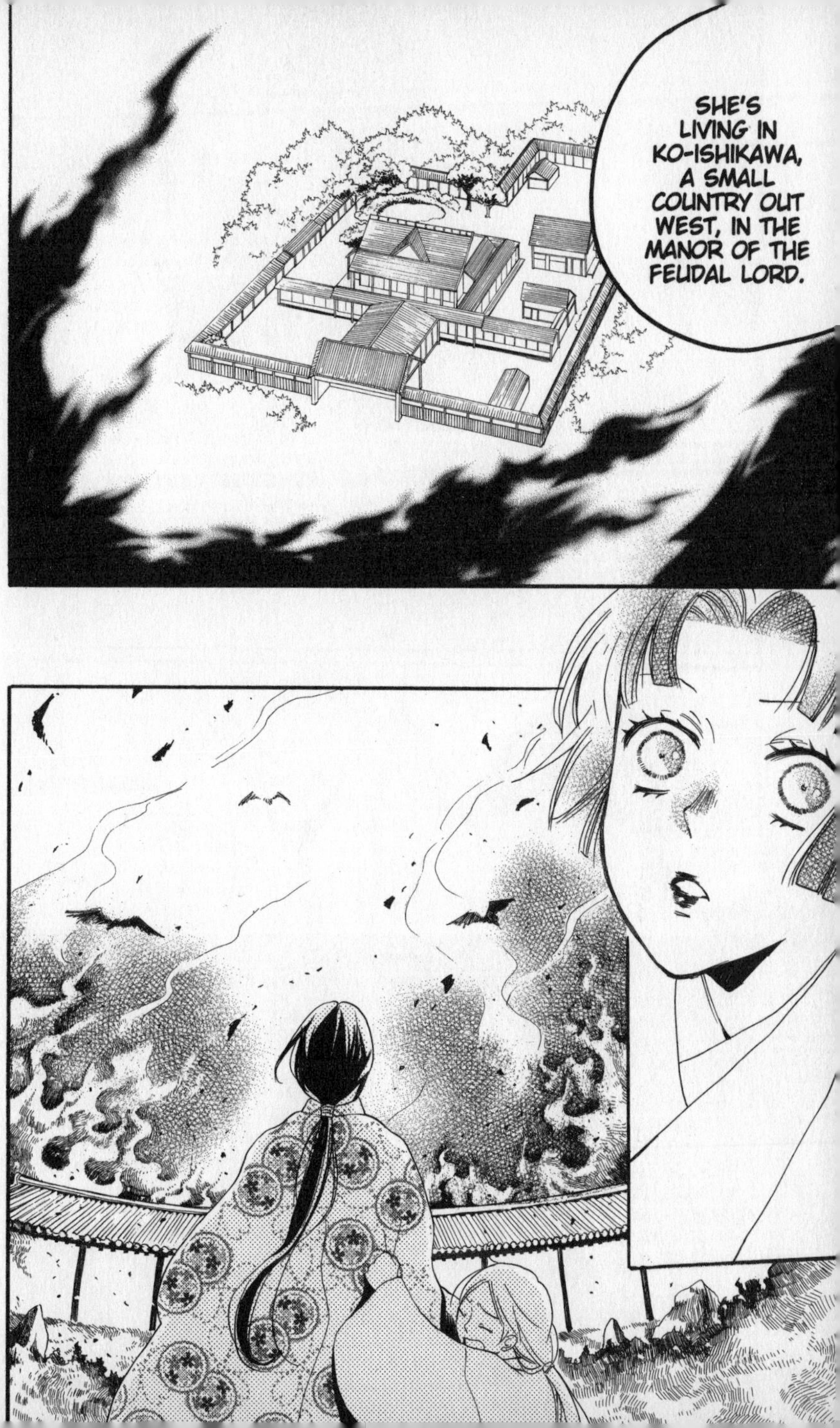
SHE'S LIVING IN KO-ISHIKAWA, A SMALL COUNTRY OUT WEST, IN THE MANOR OF THE FEUDAL LORD.

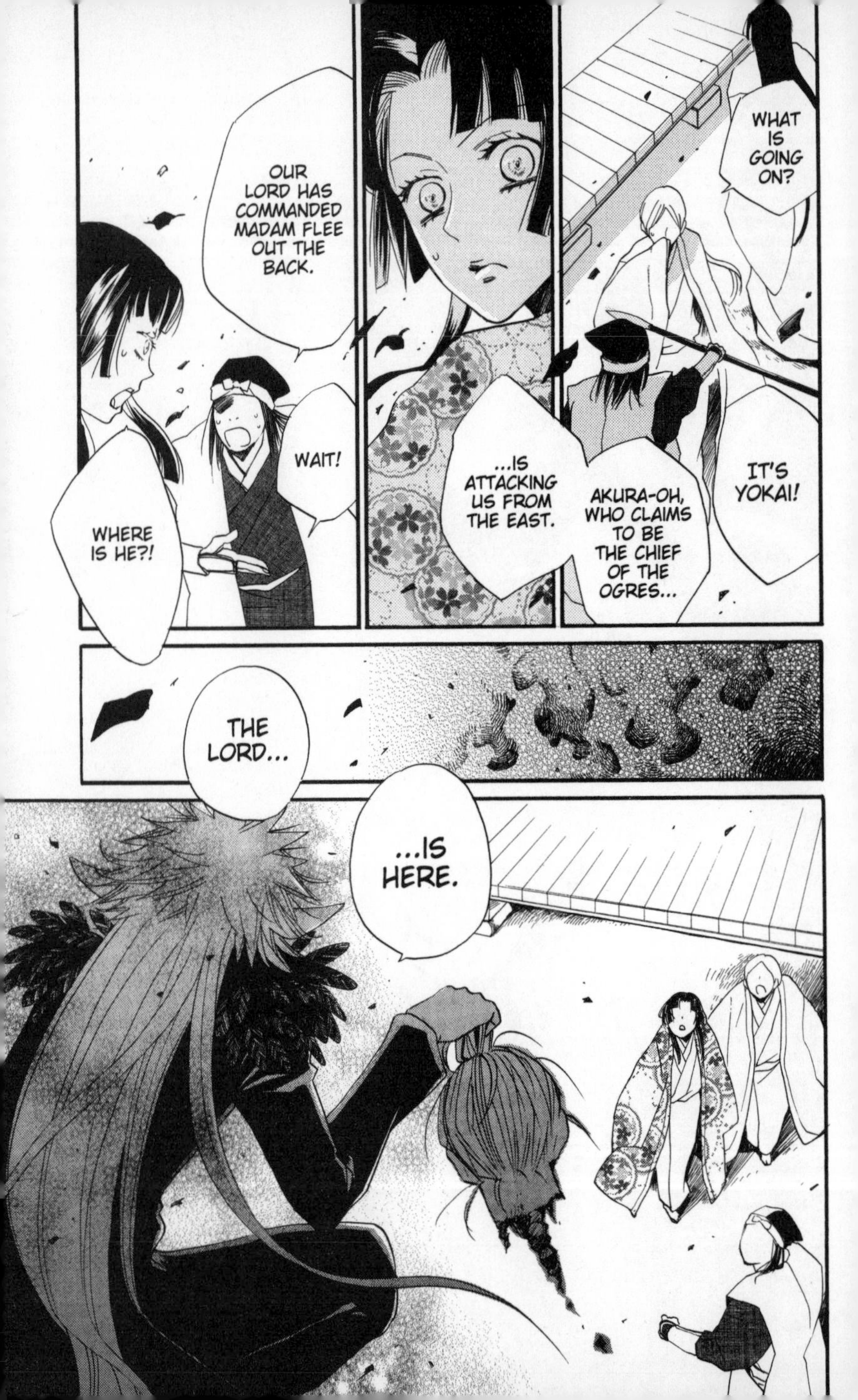
WHAT IS GOING ON?
IT'S YOKAI!
AKURA-OH, WHO CLAIMS TO BE THE CHIEF OF THE OGRES...
...IS ATTACKING US FROM THE EAST.
OUR LORD HAS COMMANDED MADAM FLEE OUT THE BACK.
WAIT!
WHERE IS HE?!
THE LORD...
...IS HERE.

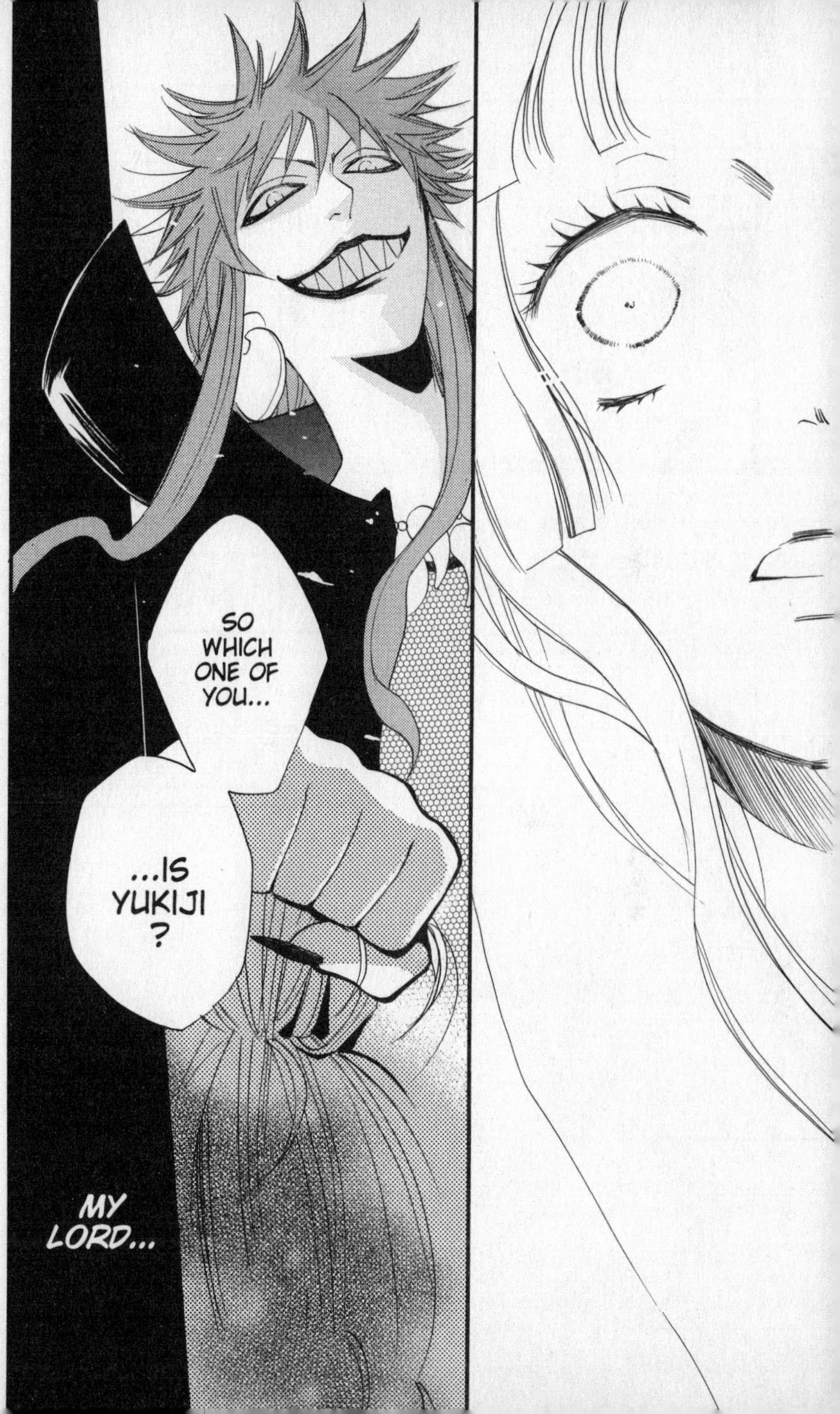
SO WHICH ONE OF YOU...
...IS YUKIJI ?
MY LORD...

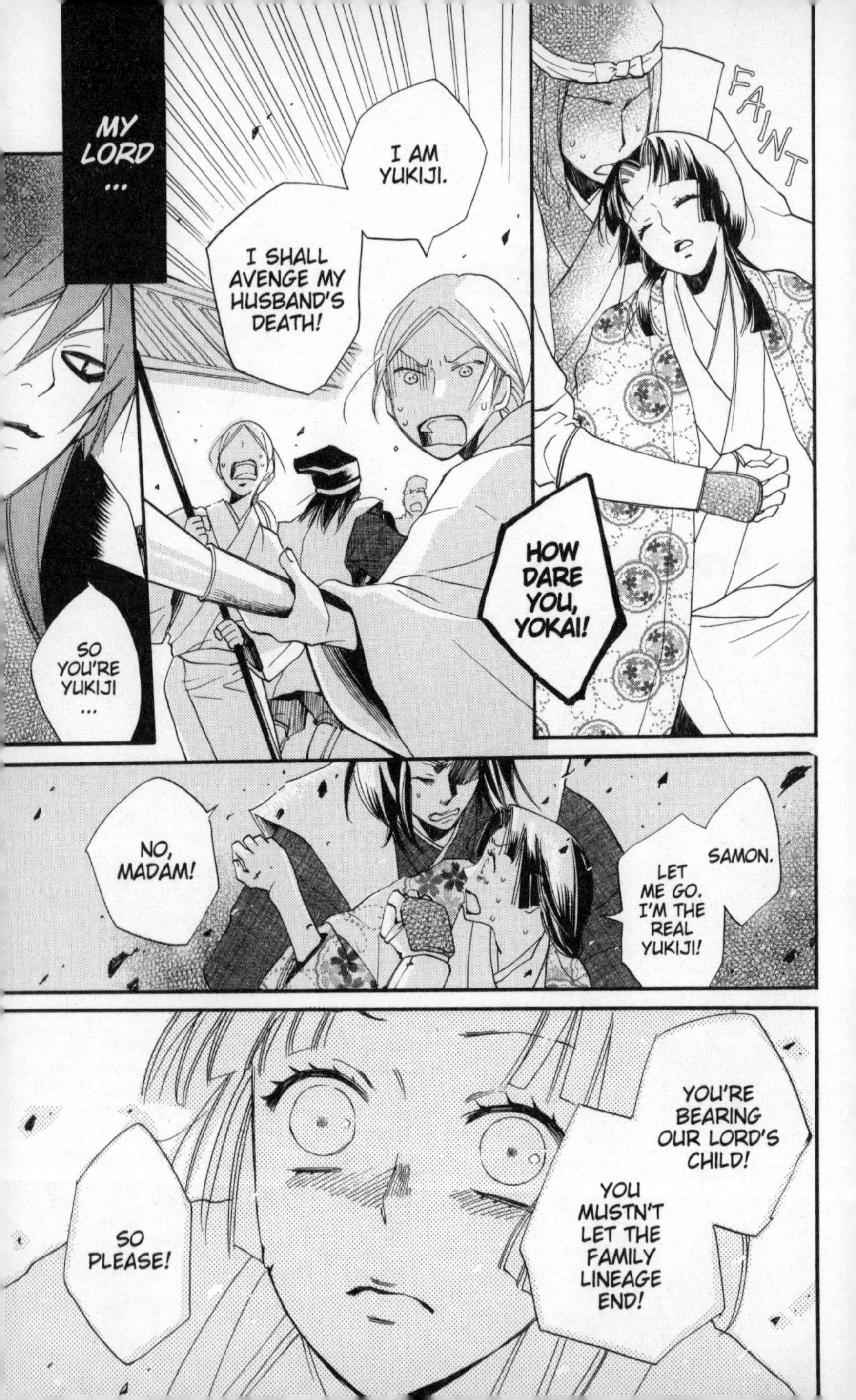
FAINT
I AM YUKIJI.
I SHALL AVENGE MY HUSBAND'S DEATH!
HOW DARE YOU, YOKAI!
MY LORD ...
SO YOU'RE YUKIJI ...
SAMON.
LET ME GO. I'M THE REAL YUKIJI!
NO, MADAM!
YOU'RE BEARING OUR LORD'S CHILD!
YOU MUSTN'T LET THE FAMILY LINEAGE END!
SO PLEASE!

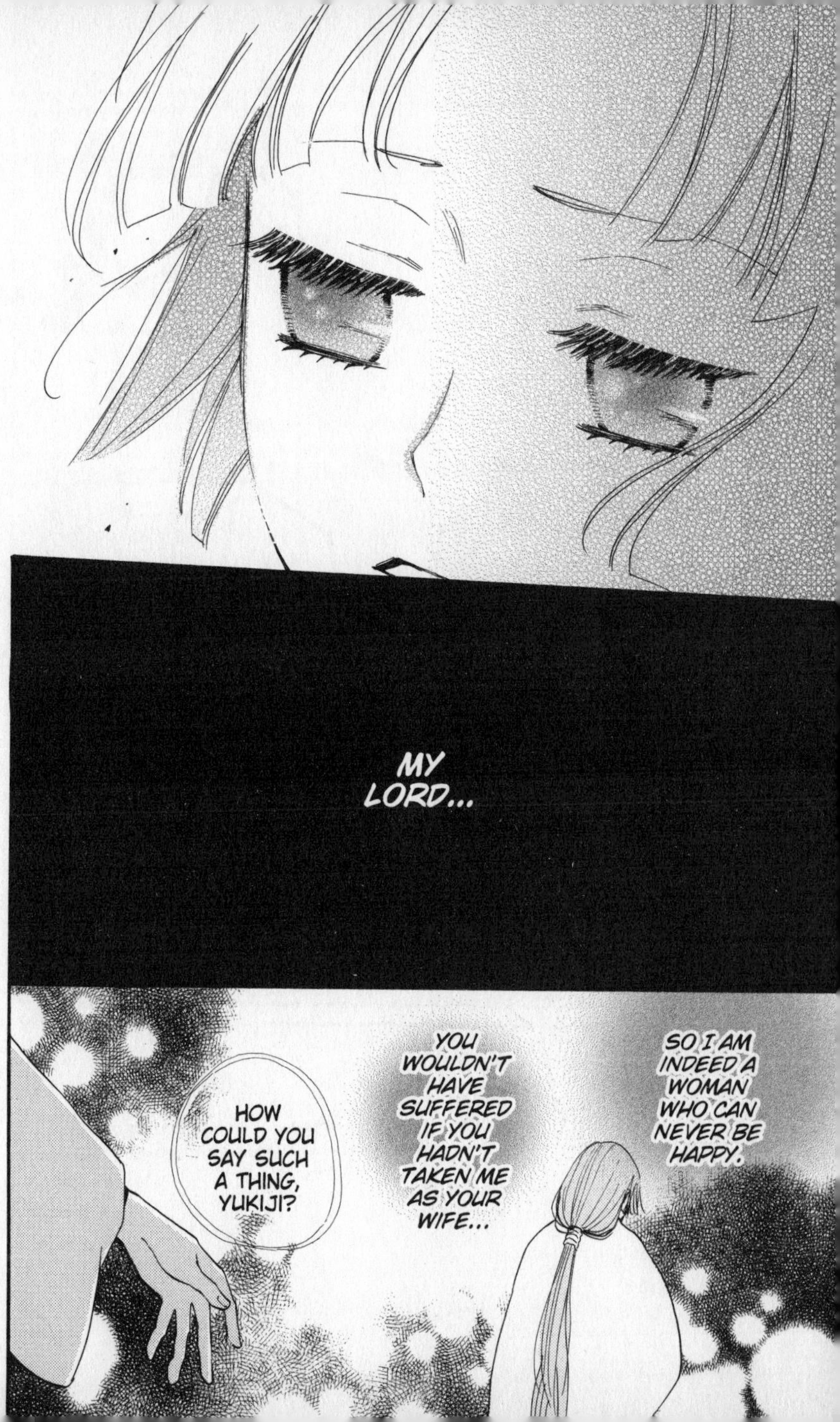
MY LORD...
SO I AM INDEED A WOMAN WHO CAN NEVER BE HAPPY.
YOU WOULDN'T HAVE SUFFERED IF YOU HADN'T TAKEN ME AS YOUR WIFE...
HOW COULD YOU SAY SUCH A THING, YUKIJI?

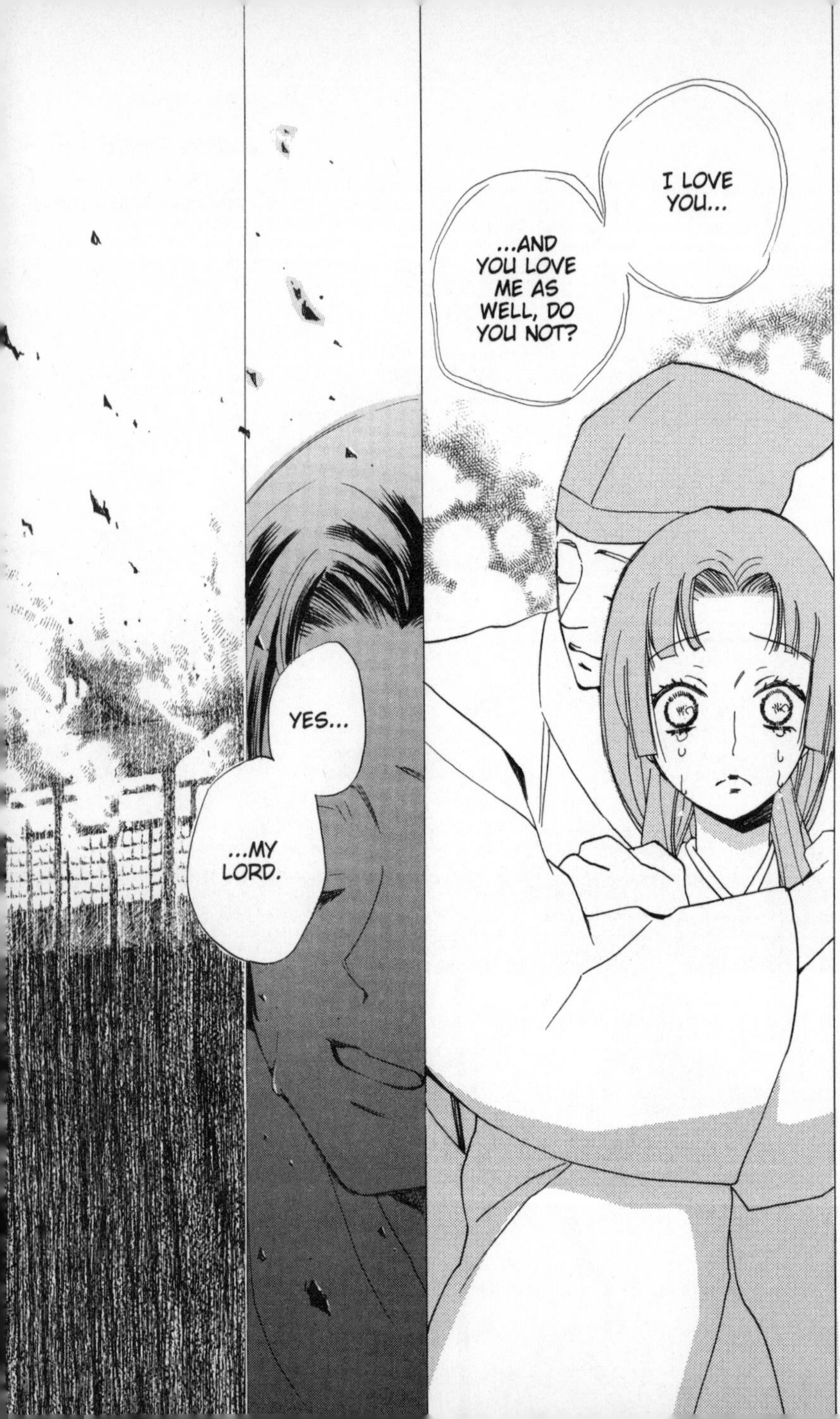
I LOVE YOU...
...AND YOU LOVE ME AS WELL, DO YOU NOT?
YES...
...MY LORD.

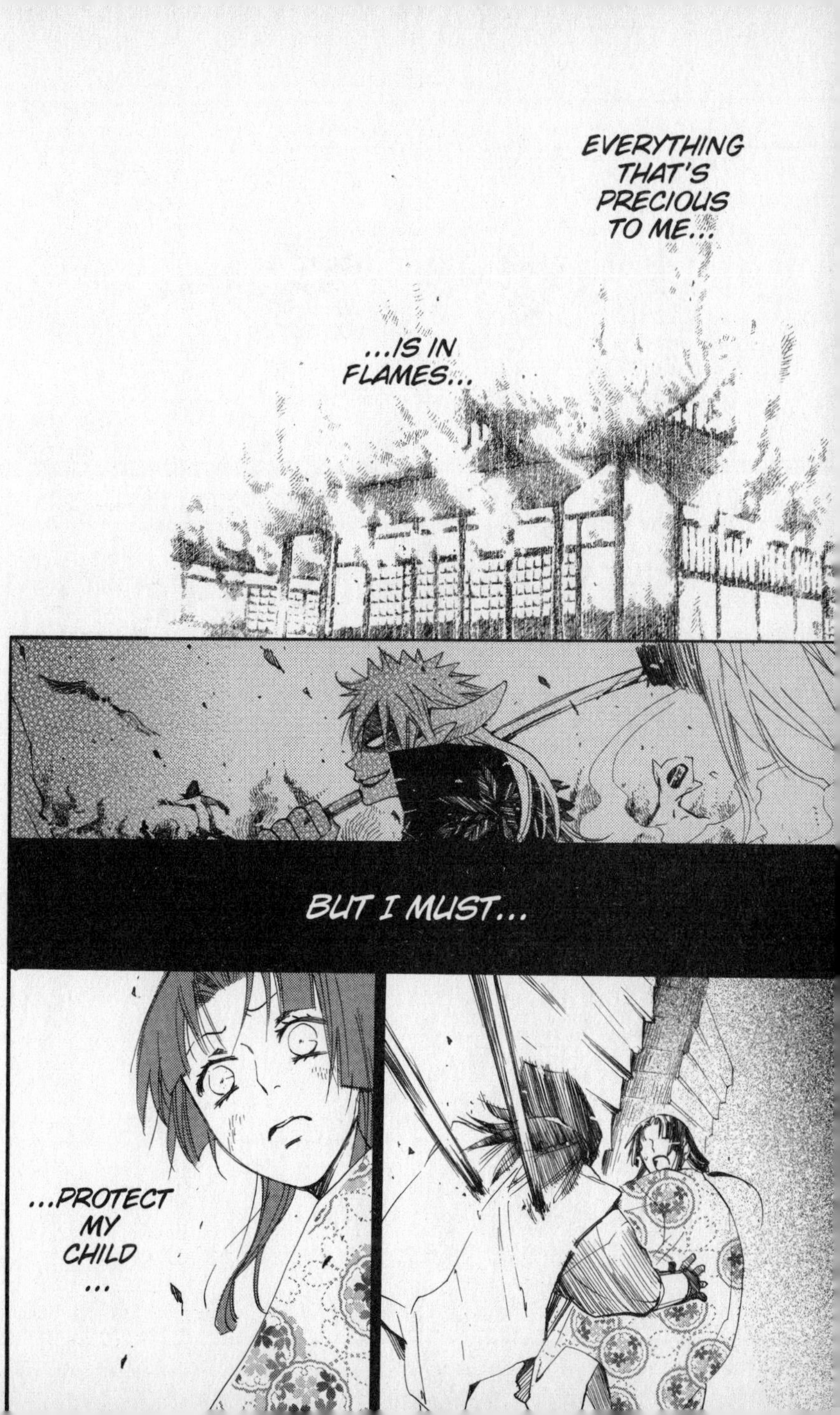
EVERYTHING THAT'S PRECIOUS TO ME...
...IS IN FLAMES...
BUT I MUST...
...PROTECT MY CHILD ...

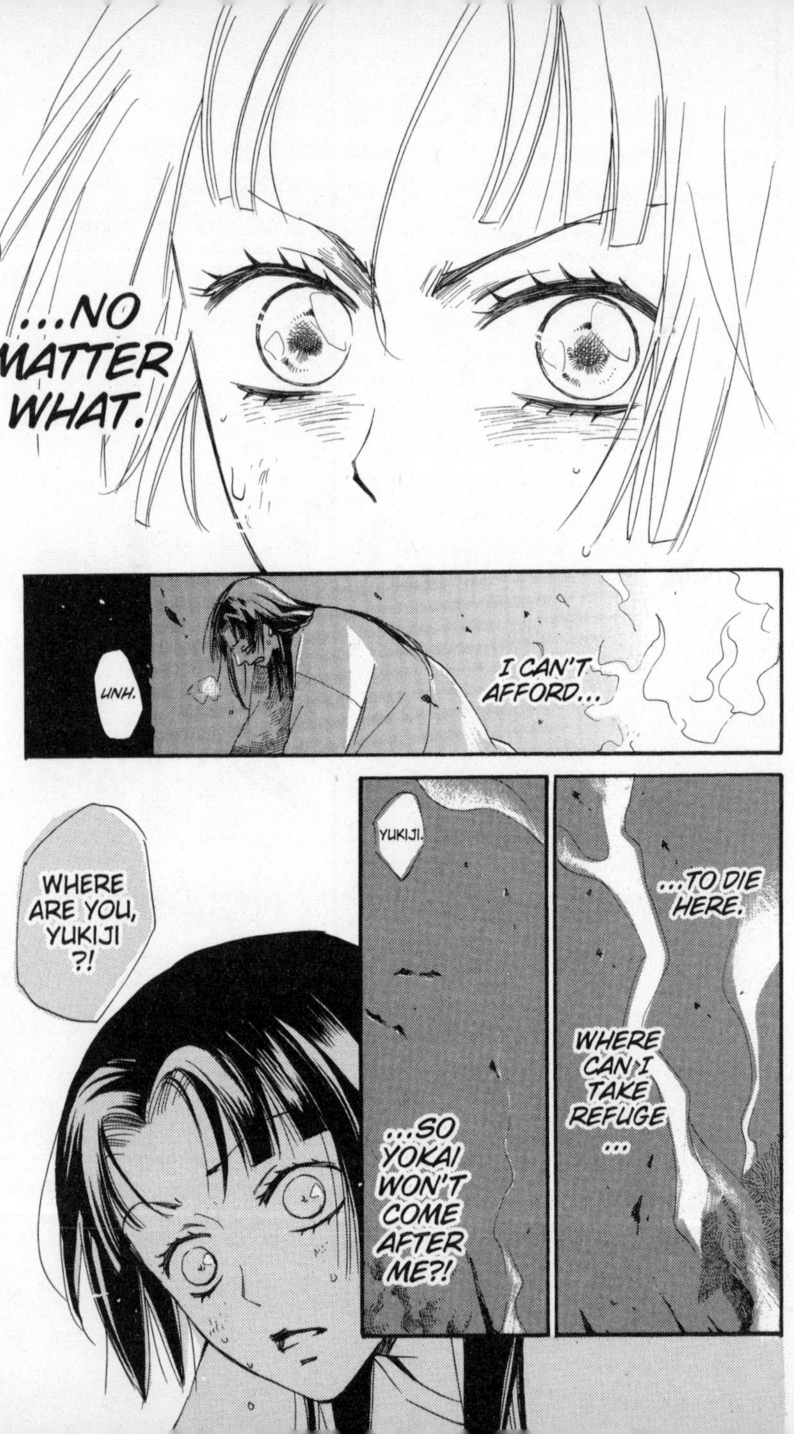
...NO MATTER WHAT.
I CAN'T AFFORD...
UNH.
...TO DIE HERE.
WHERE CAN I TAKE REFUGE...
YUKIJI.
...SO YOKAI WON'T COME AFTER ME?!
WHERE ARE YOU, YUKIJI?!

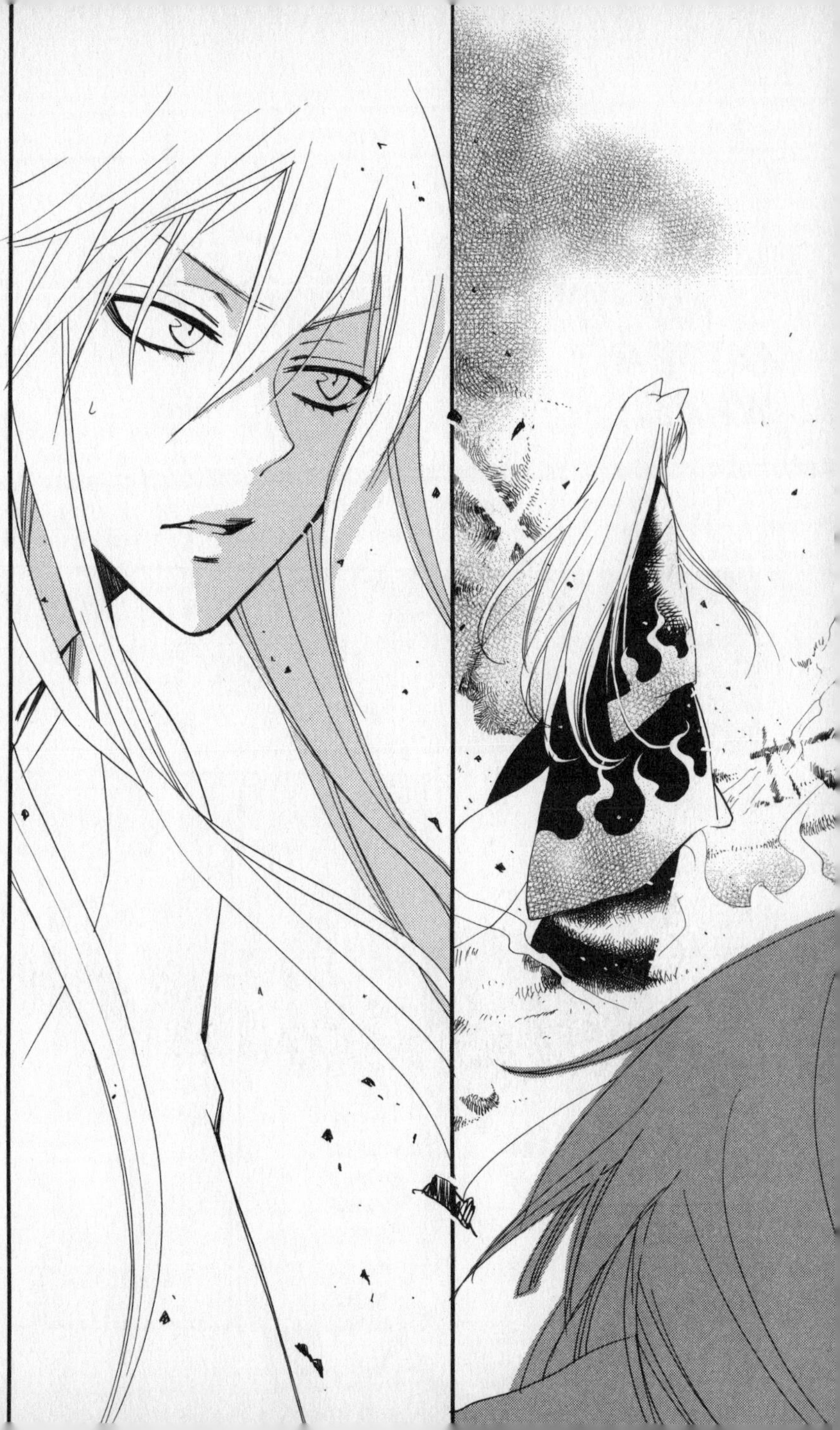

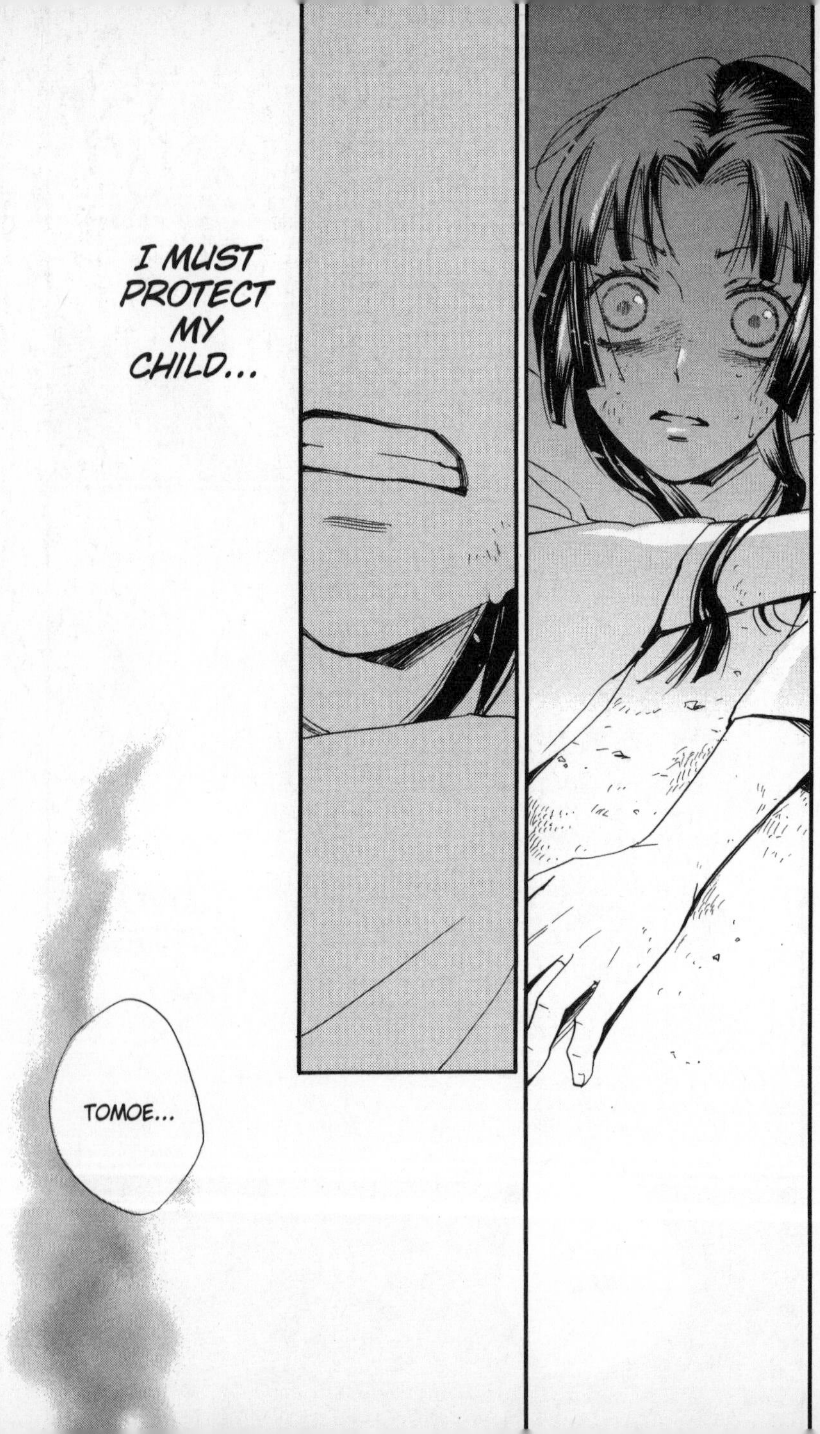
I MUST PROTECT MY CHILD...
TOMOE...

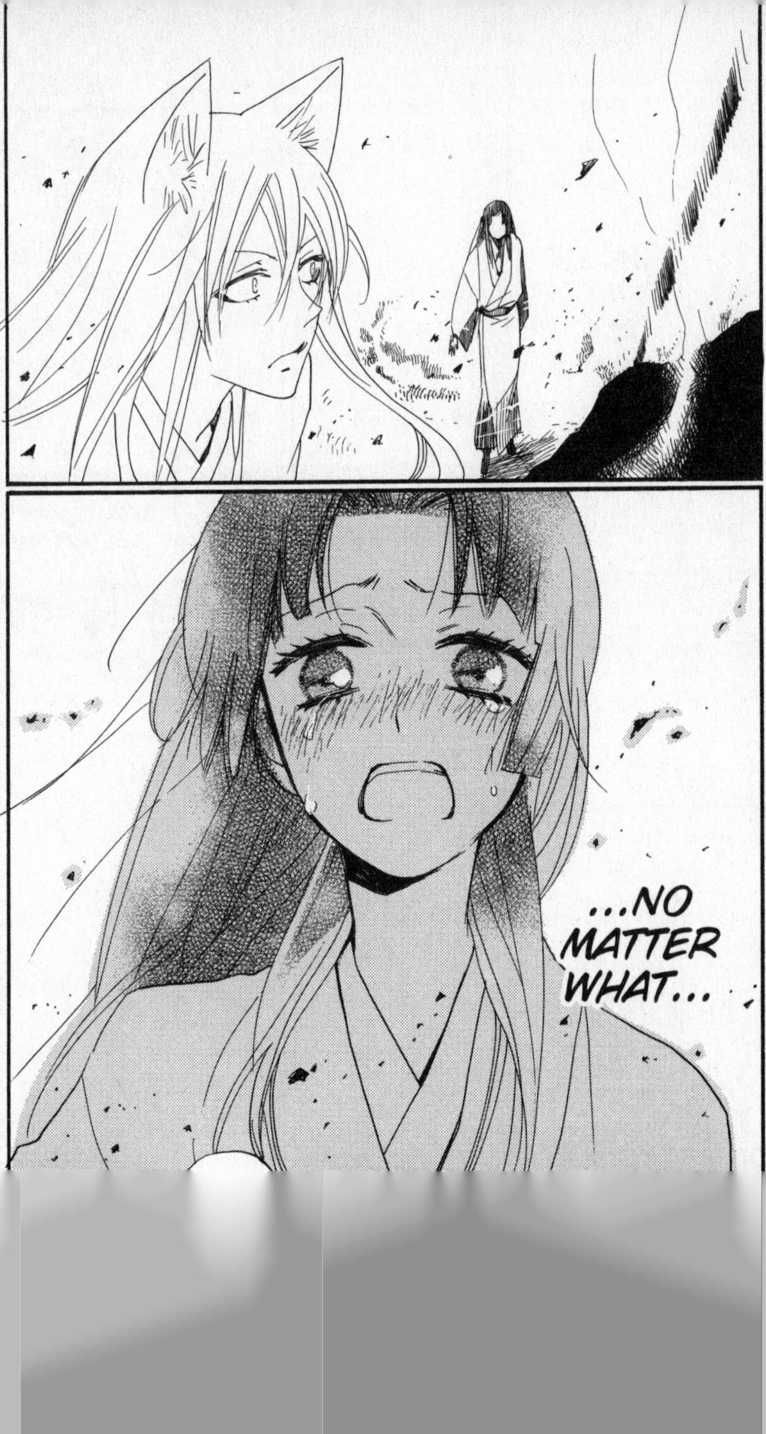
...NO MATTER WHAT...

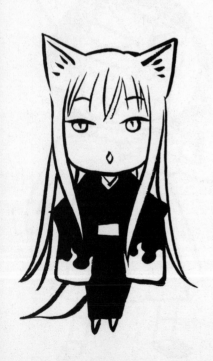

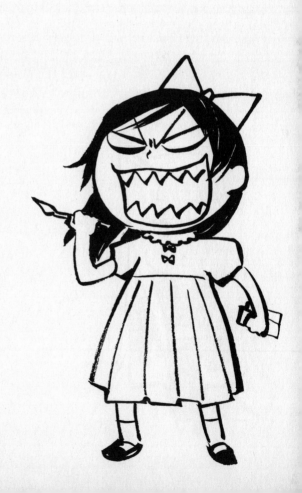

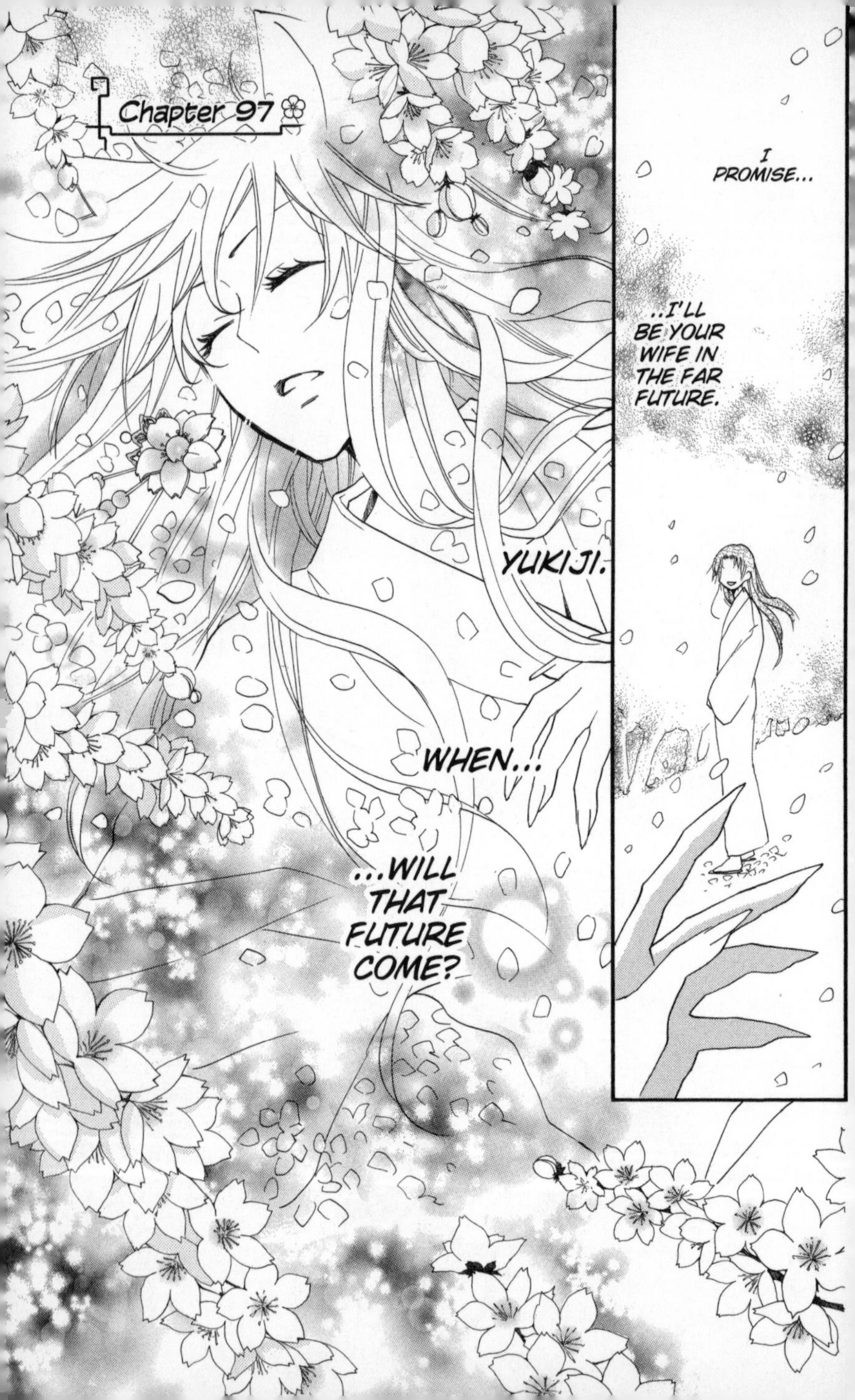
I PROMISE...
..I'LL BE YOUR WIFE IN THE FAR FUTURE.
Chapter 97
YUKIJI.
WHEN...
...WILL THAT FUTURE COME?

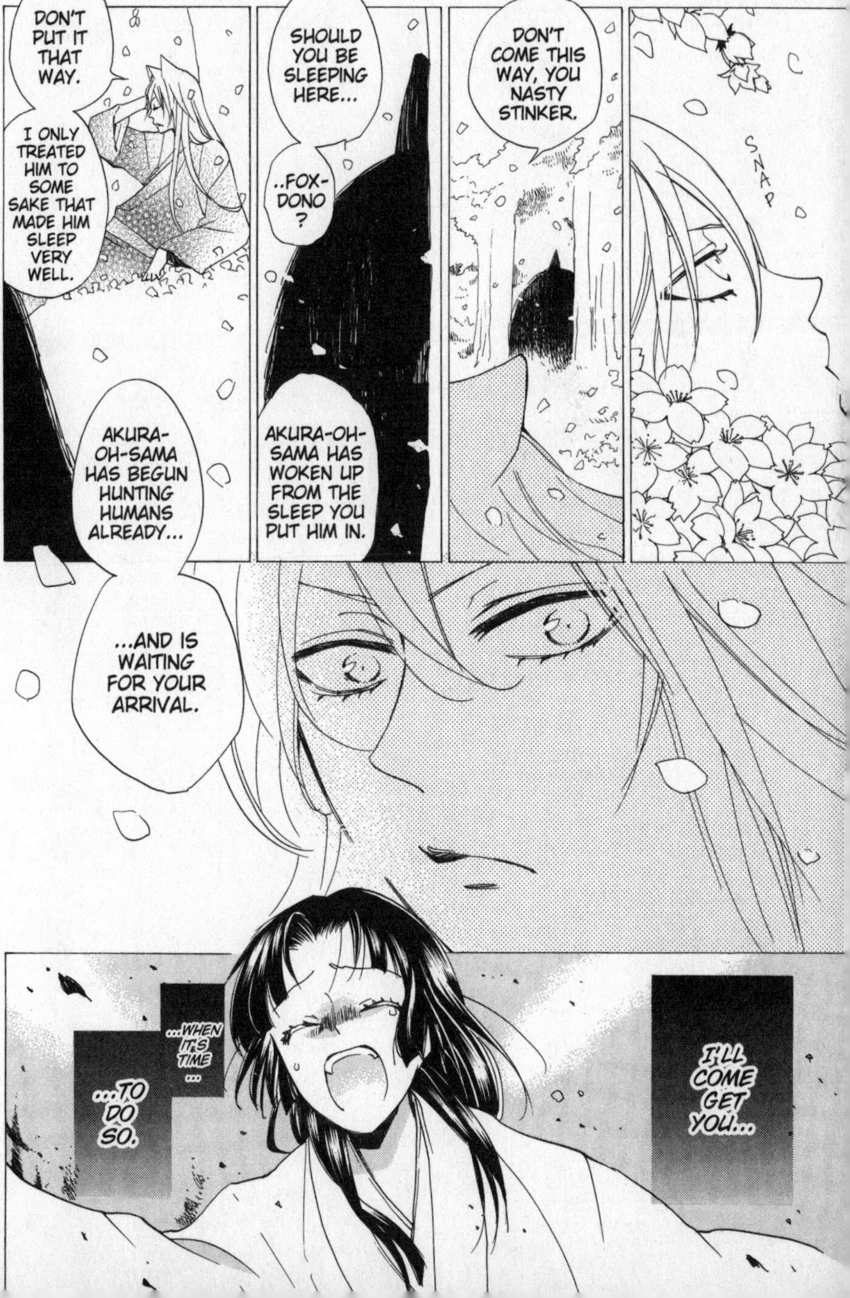
SNAP
DON'T COME THIS WAY, YOU NASTY STINKER.
SHOULD YOU BE SLEEPING HERE...
..FOX-DONO?
AKURA-OH-SAMA HAS WOKEN UP FROM THE SLEEP YOU PUT HIM IN.
DON'T PUT IT THAT WAY.
I ONLY TREATED HIM TO SOME SAKE THAT MADE HIM SLEEP VERY WELL.
AKURA-OH-SAMA HAS BEGUN HUNTING HUMANS ALREADY...
...AND IS WAITING FOR YOUR ARRIVAL.
I'LL COME GET YOU...
...WHEN IT'S TIME...
...TO DO SO.

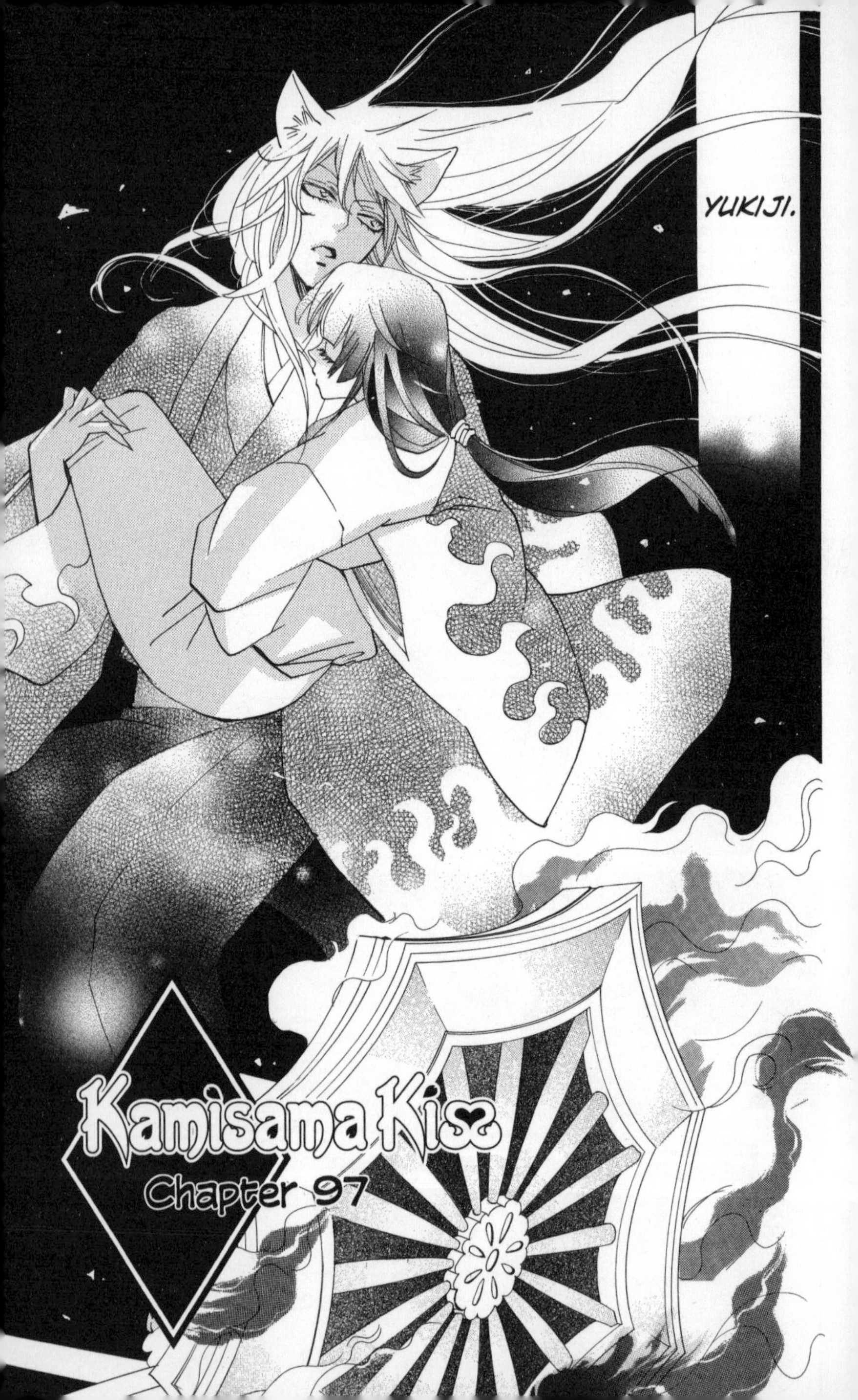
YUKIJI.
Kamisama Kiss
Chapter 97

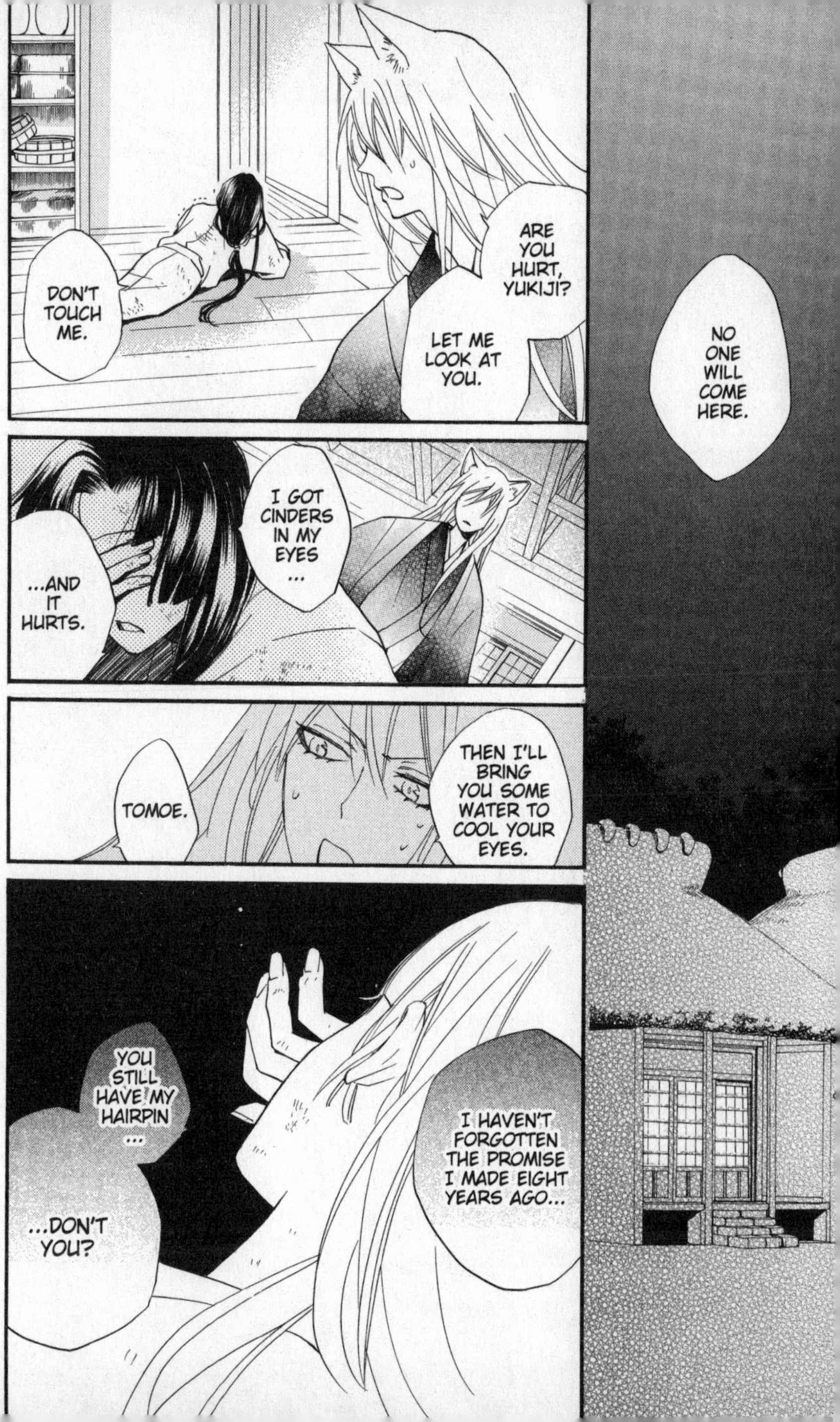
NO ONE WILL COME HERE.
ARE YOU HURT, YUKIJI?
LET ME LOOK AT YOU.
DON'T TOUCH ME.
I GOT CINDERS IN MY EYES...
...AND IT HURTS.
THEN I'LL BRING YOU SOME WATER TO COOL YOUR EYES.
TOMOE.
I HAVEN'T FORGOTTEN THE PROMISE I MADE EIGHT YEARS AGO...
YOU STILL HAVE MY HAIRPIN...
...DON'T YOU?

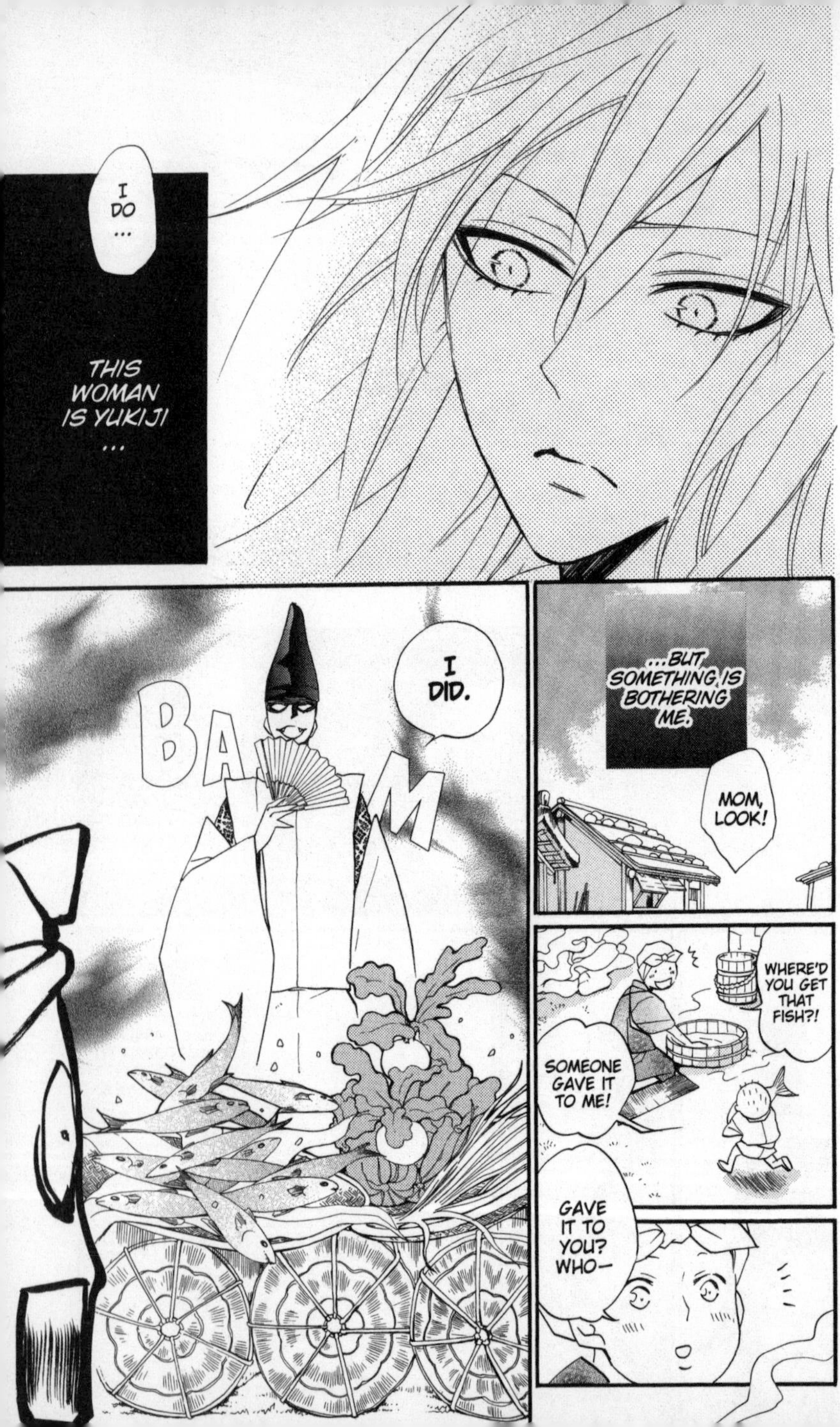
I DO...
THIS WOMAN IS YUKIJI...
...BUT SOMETHING IS BOTHERING ME.
MOM, LOOK!
WHERE'D YOU GET THAT FISH?!
SOMEONE GAVE IT TO ME!
GAVE IT TO YOU? WHO—
I DID.
BAM

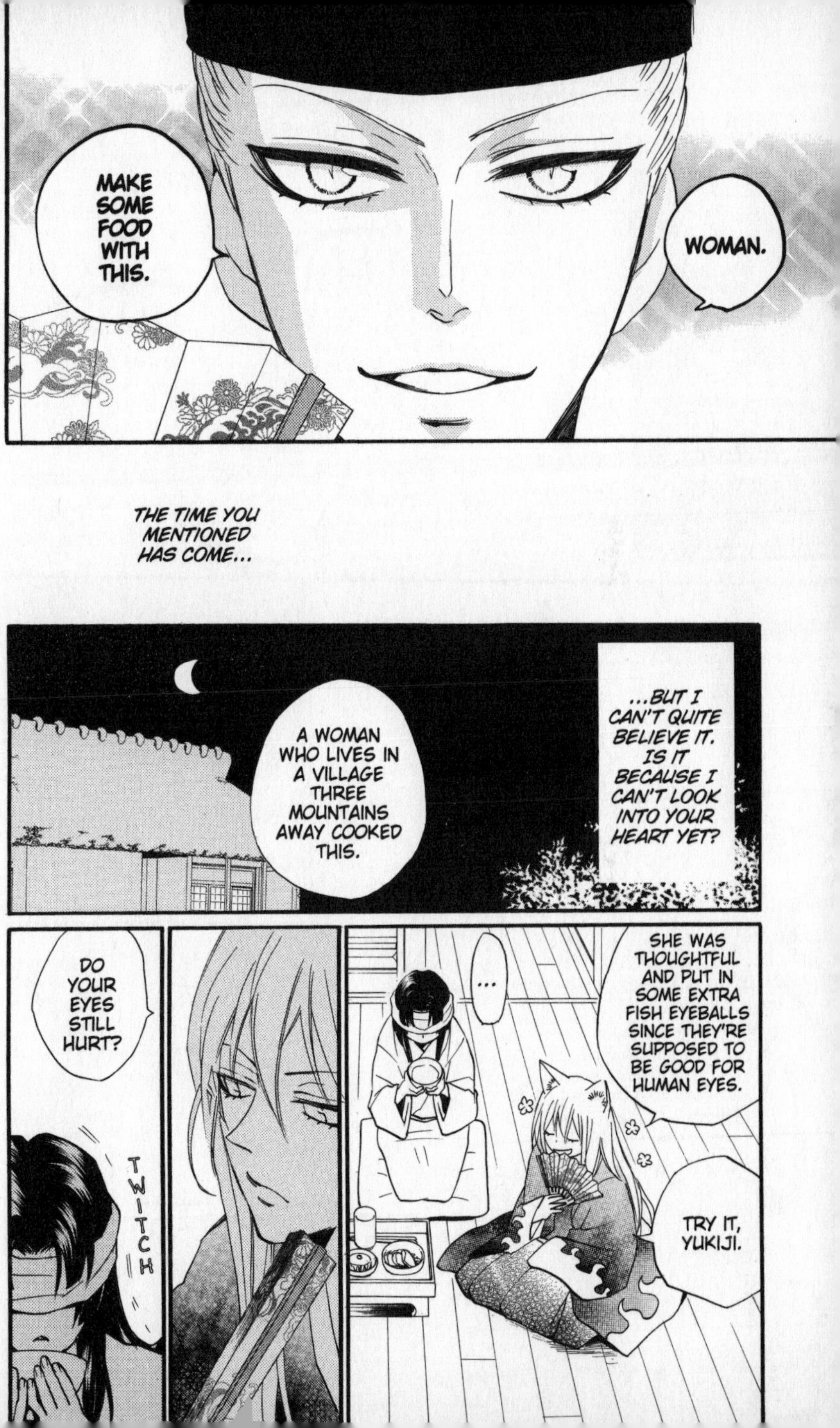
WOMAN.
MAKE SOME FOOD WITH THIS.
THE TIME YOU MENTIONED HAS COME...
...BUT I CAN'T QUITE BELIEVE IT. IS IT BECAUSE I CAN'T LOOK INTO YOUR HEART YET?
A WOMAN WHO LIVES IN A VILLAGE THREE MOUNTAINS AWAY COOKED THIS.
SHE WAS THOUGHTFUL AND PUT IN SOME EXTRA FISH EYEBALLS SINCE THEY'RE SUPPOSED TO BE GOOD FOR HUMAN EYES.
...
TRY IT, YUKIJI.
DO YOUR EYES STILL HURT?
TWITCH

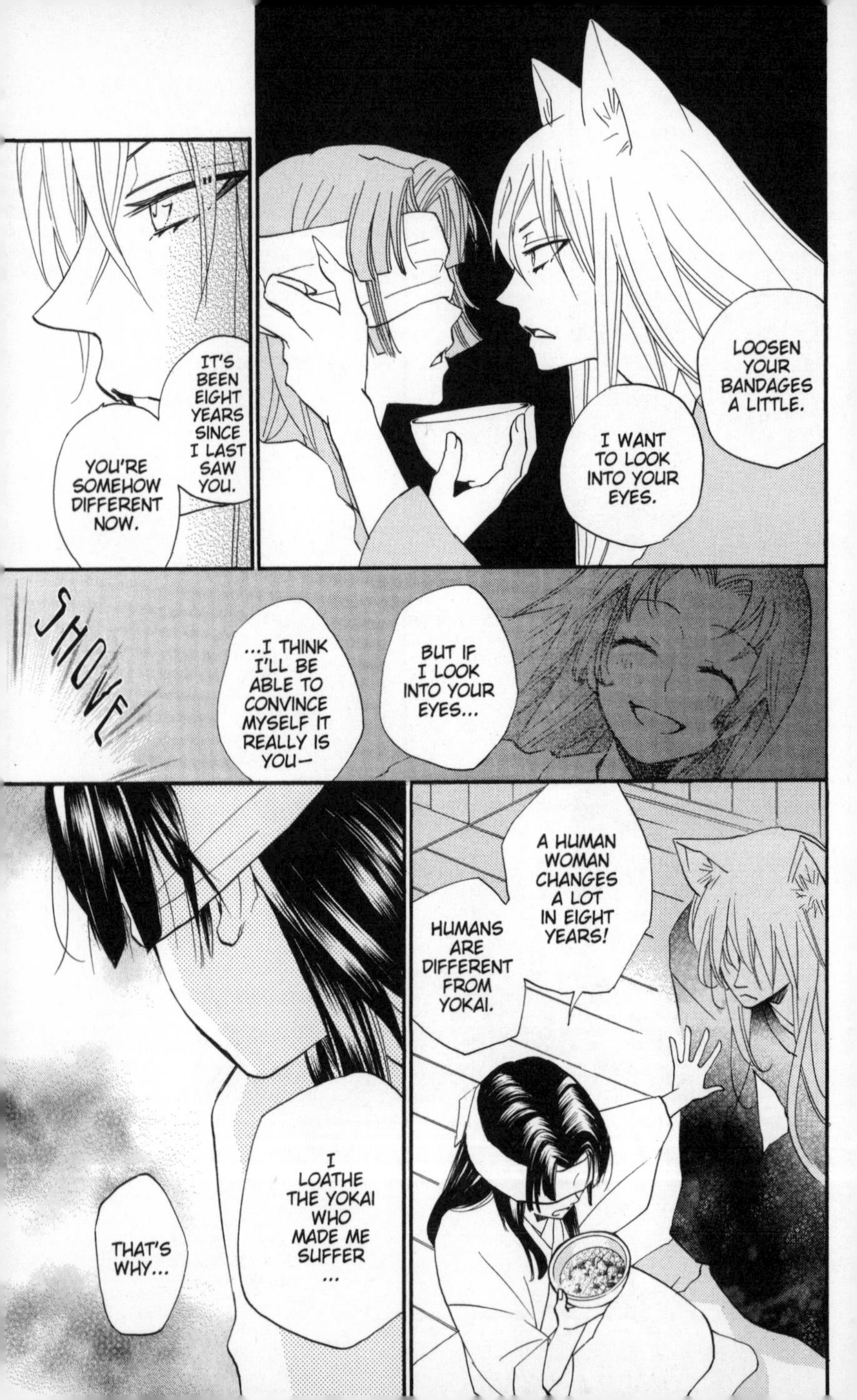
LOOSEN YOUR BANDAGES A LITTLE.
I WANT TO LOOK INTO YOUR EYES.
IT'S BEEN EIGHT YEARS SINCE I LAST SAW YOU.
YOU'RE SOMEHOW DIFFERENT NOW.
BUT IF I LOOK INTO YOUR EYES...
...I THINK I'LL BE ABLE TO CONVINCE MYSELF IT REALLY IS YOU—
SHOVE
A HUMAN WOMAN CHANGES A LOT IN EIGHT YEARS!
HUMANS ARE DIFFERENT FROM YOKAI.
I LOATHE THE YOKAI WHO MADE ME SUFFER...
THAT'S WHY...

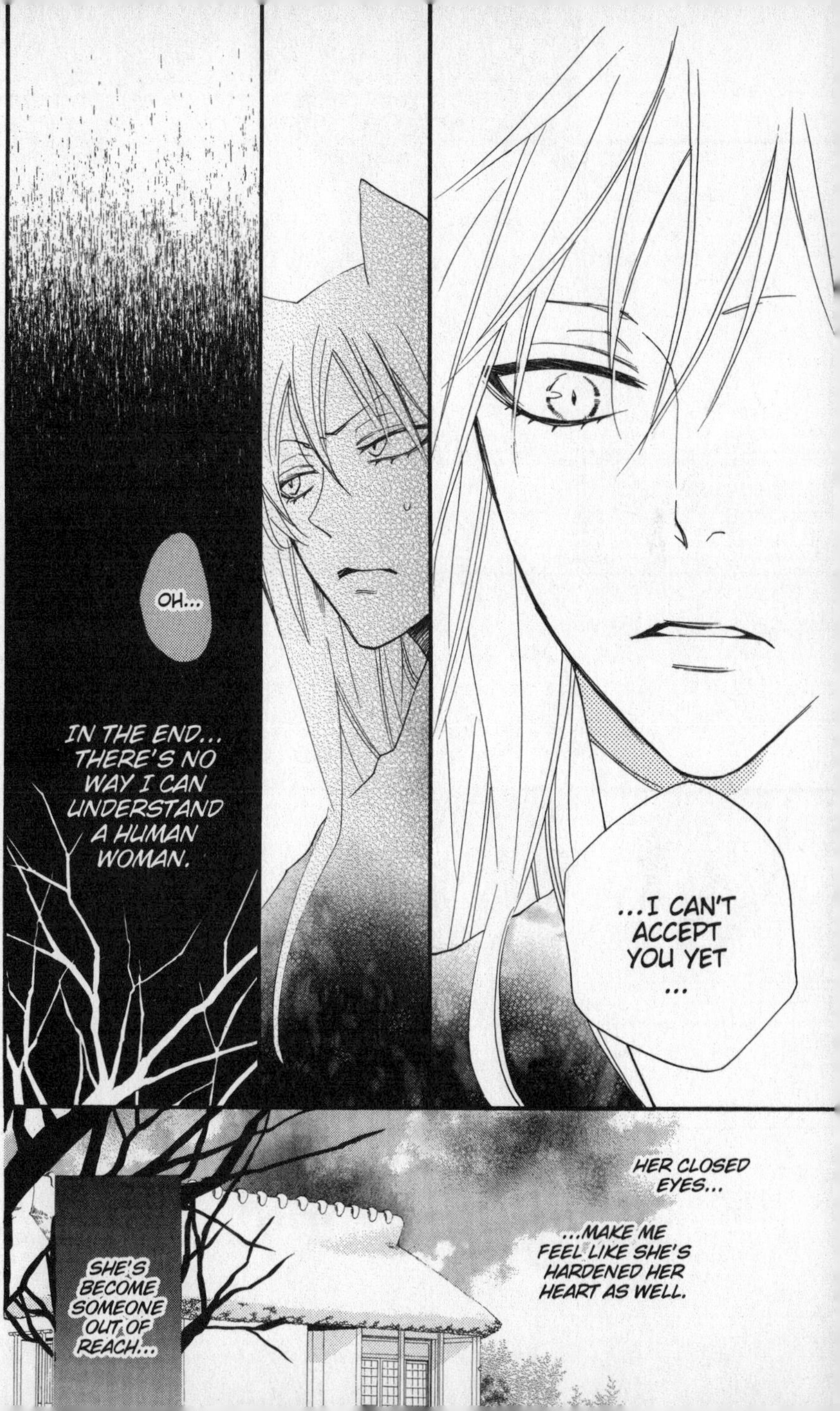
...I CAN'T ACCEPT YOU YET ...
OH...
IN THE END... THERE'S NO WAY I CAN UNDERSTAND A HUMAN WOMAN.
HER CLOSED EYES...
...MAKE ME FEEL LIKE SHE'S HARDENED HER HEART AS WELL.
SHE'S BECOME SOMEONE OUT OF REACH...

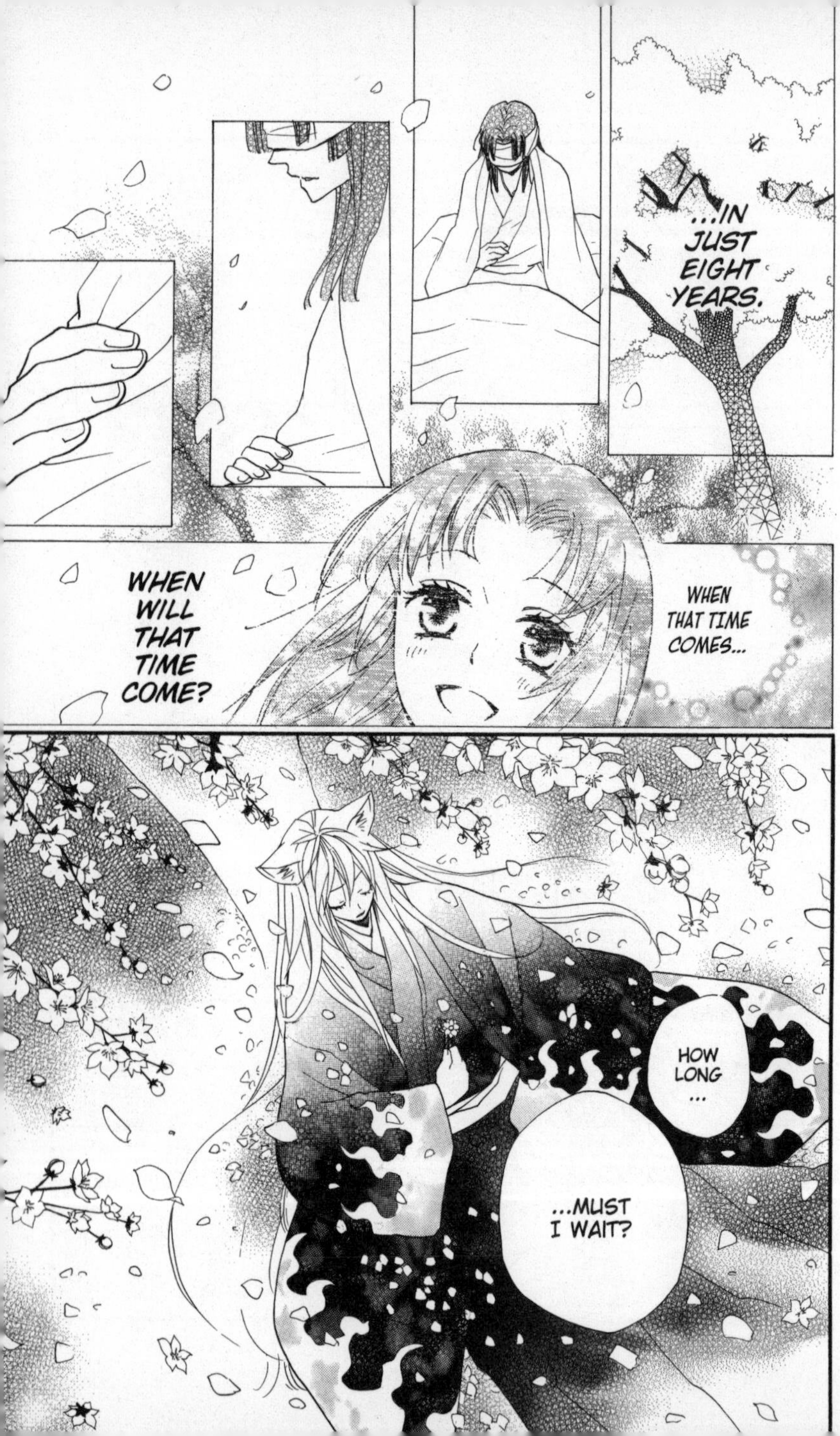
...IN JUST EIGHT YEARS.
WHEN THAT TIME COMES...
WHEN WILL THAT TIME COME?
HOW LONG ...
...MUST I WAIT?

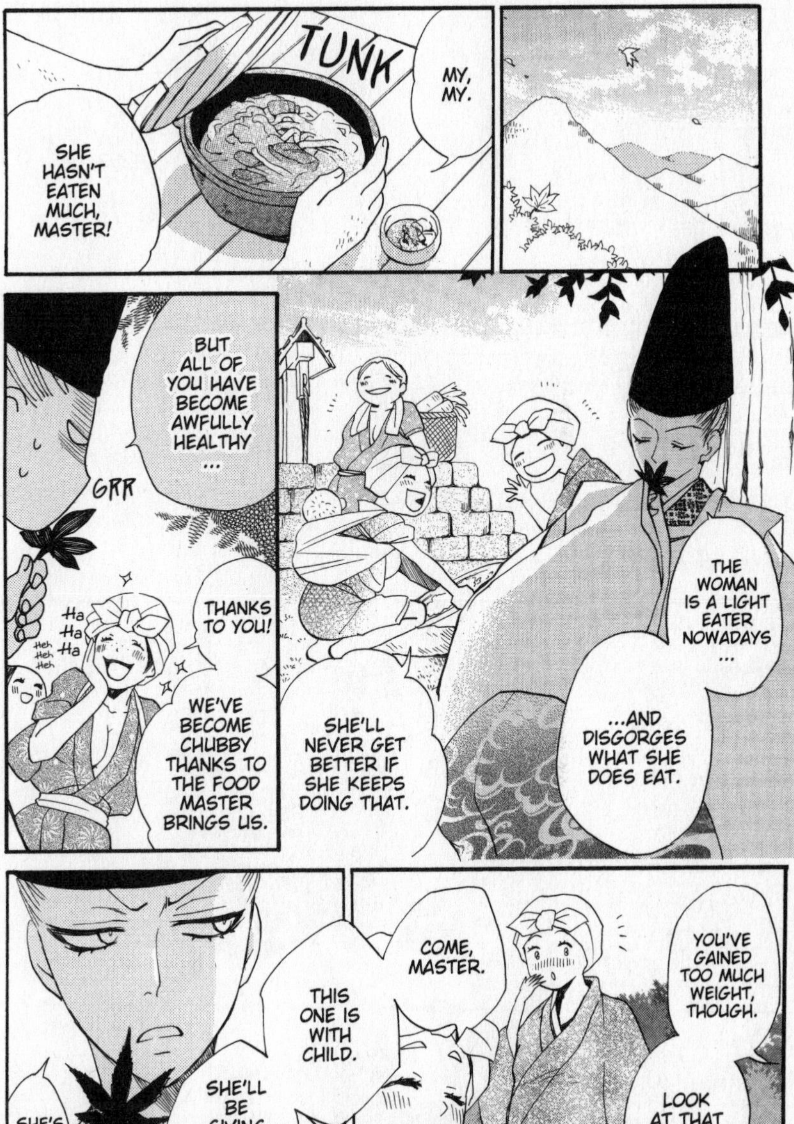

MY, MY.
TUNK
SHE HASN'T EATEN MUCH, MASTER!
THE WOMAN IS A LIGHT EATER NOWADAYS ...
...AND DISGORGES WHAT SHE DOES EAT.
SHE'LL NEVER GET BETTER IF SHE KEEPS DOING THAT.
BUT ALL OF YOU HAVE BECOME AWFULLY HEALTHY ...
GRR
THANKS TO YOU!
Ha Ha Ha
Heh Heh Heh
WE'VE BECOME CHUBBY THANKS TO THE FOOD MASTER BRINGS US.
YOU'VE GAINED TOO MUCH WEIGHT, THOUGH.
COME, MASTER.
LOOK AT THAT BELLY.
THIS ONE IS WITH CHILD.
SHE'LL BE GIVING BIRTH SOON.
SHE'S WITH CHILD?

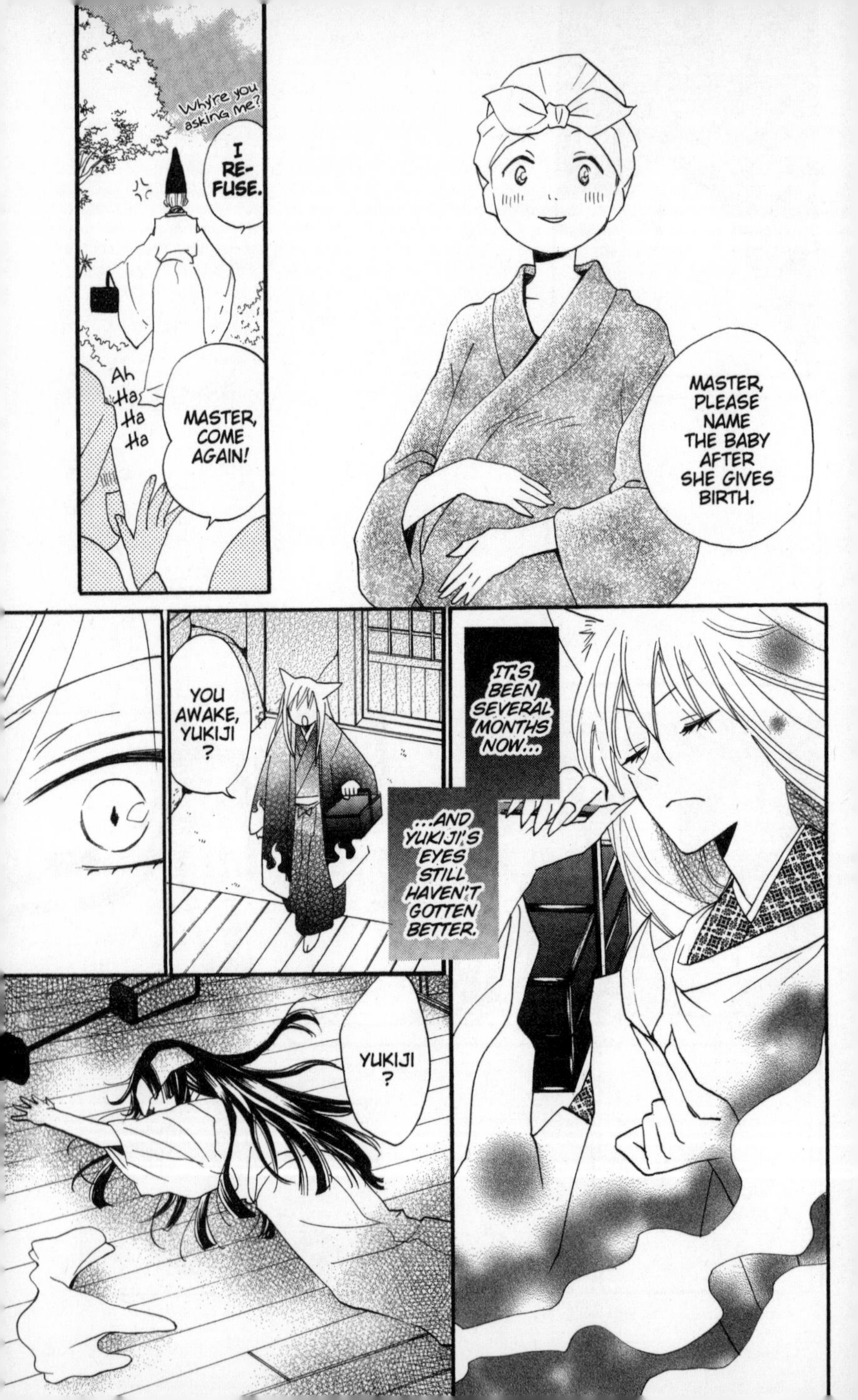
MASTER, PLEASE NAME THE BABY AFTER SHE GIVES BIRTH.
Why're you asking me?
I RE-FUSE.
MASTER, COME AGAIN!
Ah Ha Ha Ha
IT'S BEEN SEVERAL MONTHS NOW...
...AND YUKIJI'S EYES STILL HAVEN'T GOTTEN BETTER.
YOU AWAKE, YUKIJI?
YUKIJI?

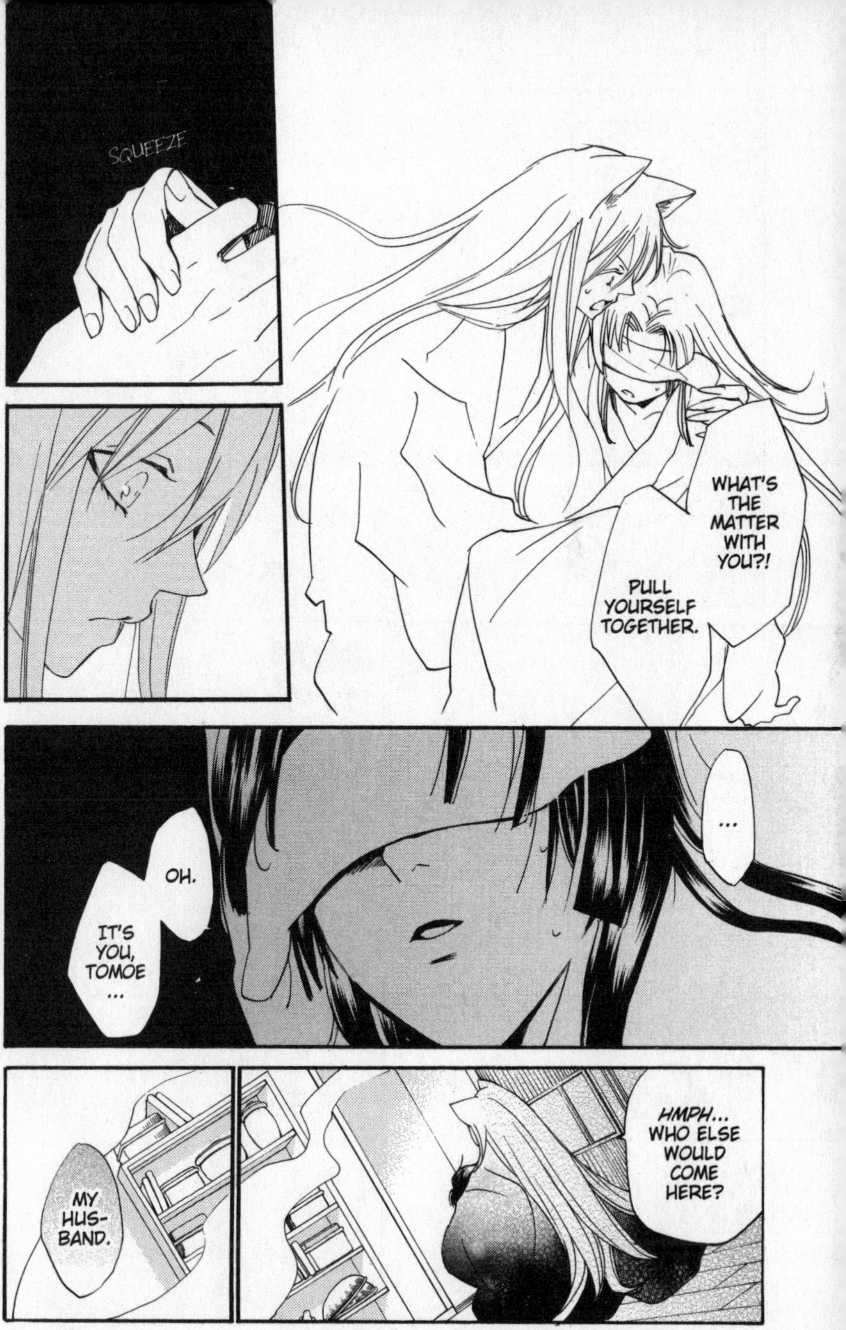
WHAT'S THE MATTER WITH YOU?!
PULL YOURSELF TOGETHER.
SQUEEZE
...
OH.
IT'S YOU, TOMOE ...
HMPH... WHO ELSE WOULD COME HERE?
MY HUS-BAND.

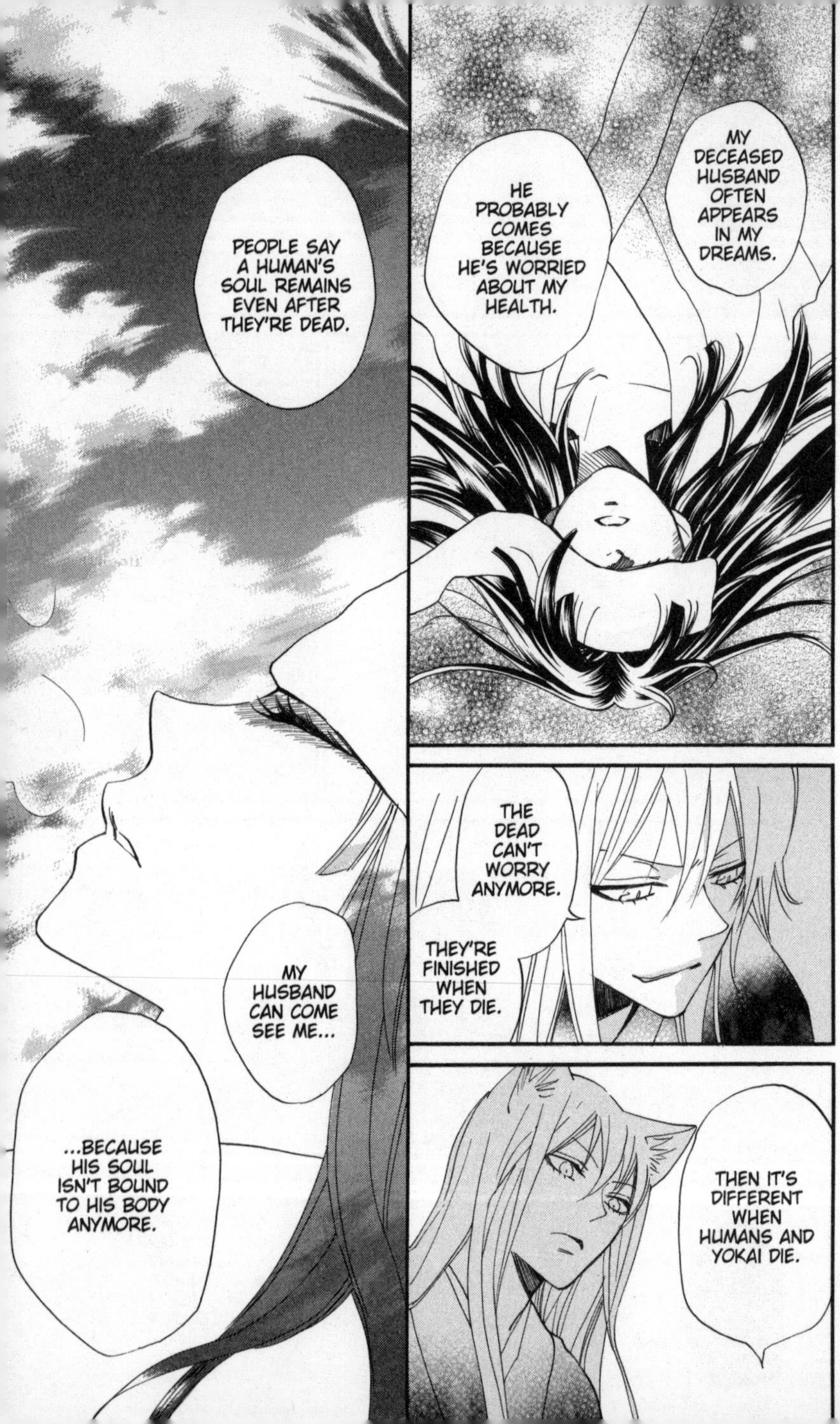
MY DECEASED HUSBAND OFTEN APPEARS IN MY DREAMS.
HE PROBABLY COMES BECAUSE HE'S WORRIED ABOUT MY HEALTH.
THE DEAD CAN'T WORRY ANYMORE.
THEY'RE FINISHED WHEN THEY DIE.
THEN IT'S DIFFERENT WHEN HUMANS AND YOKAI DIE.
PEOPLE SAY A HUMAN'S SOUL REMAINS EVEN AFTER THEY'RE DEAD.
MY HUSBAND CAN COME SEE ME...
...BECAUSE HIS SOUL ISN'T BOUND TO HIS BODY ANYMORE.

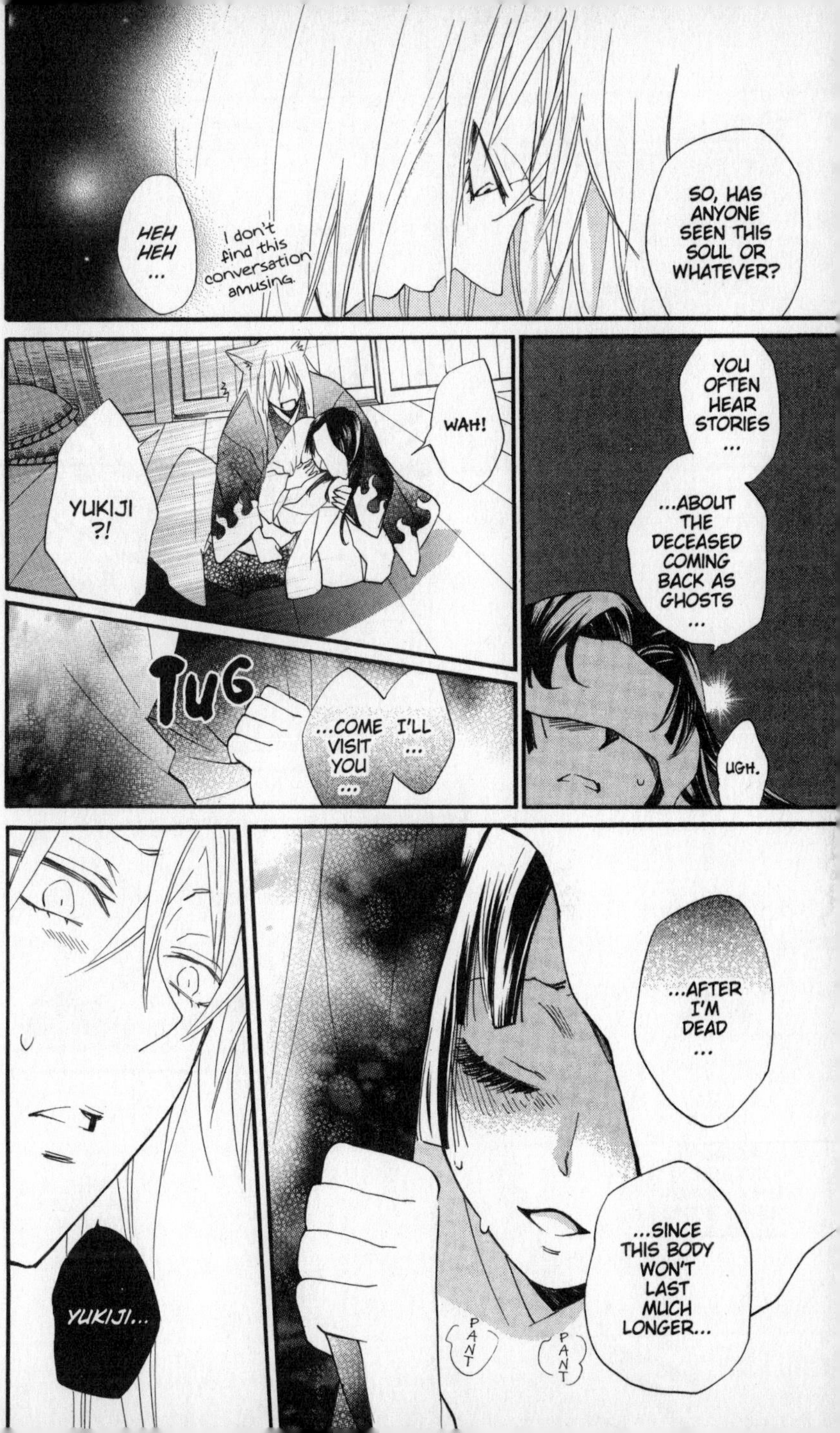
SO, HAS ANYONE SEEN THIS SOUL OR WHATEVER?
I don't find this conversation amusing.
HEH HEH ...
YOU OFTEN HEAR STORIES ...
...ABOUT THE DECEASED COMING BACK AS GHOSTS ...
UGH.
WAH!
YUKIJI ?!
I'LL ...
...COME VISIT YOU ...
TUG
...AFTER I'M DEAD ...
...SINCE THIS BODY WON'T LAST MUCH LONGER...
PANT
PANT
YUKIJI...

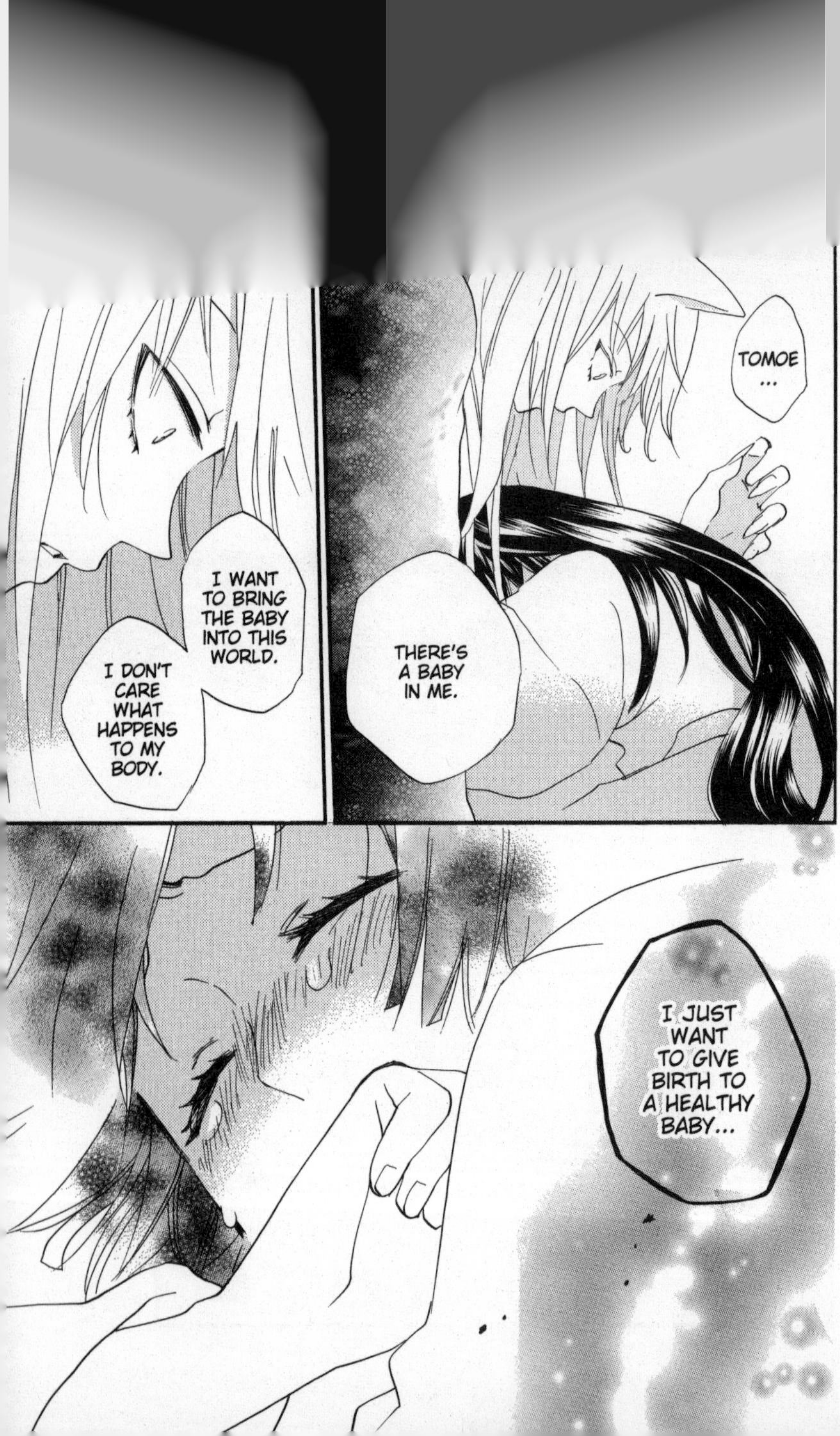
TOMOE ...
THERE'S A BABY IN ME.
I WANT TO BRING THE BABY INTO THIS WORLD.
I DON'T CARE WHAT HAPPENS TO MY BODY.
I JUST WANT TO GIVE BIRTH TO A HEALTHY BABY...

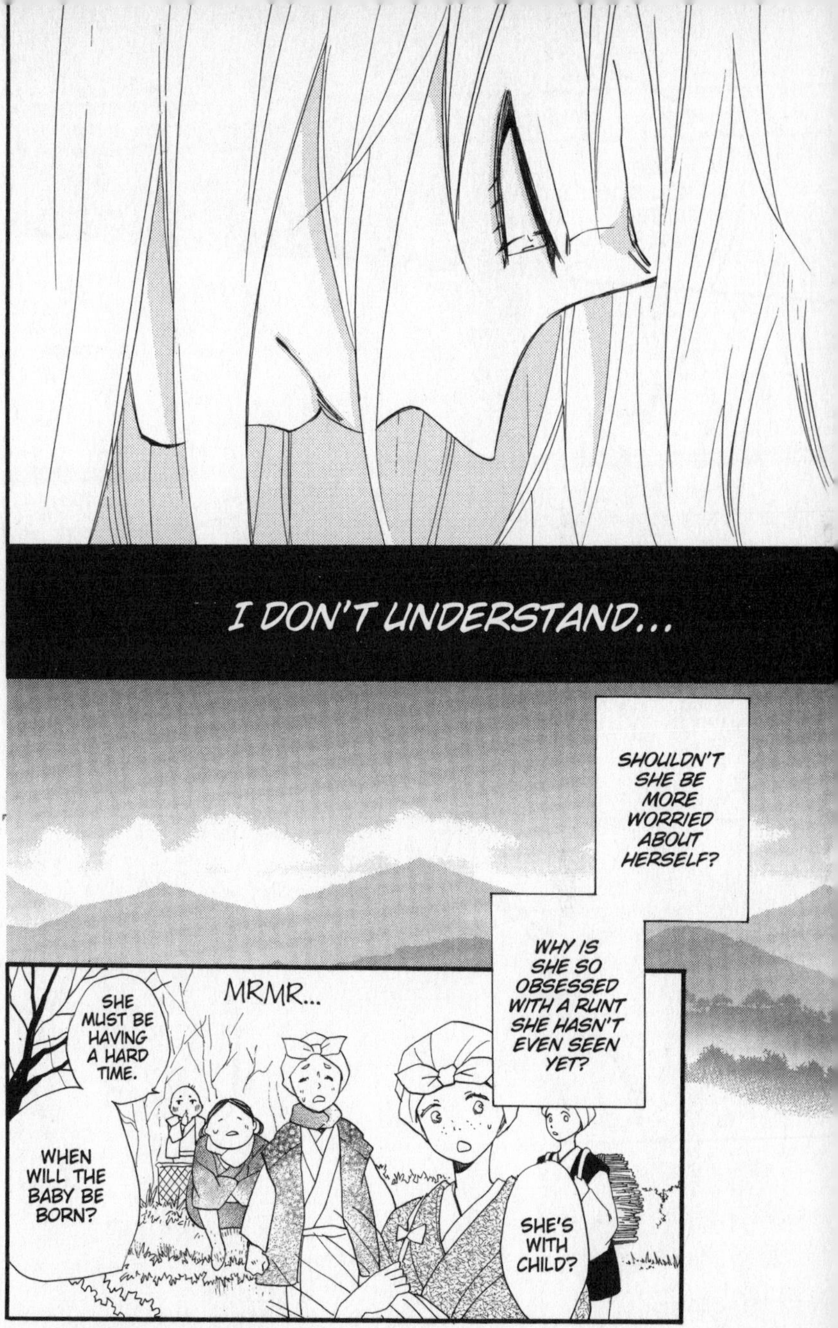
I DON'T UNDERSTAND...
SHOULDN'T SHE BE MORE WORRIED ABOUT HERSELF?
WHY IS SHE SO OBSESSED WITH A RUNT SHE HASN'T EVEN SEEN YET?
SHE'S WITH CHILD?
MRMR...
SHE MUST BE HAVING A HARD TIME.
WHEN WILL THE BABY BE BORN?

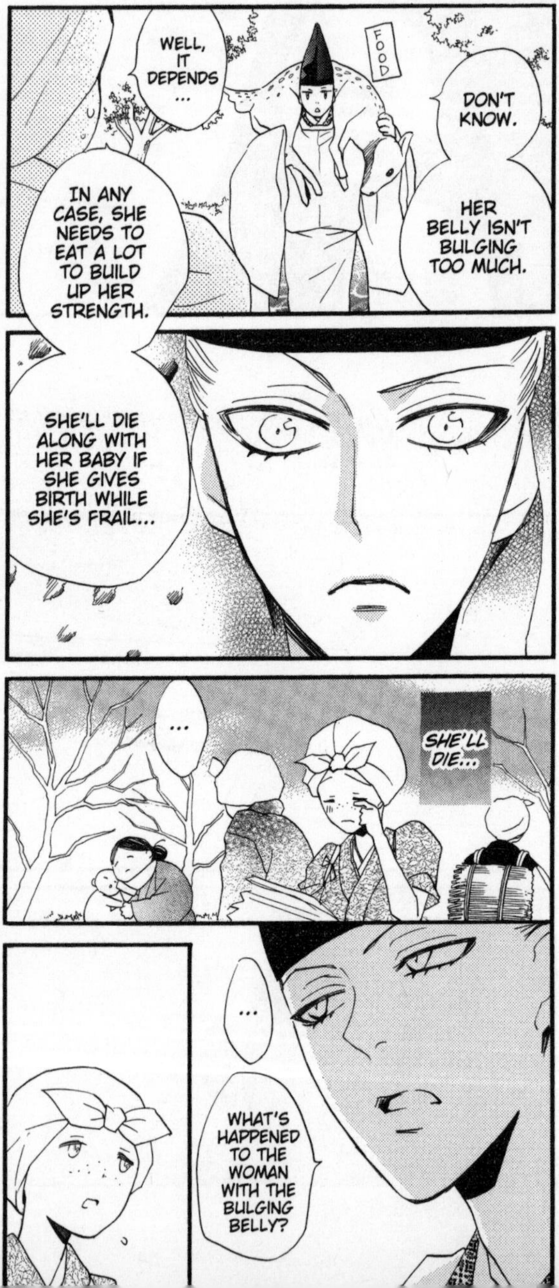
DON'T KNOW.
HER BELLY ISN'T BULGING TOO MUCH.
FOOD
WELL, IT DEPENDS ...
IN ANY CASE, SHE NEEDS TO EAT A LOT TO BUILD UP HER STRENGTH.
SHE'LL DIE ALONG WITH HER BABY IF SHE GIVES BIRTH WHILE SHE'S FRAIL...
SHE'LL DIE...
...
...
WHAT'S HAPPENED TO THE WOMAN WITH THE BULGING BELLY?

After thinking about it for a long time, I recently began to visit a dentist.

I had cavities under all my silver fillings.

I knew I did!

I had 12! of them.

Everyone should get dental checkups...

By the way, the treatments have been going well, and I only have one more cavity left.

I'm very happy I can now eat my favorite yoriyori again...!

But I still find dentists scary.

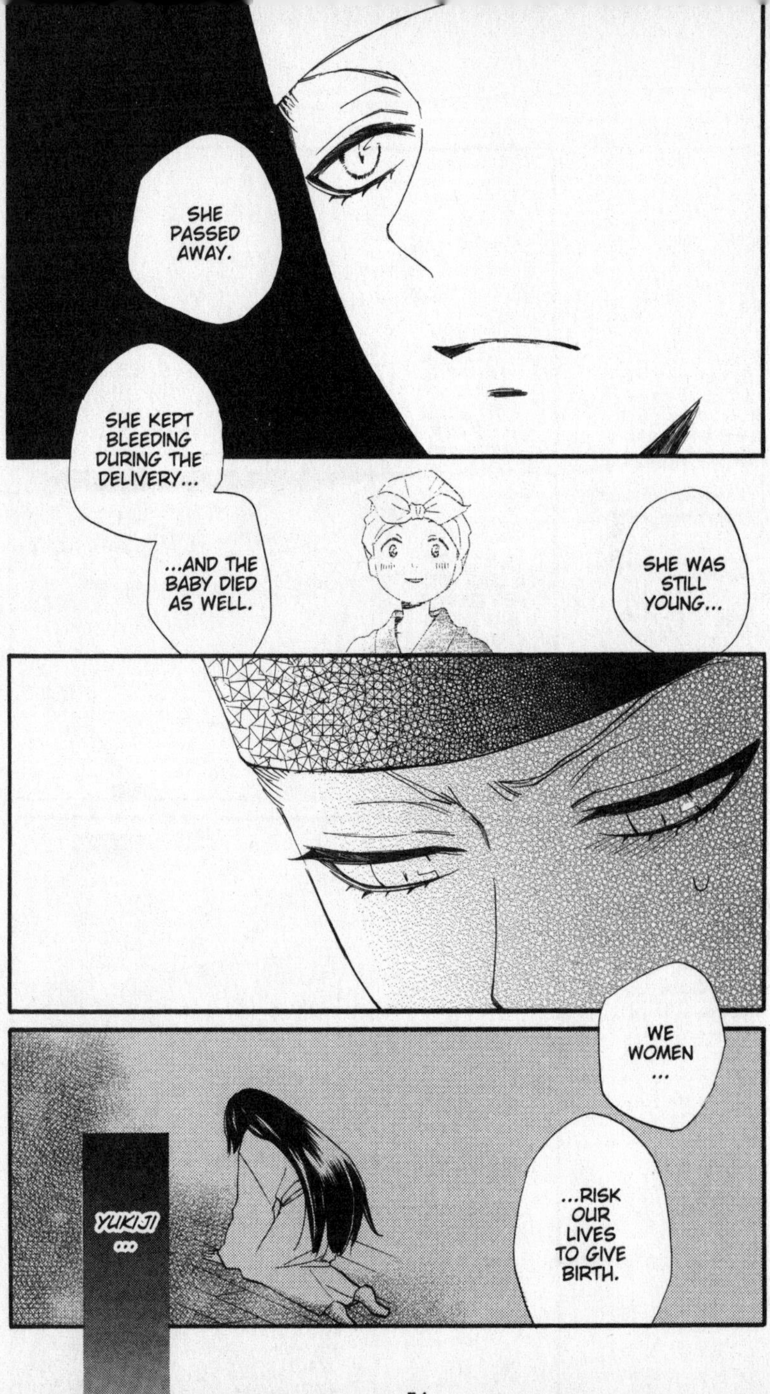
SHE PASSED AWAY.
SHE KEPT BLEEDING DURING THE DELIVERY...
...AND THE BABY DIED AS WELL.
SHE WAS STILL YOUNG...
WE WOMEN ...
...RISK OUR LIVES TO GIVE BIRTH.
YUKIJI ...

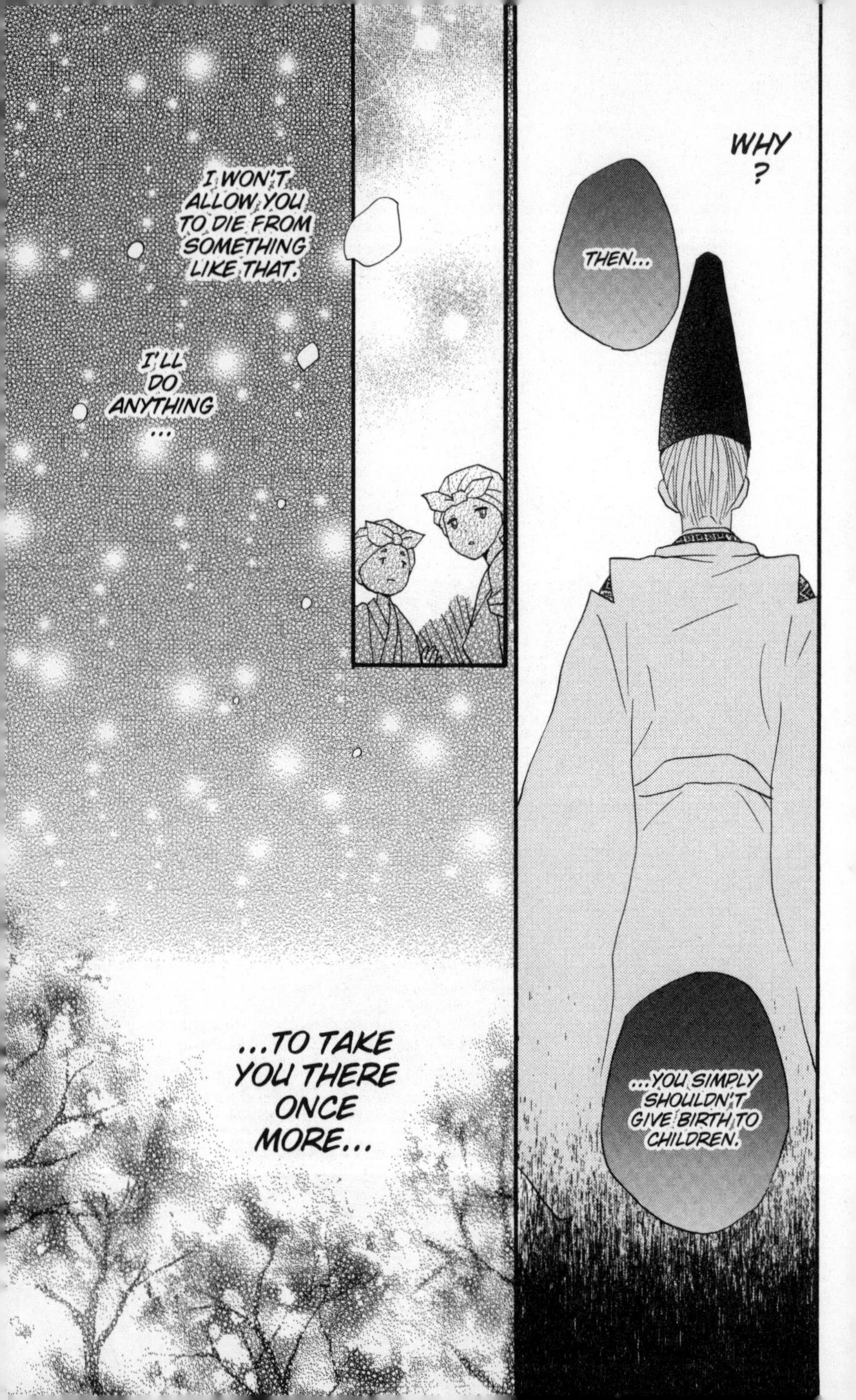
WHY?
THEN...
...YOU SIMPLY SHOULDN'T GIVE BIRTH TO CHILDREN.
I WON'T ALLOW YOU TO DIE FROM SOMETHING LIKE THAT.
I'LL DO ANYTHING...
...TO TAKE YOU THERE ONCE MORE...

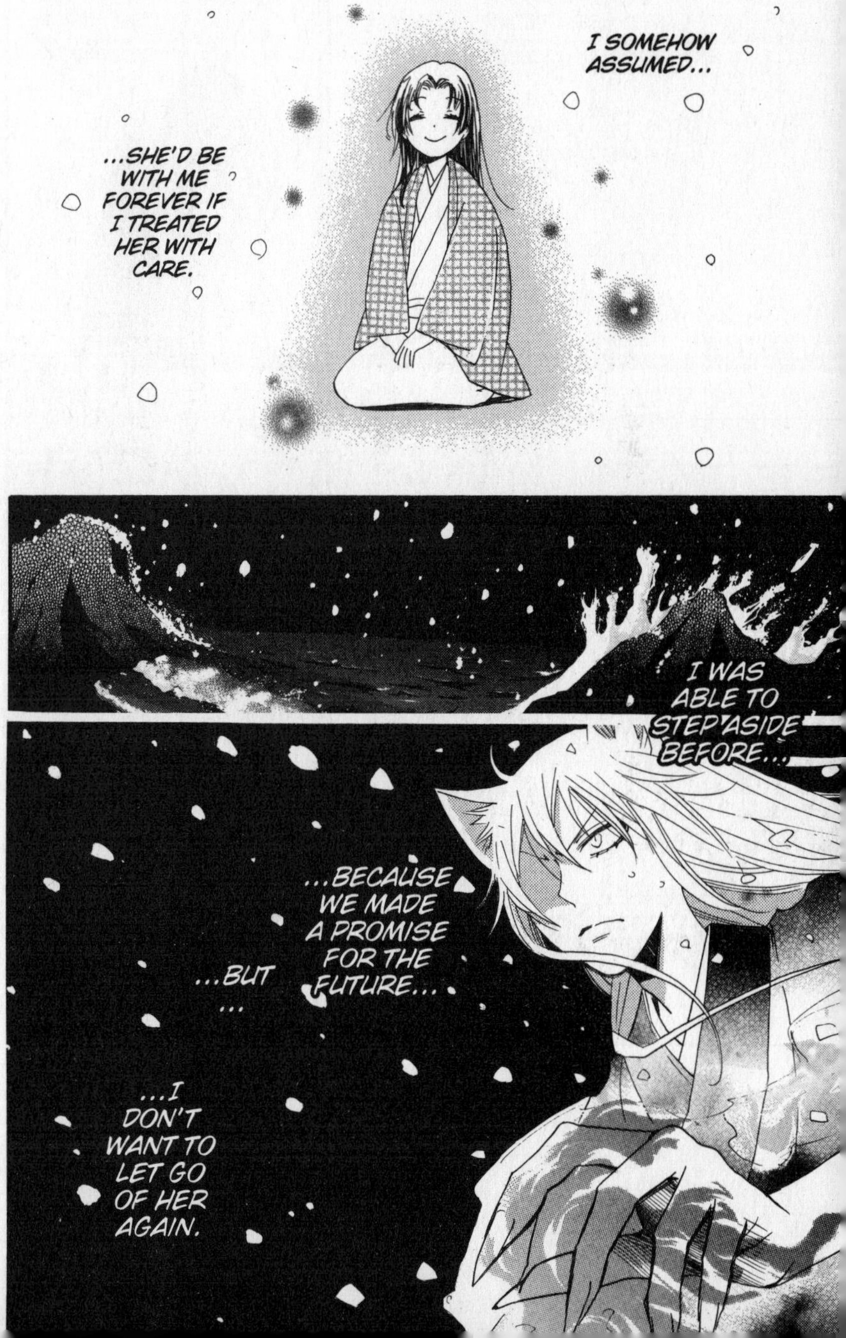
I SOMEHOW ASSUMED...
...SHE'D BE WITH ME FOREVER IF I TREATED HER WITH CARE.
I WAS ABLE TO STEP ASIDE BEFORE...
...BECAUSE WE MADE A PROMISE FOR THE FUTURE...
...BUT ...
...I DON'T WANT TO LET GO OF HER AGAIN.

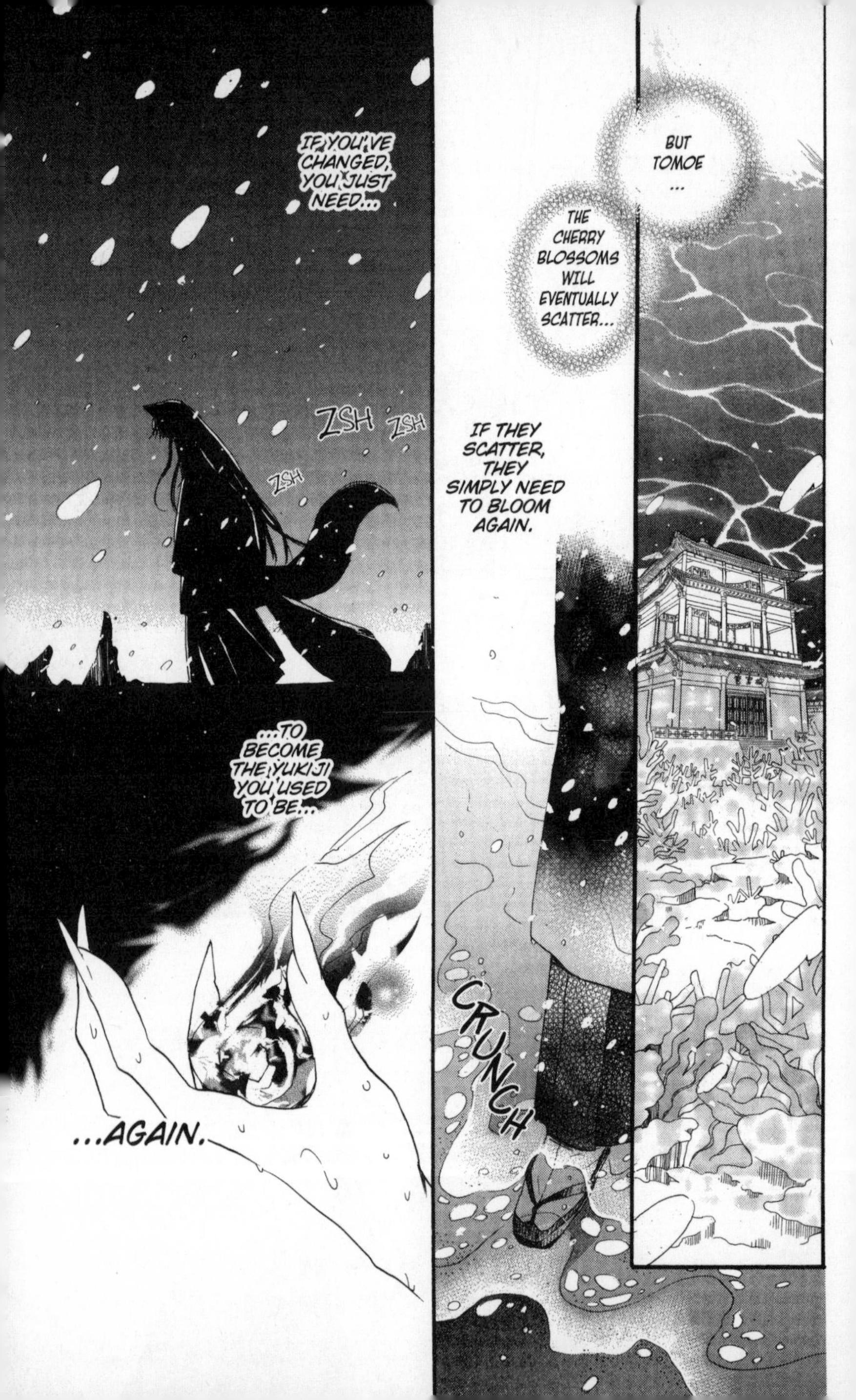
BUT TOMOE ...
THE CHERRY BLOSSOMS WILL EVENTUALLY SCATTER...
IF THEY SCATTER, THEY SIMPLY NEED TO BLOOM AGAIN.
CRUNCH
IF YOU'VE CHANGED, YOU JUST NEED...
ZSH
ZSH
ZSH
...TO BECOME THE YUKIJI YOU USED TO BE...
...AGAIN.

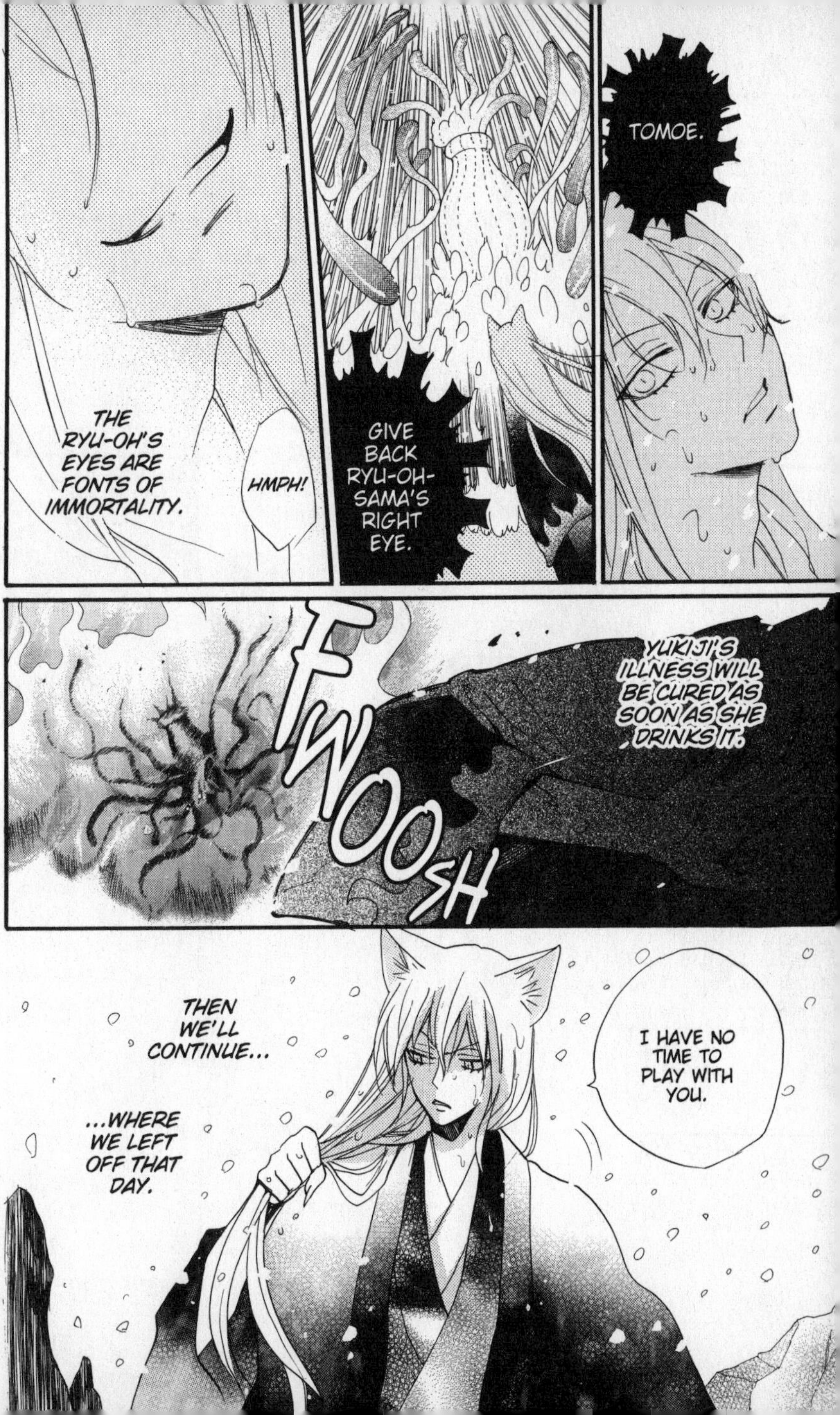
TOMOE.
GIVE BACK RYU-OH-SAMA'S RIGHT EYE.
HMPH!
THE RYU-OH'S EYES ARE FONTS OF IMMORTALITY.
YUKIJI'S ILLNESS WILL BE CURED AS SOON AS SHE DRINKS IT.
FWOOSH
I HAVE NO TIME TO PLAY WITH YOU.
THEN WE'LL CONTINUE...
...WHERE WE LEFT OFF THAT DAY.

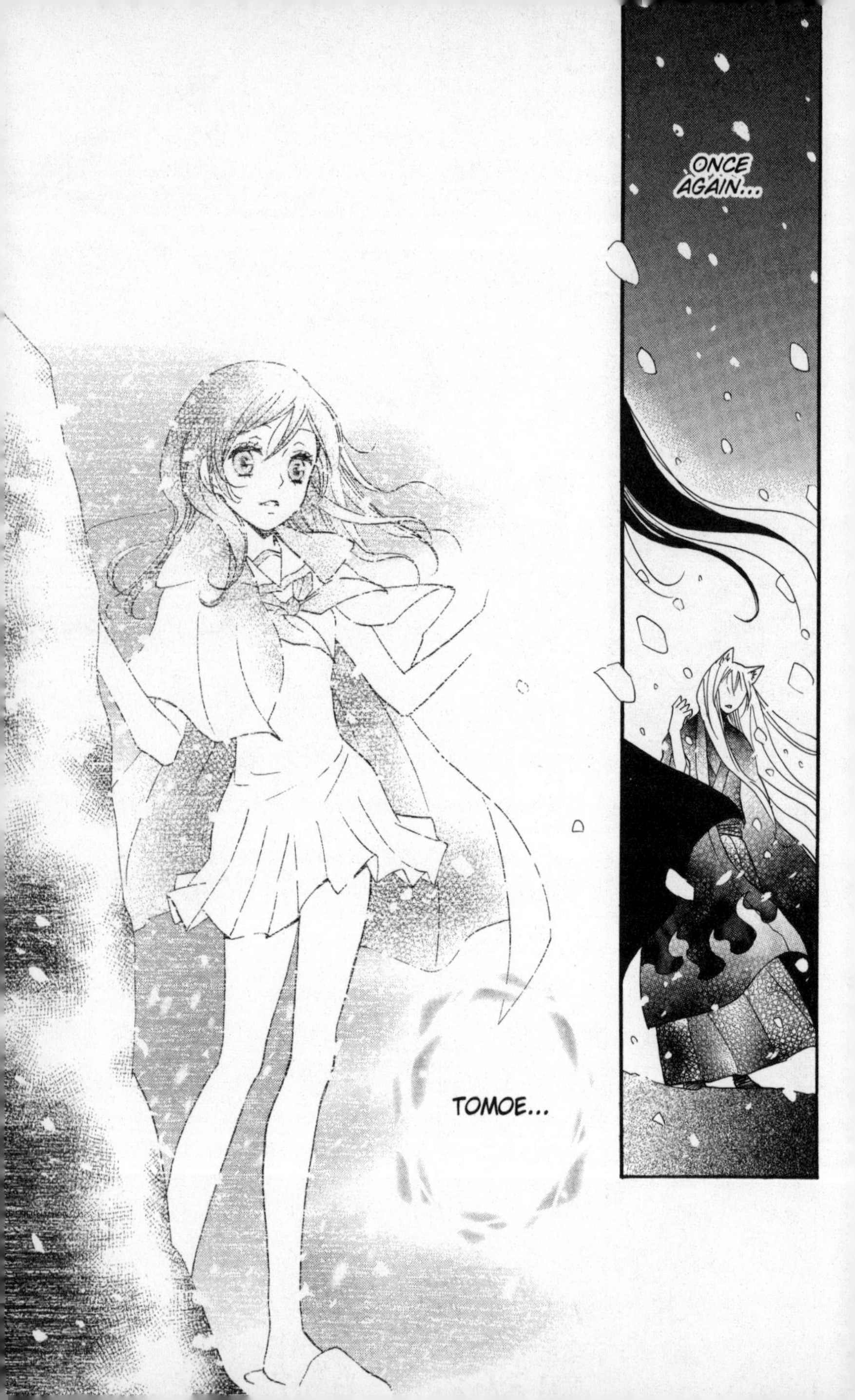
ONCE AGAIN...
TOMOE...

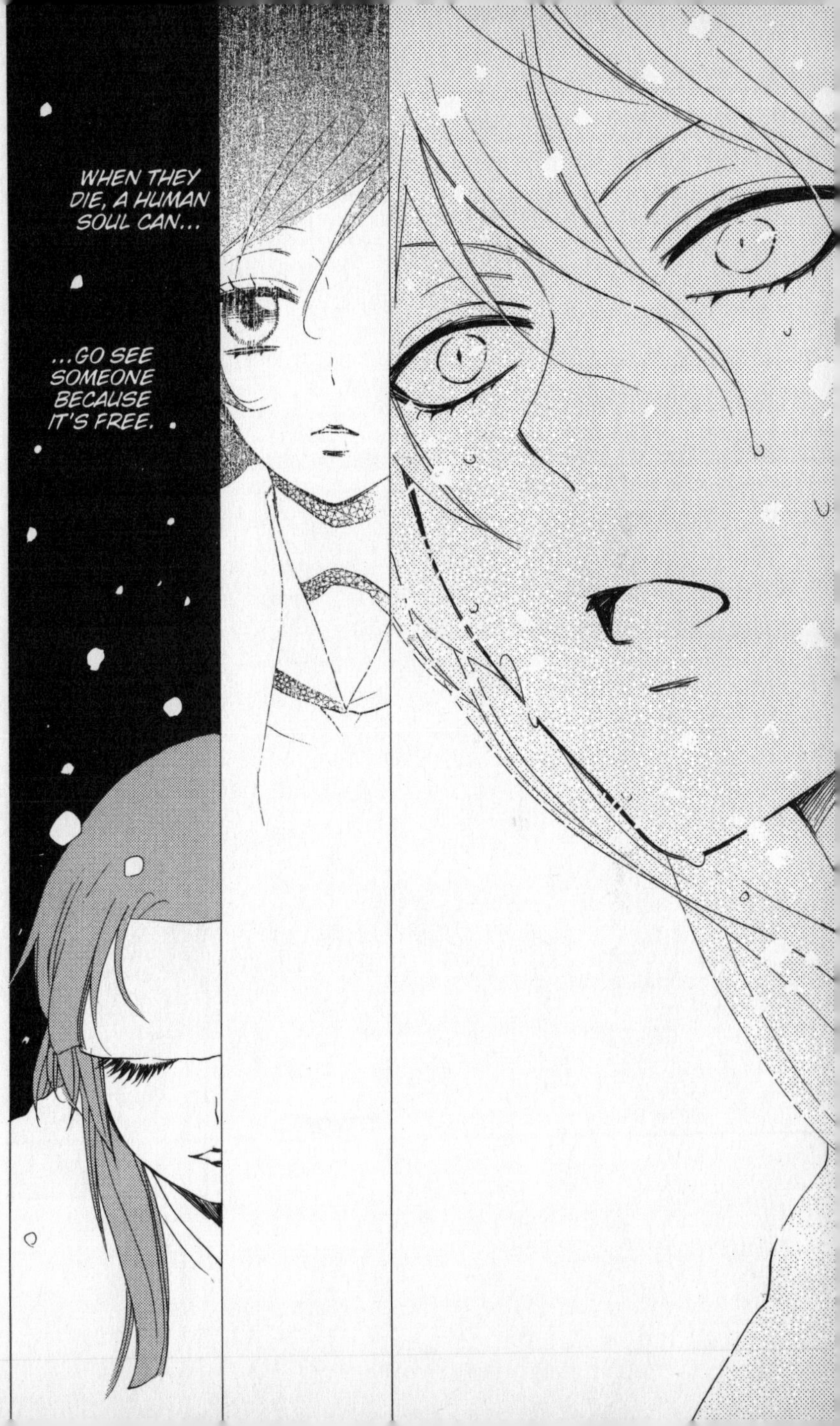
WHEN THEY DIE, A HUMAN SOUL CAN...
...GO SEE SOMEONE BECAUSE IT'S FREE.

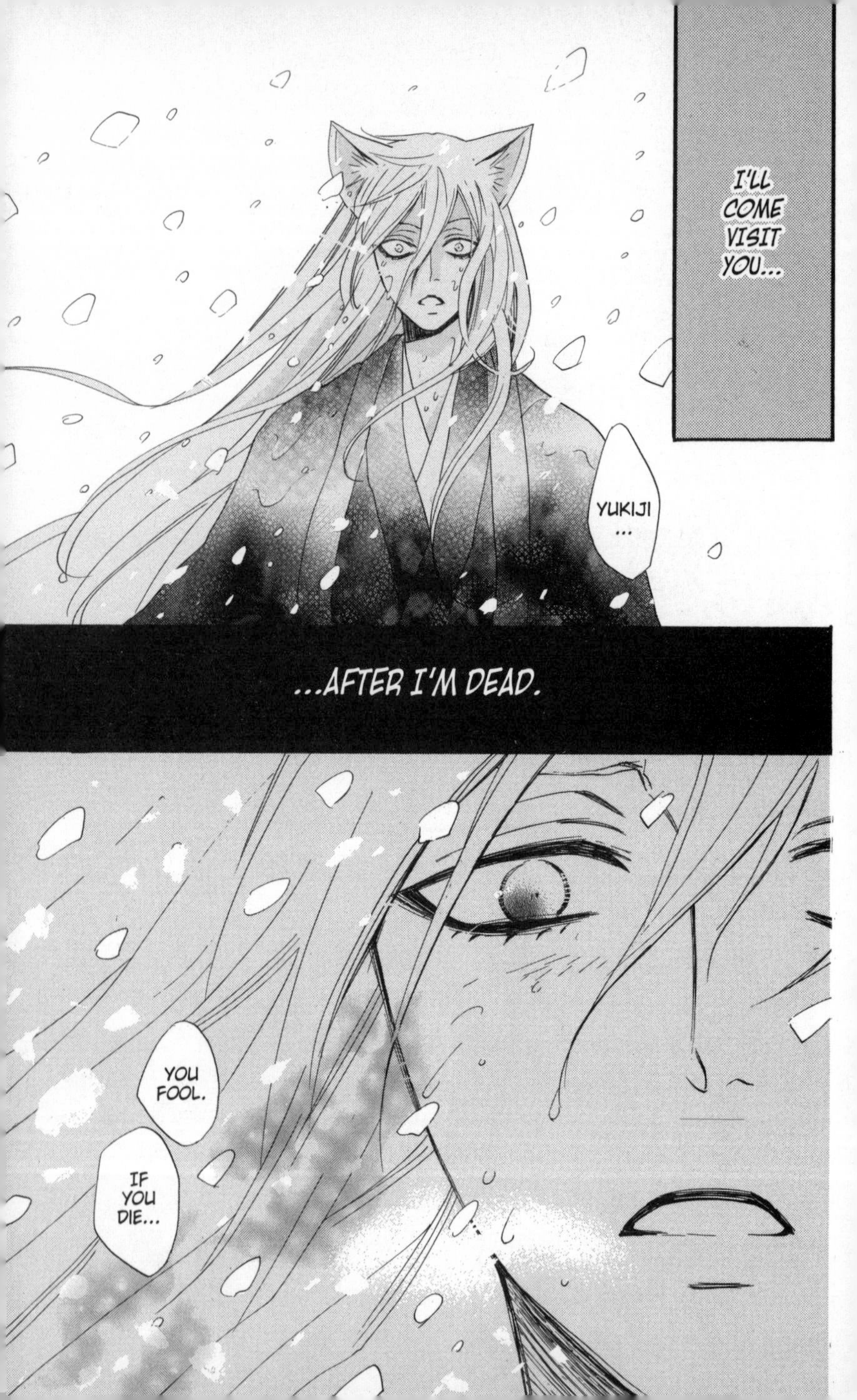
I'LL COME VISIT YOU...
YUKIJI...
...AFTER I'M DEAD.
YOU FOOL.
IF YOU DIE...

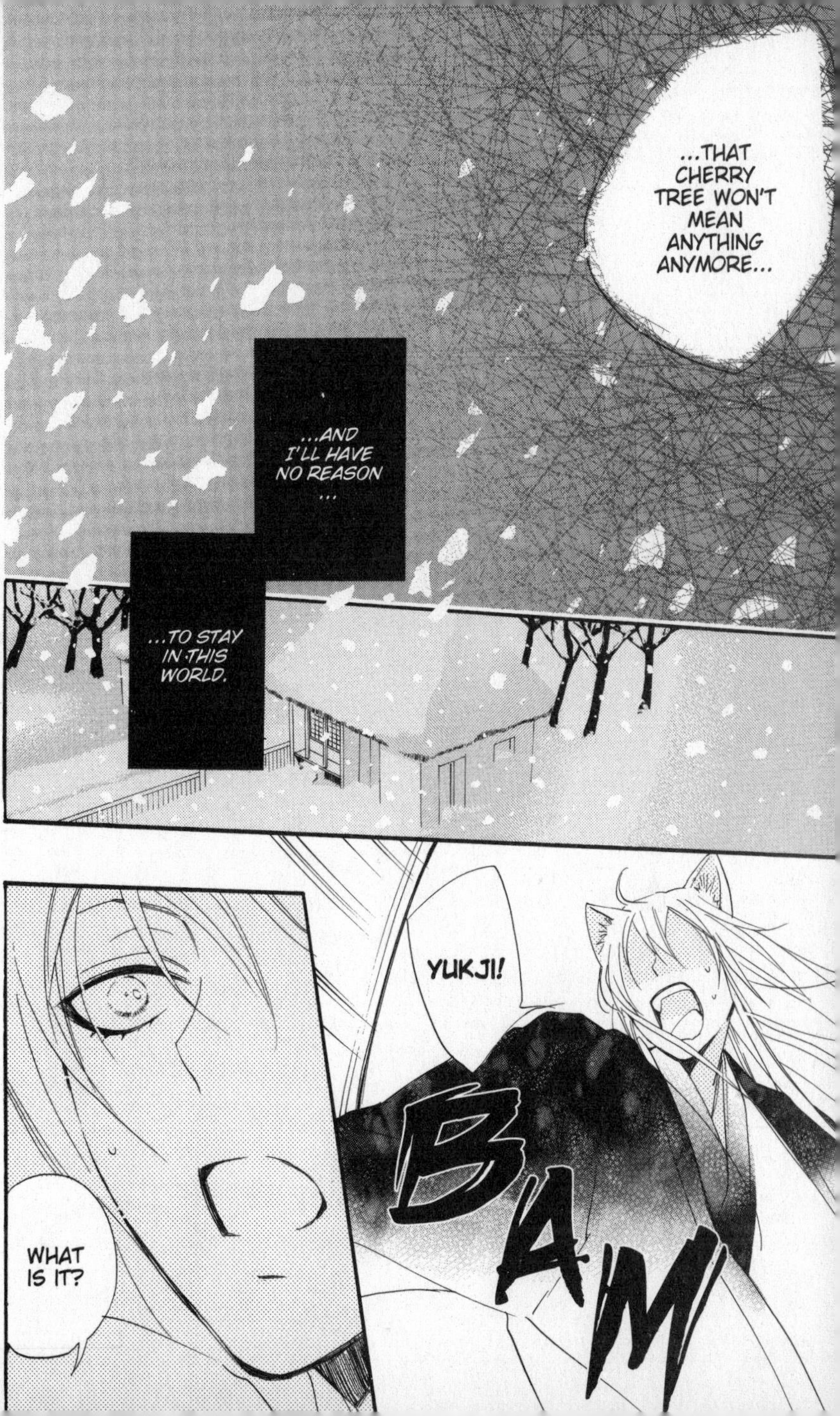
...THAT CHERRY TREE WON'T MEAN ANYTHING ANYMORE...
...AND I'LL HAVE NO REASON ...
...TO STAY IN THIS WORLD.
YUKJI!
BAM
WHAT IS IT?

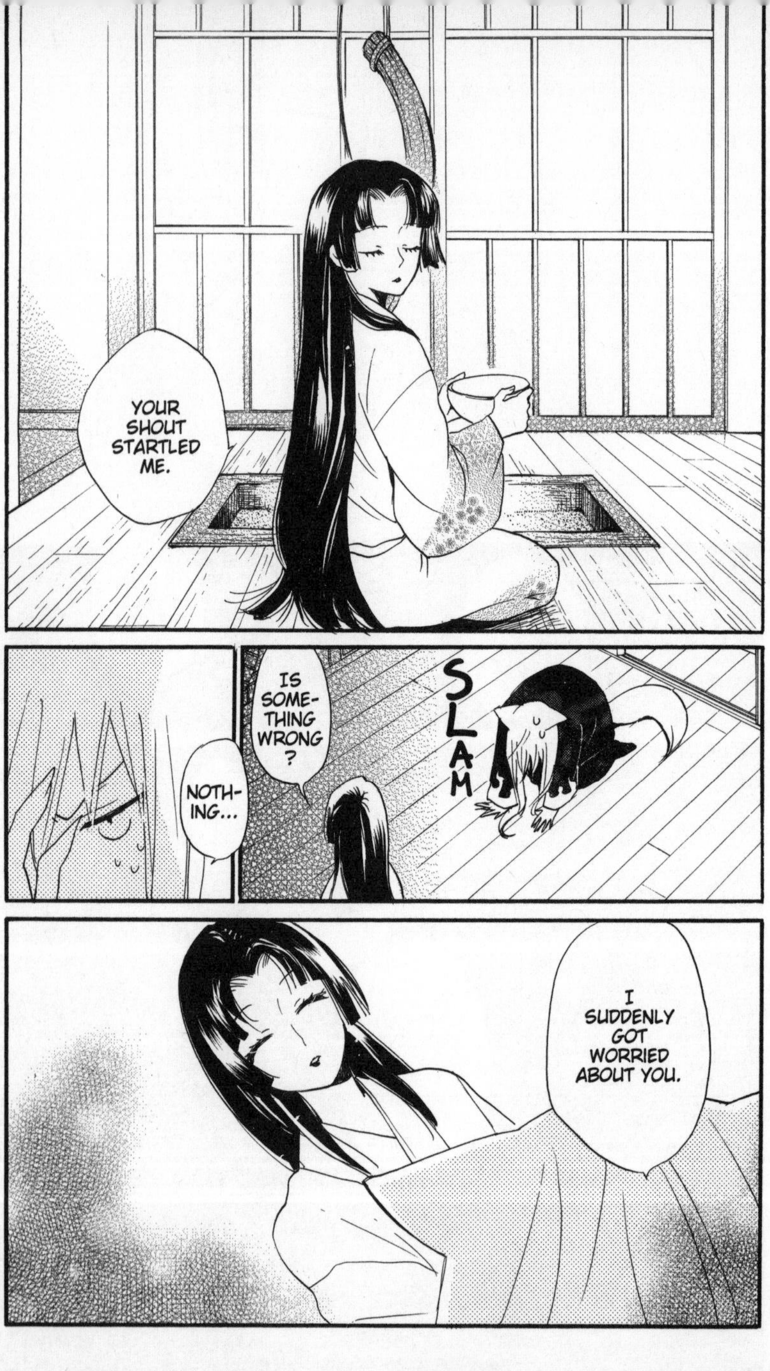
YOUR SHOUT STARTLED ME.
SLAM
IS SOME-THING WRONG?
NOTH-ING...
I SUDDENLY GOT WORRIED ABOUT YOU.

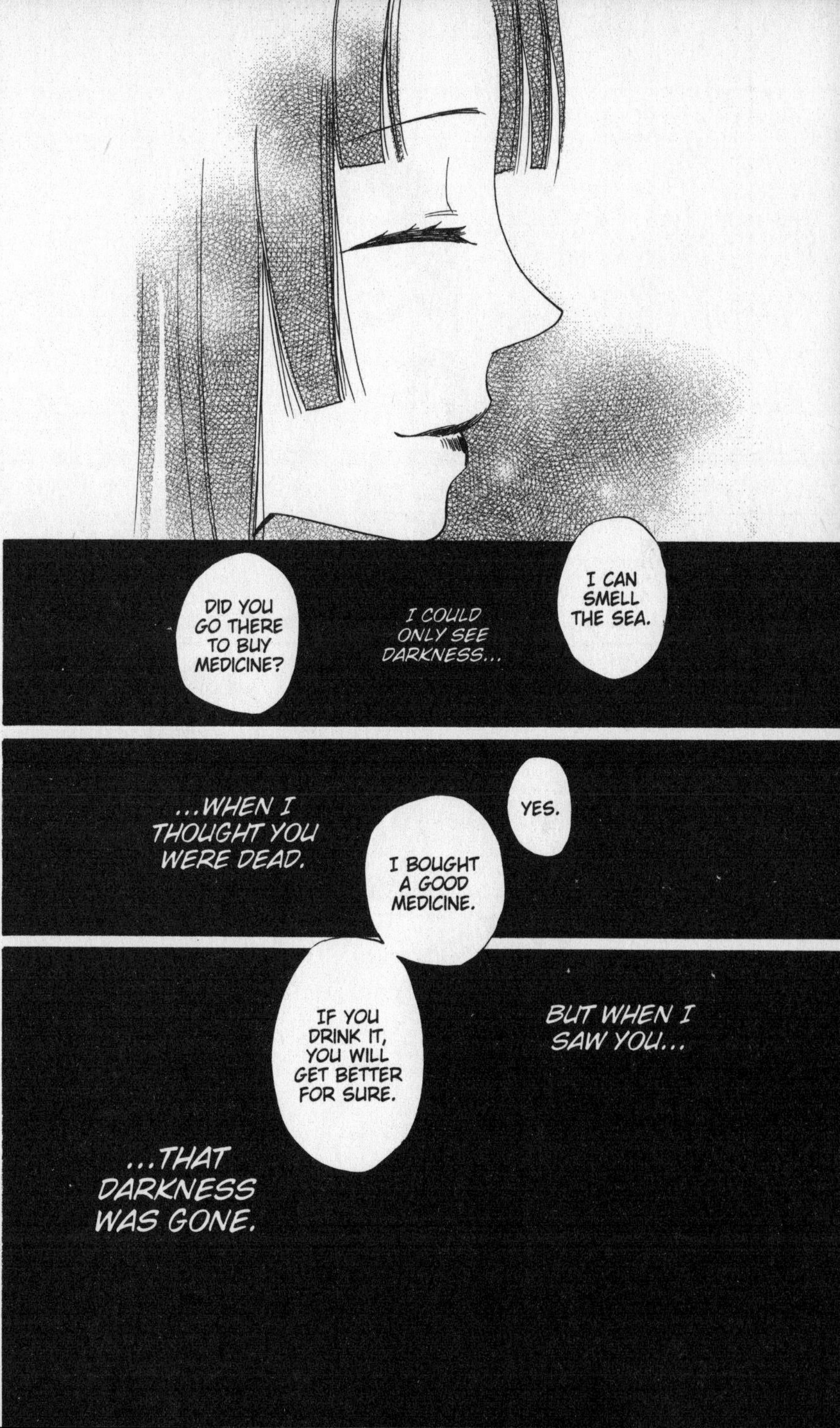
I CAN SMELL THE SEA.
I COULD ONLY SEE DARKNESS...
DID YOU GO THERE TO BUY MEDICINE?
YES.
I BOUGHT A GOOD MEDICINE.
...WHEN I THOUGHT YOU WERE DEAD.
BUT WHEN I SAW YOU...
IF YOU DRINK IT, YOU WILL GET BETTER FOR SURE.
...THAT DARKNESS WAS GONE.

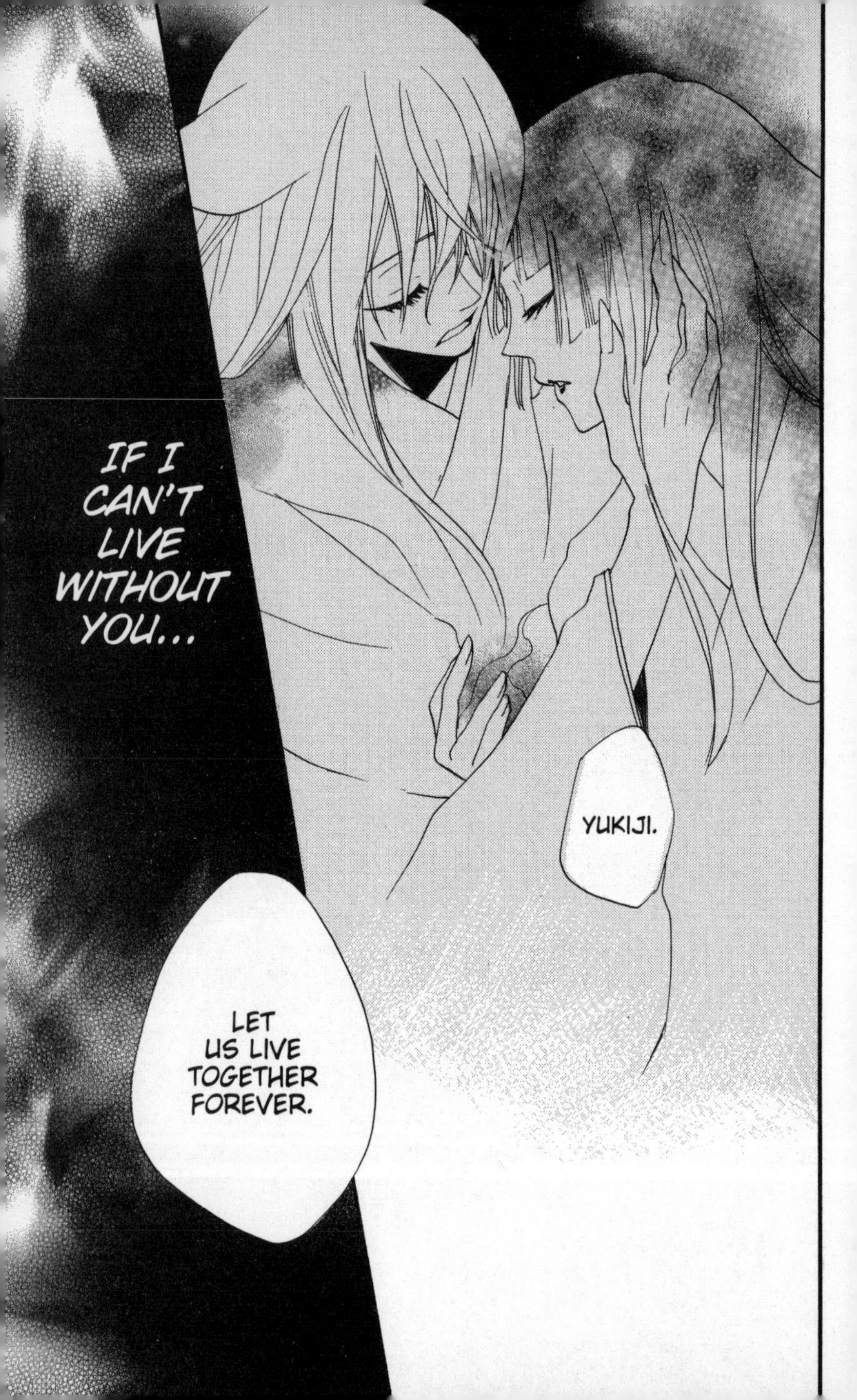
YUKIJI.
IF I CAN'T LIVE WITHOUT YOU...
LET US LIVE TOGETHER FOREVER.

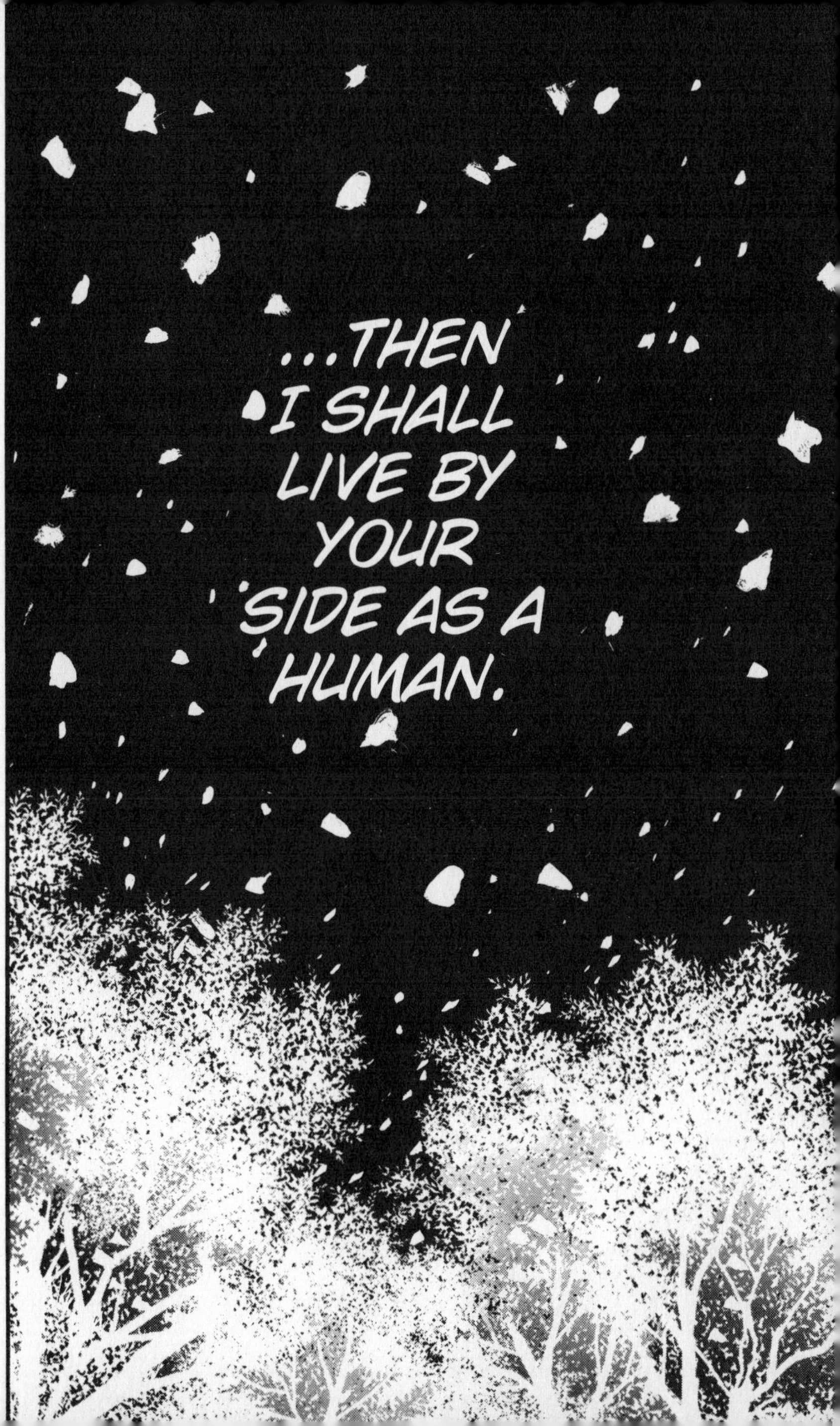
...THEN I SHALL LIVE BY YOUR SIDE AS A HUMAN.

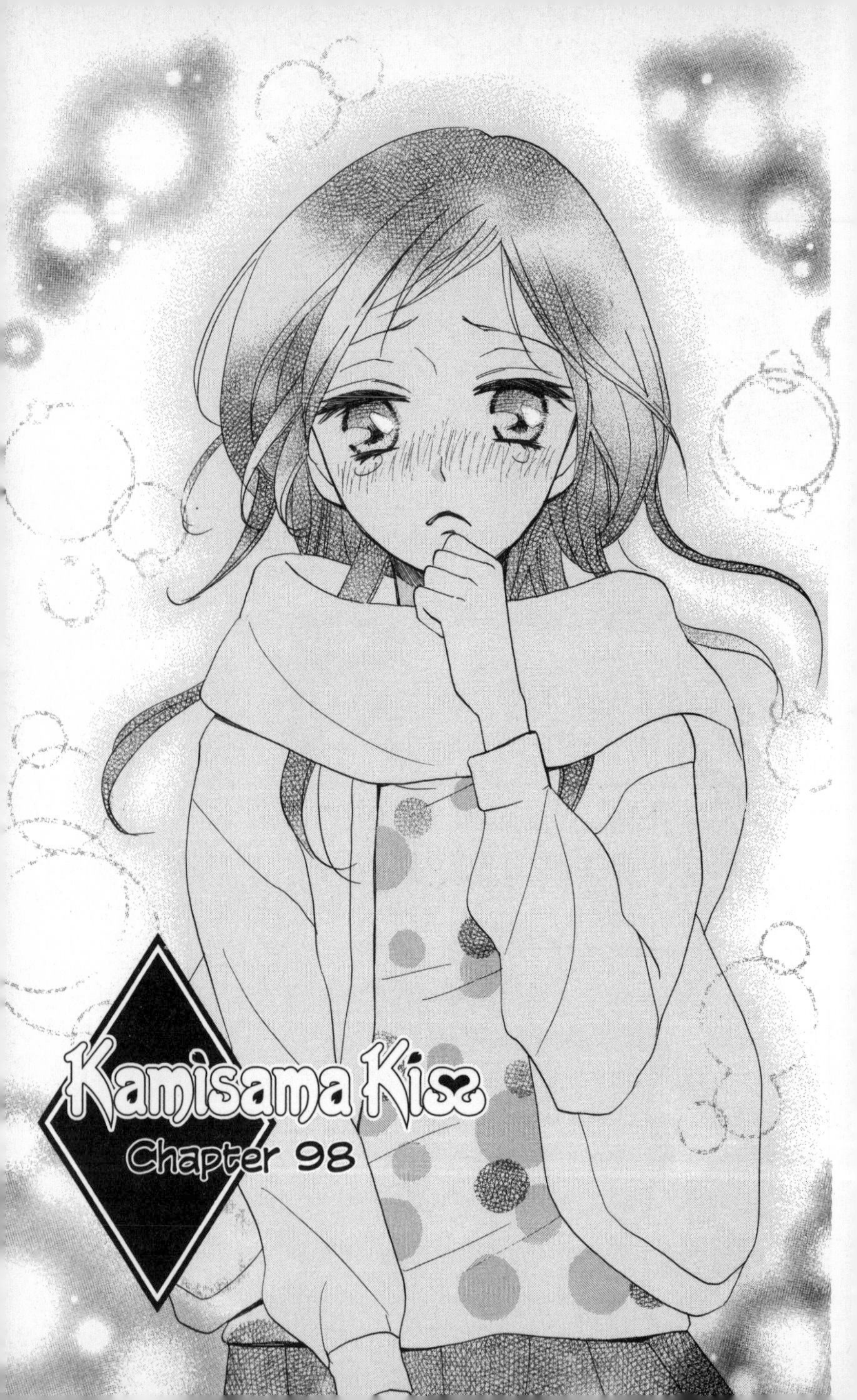
Kamisama Kiss
Chapter 98

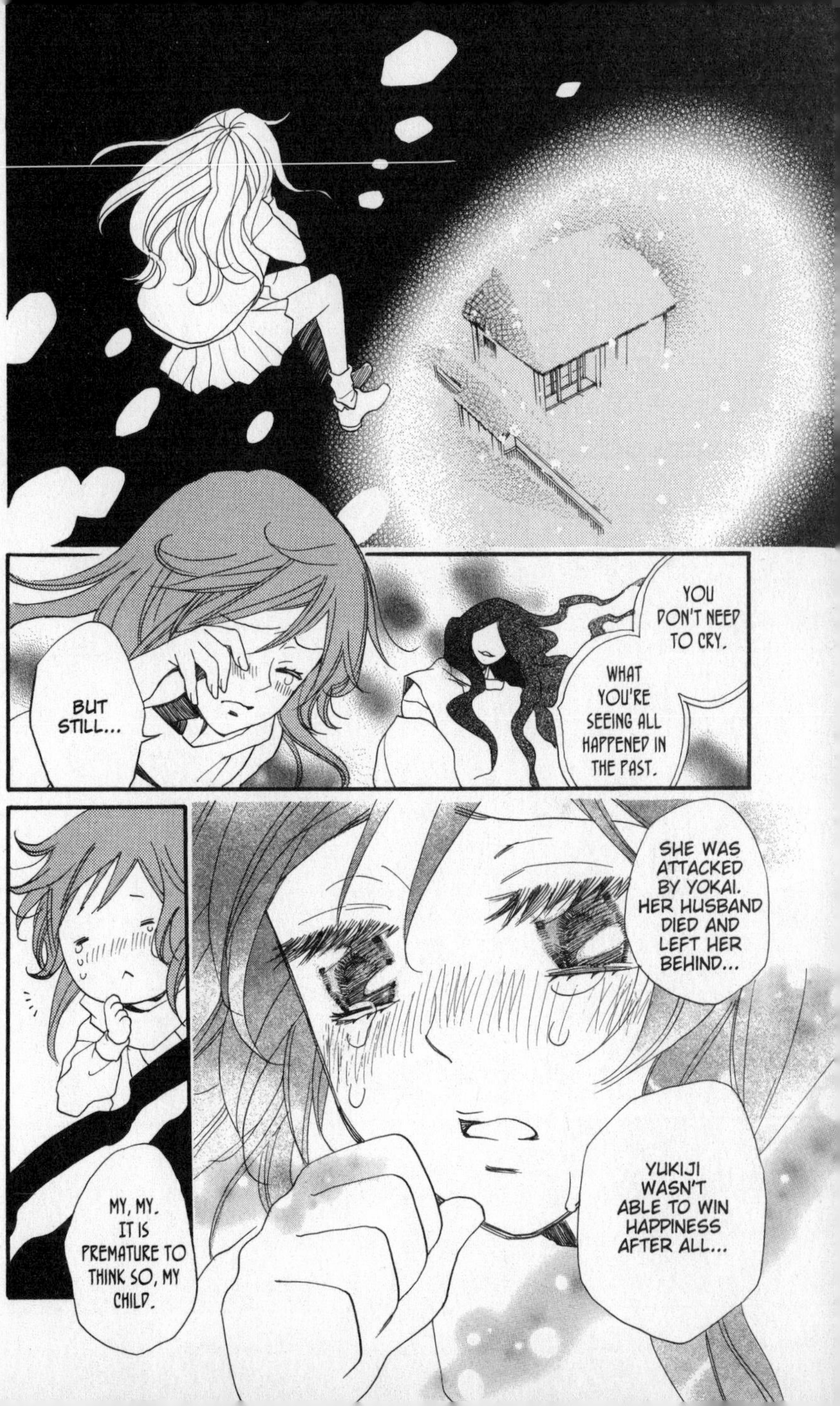
YOU DON'T NEED TO CRY.
WHAT YOU'RE SEEING ALL HAPPENED IN THE PAST.
BUT STILL...
SHE WAS ATTACKED BY YOKAI. HER HUSBAND DIED AND LEFT HER BEHIND...
YUKIJI WASN'T ABLE TO WIN HAPPINESS AFTER ALL...
MY, MY. IT IS PREMATURE TO THINK SO, MY CHILD.

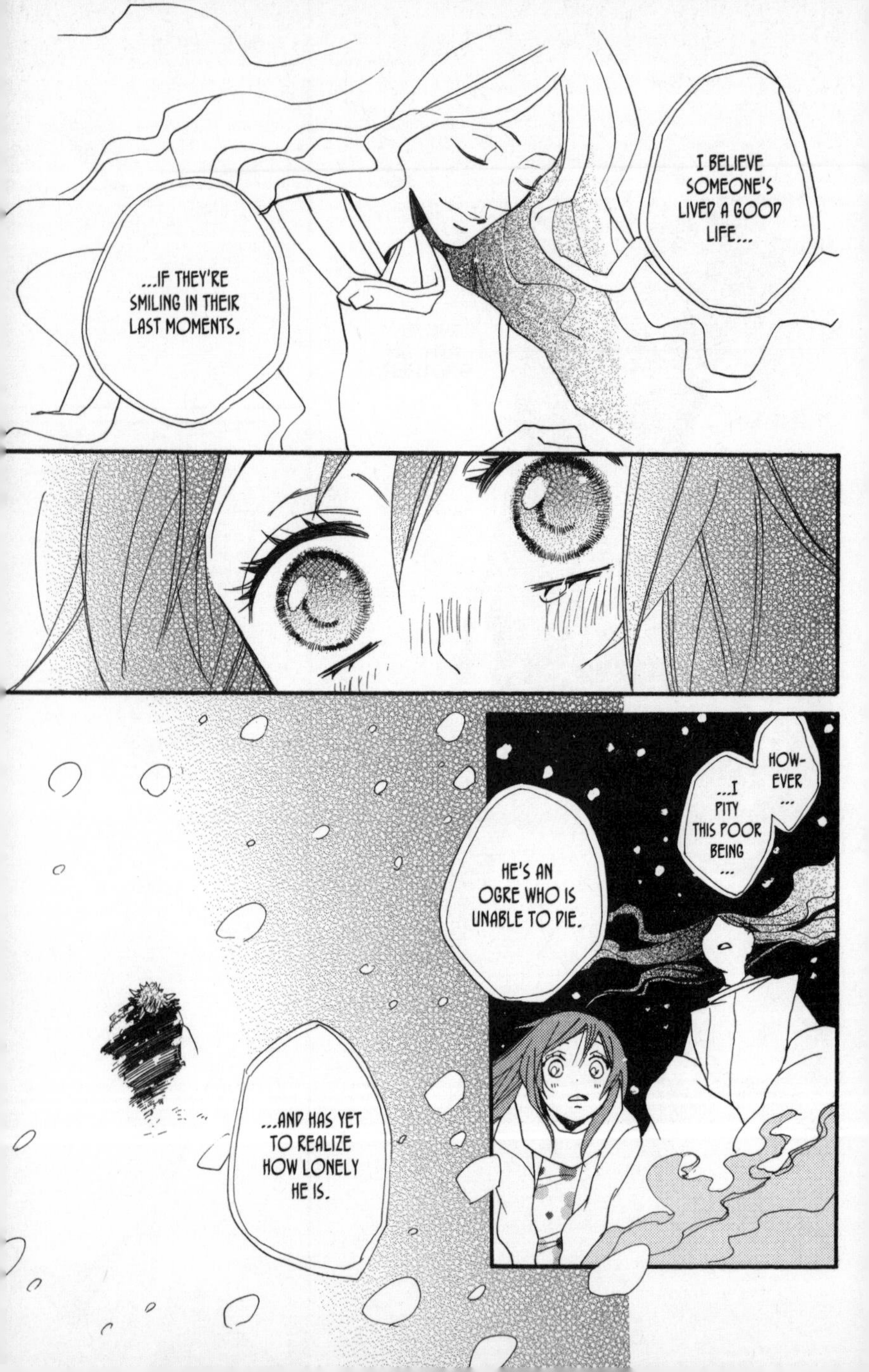
I BELIEVE SOMEONE'S LIVED A GOOD LIFE...
...IF THEY'RE SMILING IN THEIR LAST MOMENTS.
HOW-EVER...
...I PITY THIS POOR BEING...
HE'S AN OGRE WHO IS UNABLE TO DIE.
...AND HAS YET TO REALIZE HOW LONELY HE IS.

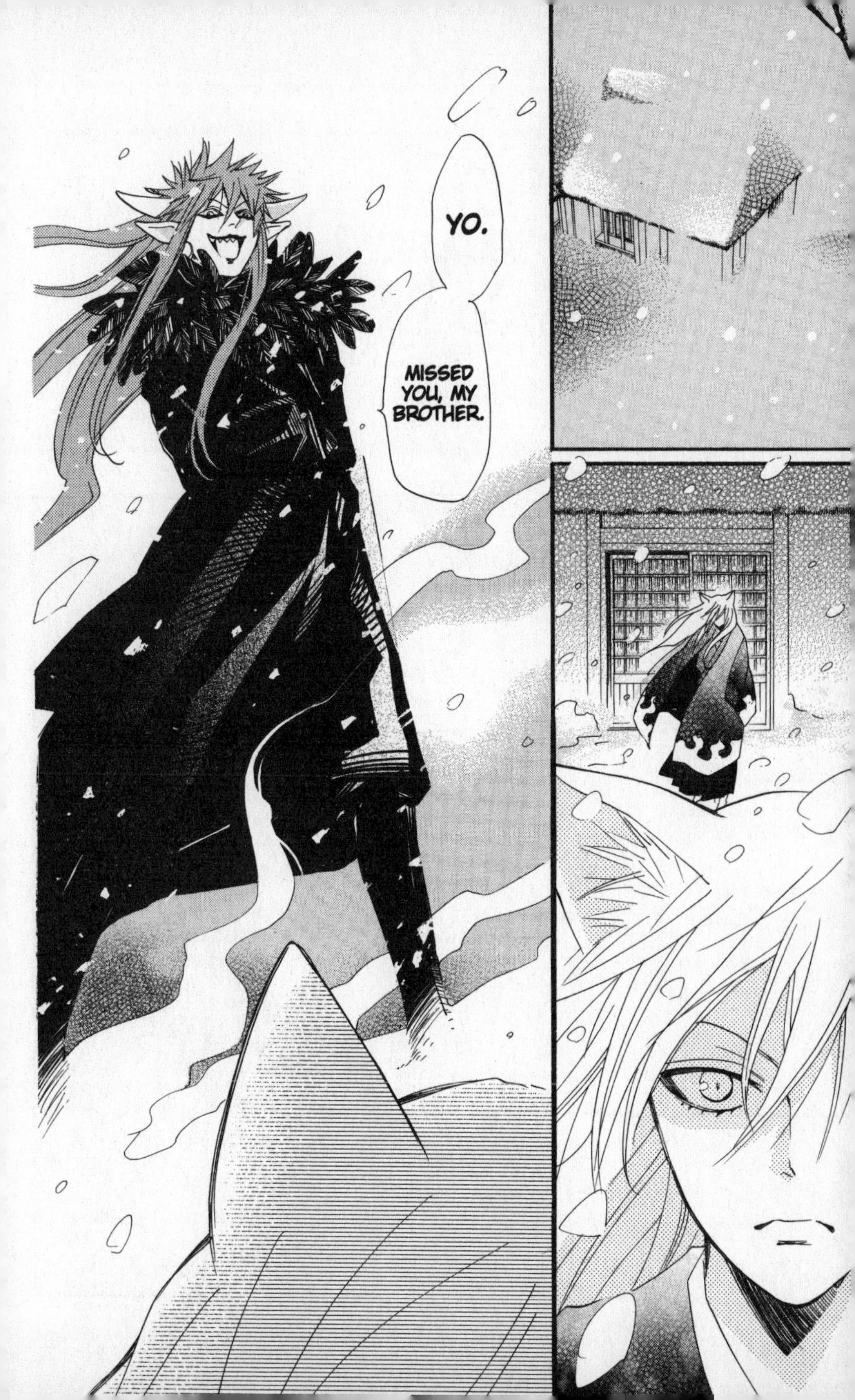
YO.
MISSED YOU, MY BROTHER.

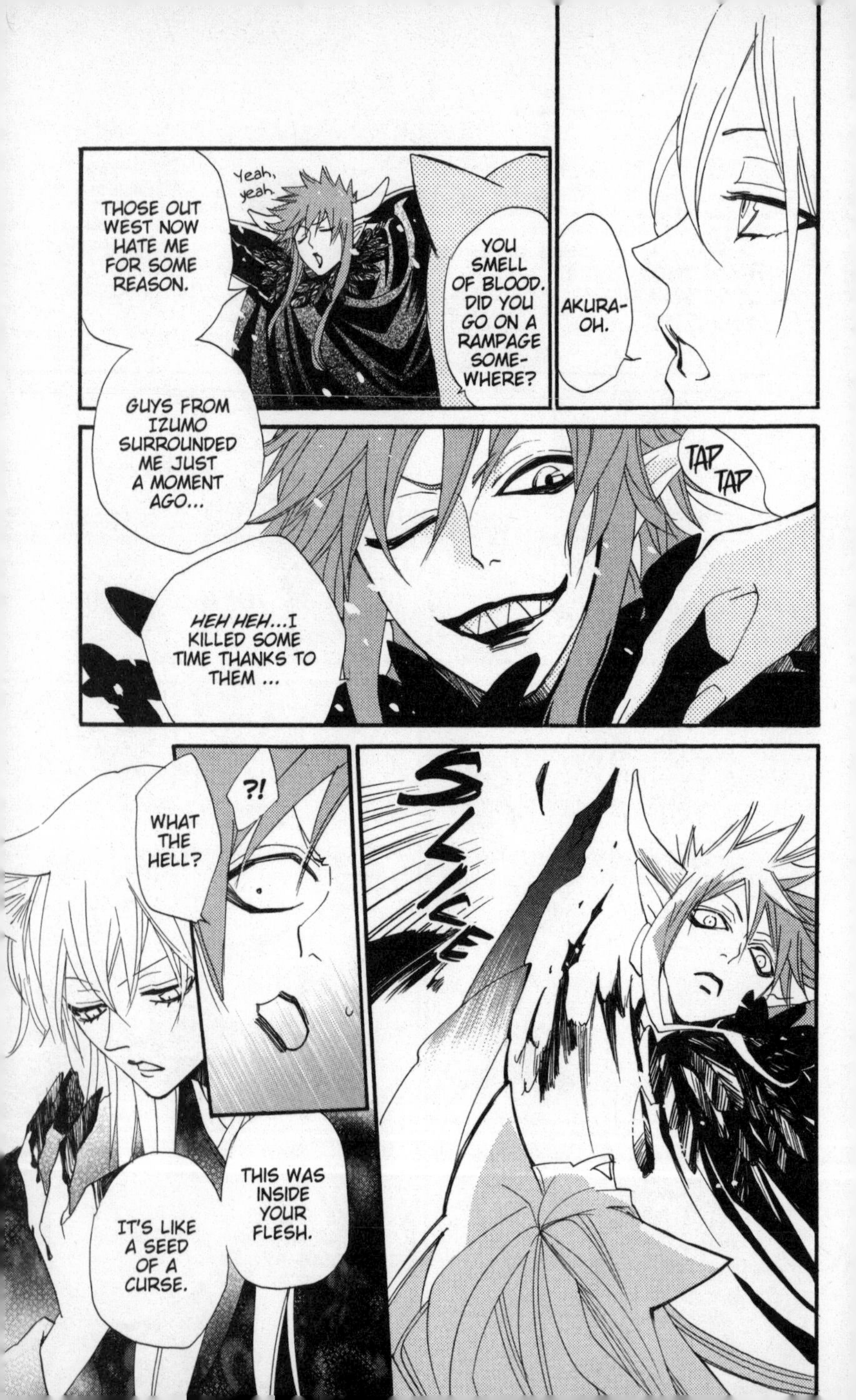
AKURA-OH.
YOU SMELL OF BLOOD. DID YOU GO ON A RAMPAGE SOMEWHERE?
Yeah, yeah.
THOSE OUT WEST NOW HATE ME FOR SOME REASON.
TAP TAP
GUYS FROM IZUMO SURROUNDED ME JUST A MOMENT AGO...
HEH HEH...I KILLED SOME TIME THANKS TO THEM ...
SLICE
?!
WHAT THE HELL?
THIS WAS INSIDE YOUR FLESH.
IT'S LIKE A SEED OF A CURSE.

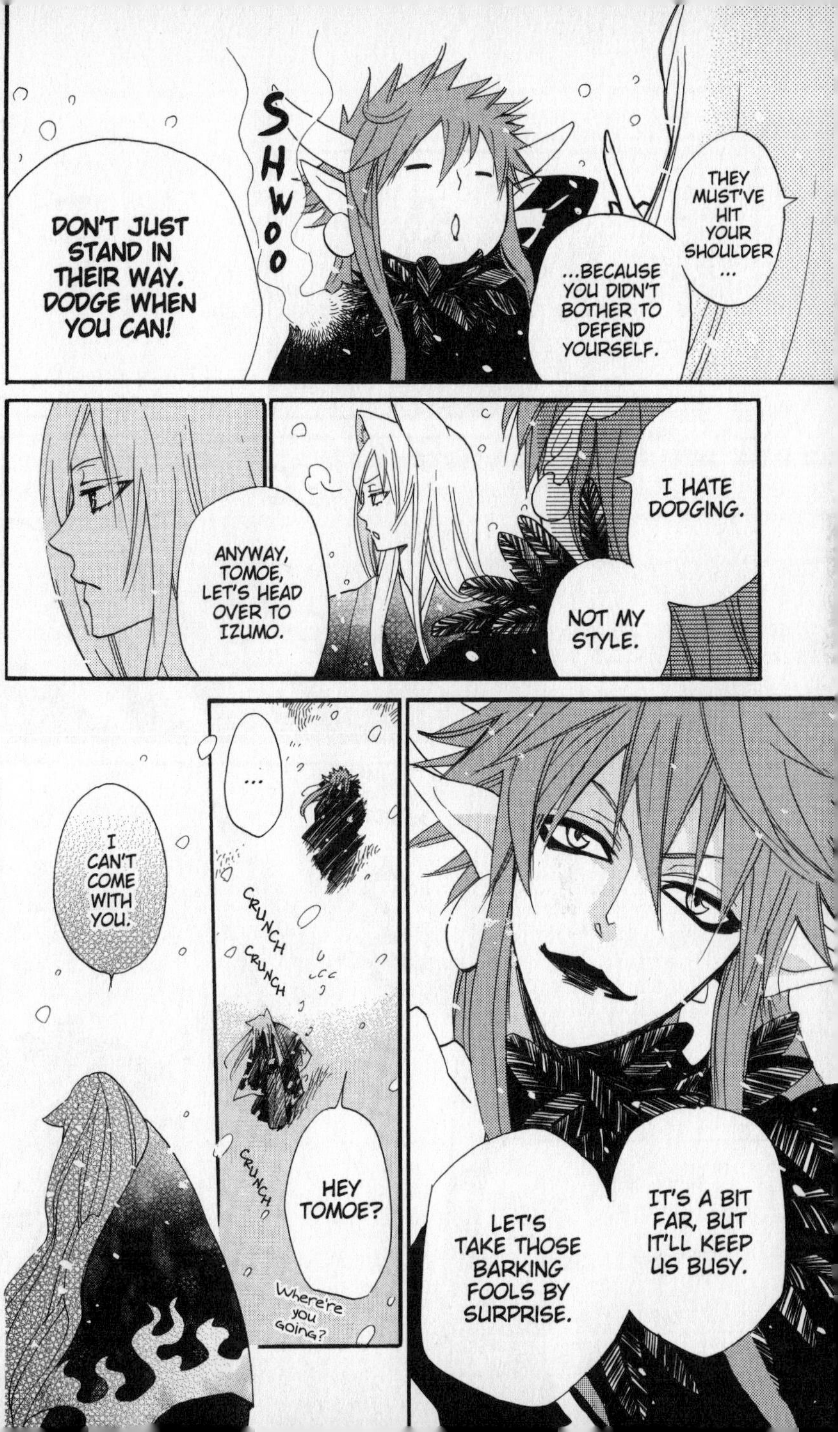
THEY MUST'VE HIT YOUR SHOULDER...
...BECAUSE YOU DIDN'T BOTHER TO DEFEND YOURSELF.
SHWOO
DON'T JUST STAND IN THEIR WAY. DODGE WHEN YOU CAN!
I HATE DODGING.
NOT MY STYLE.
ANYWAY, TOMOE, LET'S HEAD OVER TO IZUMO.
IT'S A BIT FAR, BUT IT'LL KEEP US BUSY.
LET'S TAKE THOSE BARKING FOOLS BY SURPRISE.
...
CRUNCH CRUNCH
HEY TOMOE?
CRUNCH
Where're you going?
I CAN'T COME WITH YOU.

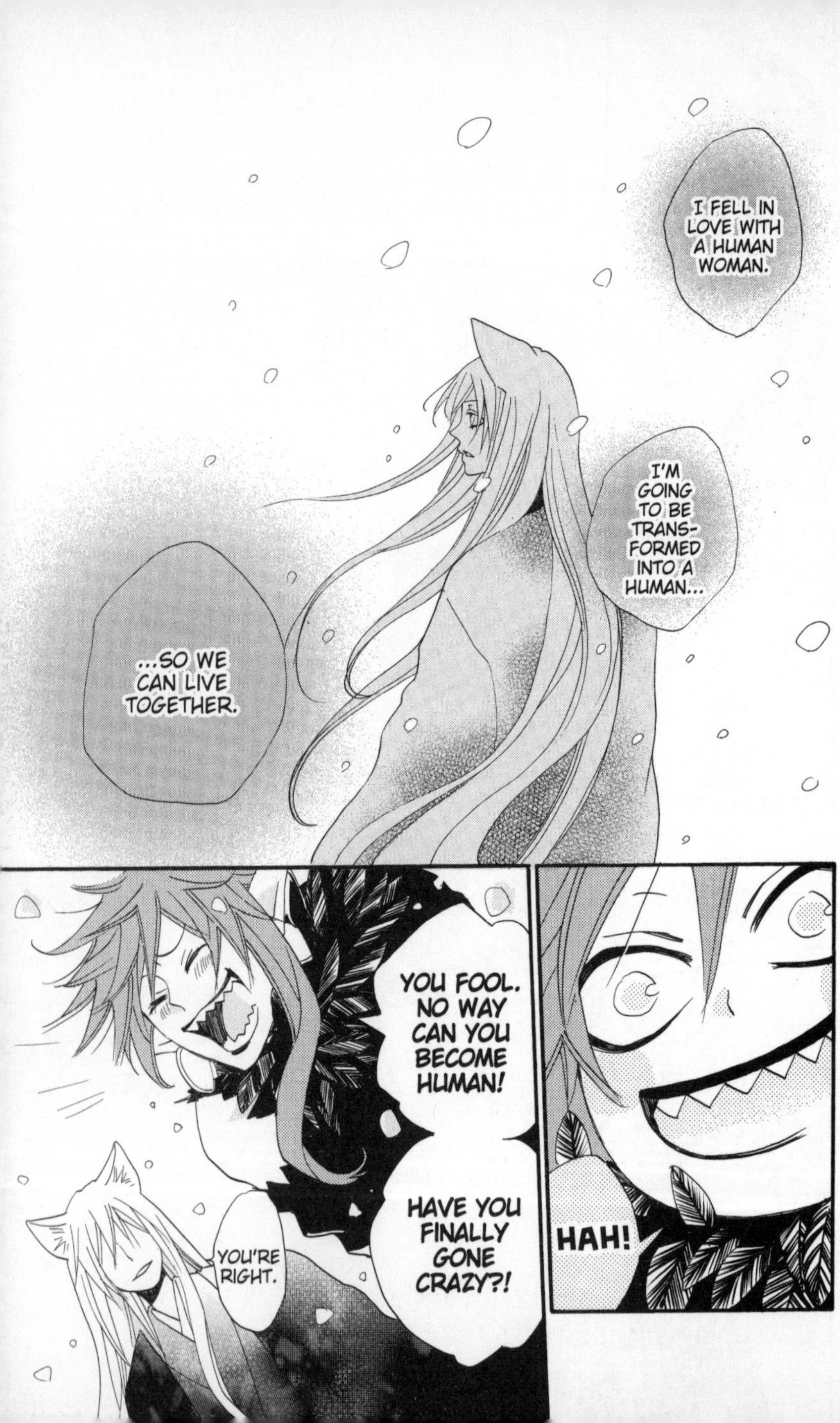

I FELL IN LOVE WITH A HUMAN WOMAN.
I'M GOING TO BE TRANS-FORMED INTO A HUMAN...
...SO WE CAN LIVE TOGETHER.
HAH!
YOU FOOL. NO WAY CAN YOU BECOME HUMAN!
HAVE YOU FINALLY GONE CRAZY?!
YOU'RE RIGHT.

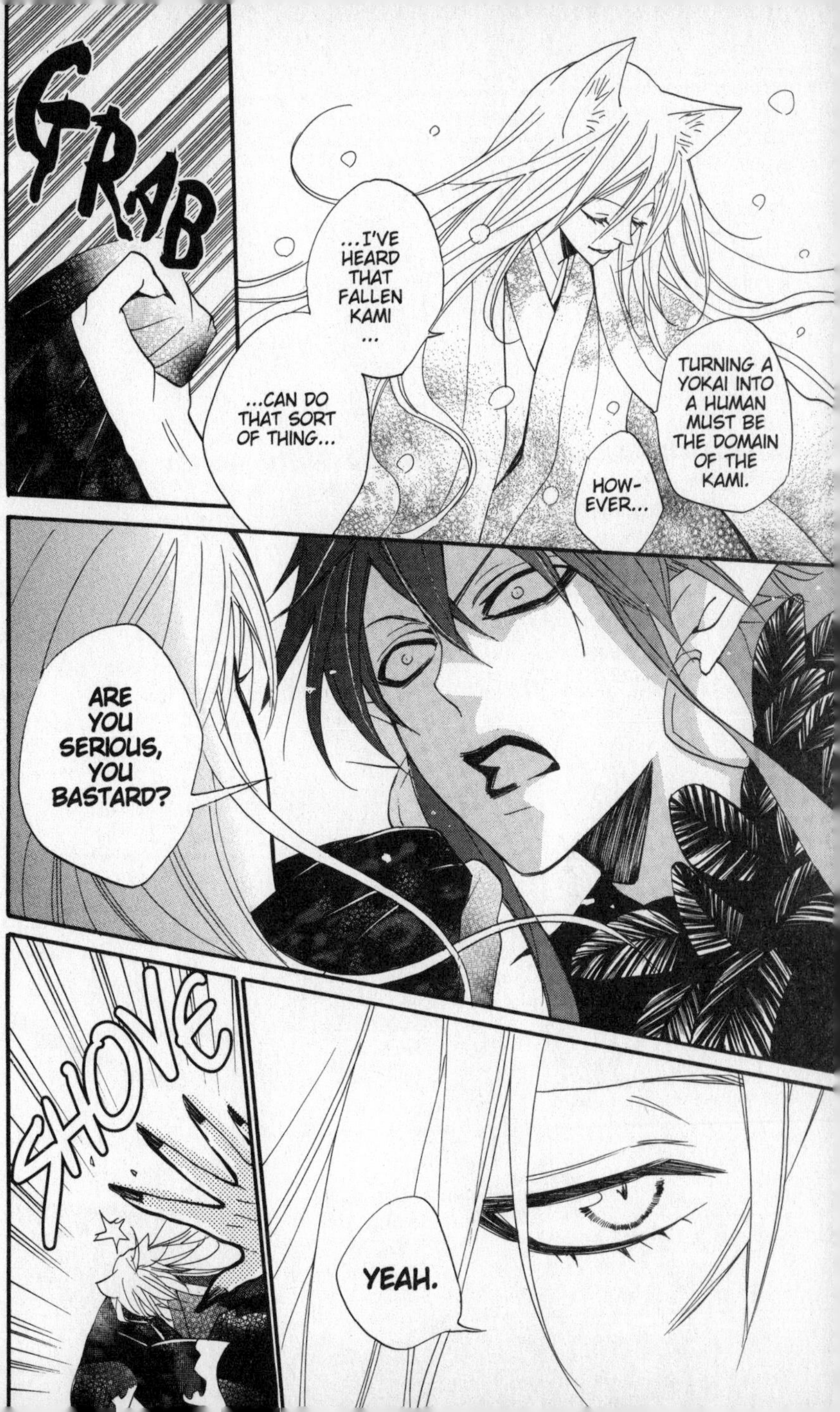
TURNING A YOKAI INTO A HUMAN MUST BE THE DOMAIN OF THE KAMI.
HOW-EVER...
...I'VE HEARD THAT FALLEN KAMI...
...CAN DO THAT SORT OF THING...
GRAB
ARE YOU SERIOUS, YOU BASTARD?
YEAH.
SHOVE

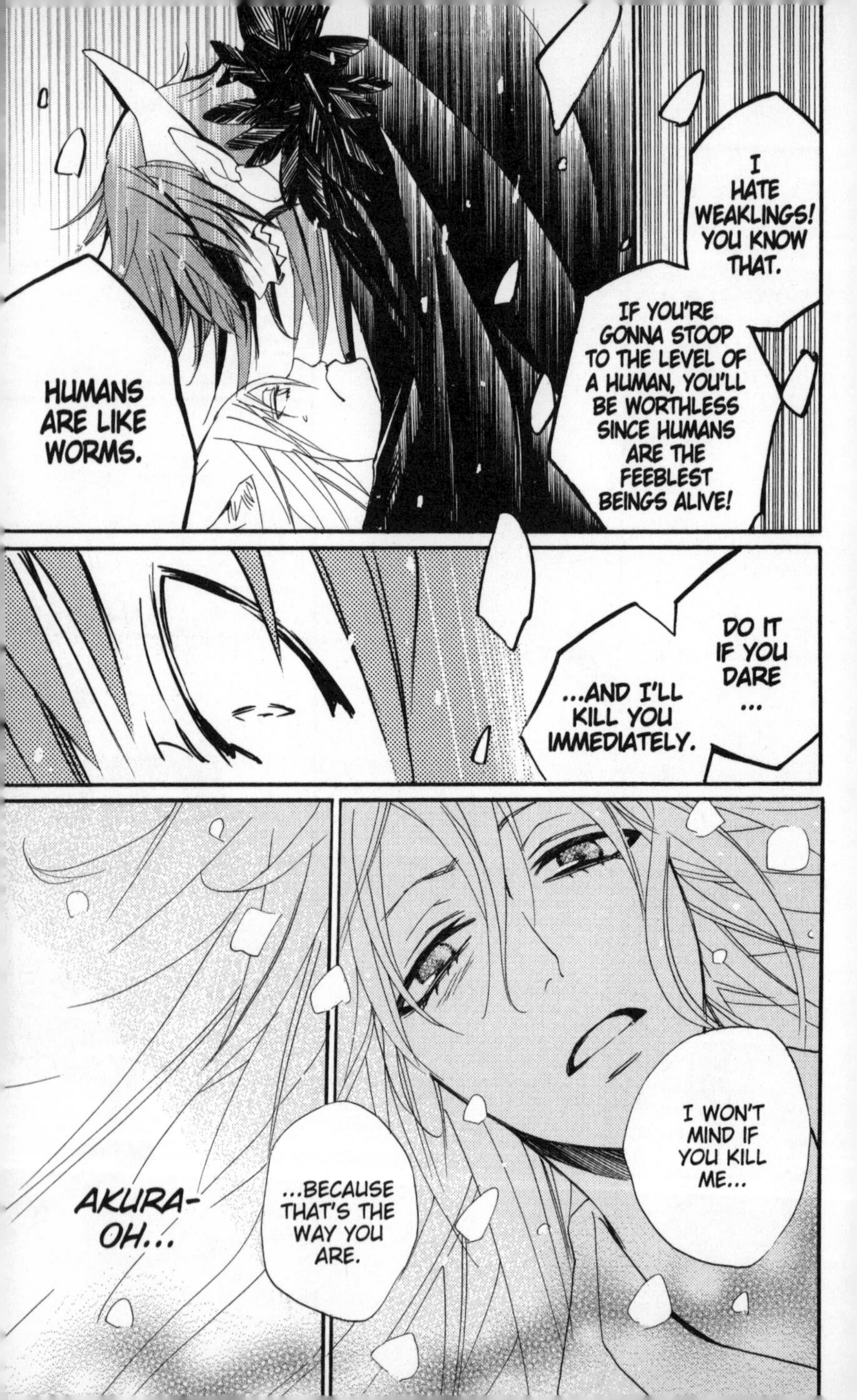
I HATE WEAKLINGS! YOU KNOW THAT.
IF YOU'RE GONNA STOOP TO THE LEVEL OF A HUMAN, YOU'LL BE WORTHLESS SINCE HUMANS ARE THE FEEBLEST BEINGS ALIVE!
HUMANS ARE LIKE WORMS.
DO IT IF YOU DARE...
...AND I'LL KILL YOU IMMEDIATELY.
I WON'T MIND IF YOU KILL ME...
...BECAUSE THAT'S THE WAY YOU ARE.
AKURA-OH...

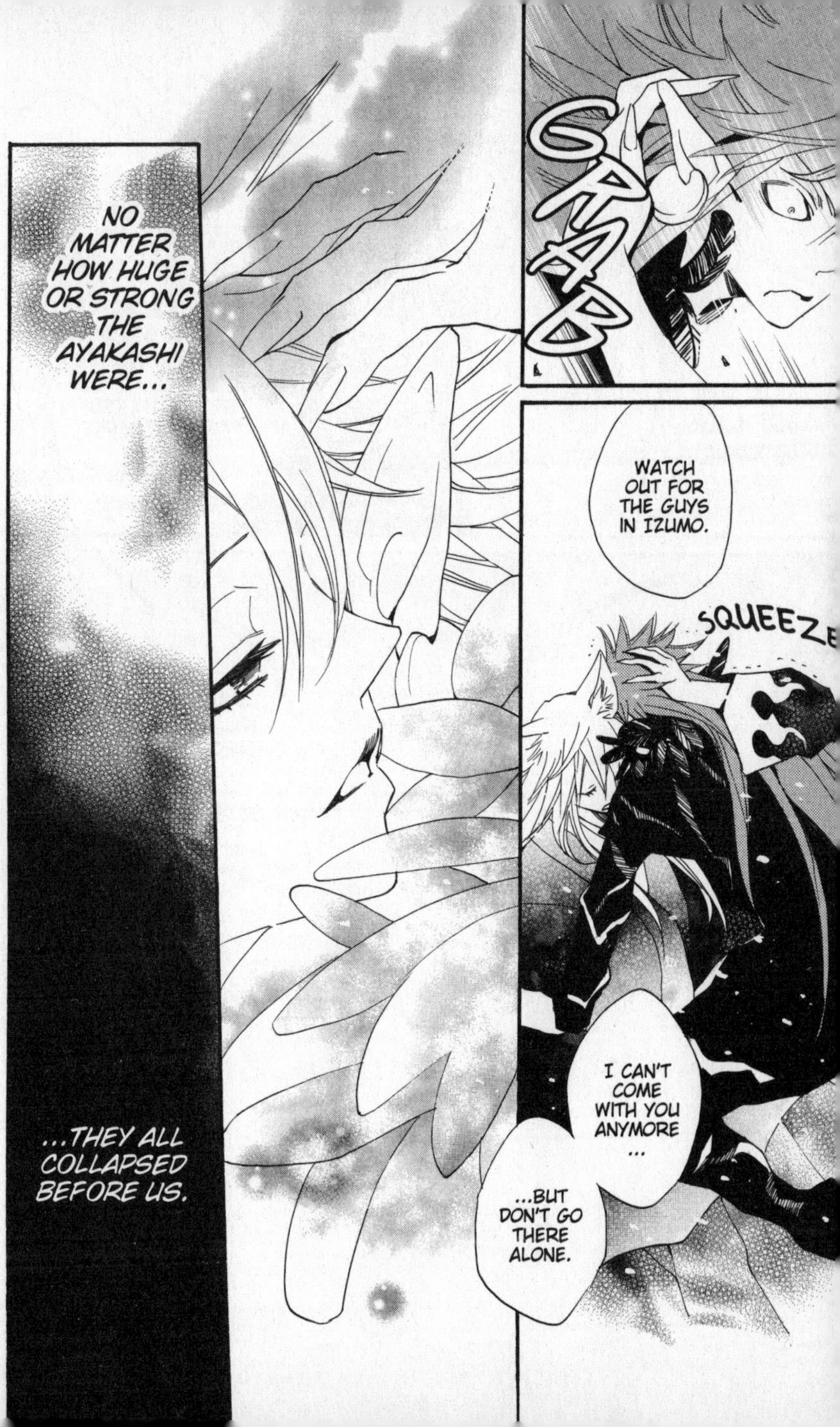
GRAB
WATCH OUT FOR THE GUYS IN IZUMO.
SQUEEZE
I CAN'T COME WITH YOU ANYMORE ...
...BUT DON'T GO THERE ALONE.
NO MATTER HOW HUGE OR STRONG THE AYAKASHI WERE...
...THEY ALL COLLAPSED BEFORE US.

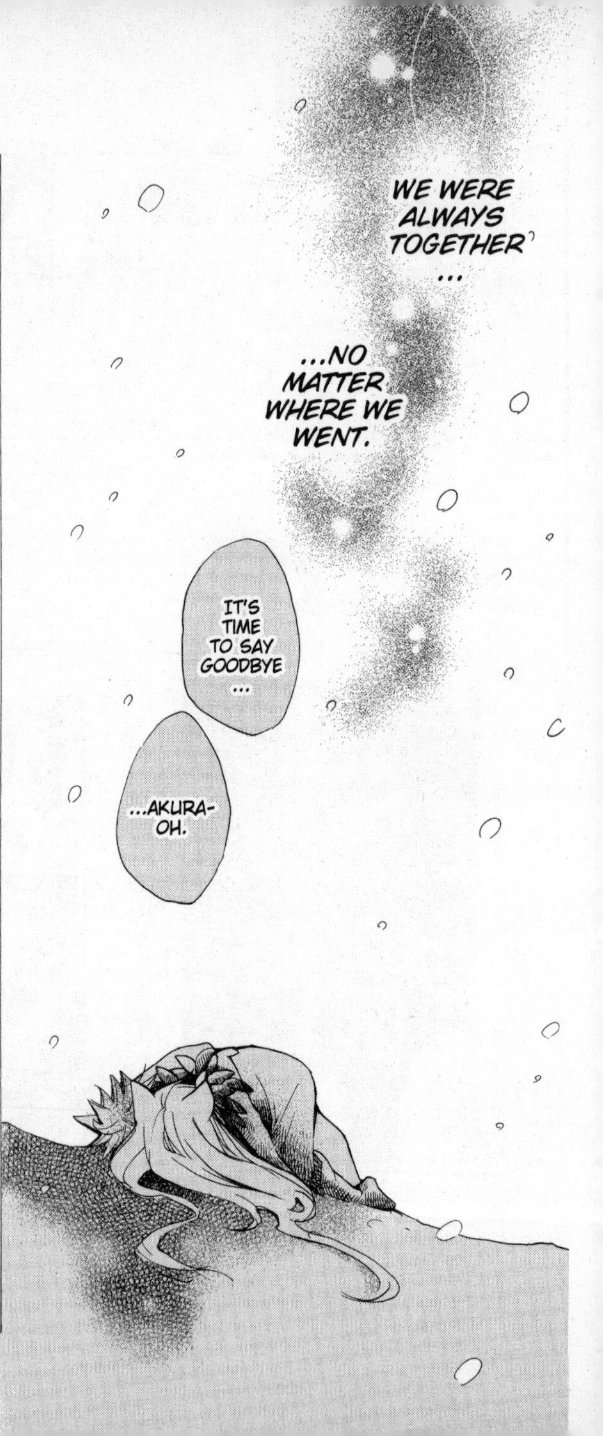
WE WERE ALWAYS TOGETHER...
...NO MATTER WHERE WE WENT.
IT'S TIME TO SAY GOODBYE...
...AKURA-OH.

I can't help wanting to see Moomin when the weather gets cold.

I'm referring to Moomin the TV show.

I'm watching a Moomin DVD right this moment as I'm writing this sidebar.

I want to live in Moominvalley too!

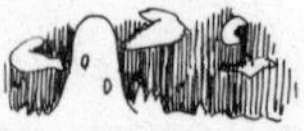

I wish my workplace was like Moomin House at least.

I wish Moomin Mama would make me late-night snacks when I'm working.

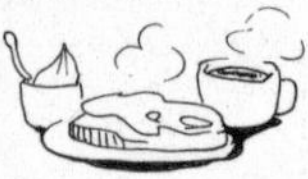

That is my dream.

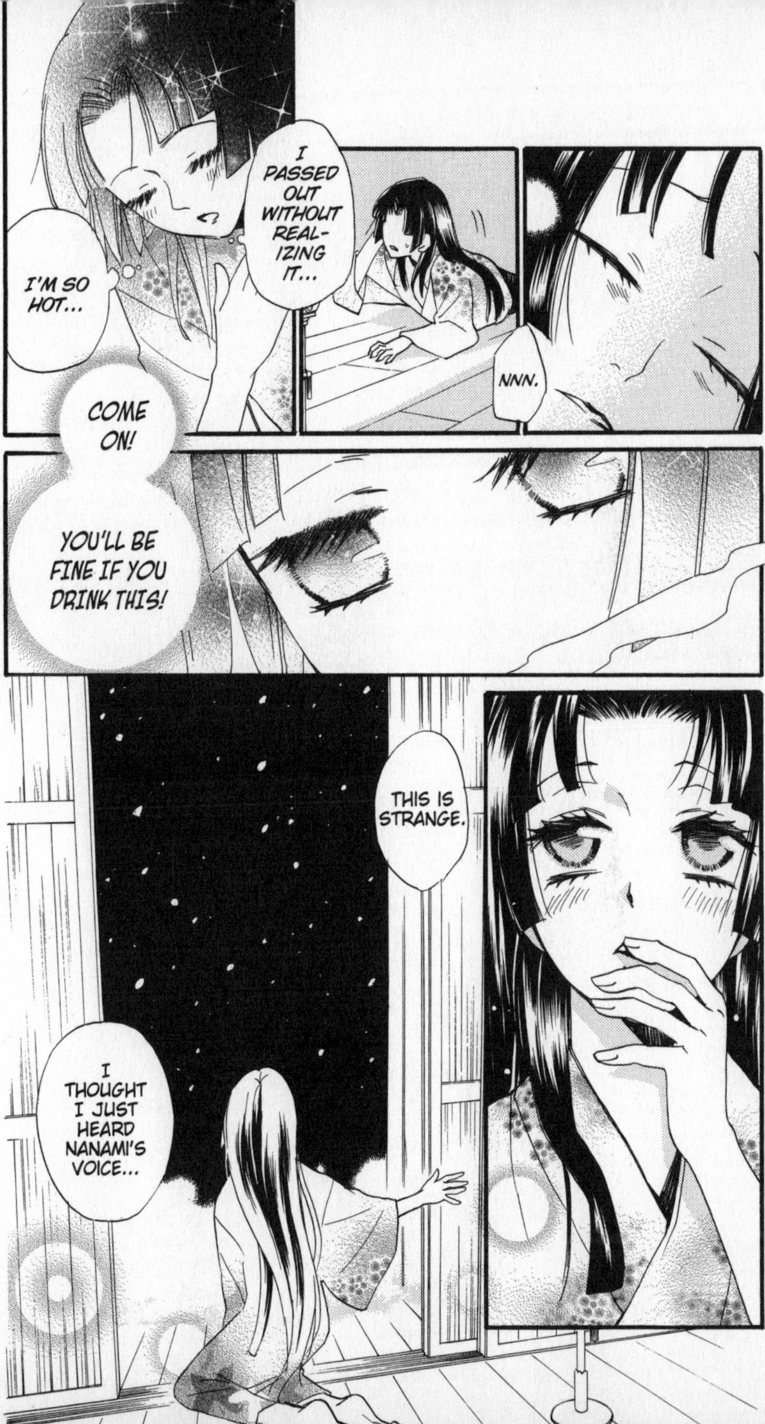

NNN.
I PASSED OUT WITHOUT REALIZING IT...
I'M SO HOT...
COME ON!
YOU'LL BE FINE IF YOU DRINK THIS!
THIS IS STRANGE.
I THOUGHT I JUST HEARD NANAMI'S VOICE...

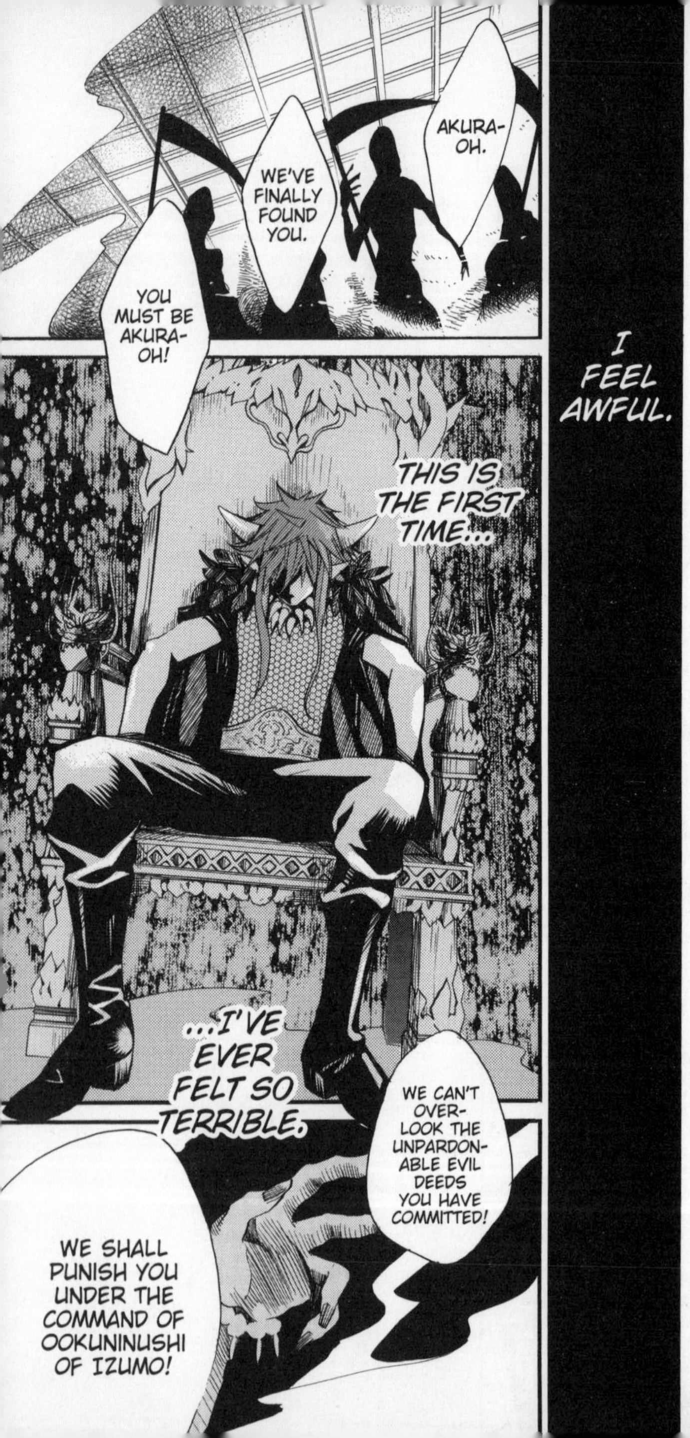
I FEEL AWFUL.
AKURA-OH.
WE'VE FINALLY FOUND YOU.
YOU MUST BE AKURA-OH!
THIS IS THE FIRST TIME...
...I'VE EVER FELT SO TERRIBLE.
WE CAN'T OVER-LOOK THE UNPARDON-ABLE EVIL DEEDS YOU HAVE COMMITTED!
WE SHALL PUNISH YOU UNDER THE COMMAND OF OOKUNINUSHI OF IZUMO!

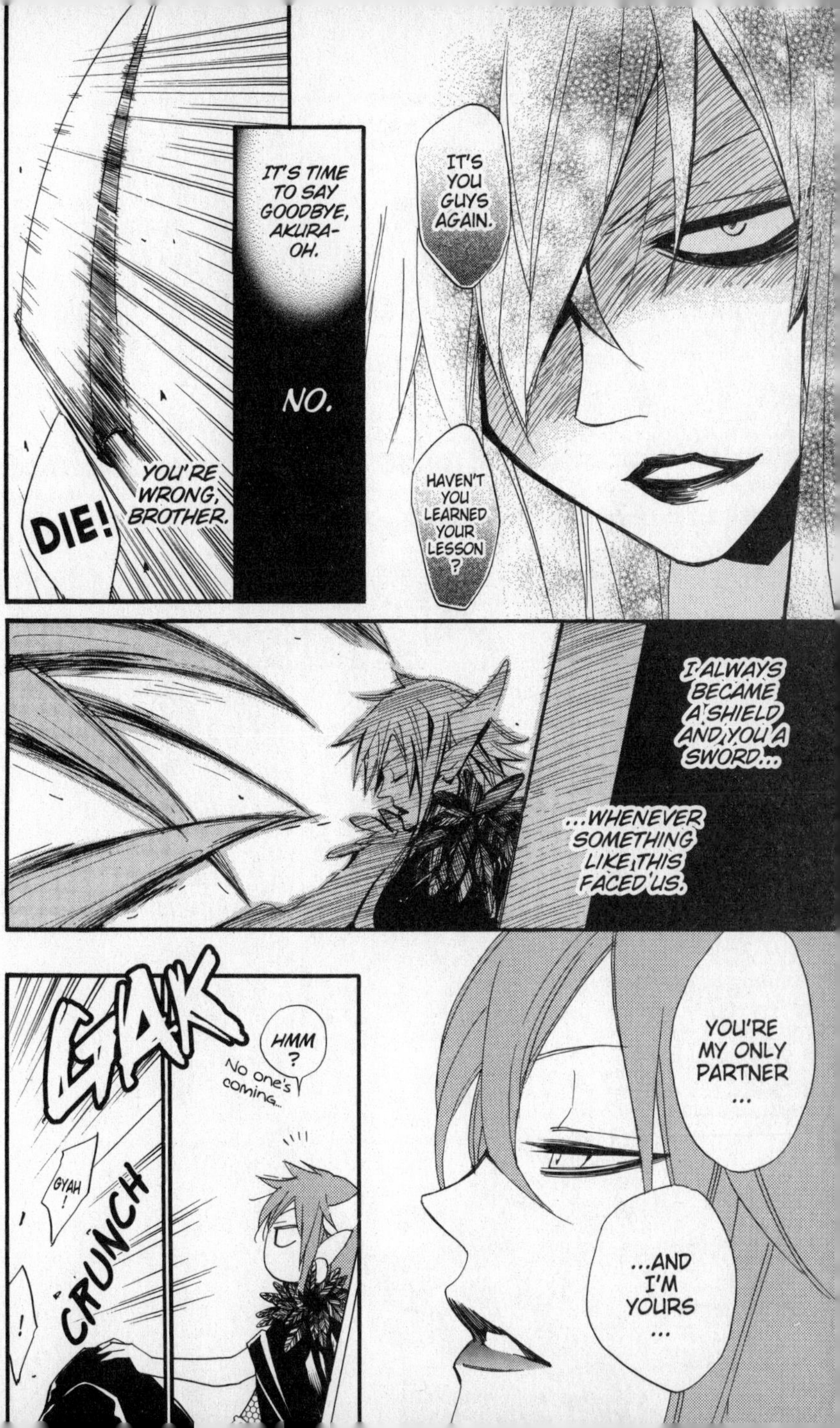

IT'S YOU GUYS AGAIN.
HAVEN'T YOU LEARNED YOUR LESSON?
IT'S TIME TO SAY GOODBYE, AKURA-OH.
NO.
YOU'RE WRONG, BROTHER.
DIE!
I ALWAYS BECAME A SHIELD AND YOU A SWORD...
...WHENEVER SOMETHING LIKE THIS FACED US.
YOU'RE MY ONLY PARTNER...
...AND I'M YOURS...
GAK
HMM?
No one's coming...
GYAH!
CRUNCH
!

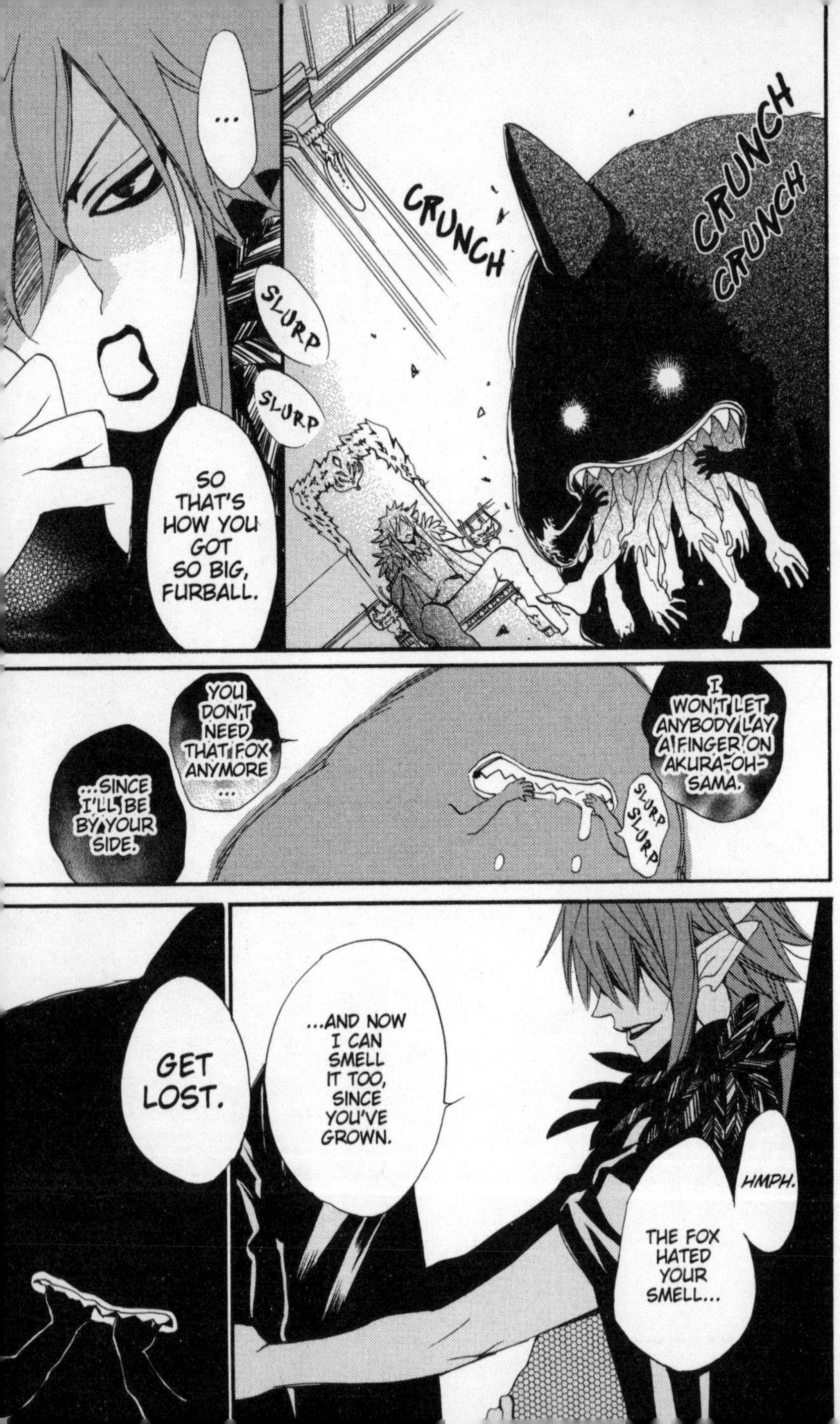
CRUNCH CRUNCH
CRUNCH
...
SLURP
SLURP
SO THAT'S HOW YOU GOT SO BIG, FURBALL.
I WON'T LET ANYBODY LAY A FINGER ON AKURA-OH-SAMA.
SLURP SLURP
YOU DON'T NEED THAT FOX ANYMORE...
...SINCE I'LL BE BY YOUR SIDE.
HMPH.
THE FOX HATED YOUR SMELL...
...AND NOW I CAN SMELL IT TOO, SINCE YOU'VE GROWN.
GET LOST.

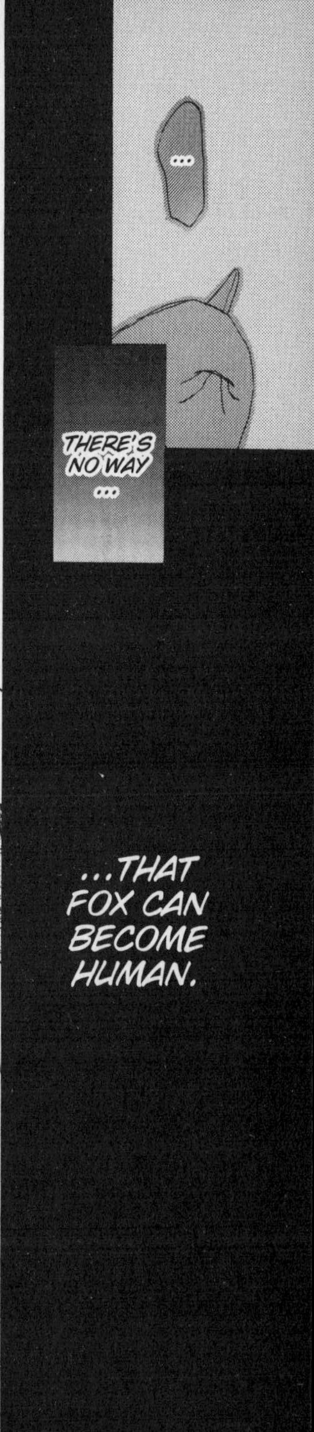
...
THERE'S NO WAY ...
...THAT FOX CAN BECOME HUMAN.
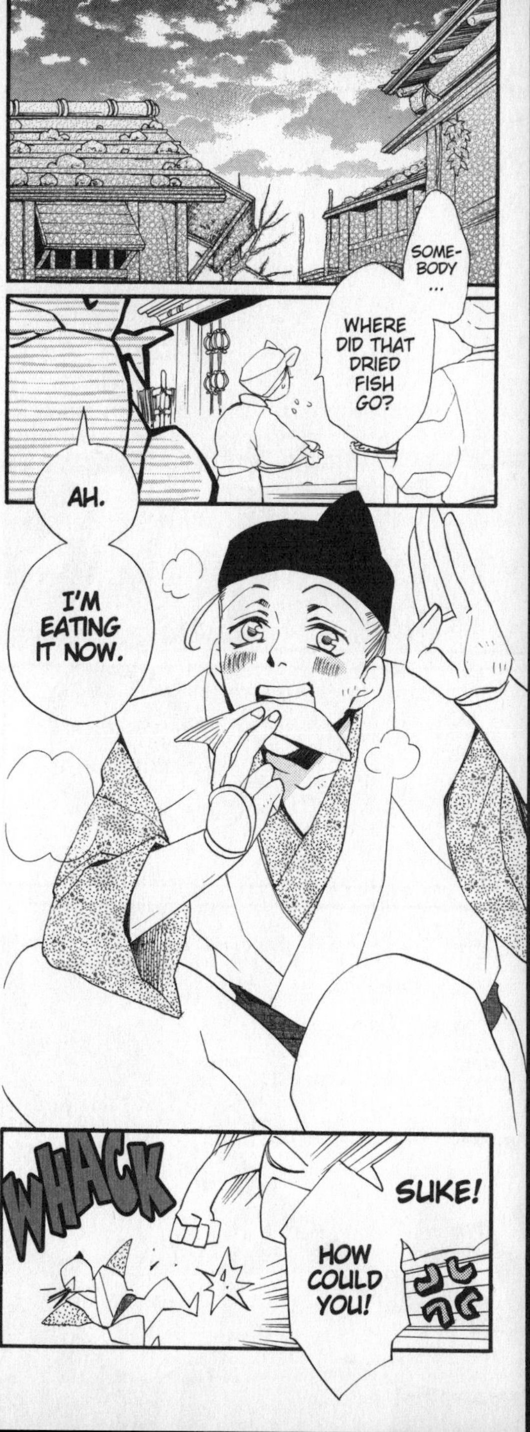
SOME-BODY ...
WHERE DID THAT DRIED FISH GO?
AH.
I'M EATING IT NOW.
WHACK
SUKE!
HOW COULD YOU!

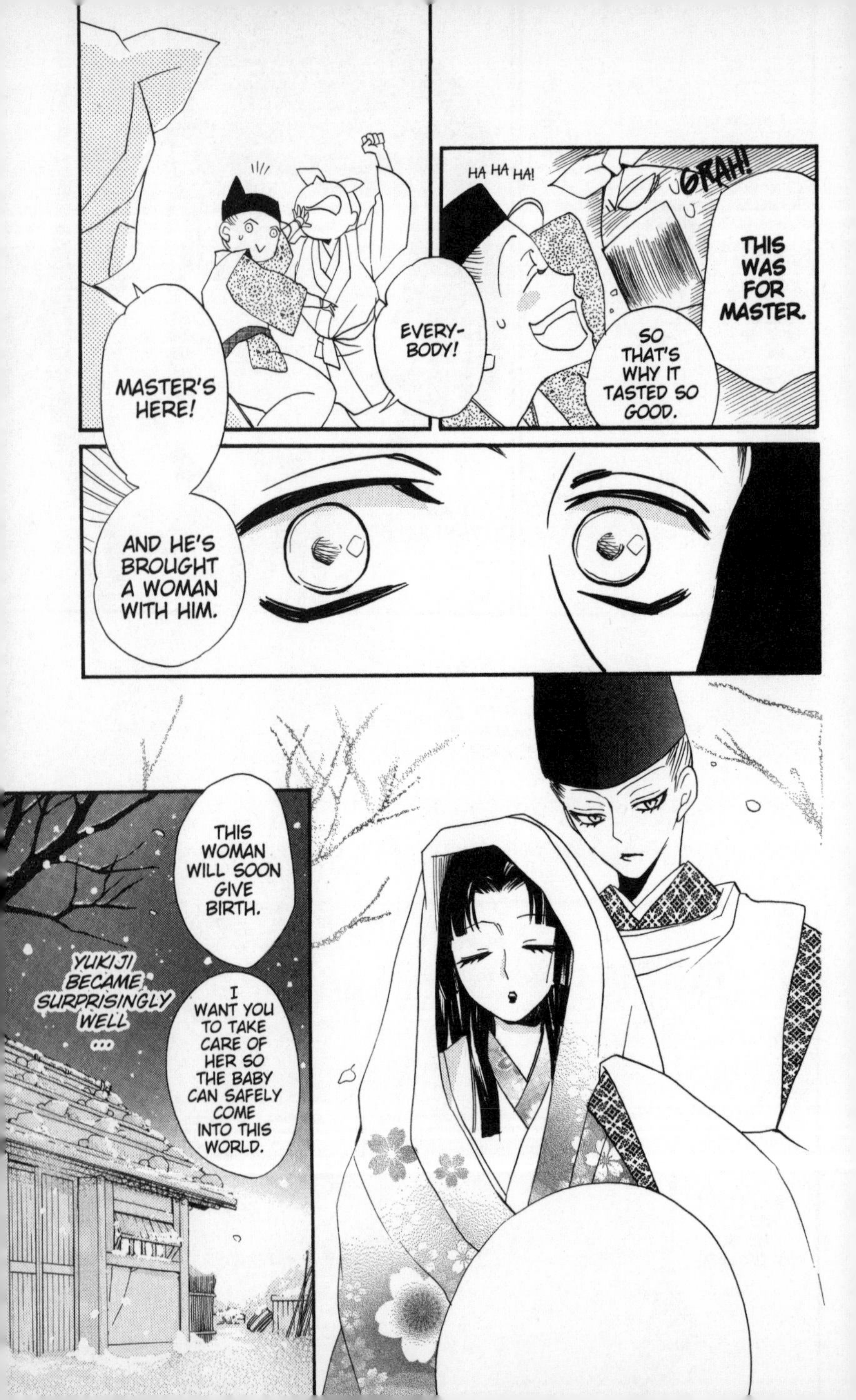
GRAH!
THIS WAS FOR MASTER.
HA HA HA!
SO THAT'S WHY IT TASTED SO GOOD.
EVERY-BODY!
MASTER'S HERE!
AND HE'S BROUGHT A WOMAN WITH HIM.
THIS WOMAN WILL SOON GIVE BIRTH.
I WANT YOU TO TAKE CARE OF HER SO THE BABY CAN SAFELY COME INTO THIS WORLD.
YUKIJI BECAME SURPRISINGLY WELL ...

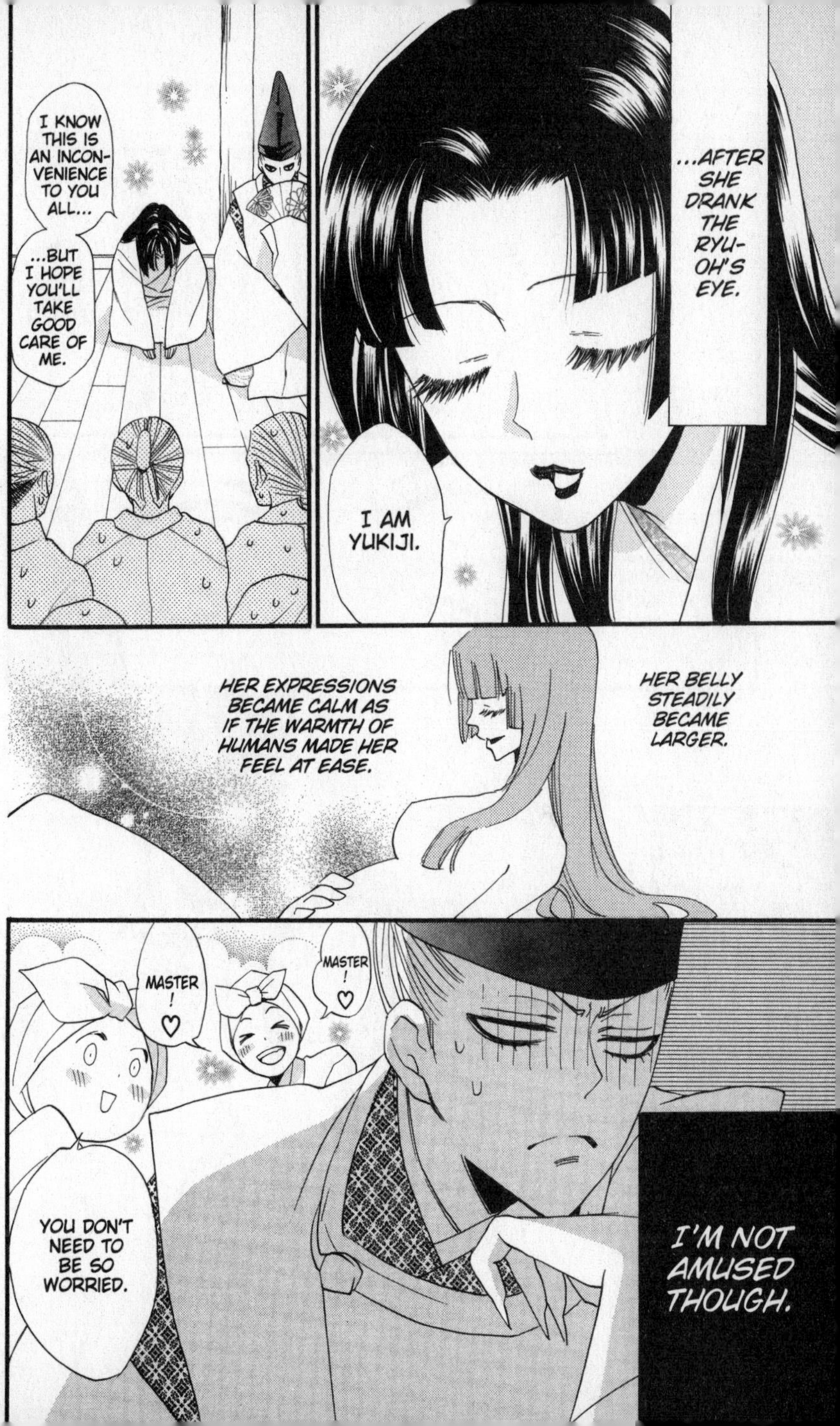
...AFTER SHE DRANK THE RYU-OH'S EYE.
I AM YUKIJI.
I KNOW THIS IS AN INCONVENIENCE TO YOU ALL...
...BUT I HOPE YOU'LL TAKE GOOD CARE OF ME.
HER BELLY STEADILY BECAME LARGER.
HER EXPRESSIONS BECAME CALM AS IF THE WARMTH OF HUMANS MADE HER FEEL AT EASE.
I'M NOT AMUSED THOUGH.
MASTER! ♡
MASTER! ♡
YOU DON'T NEED TO BE SO WORRIED.

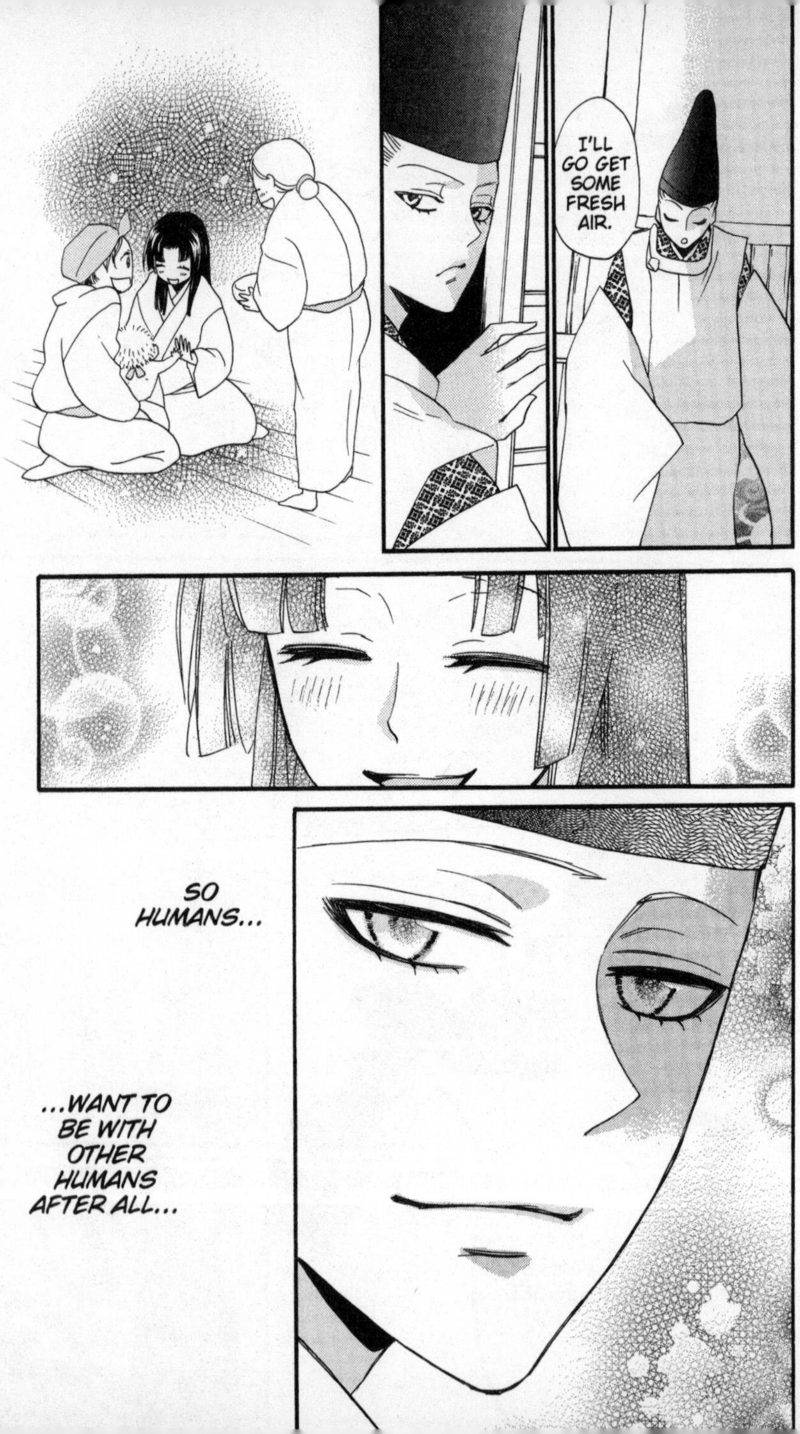
I'LL GO GET SOME FRESH AIR.
SO HUMANS...
...WANT TO BE WITH OTHER HUMANS AFTER ALL...

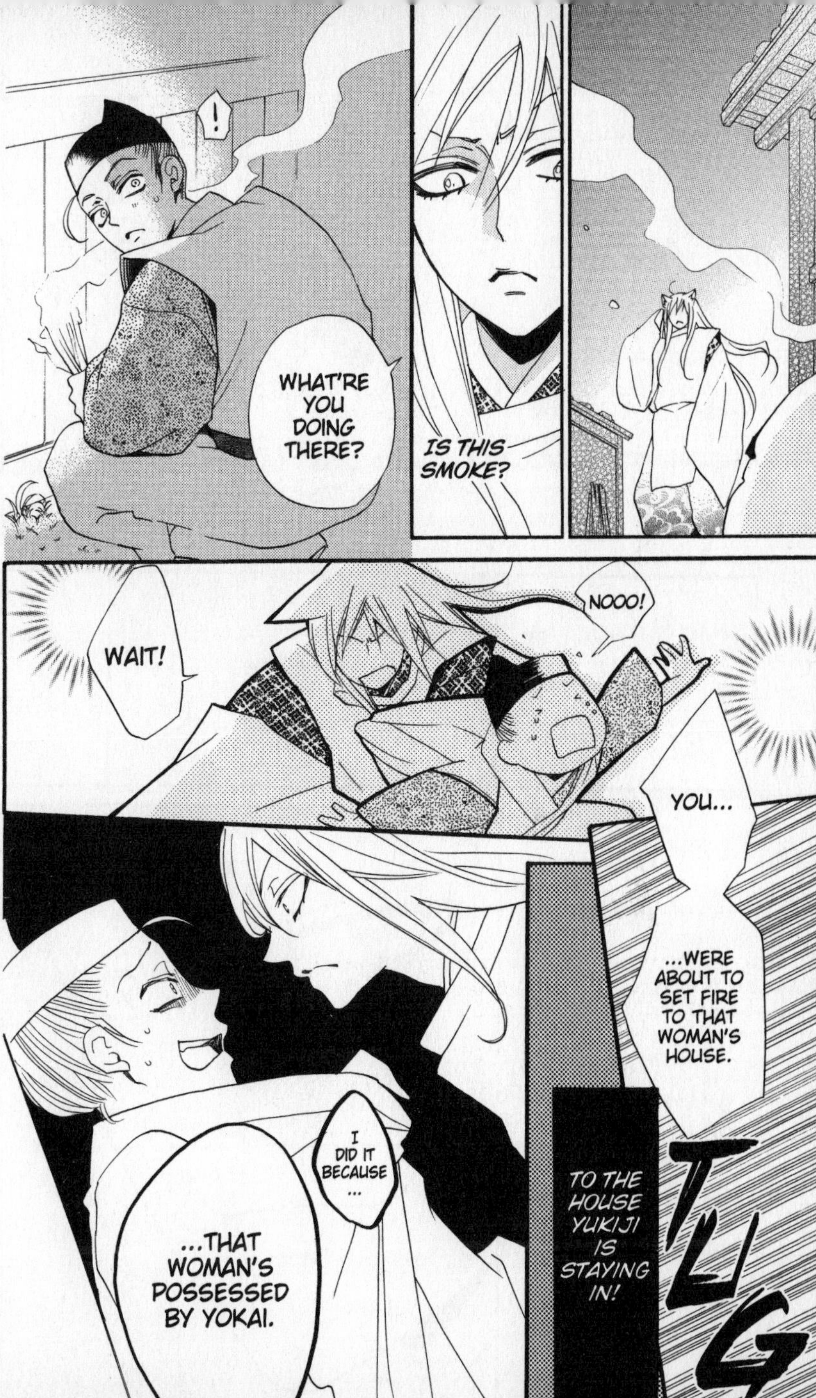
IS THIS SMOKE?
!
WHAT'RE YOU DOING THERE?
NOOO!
WAIT!
YOU...
...WERE ABOUT TO SET FIRE TO THAT WOMAN'S HOUSE.
TO THE HOUSE YUKIJI IS STAYING IN!
TUG
I DID IT BECAUSE...
...THAT WOMAN'S POSSESSED BY YOKAI.

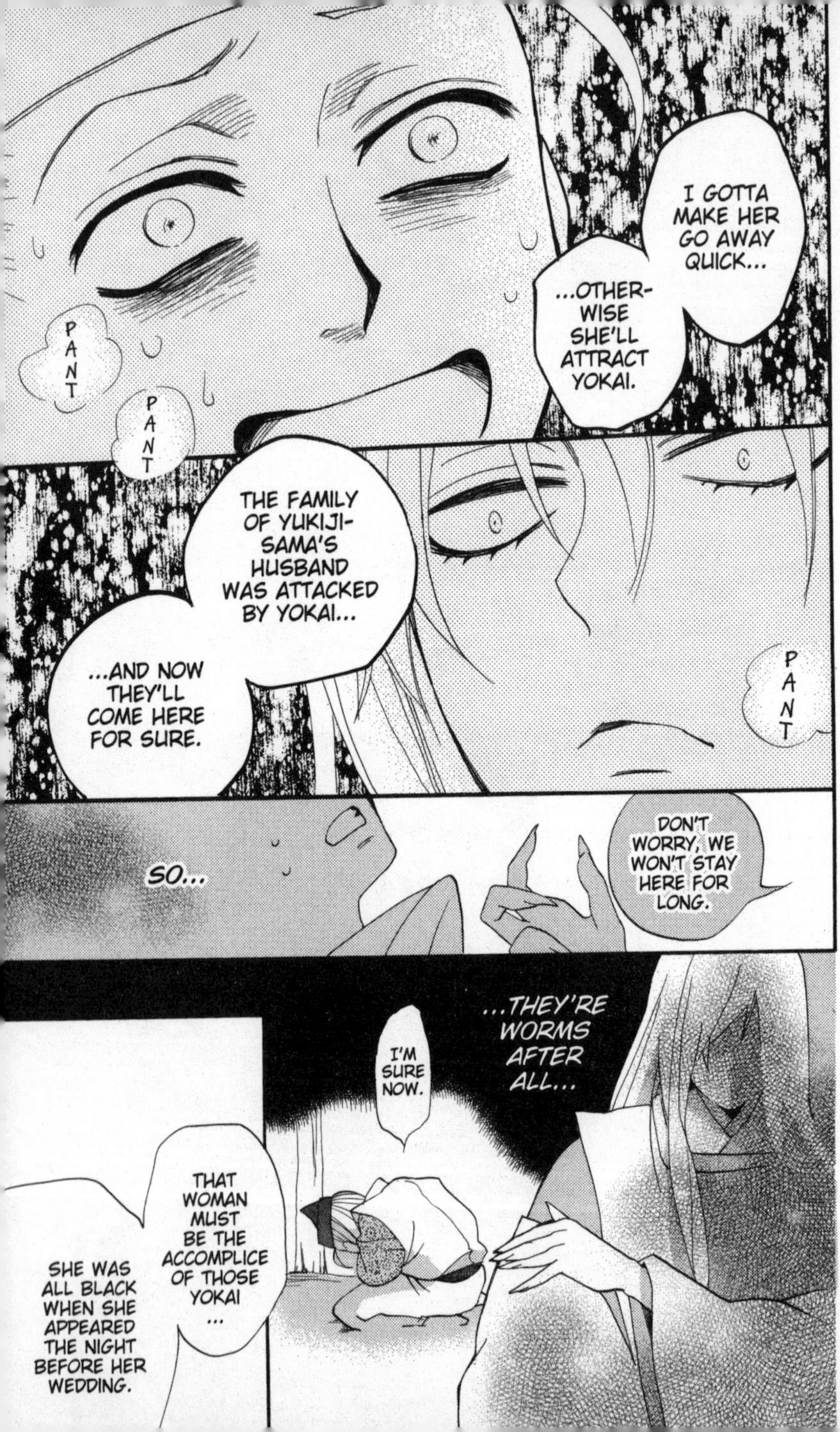
I GOTTA MAKE HER GO AWAY QUICK...
...OTHER-WISE SHE'LL ATTRACT YOKAI.
PANT
PANT
PANT
THE FAMILY OF YUKIJI-SAMA'S HUSBAND WAS ATTACKED BY YOKAI...
...AND NOW THEY'LL COME HERE FOR SURE.
DON'T WORRY, WE WON'T STAY HERE FOR LONG.
SO...
...THEY'RE WORMS AFTER ALL...
I'M SURE NOW.
THAT WOMAN MUST BE THE ACCOMPLICE OF THOSE YOKAI ...
SHE WAS ALL BLACK WHEN SHE APPEARED THE NIGHT BEFORE HER WEDDING.

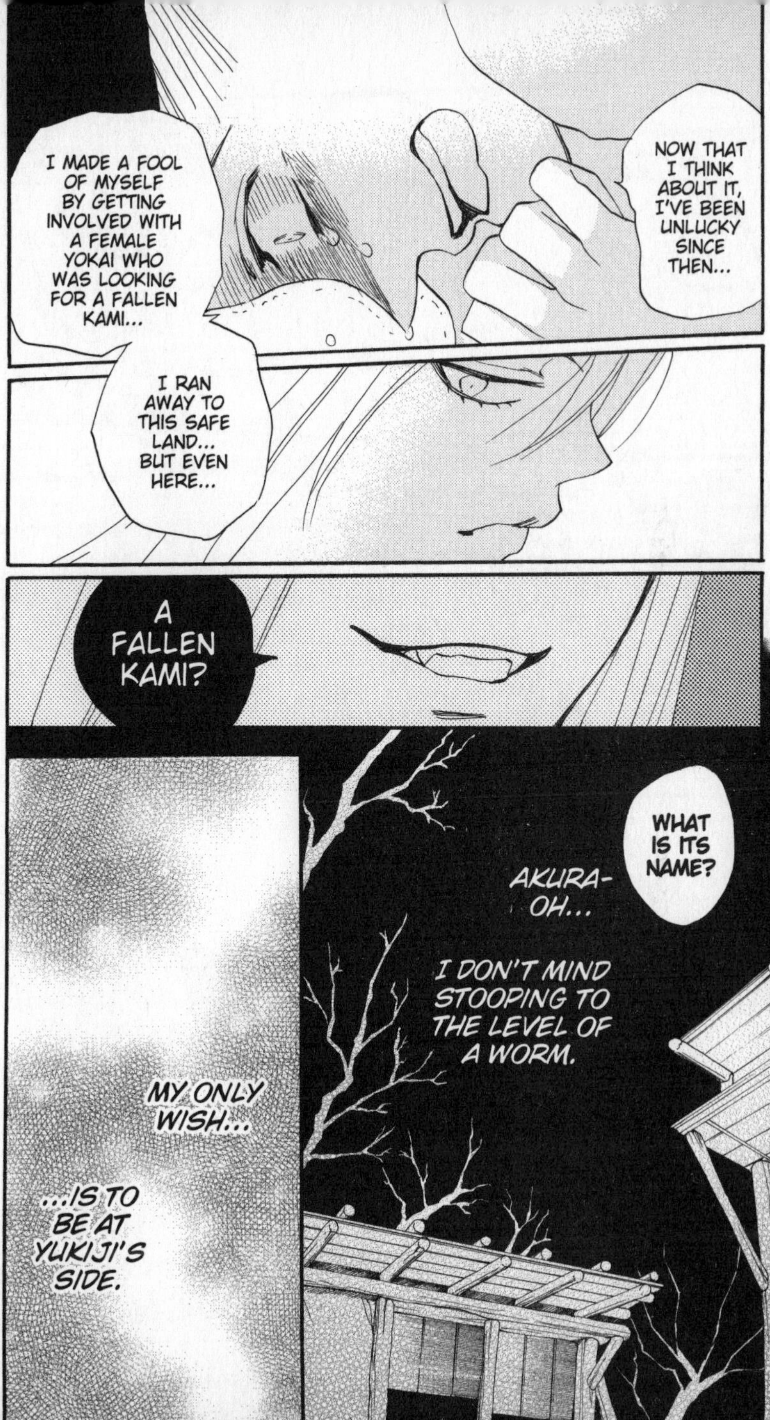
NOW THAT I THINK ABOUT IT, I'VE BEEN UNLUCKY SINCE THEN...
I MADE A FOOL OF MYSELF BY GETTING INVOLVED WITH A FEMALE YOKAI WHO WAS LOOKING FOR A FALLEN KAMI...
I RAN AWAY TO THIS SAFE LAND... BUT EVEN HERE...
A FALLEN KAMI?
WHAT IS ITS NAME?
AKURA-OH...
I DON'T MIND STOOPING TO THE LEVEL OF A WORM.
MY ONLY WISH...
...IS TO BE AT YUKIJI'S SIDE.

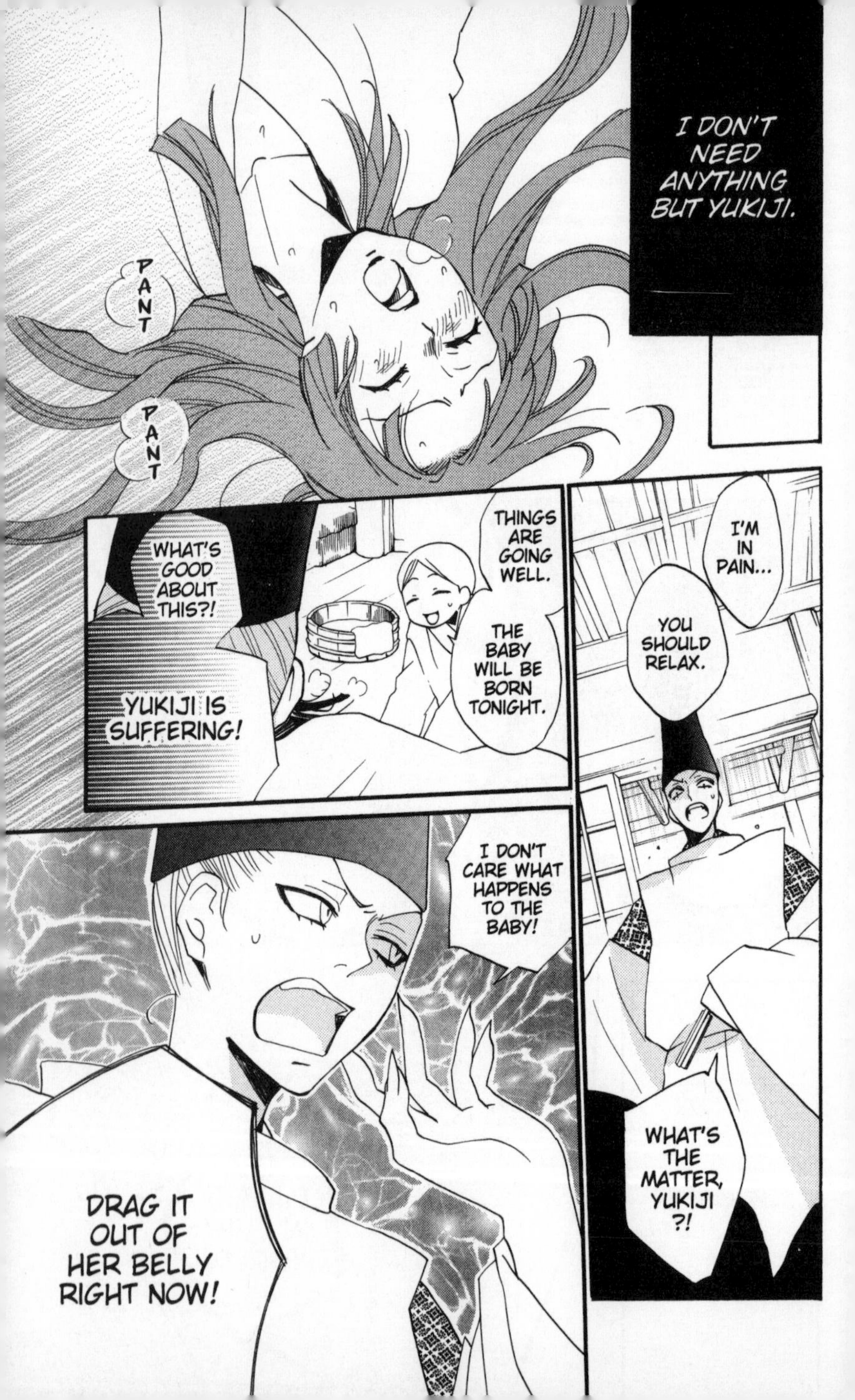
I DON'T NEED ANYTHING BUT YUKIJI.
PANT
PANT
I'M IN PAIN...
YOU SHOULD RELAX.
WHAT'S THE MATTER, YUKIJI?!
THINGS ARE GOING WELL.
THE BABY WILL BE BORN TONIGHT.
WHAT'S GOOD ABOUT THIS?!
YUKIJI IS SUFFERING!
I DON'T CARE WHAT HAPPENS TO THE BABY!
DRAG IT OUT OF HER BELLY RIGHT NOW!

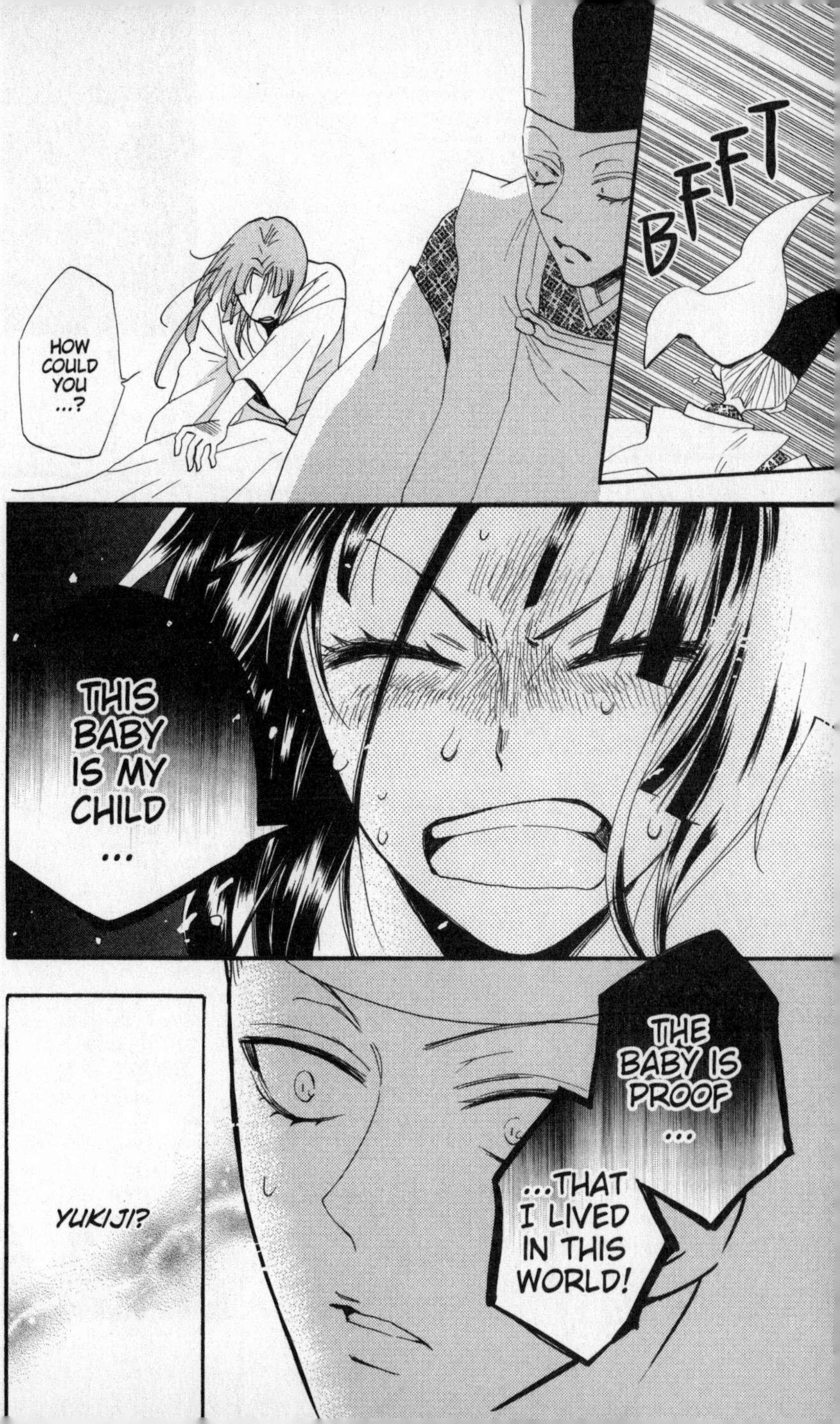
BFFT
HOW COULD YOU ...?
THIS BABY IS MY CHILD ...
THE BABY IS PROOF ...
...THAT I LIVED IN THIS WORLD!
YUKIJI?

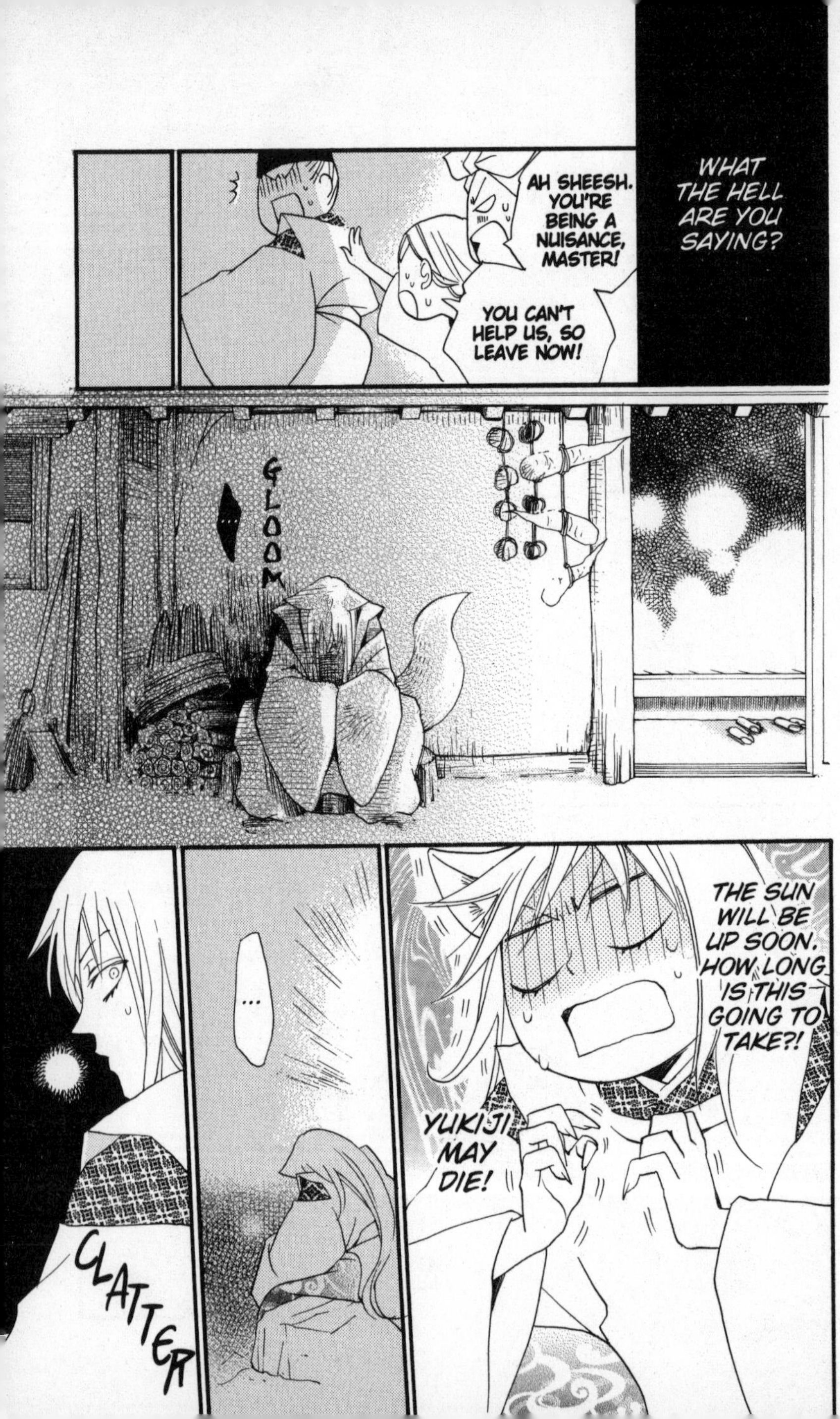
WHAT THE HELL ARE YOU SAYING?
AH SHEESH. YOU'RE BEING A NUISANCE, MASTER!
YOU CAN'T HELP US, SO LEAVE NOW!
GLOOM
...
THE SUN WILL BE UP SOON. HOW LONG IS THIS GOING TO TAKE?!
YUKIJI MAY DIE!
...
CLATTER

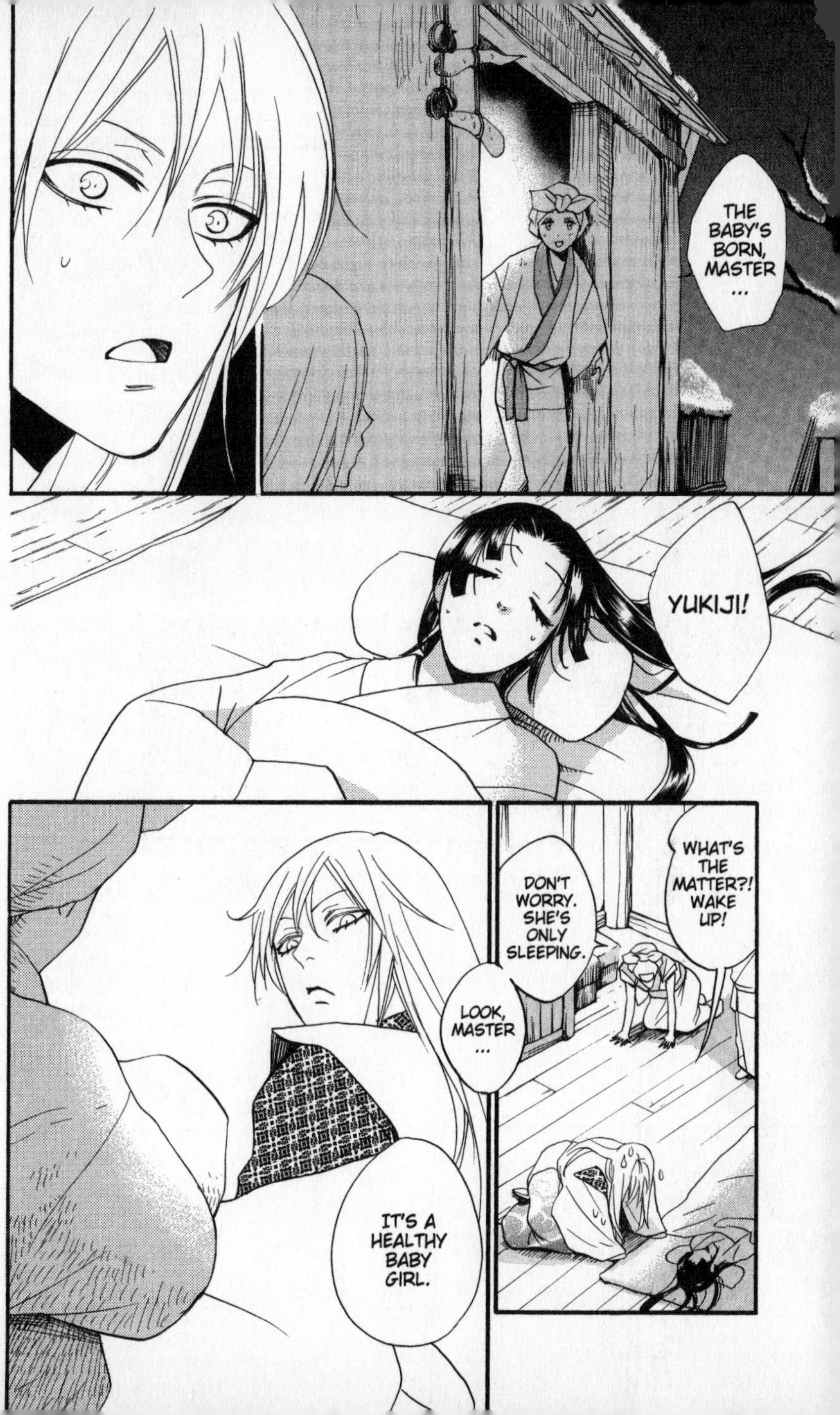
THE BABY'S BORN, MASTER ...
YUKIJI!
WHAT'S THE MATTER?! WAKE UP!
DON'T WORRY. SHE'S ONLY SLEEPING.
LOOK, MASTER ...
IT'S A HEALTHY BABY GIRL.

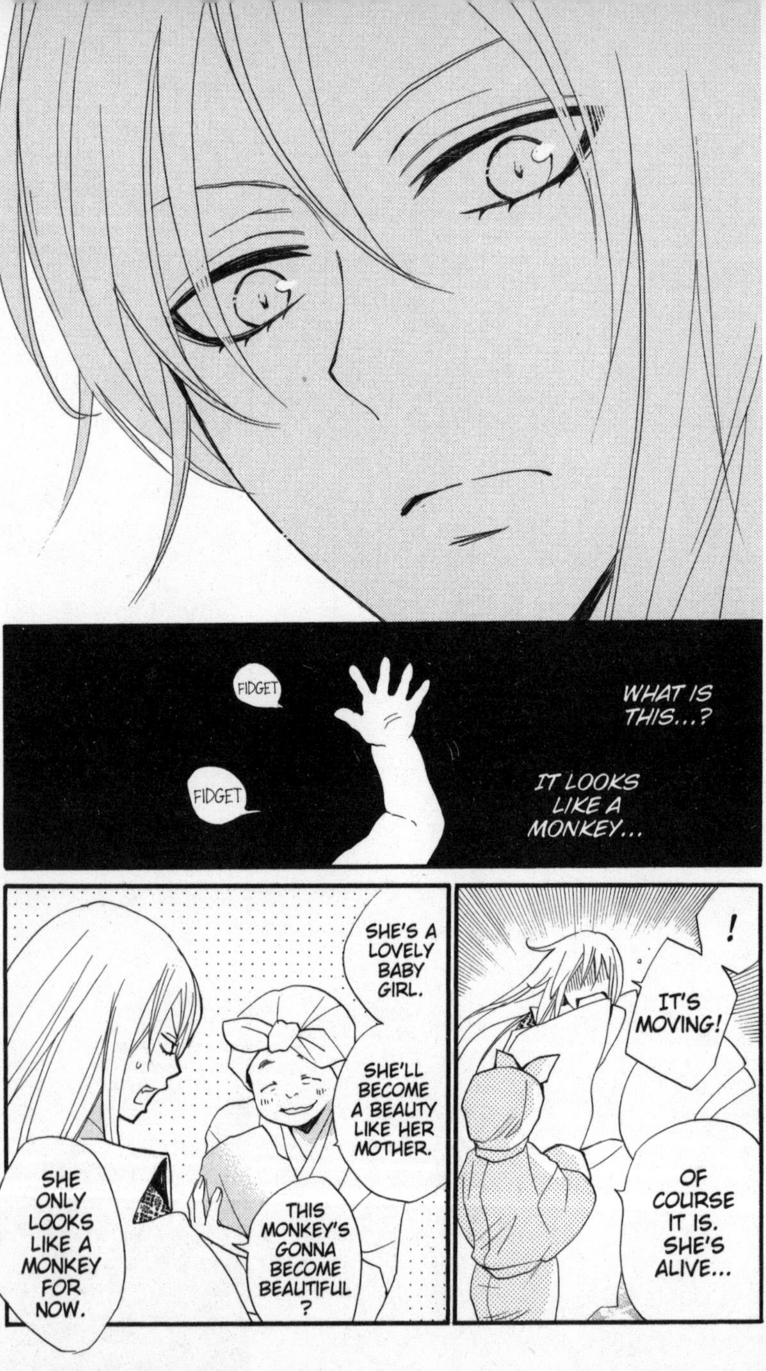
WHAT IS THIS...?
IT LOOKS LIKE A MONKEY...
FIDGET
FIDGET
!
IT'S MOVING!
OF COURSE IT IS. SHE'S ALIVE...
SHE'S A LOVELY BABY GIRL.
SHE'LL BECOME A BEAUTY LIKE HER MOTHER.
THIS MONKEY'S GONNA BECOME BEAUTIFUL?
SHE ONLY LOOKS LIKE A MONKEY FOR NOW.

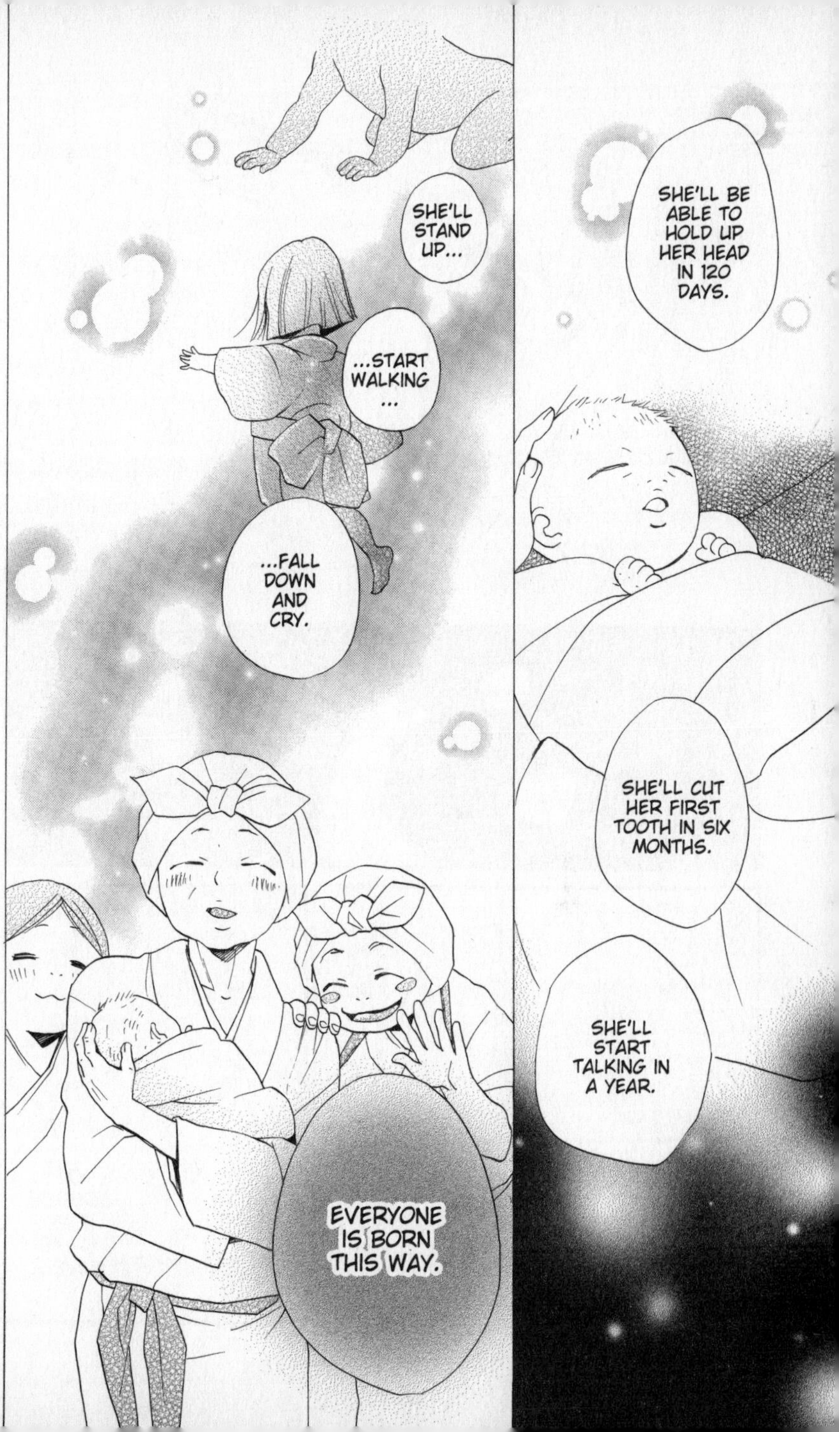
SHE'LL BE ABLE TO HOLD UP HER HEAD IN 120 DAYS.
SHE'LL CUT HER FIRST TOOTH IN SIX MONTHS.
SHE'LL START TALKING IN A YEAR.
SHE'LL STAND UP...
...START WALKING ...
...FALL DOWN AND CRY.
EVERYONE IS BORN THIS WAY.

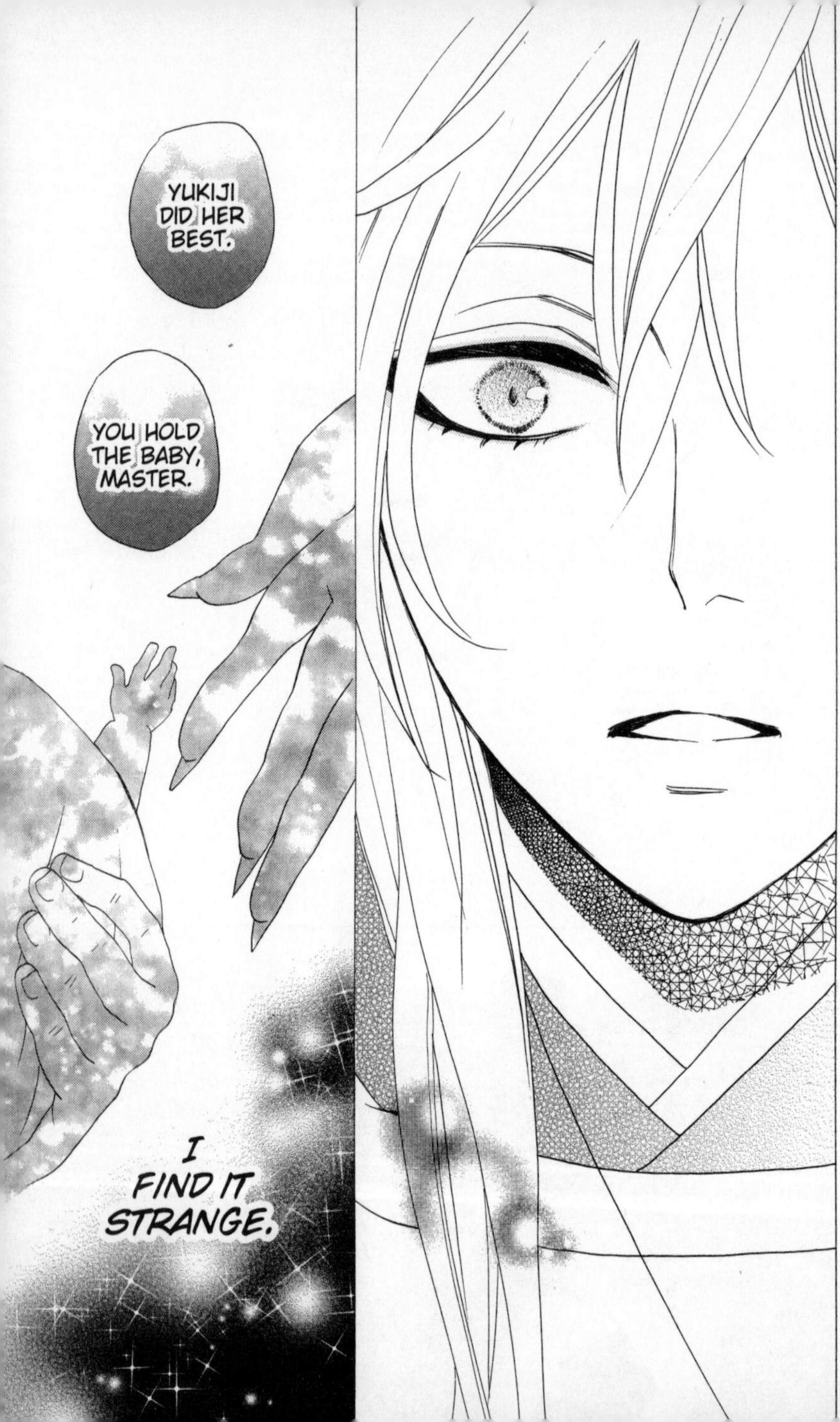
YUKIJI DID HER BEST.
YOU HOLD THE BABY, MASTER.
I FIND IT STRANGE.

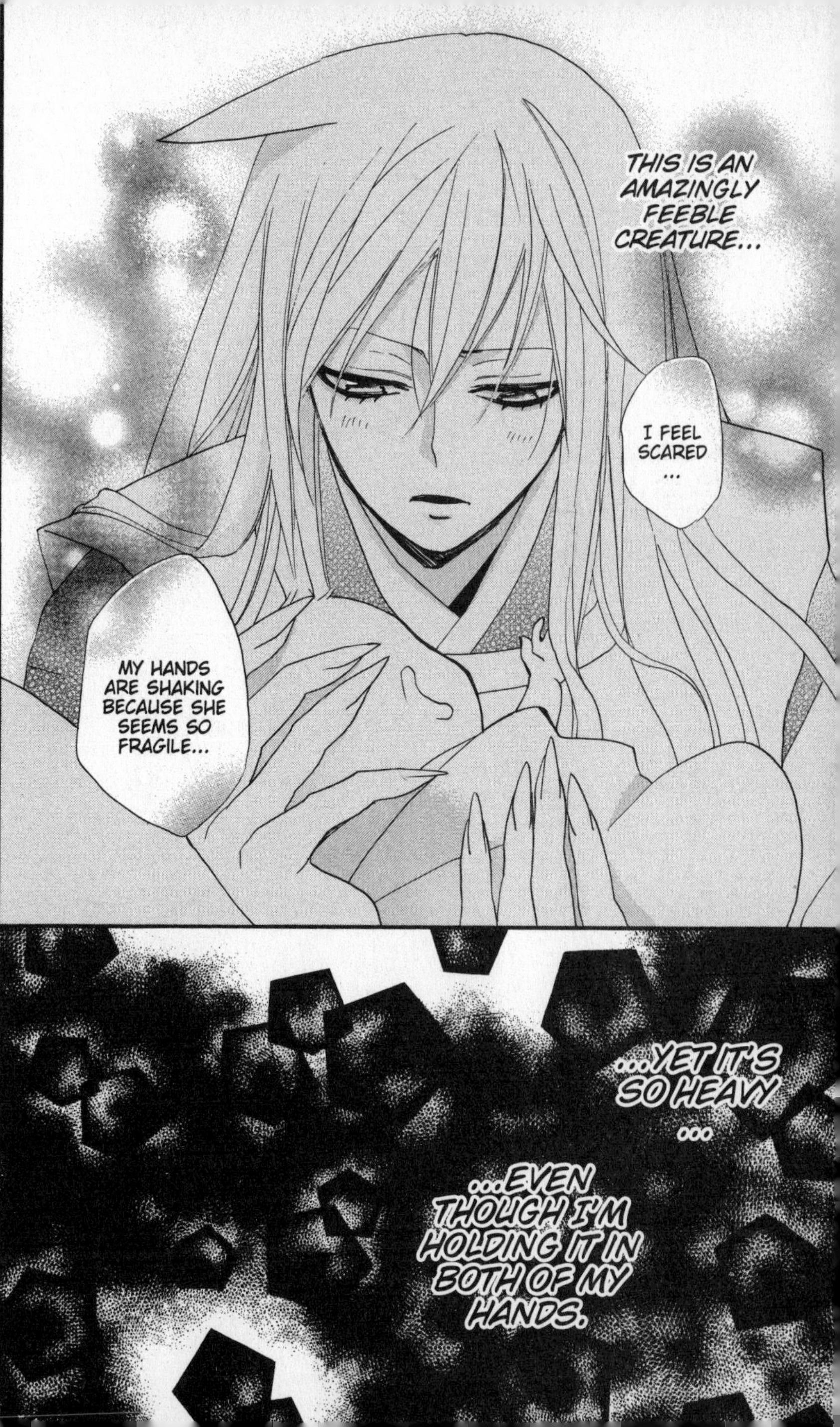
THIS IS AN AMAZINGLY FEEBLE CREATURE...
I FEEL SCARED ...
MY HANDS ARE SHAKING BECAUSE SHE SEEMS SO FRAGILE...
...YET IT'S SO HEAVY ...
...EVEN THOUGH I'M HOLDING IT IN BOTH OF MY HANDS.

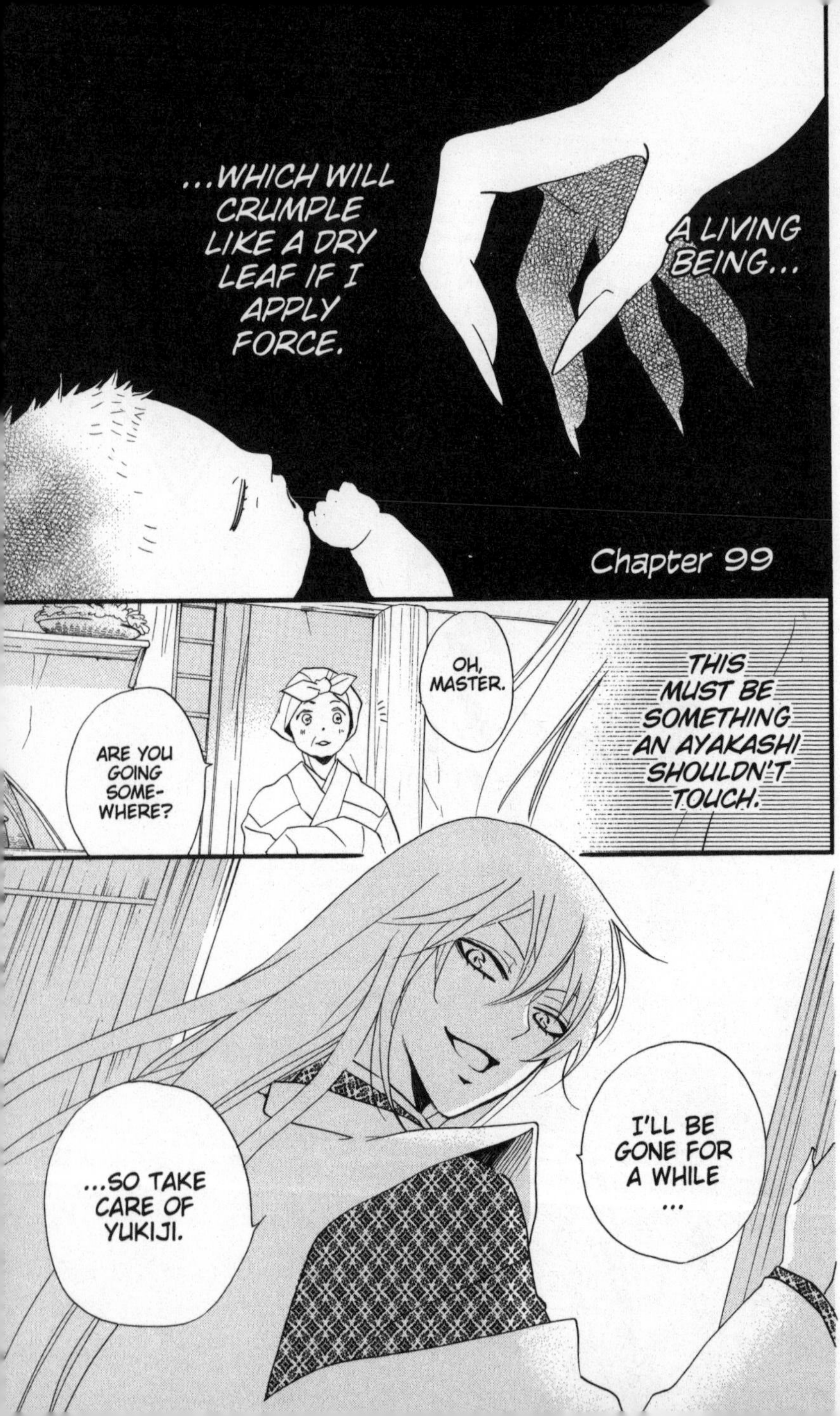
A LIVING BEING...
...WHICH WILL CRUMPLE LIKE A DRY LEAF IF I APPLY FORCE.
Chapter 99
THIS MUST BE SOMETHING AN AYAKASHI SHOULDN'T TOUCH.
OH, MASTER.
ARE YOU GOING SOME-WHERE?
I'LL BE GONE FOR A WHILE ...
...SO TAKE CARE OF YUKIJI.

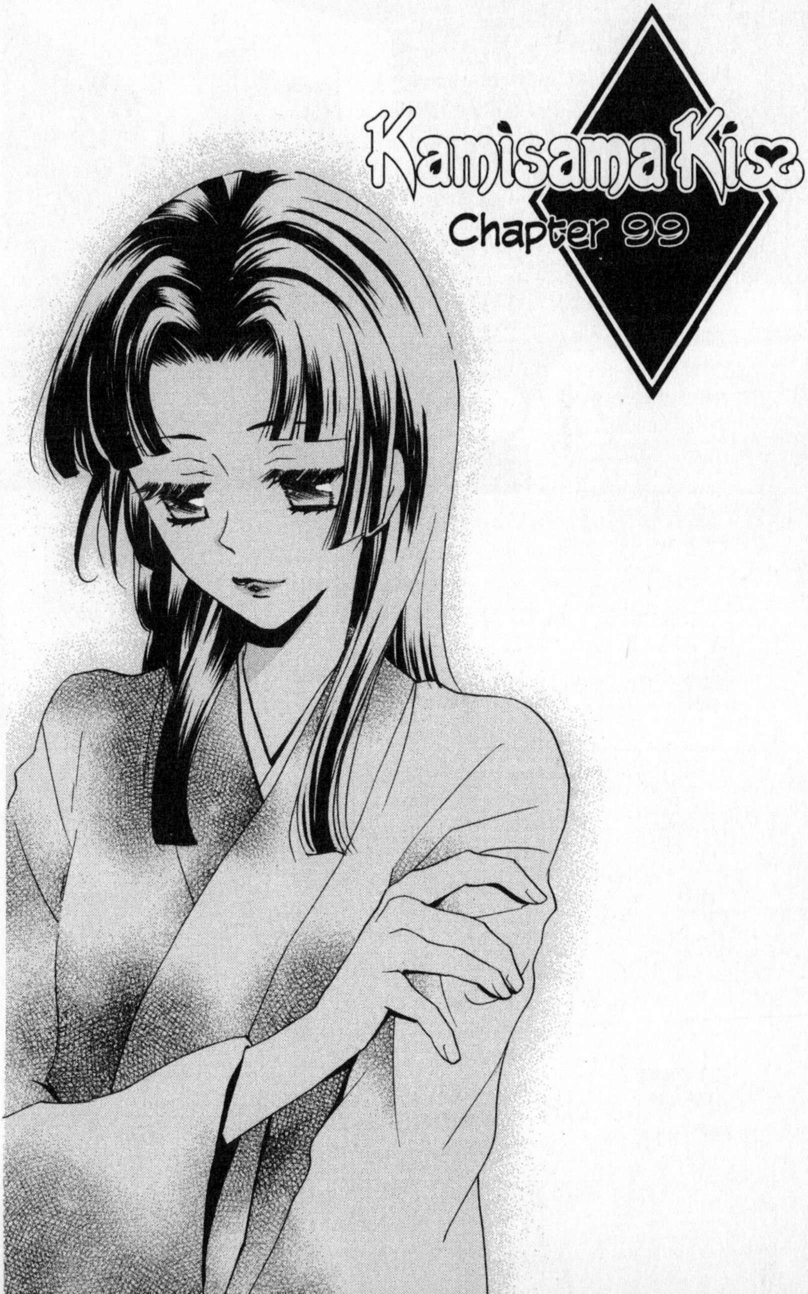
Kamisama Kiss
Chapter 99

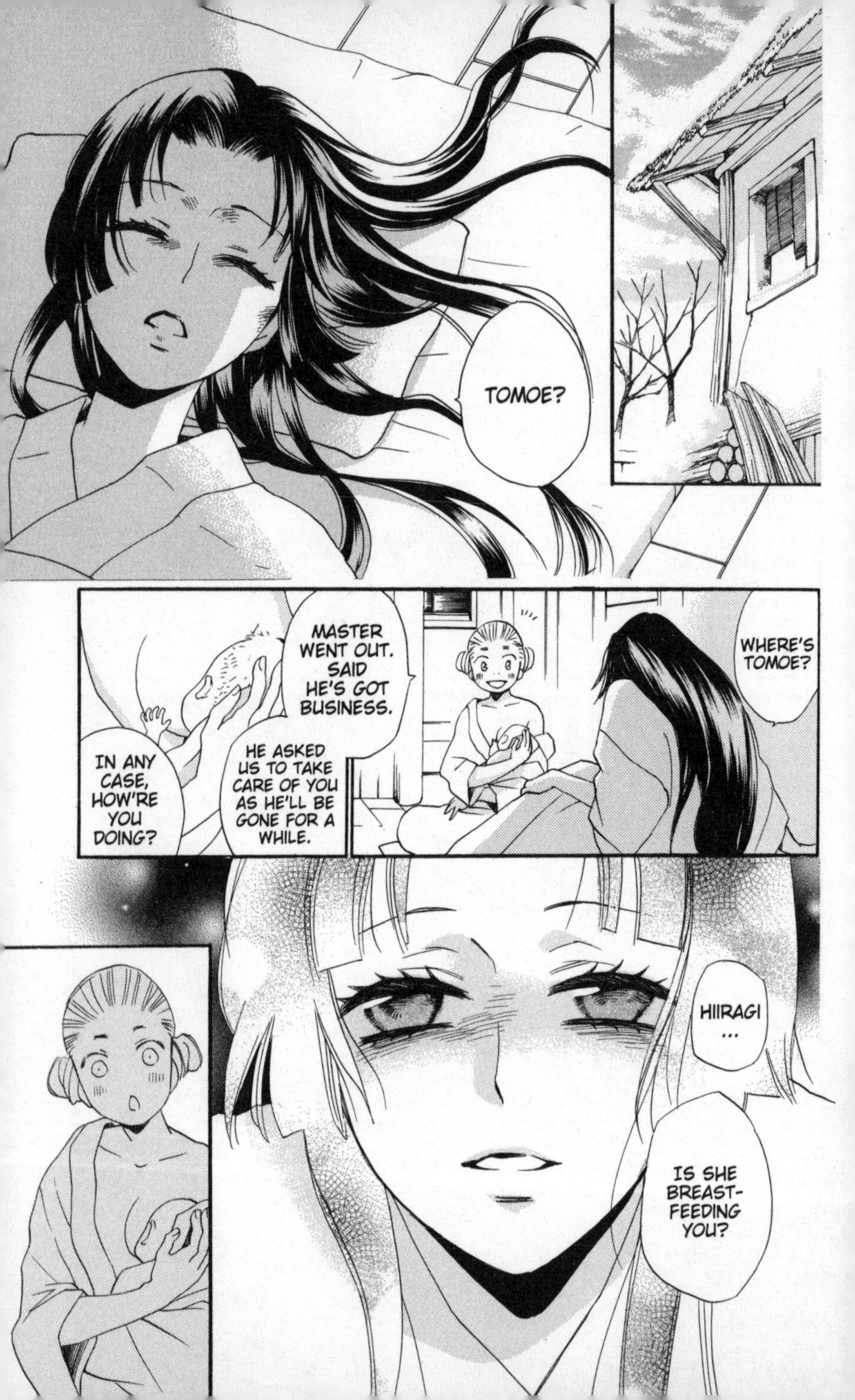
TOMOE?
WHERE'S TOMOE?
MASTER WENT OUT. SAID HE'S GOT BUSINESS.
HE ASKED US TO TAKE CARE OF YOU AS HE'LL BE GONE FOR A WHILE.
IN ANY CASE, HOW'RE YOU DOING?
HIIRAGI ...
IS SHE BREAST-FEEDING YOU?

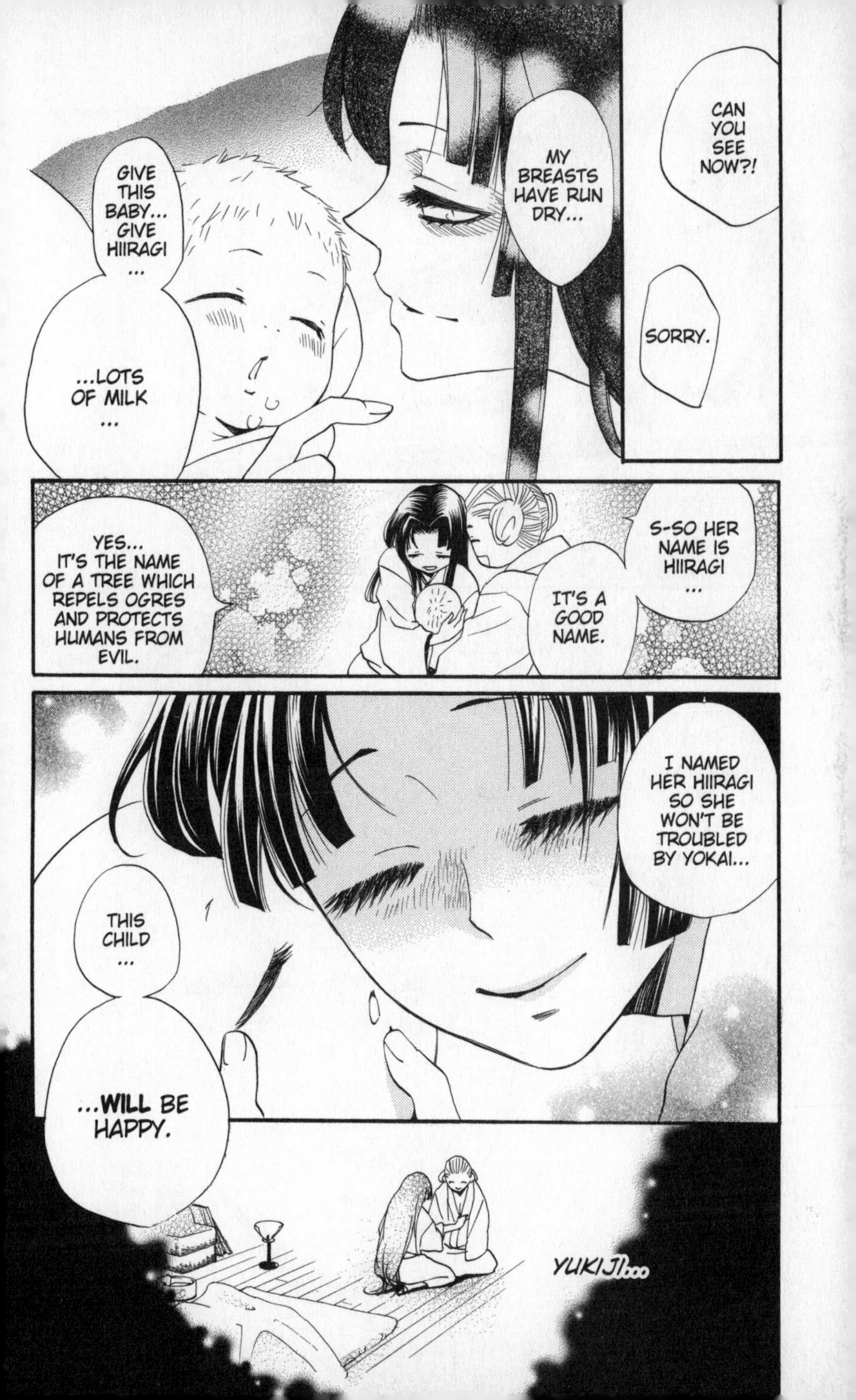
CAN YOU SEE NOW?!
SORRY.
MY BREASTS HAVE RUN DRY...
GIVE THIS BABY... GIVE HIIRAGI ...
...LOTS OF MILK ...
S-SO HER NAME IS HIIRAGI ...
IT'S A GOOD NAME.
YES... IT'S THE NAME OF A TREE WHICH REPELS OGRES AND PROTECTS HUMANS FROM EVIL.
I NAMED HER HIIRAGI SO SHE WON'T BE TROUBLED BY YOKAI...
THIS CHILD ...
...**WILL** BE HAPPY.
YUKIJI...

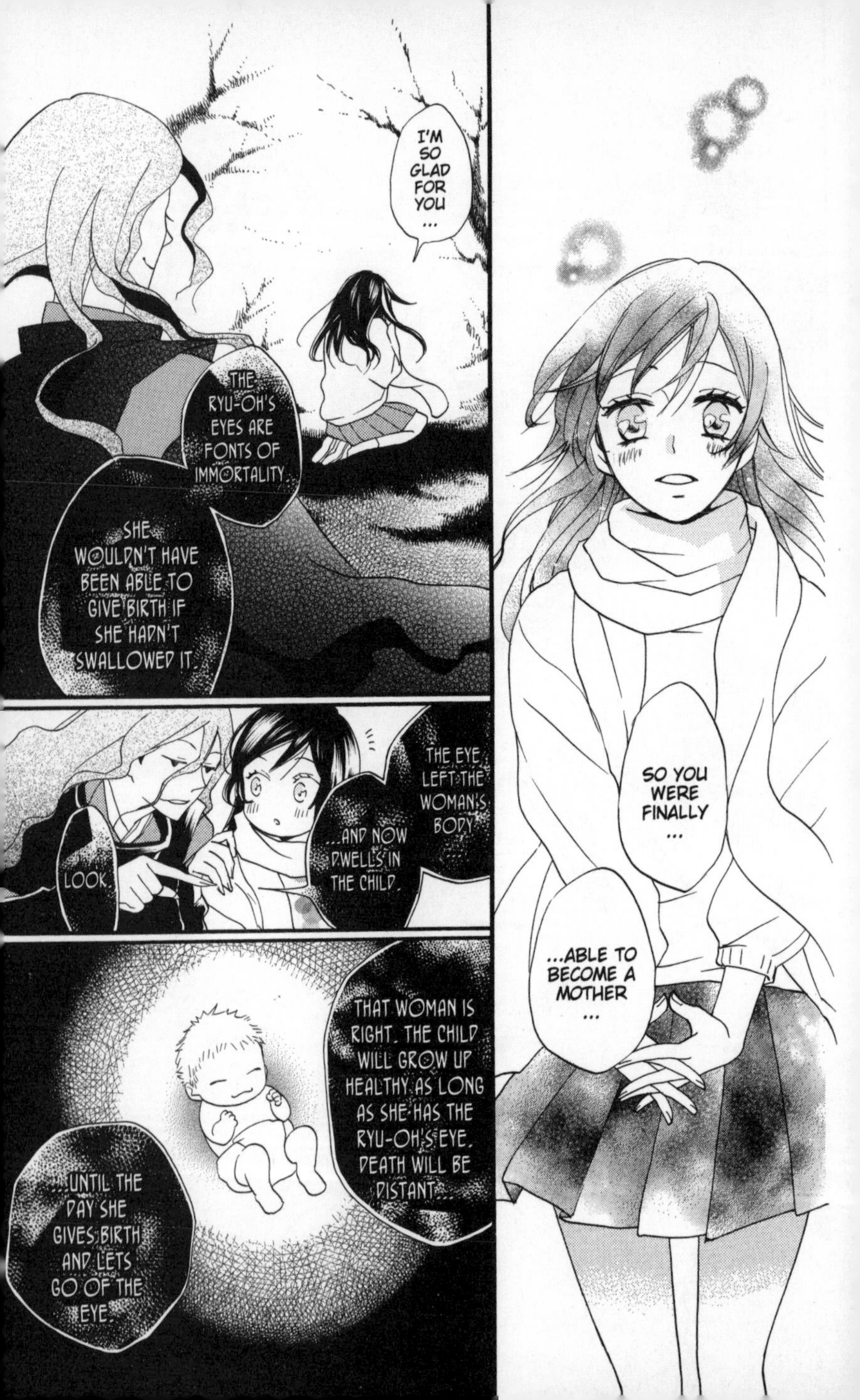
SO YOU WERE FINALLY ...
...ABLE TO BECOME A MOTHER ...
I'M SO GLAD FOR YOU ...
THE RYU-OH'S EYES ARE FONTS OF IMMORTALITY.
SHE WOULDN'T HAVE BEEN ABLE TO GIVE BIRTH IF SHE HADN'T SWALLOWED IT.
THE EYE LEFT THE WOMAN'S BODY ...
...AND NOW DWELLS IN THE CHILD.
LOOK.
THAT WOMAN IS RIGHT. THE CHILD WILL GROW UP HEALTHY AS LONG AS SHE HAS THE RYU-OH'S EYE. DEATH WILL BE DISTANT...
...UNTIL THE DAY SHE GIVES BIRTH AND LETS GO OF THE EYE.

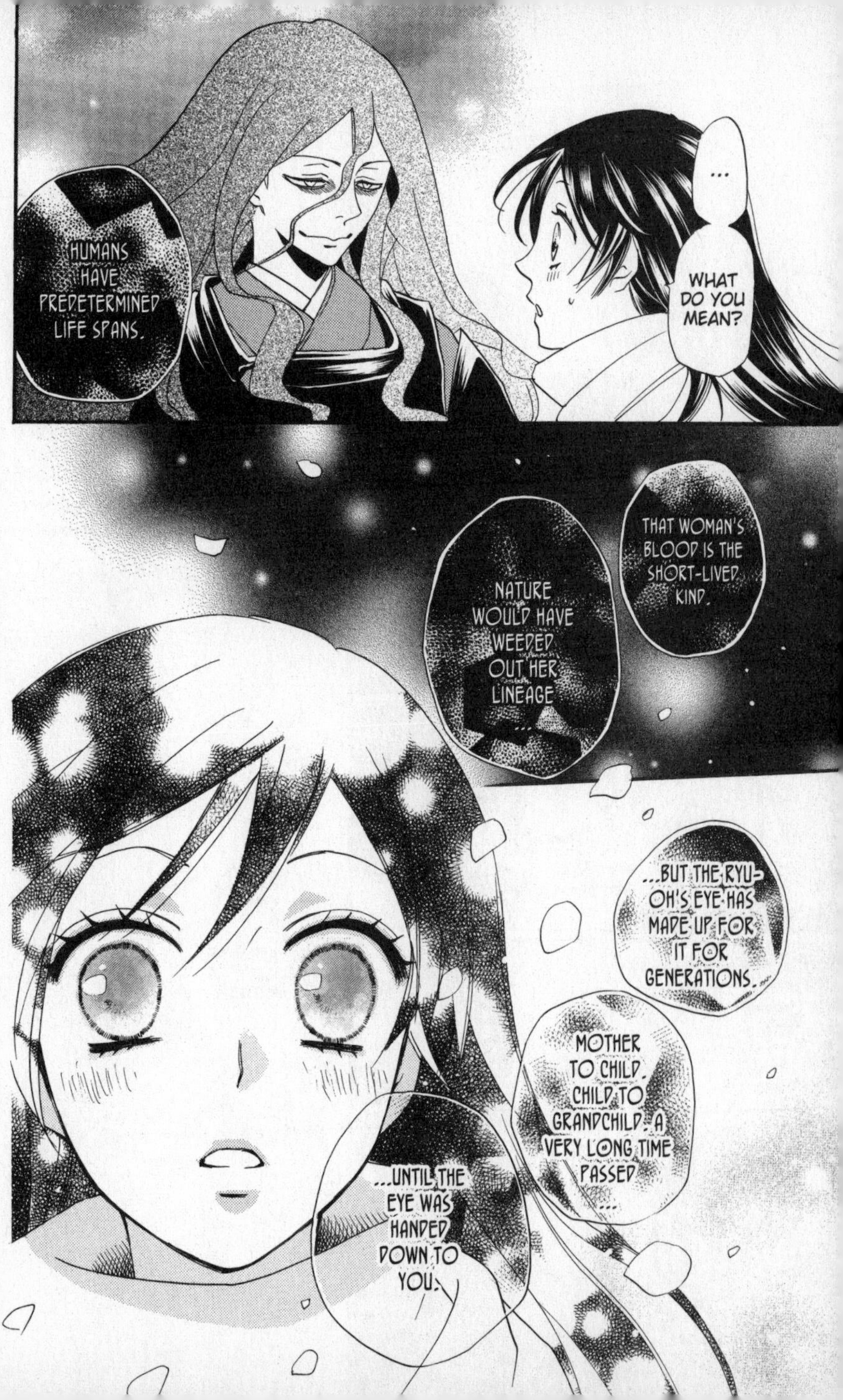
...
WHAT DO YOU MEAN?
HUMANS HAVE PREDETERMINED LIFE SPANS.
THAT WOMAN'S BLOOD IS THE SHORT-LIVED KIND.
NATURE WOULD HAVE WEEDED OUT HER LINEAGE...
...BUT THE RYU-OH'S EYE HAS MADE UP FOR IT FOR GENERATIONS.
MOTHER TO CHILD. CHILD TO GRANDCHILD. A VERY LONG TIME PASSED...
...UNTIL THE EYE WAS HANDED DOWN TO YOU.

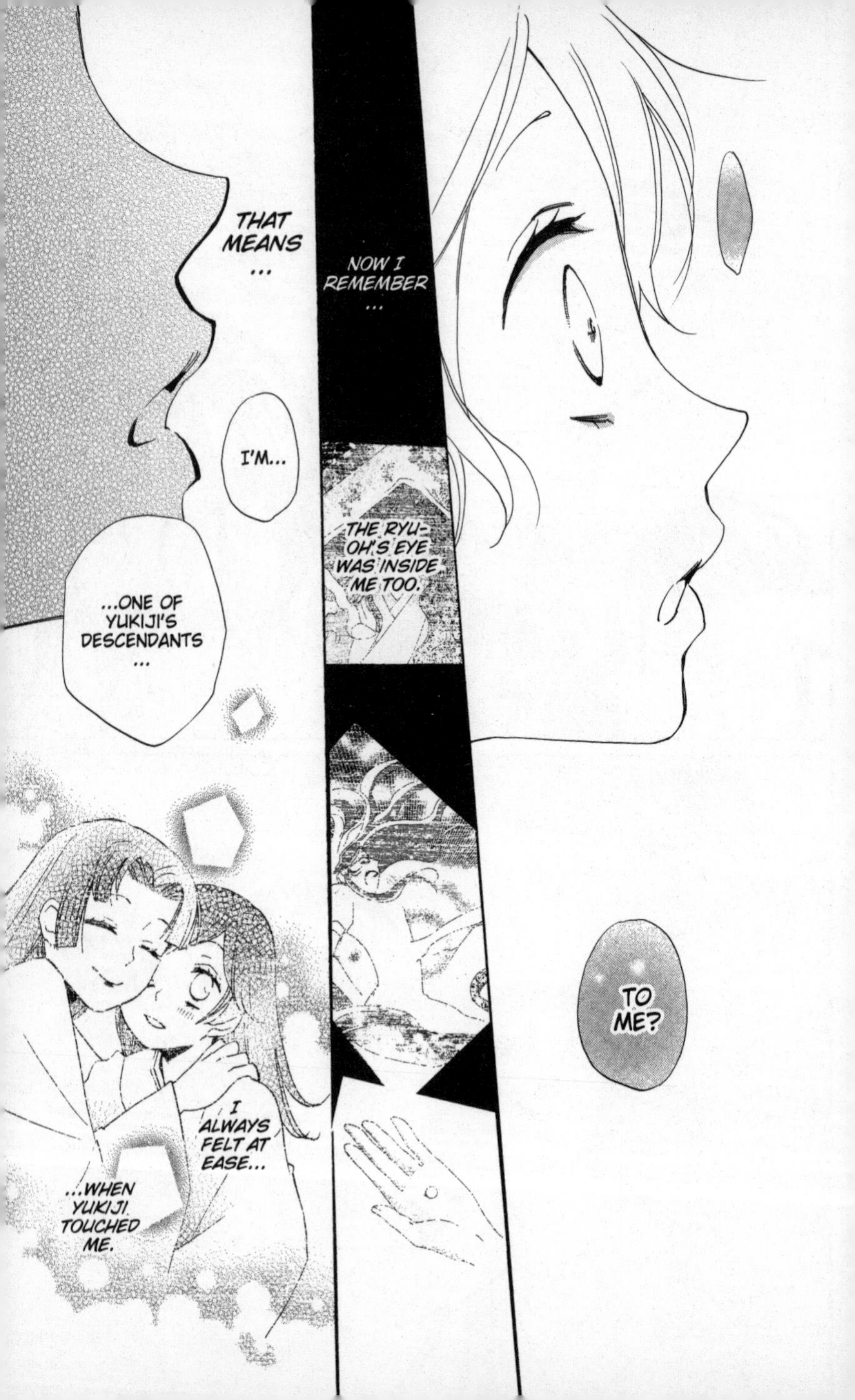
NOW I REMEMBER ...
THE RYU-OH'S EYE WAS INSIDE ME TOO.
TO ME?
THAT MEANS ...
I'M...
...ONE OF YUKIJI'S DESCENDANTS ...
I ALWAYS FELT AT EASE...
...WHEN YUKIJI TOUCHED ME.

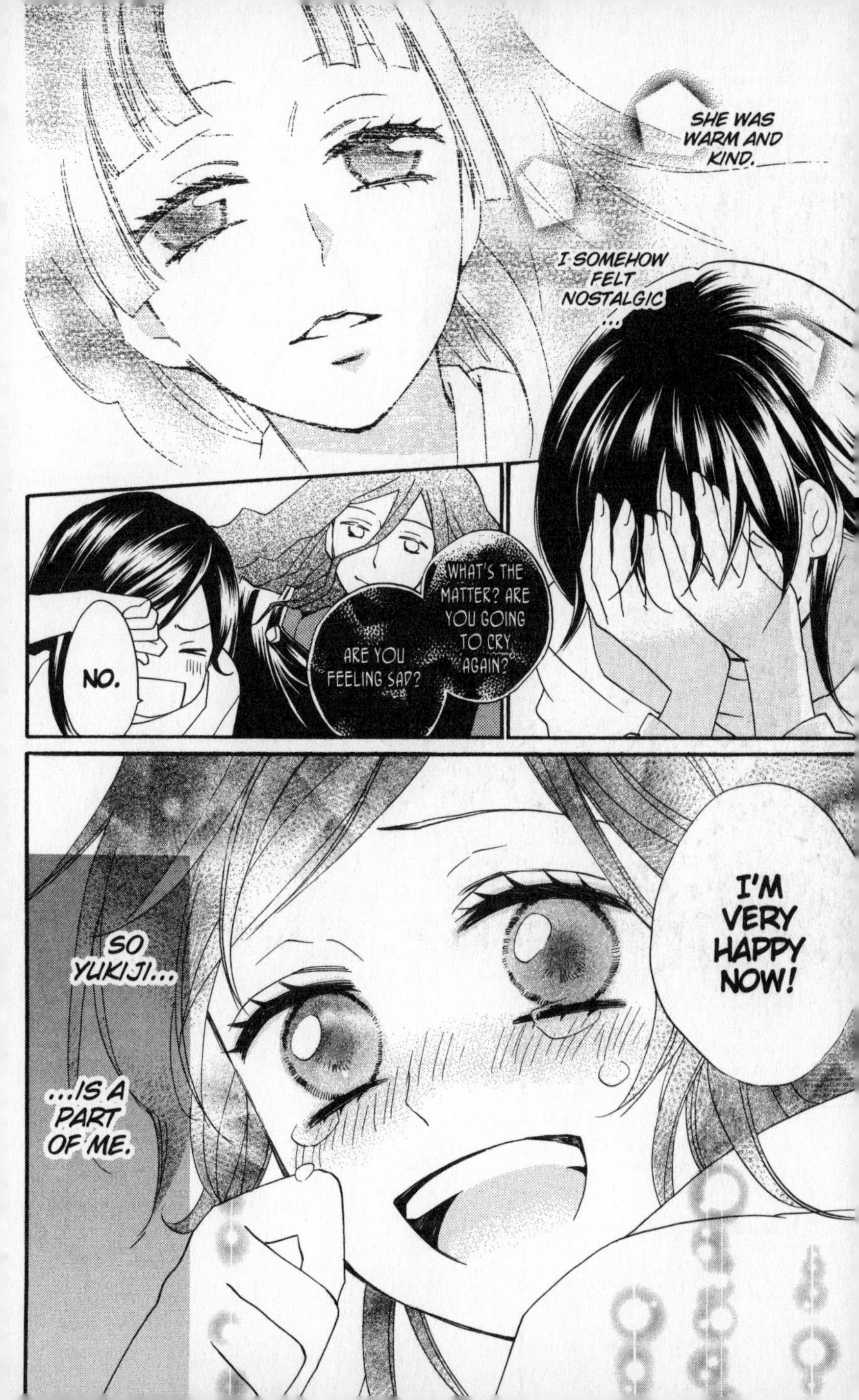
SHE WAS WARM AND KIND.
I SOMEHOW FELT NOSTALGIC...
WHAT'S THE MATTER? ARE YOU GOING TO CRY AGAIN?
ARE YOU FEELING SAD?
NO.
I'M VERY HAPPY NOW!
SO YUKIJI...
...IS A PART OF ME.

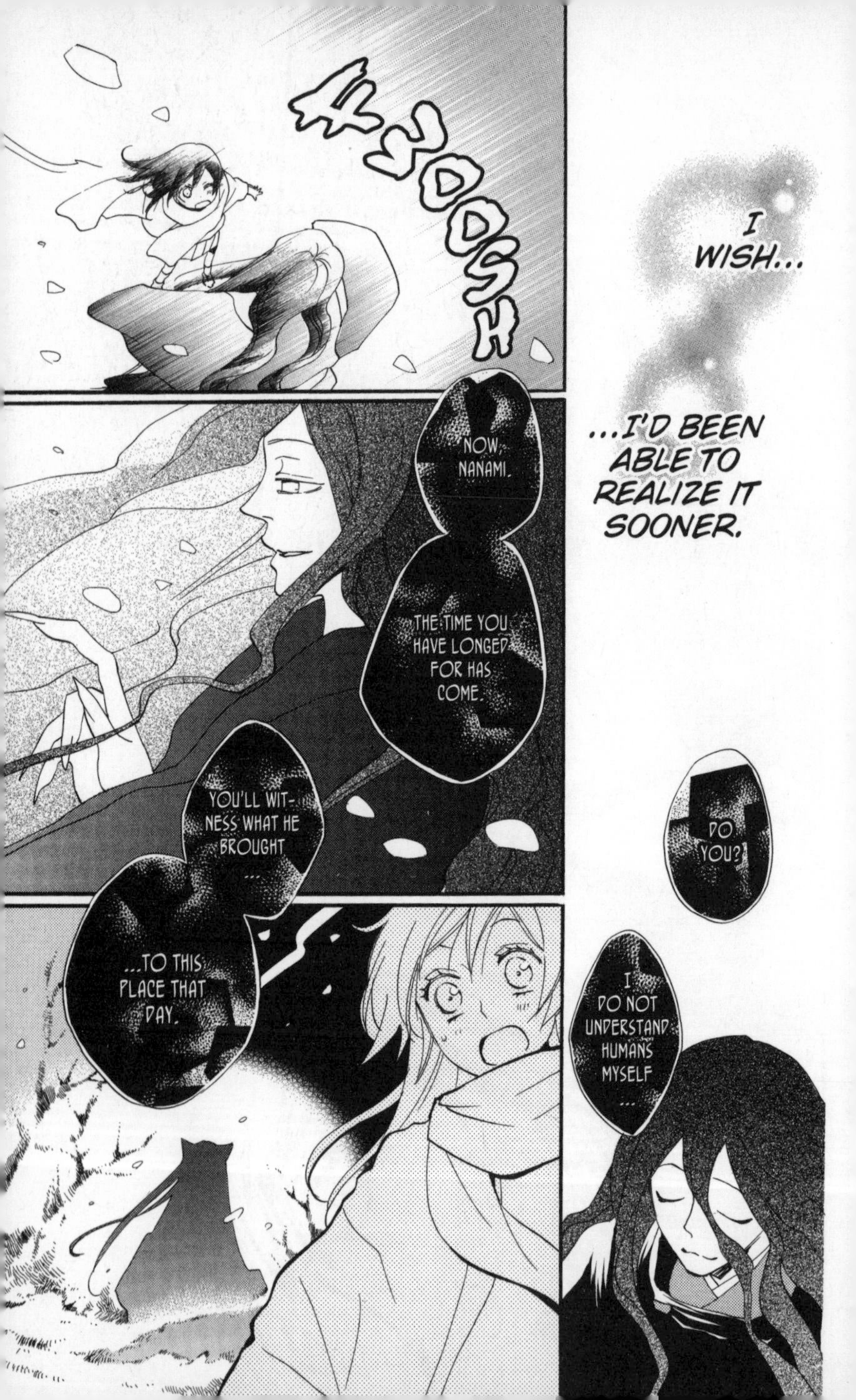
I WISH...
...I'D BEEN ABLE TO REALIZE IT SOONER.
DO YOU?
I DO NOT UNDERSTAND HUMANS MYSELF...
WHOOSH
NOW, NANAMI.
THE TIME YOU HAVE LONGED FOR HAS COME.
YOU'LL WIT- NESS WHAT HE BROUGHT...
...TO THIS PLACE THAT DAY.

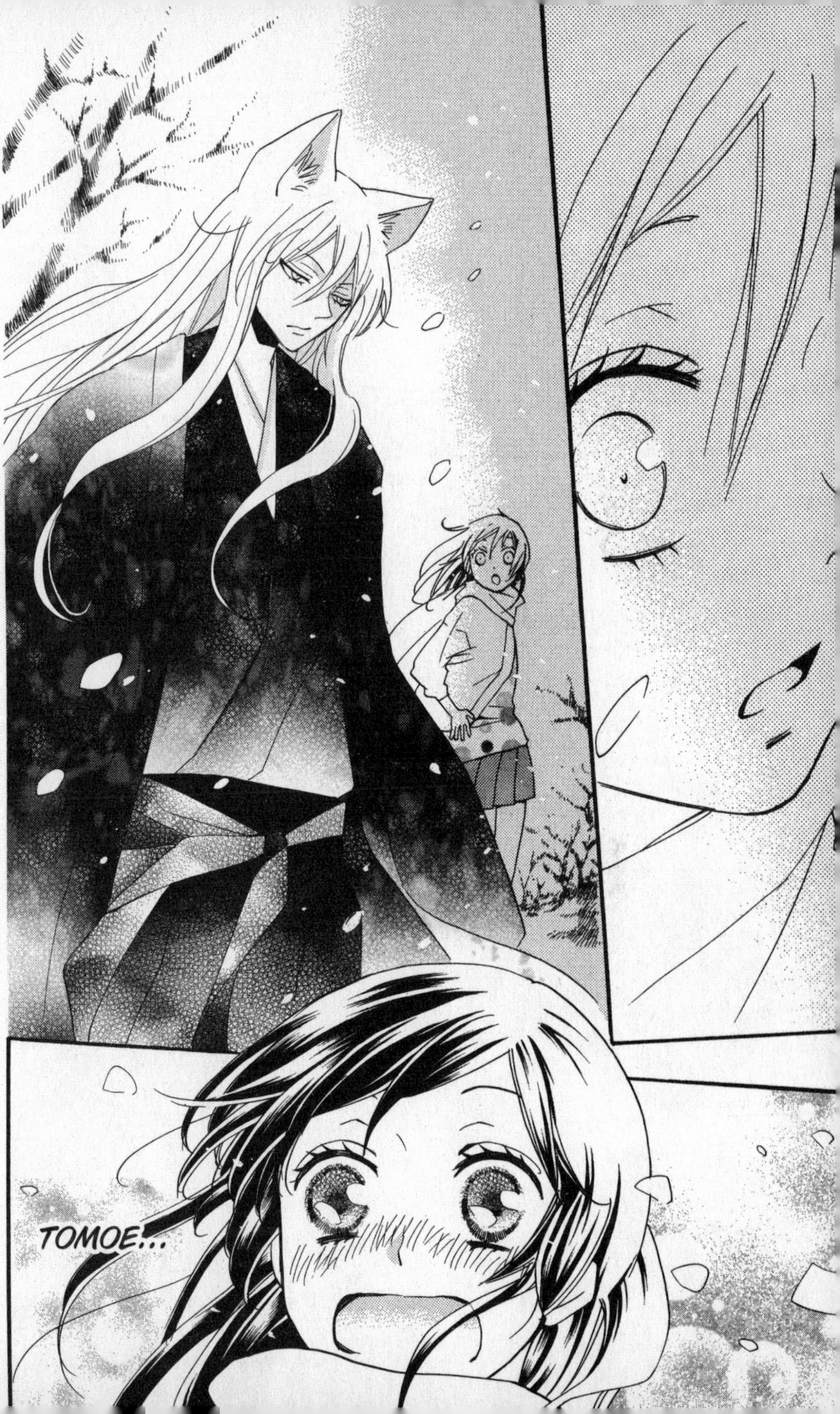
TOMOE...

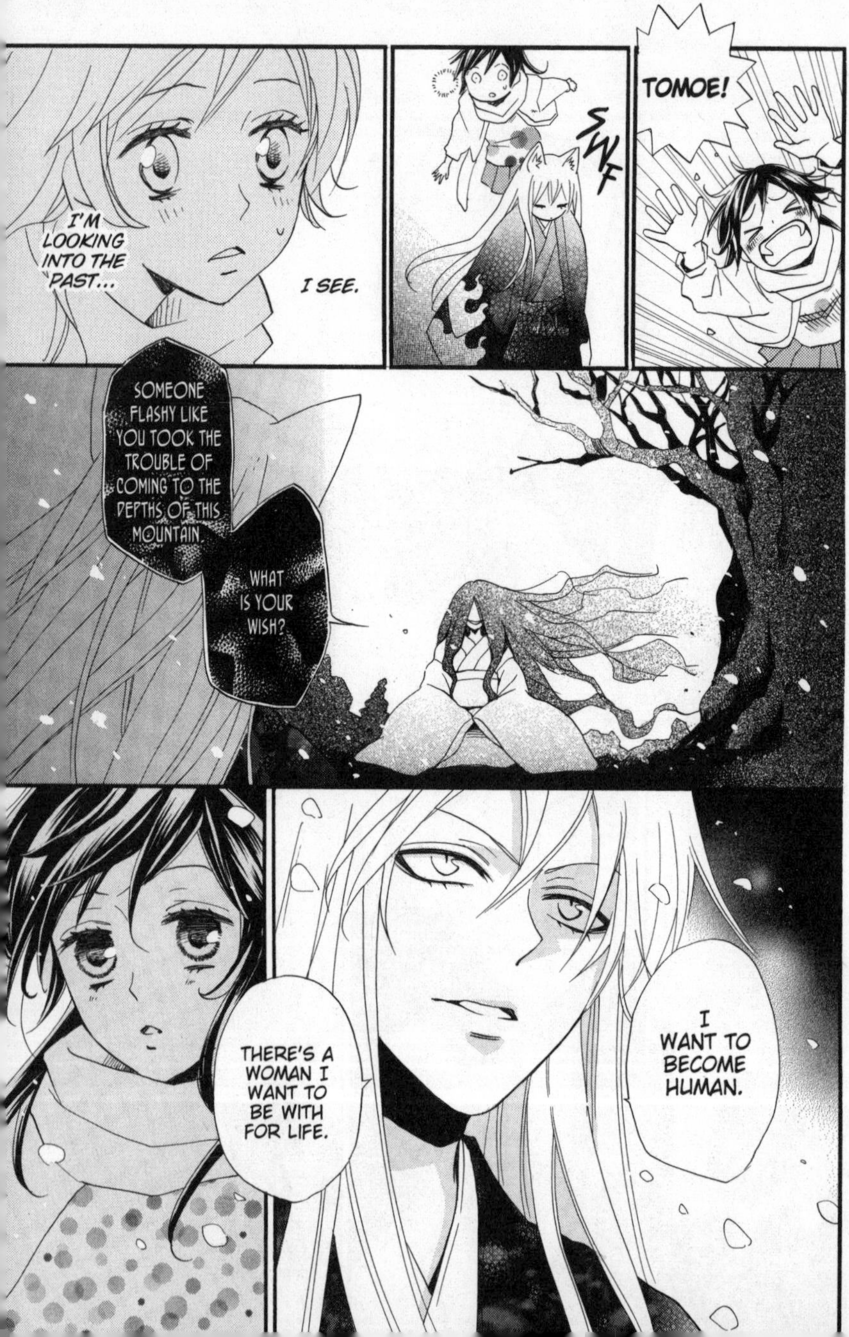
TOMOE!
SWF
I'M LOOKING INTO THE PAST...
I SEE.
SOMEONE FLASHY LIKE YOU TOOK THE TROUBLE OF COMING TO THE DEPTHS OF THIS MOUNTAIN.
WHAT IS YOUR WISH?
I WANT TO BECOME HUMAN.
THERE'S A WOMAN I WANT TO BE WITH FOR LIFE.

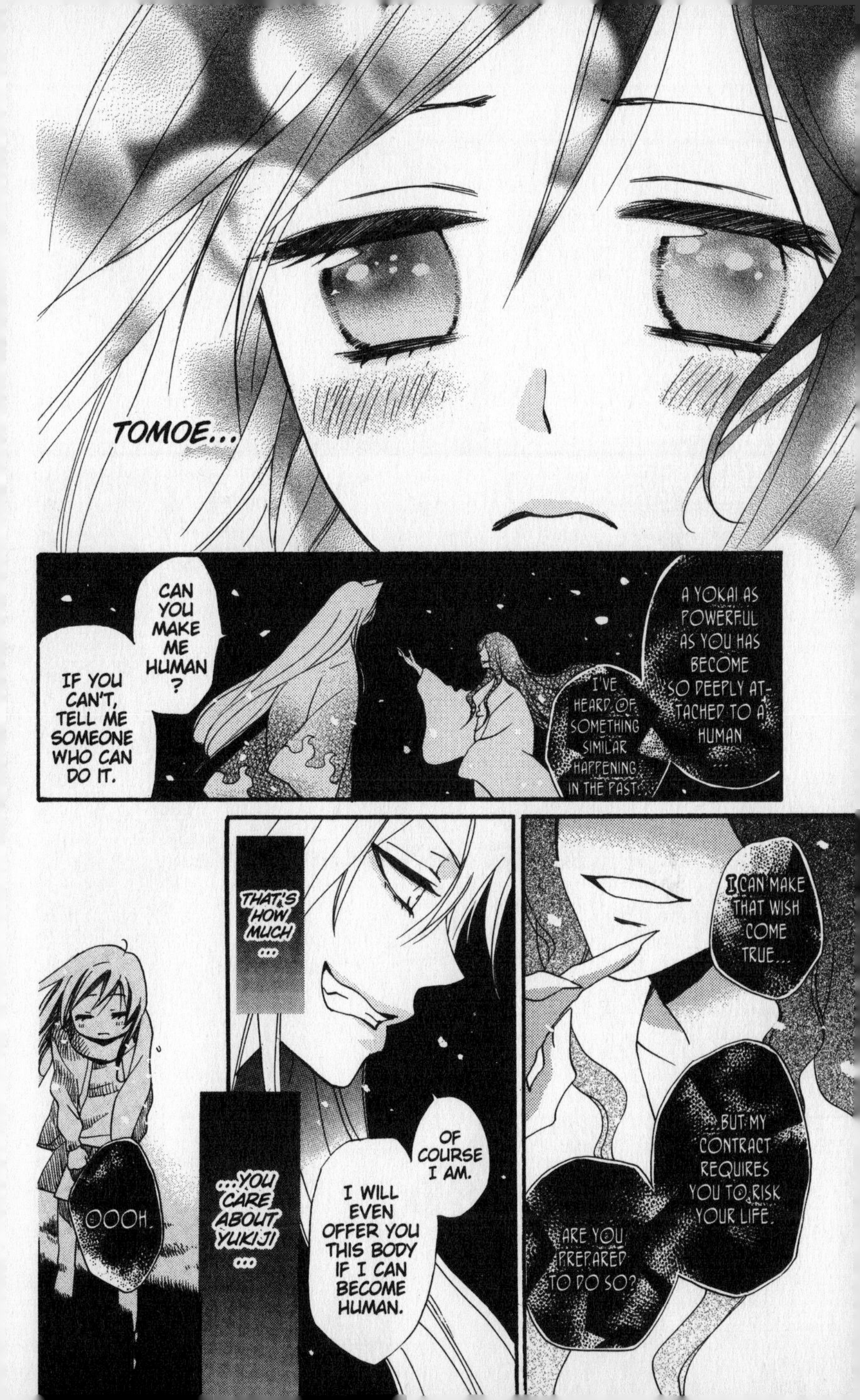
TOMOE...
A YOKAI AS POWERFUL AS YOU HAS BECOME SO DEEPLY AT-TACHED TO A HUMAN...
I'VE HEARD OF SOMETHING SIMILAR HAPPENING IN THE PAST.
CAN YOU MAKE ME HUMAN?
IF YOU CAN'T, TELL ME SOMEONE WHO CAN DO IT.
I CAN MAKE THAT WISH COME TRUE...
BUT MY CONTRACT REQUIRES YOU TO RISK YOUR LIFE.
ARE YOU PREPARED TO DO SO?
THAT'S HOW MUCH...
OF COURSE I AM.
I WILL EVEN OFFER YOU THIS BODY IF I CAN BECOME HUMAN.
...YOU CARE ABOUT YUKIJI...
OOOH.

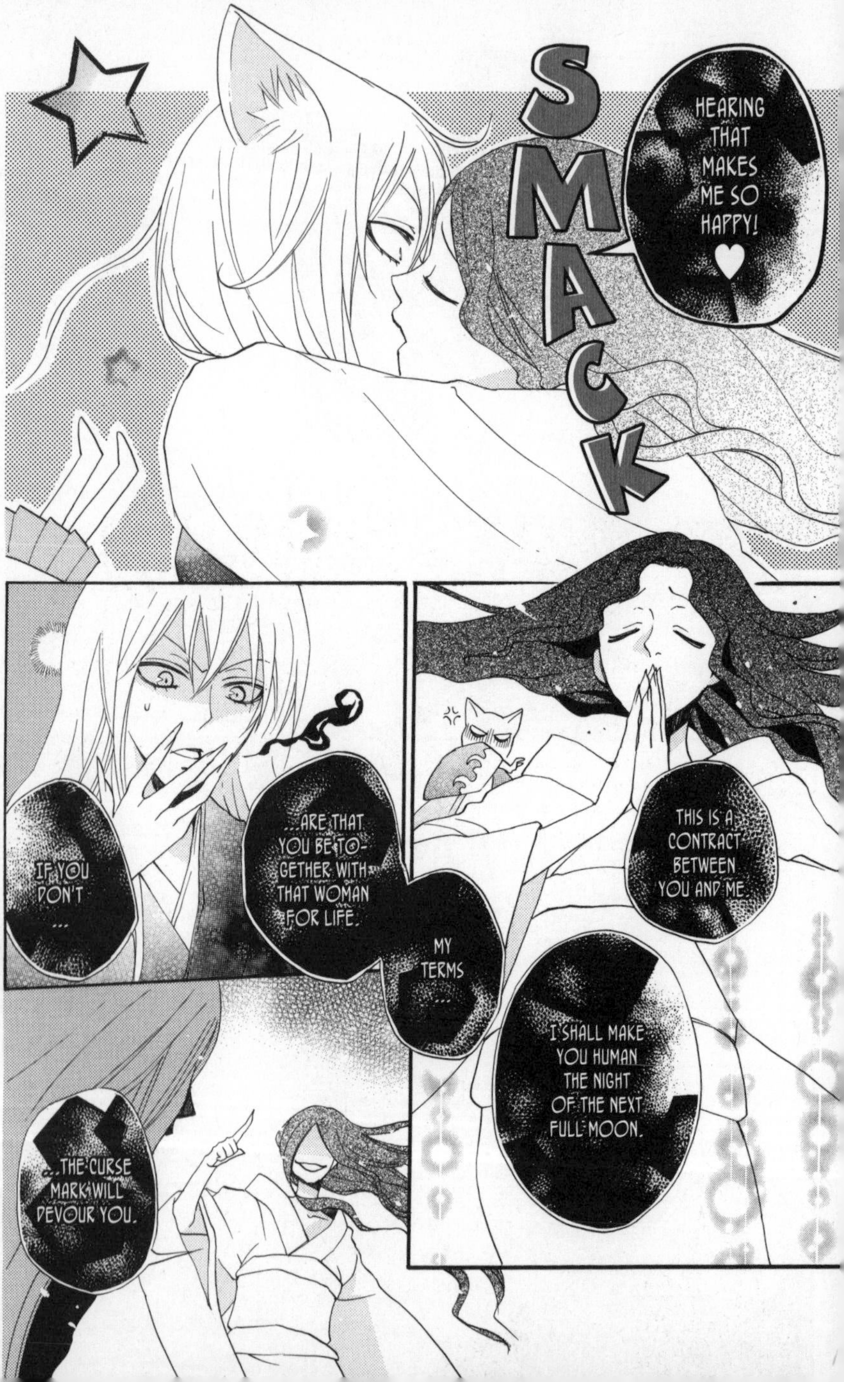
HEARING THAT MAKES ME SO HAPPY! ♥
SMACK
THIS IS A CONTRACT BETWEEN YOU AND ME.
I SHALL MAKE YOU HUMAN THE NIGHT OF THE NEXT FULL MOON.
MY TERMS...
...ARE THAT YOU BE TO-GETHER WITH THAT WOMAN FOR LIFE.
IF YOU DON'T...
...THE CURSE MARK WILL DEVOUR YOU.

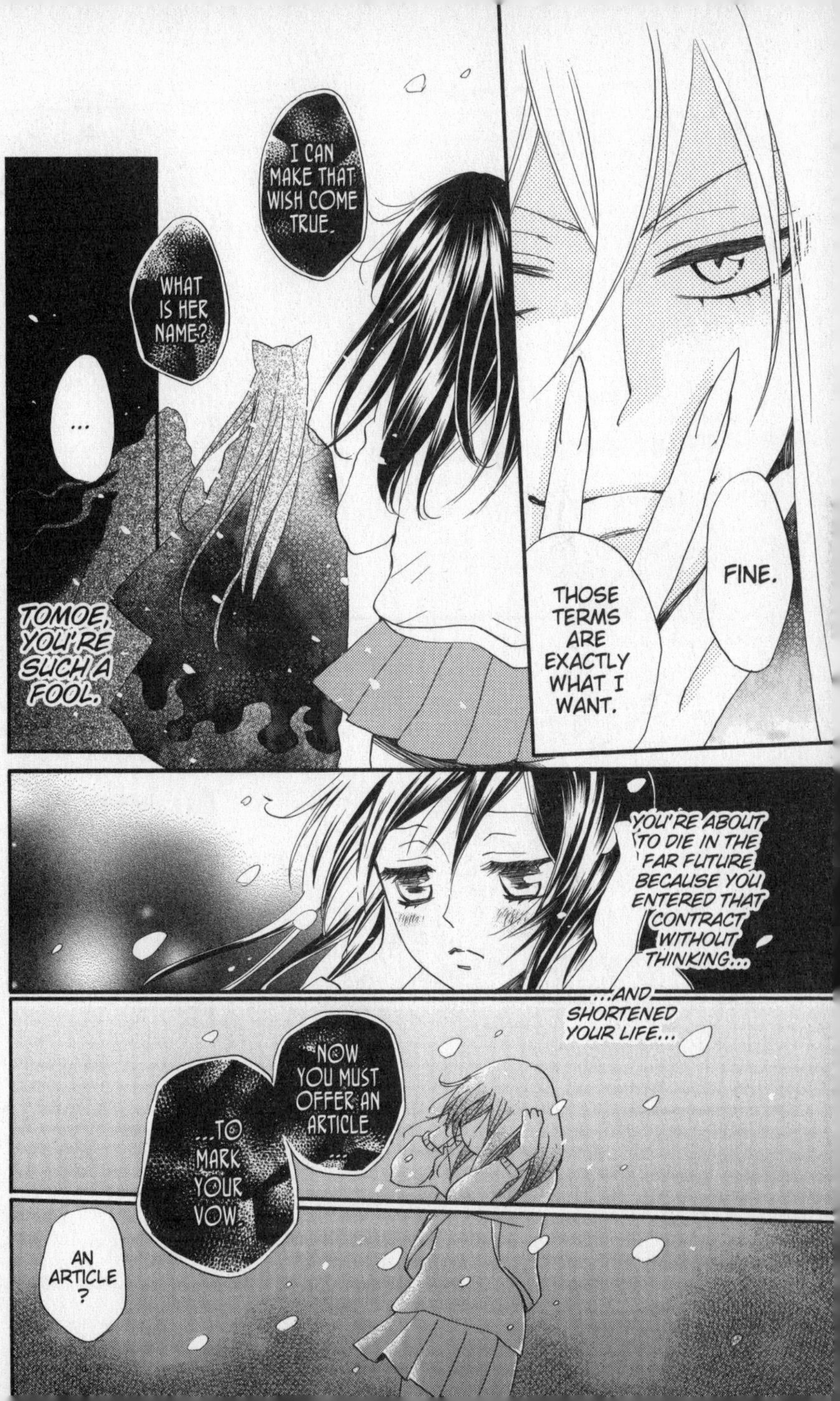
FINE.
THOSE TERMS ARE EXACTLY WHAT I WANT.
I CAN MAKE THAT WISH COME TRUE.
WHAT IS HER NAME?
...
TOMOE, YOU'RE SUCH A FOOL.
YOU'RE ABOUT TO DIE IN THE FAR FUTURE BECAUSE YOU ENTERED THAT CONTRACT WITHOUT THINKING...
...AND SHORTENED YOUR LIFE...
NOW YOU MUST OFFER AN ARTICLE...
...TO MARK YOUR VOW.
AN ARTICLE?

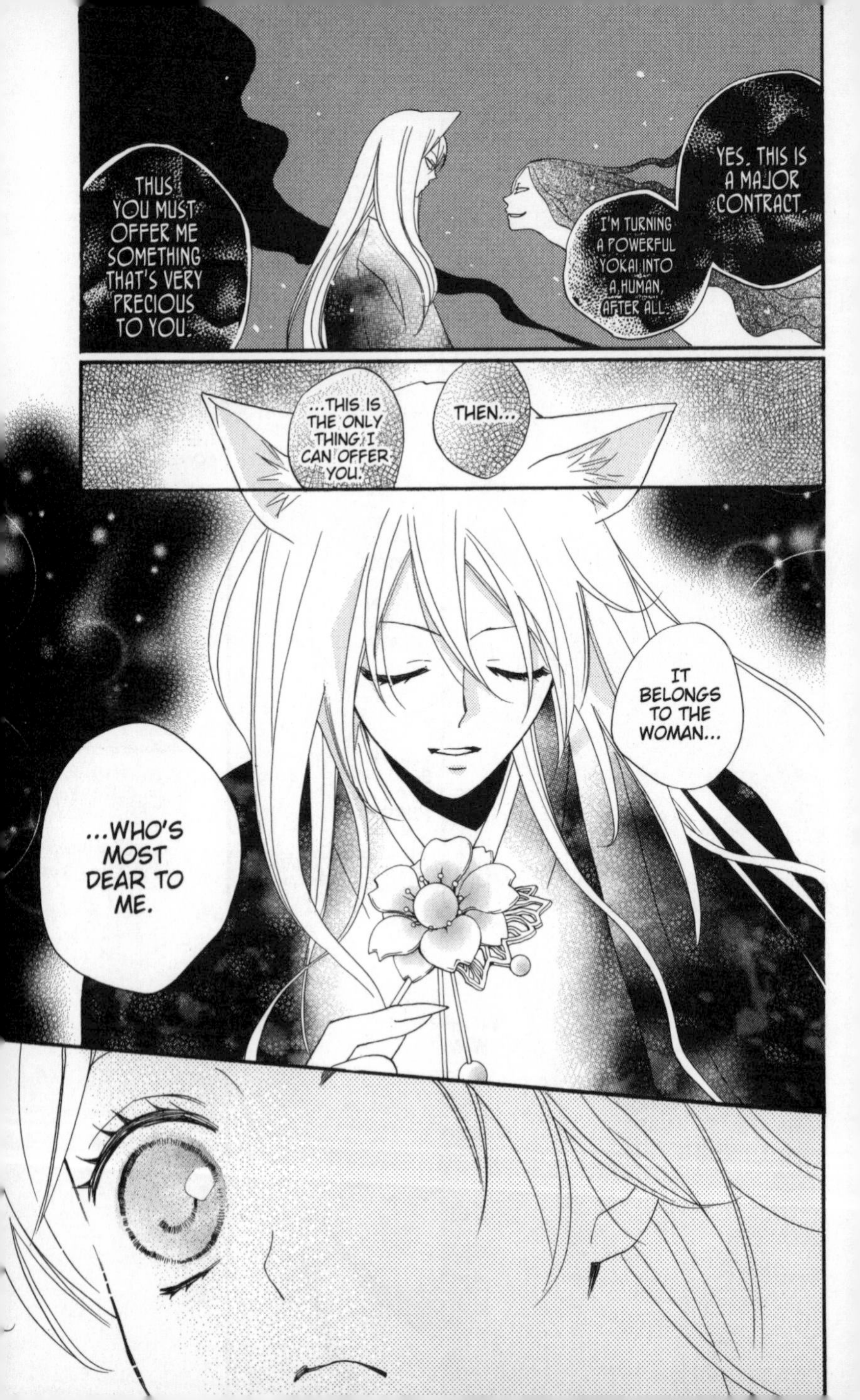
YES. THIS IS A MAJOR CONTRACT.
I'M TURNING A POWERFUL YOKAI INTO A HUMAN, AFTER ALL.
THUS YOU MUST OFFER ME SOMETHING THAT'S VERY PRECIOUS TO YOU.
THEN...
...THIS IS THE ONLY THING I CAN OFFER YOU.
IT BELONGS TO THE WOMAN...
...WHO'S MOST DEAR TO ME.

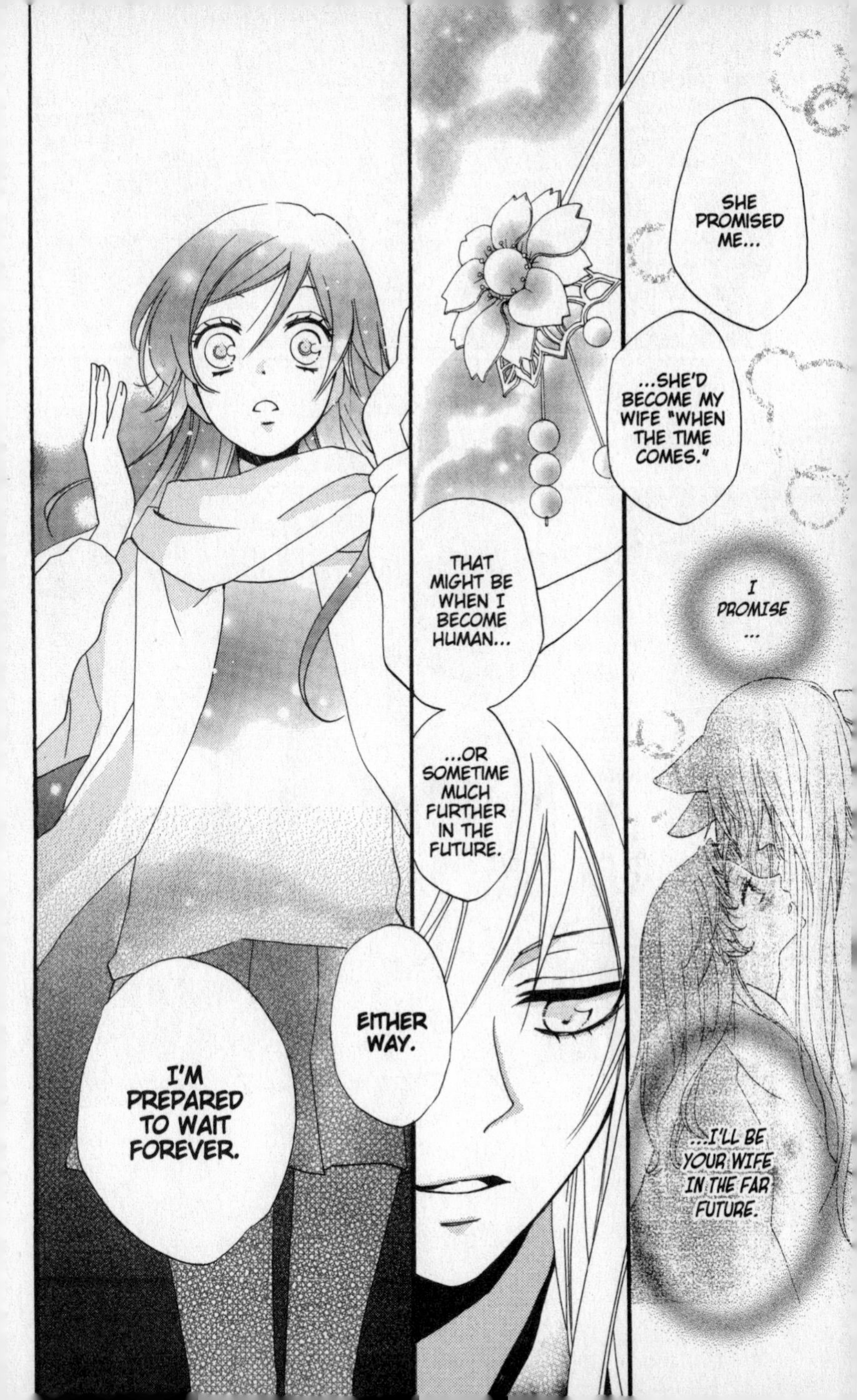
SHE PROMISED ME...
...SHE'D BECOME MY WIFE "WHEN THE TIME COMES."
I PROMISE...
...I'LL BE YOUR WIFE IN THE FAR FUTURE.
THAT MIGHT BE WHEN I BECOME HUMAN...
...OR SOMETIME MUCH FURTHER IN THE FUTURE.
EITHER WAY.
I'M PREPARED TO WAIT FOREVER.

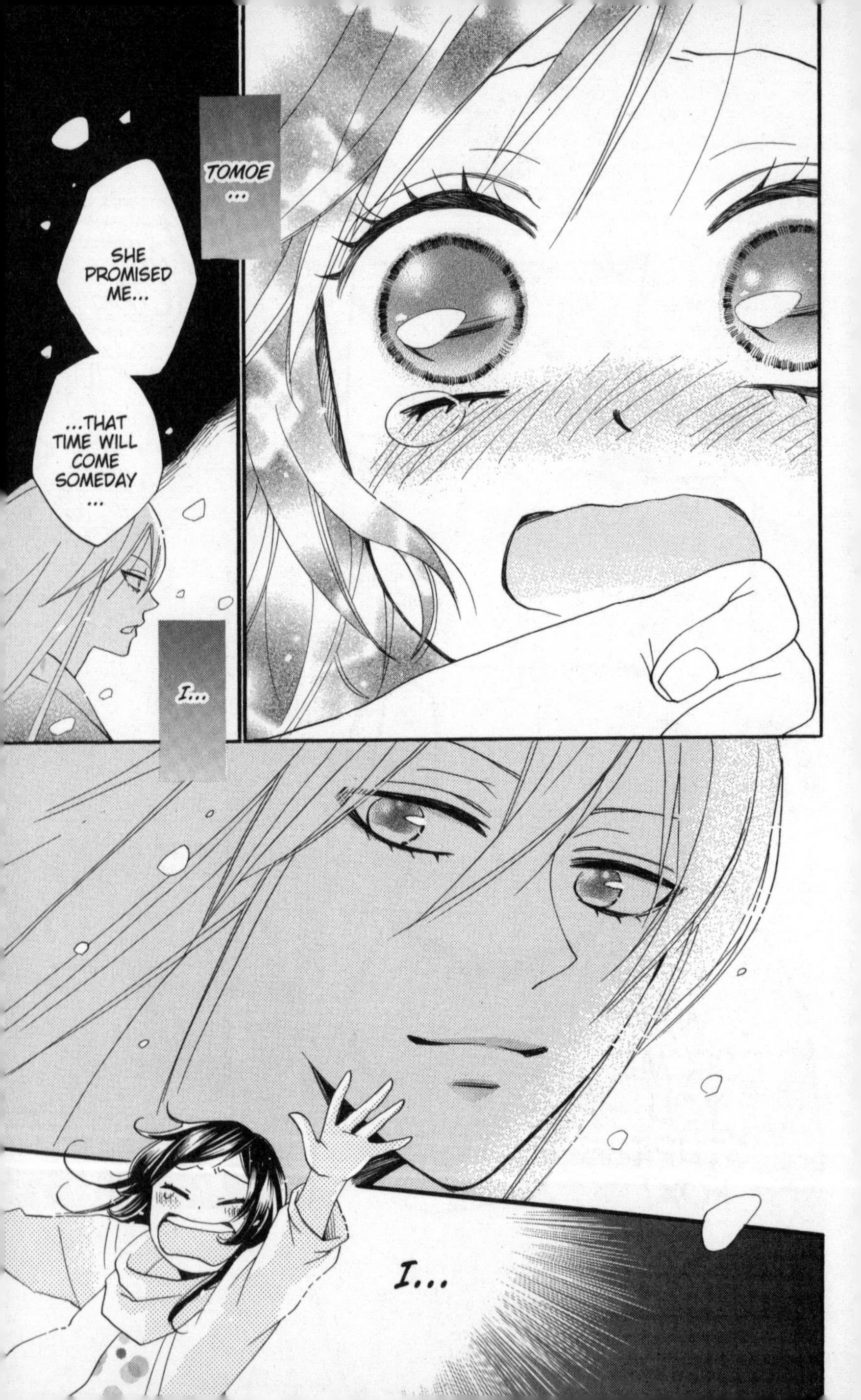
TOMOE ...
SHE PROMISED ME...
...THAT TIME WILL COME SOMEDAY ...
I...
I...

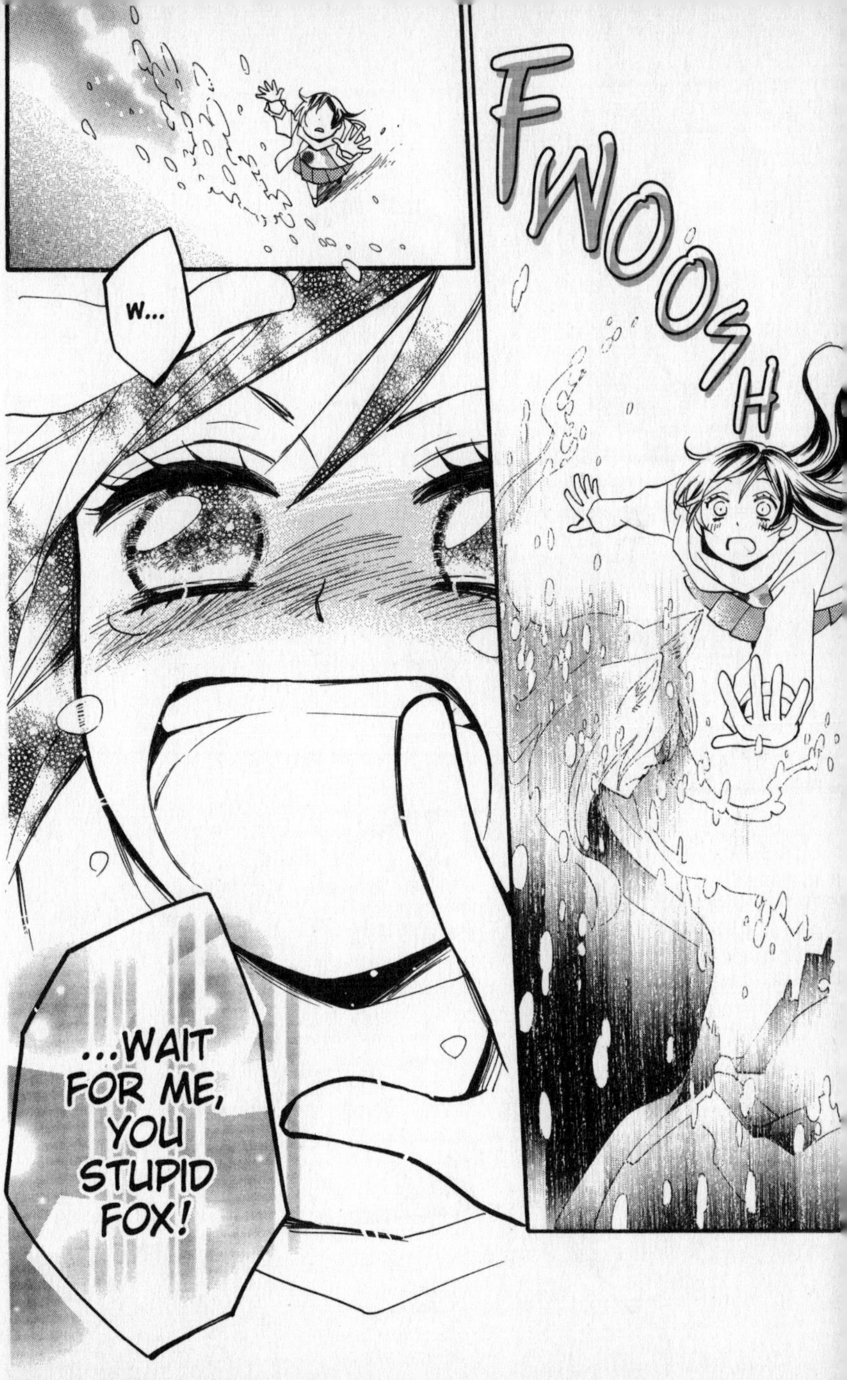
FWOOSH
W...
...WAIT FOR ME, YOU STUPID FOX!

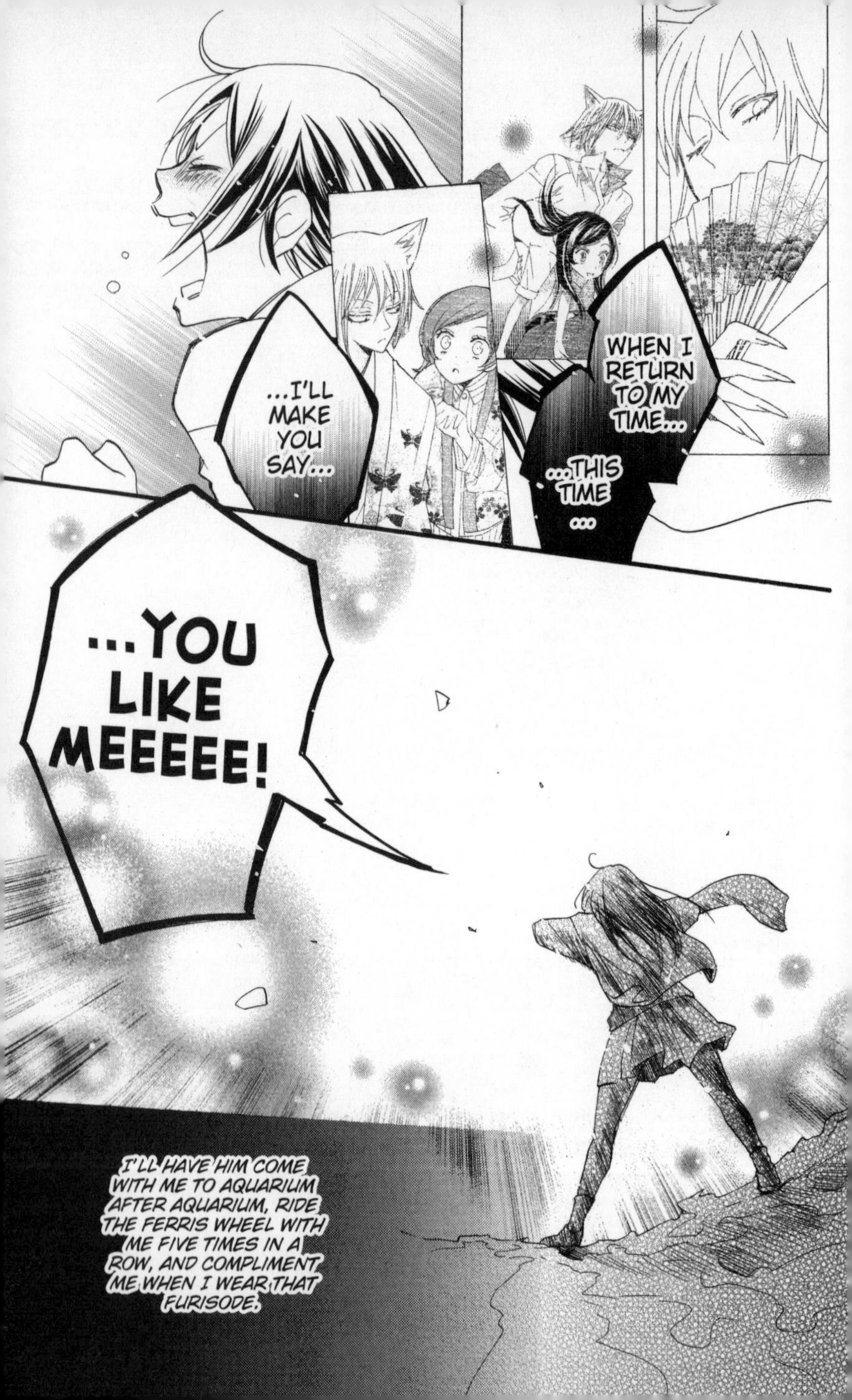
WHEN I RETURN TO MY TIME...
...THIS TIME...
...I'LL MAKE YOU SAY...
...YOU LIKE MEEEEE!
I'LL HAVE HIM COME WITH ME TO AQUARIUM AFTER AQUARIUM, RIDE THE FERRIS WHEEL WITH ME FIVE TIMES IN A ROW, AND COMPLIMENT ME WHEN I WEAR THAT FURISODE.

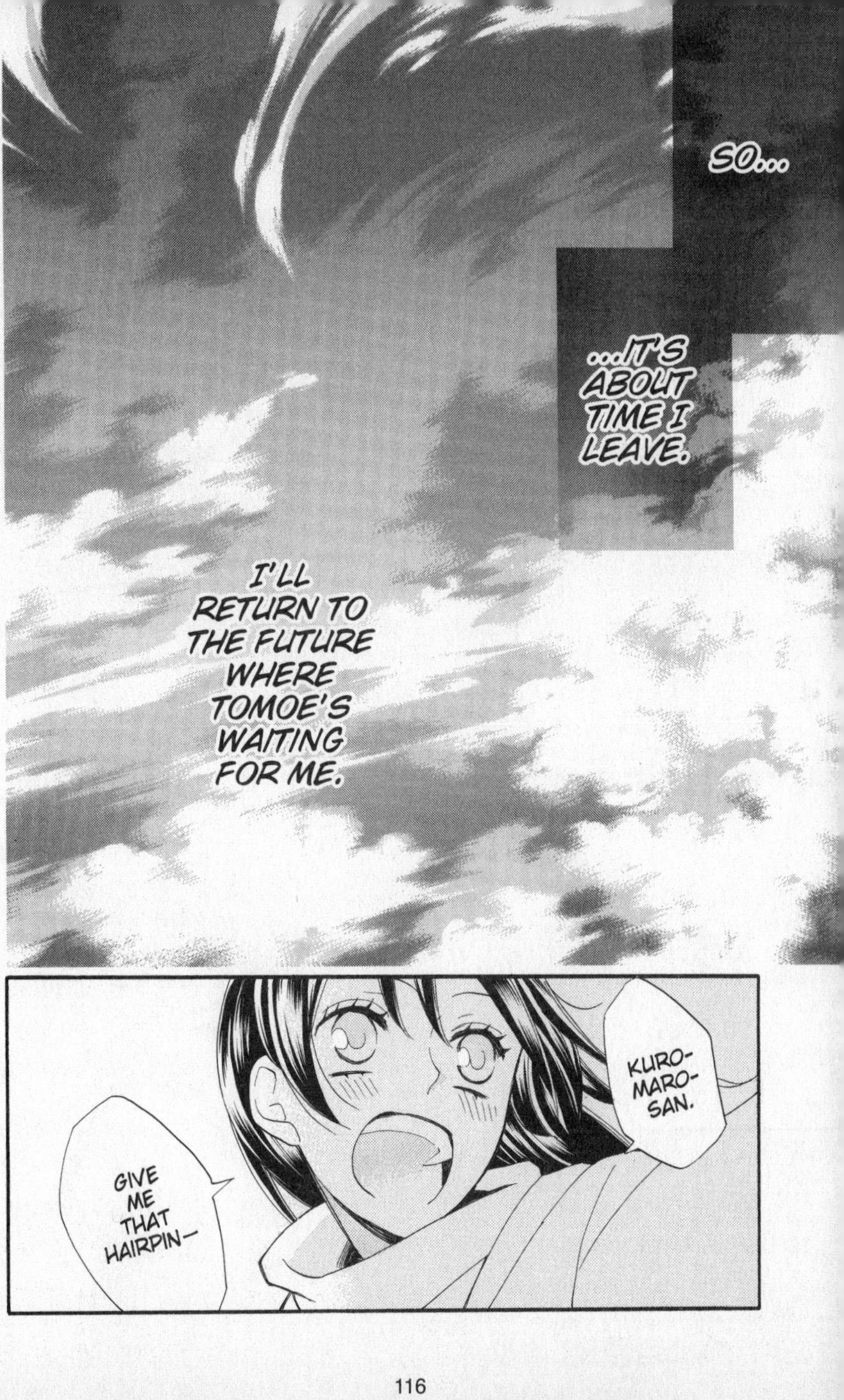
SO...
...IT'S ABOUT TIME I LEAVE.
I'LL RETURN TO THE FUTURE WHERE TOMOE'S WAITING FOR ME.
KURO-MARO-SAN.
GIVE ME THAT HAIRPIN—

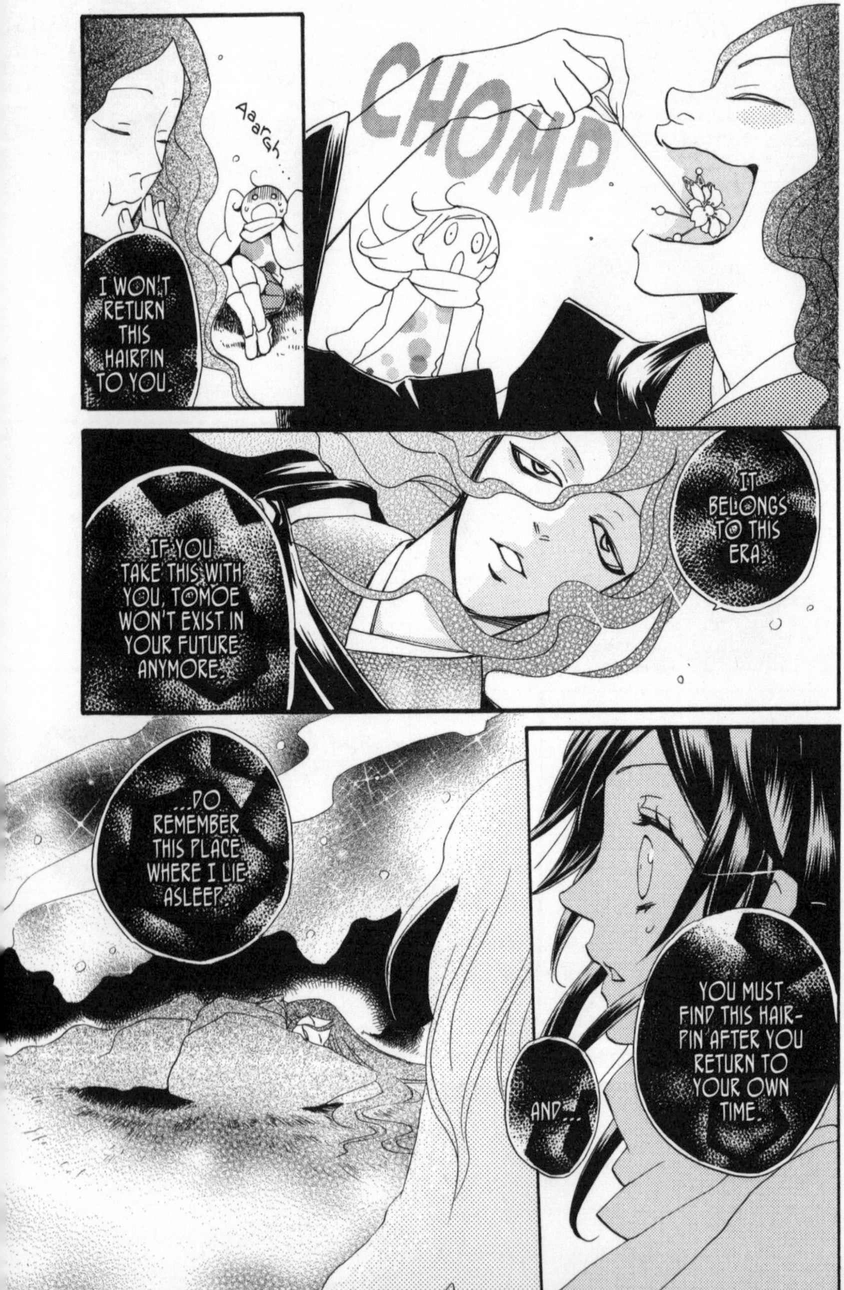
CHOMP
Aaargh...
I WON'T RETURN THIS HAIRPIN TO YOU.
IT BELONGS TO THIS ERA.
IF YOU TAKE THIS WITH YOU, TOMOE WON'T EXIST IN YOUR FUTURE ANYMORE.
YOU MUST FIND THIS HAIR-PIN AFTER YOU RETURN TO YOUR OWN TIME.
AND...
...DO REMEMBER THIS PLACE WHERE I LIE ASLEEP.

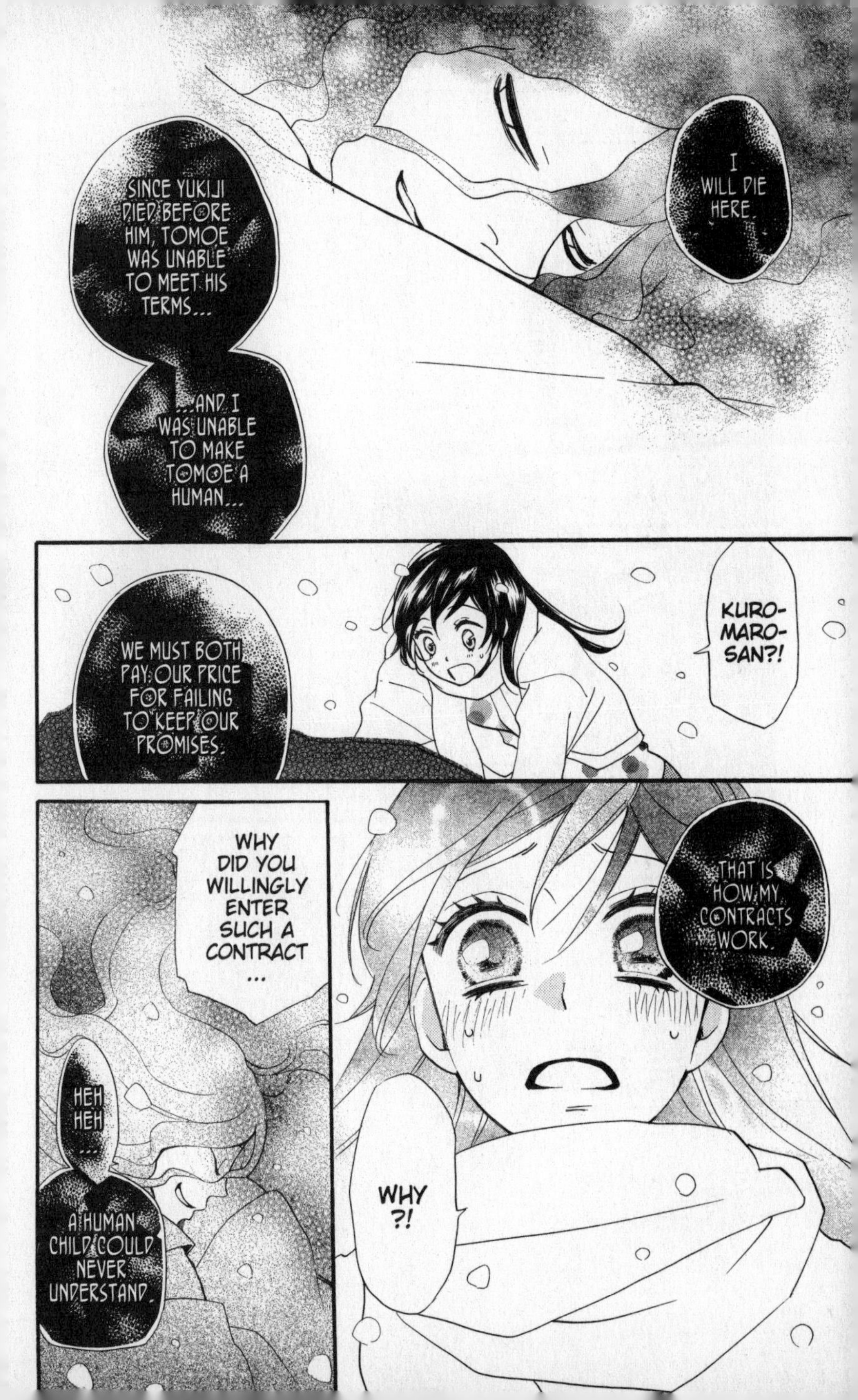
I WILL DIE HERE.
SINCE YUKIJI DIED BEFORE HIM, TOMOE WAS UNABLE TO MEET HIS TERMS...
...AND I WAS UNABLE TO MAKE TOMOE A HUMAN...
KURO-MARO-SAN?!
WE MUST BOTH PAY OUR PRICE FOR FAILING TO KEEP OUR PROMISES.
THAT IS HOW MY CONTRACTS WORK.
WHY?!
WHY DID YOU WILLINGLY ENTER SUCH A CONTRACT...
HEH HEH...
A HUMAN CHILD COULD NEVER UNDERSTAND.

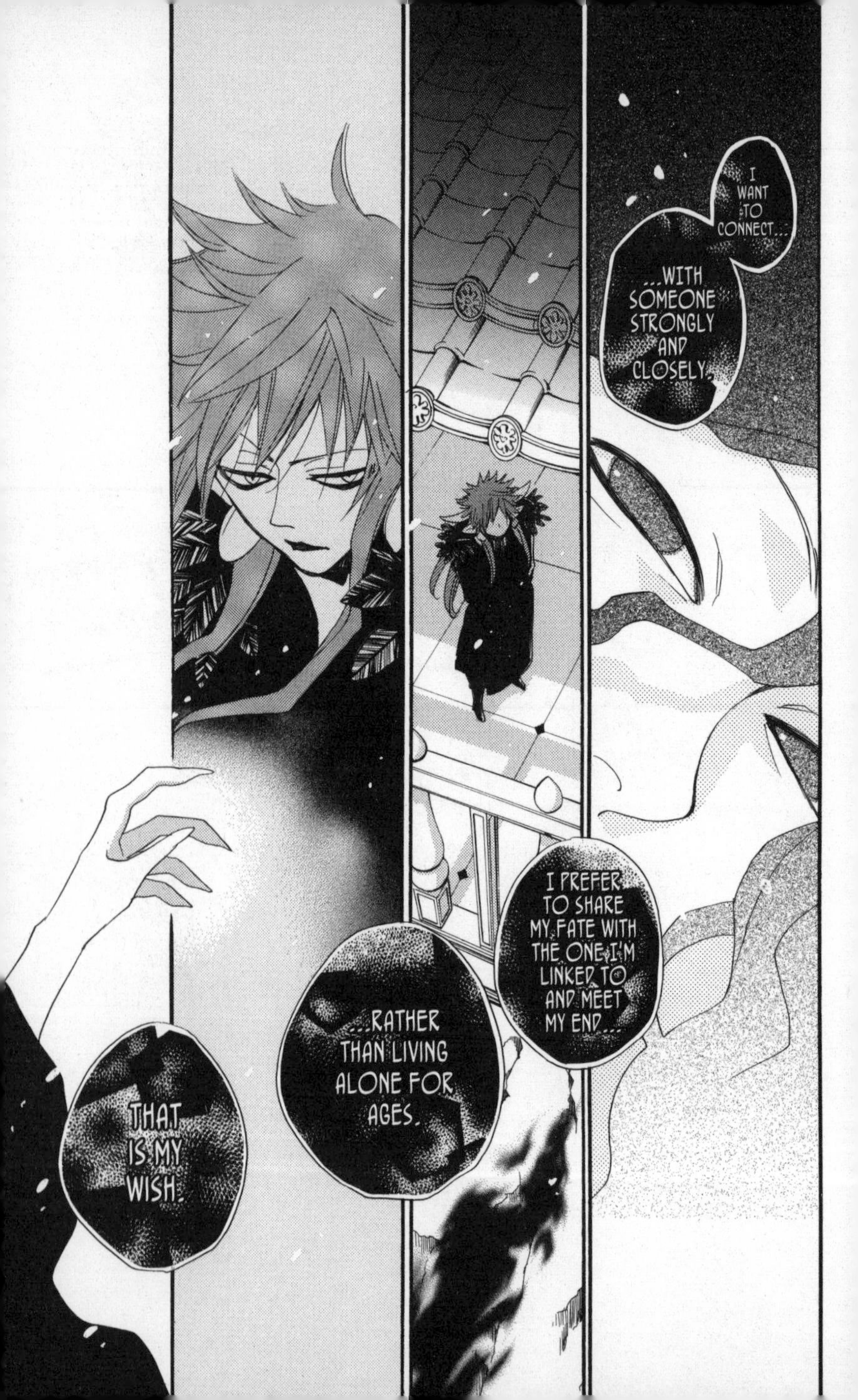
I WANT TO CONNECT...
...WITH SOMEONE STRONGLY AND CLOSELY.
I PREFER TO SHARE MY FATE WITH THE ONE I'M LINKED TO AND MEET MY END...
...RATHER THAN LIVING ALONE FOR AGES.
THAT IS MY WISH.

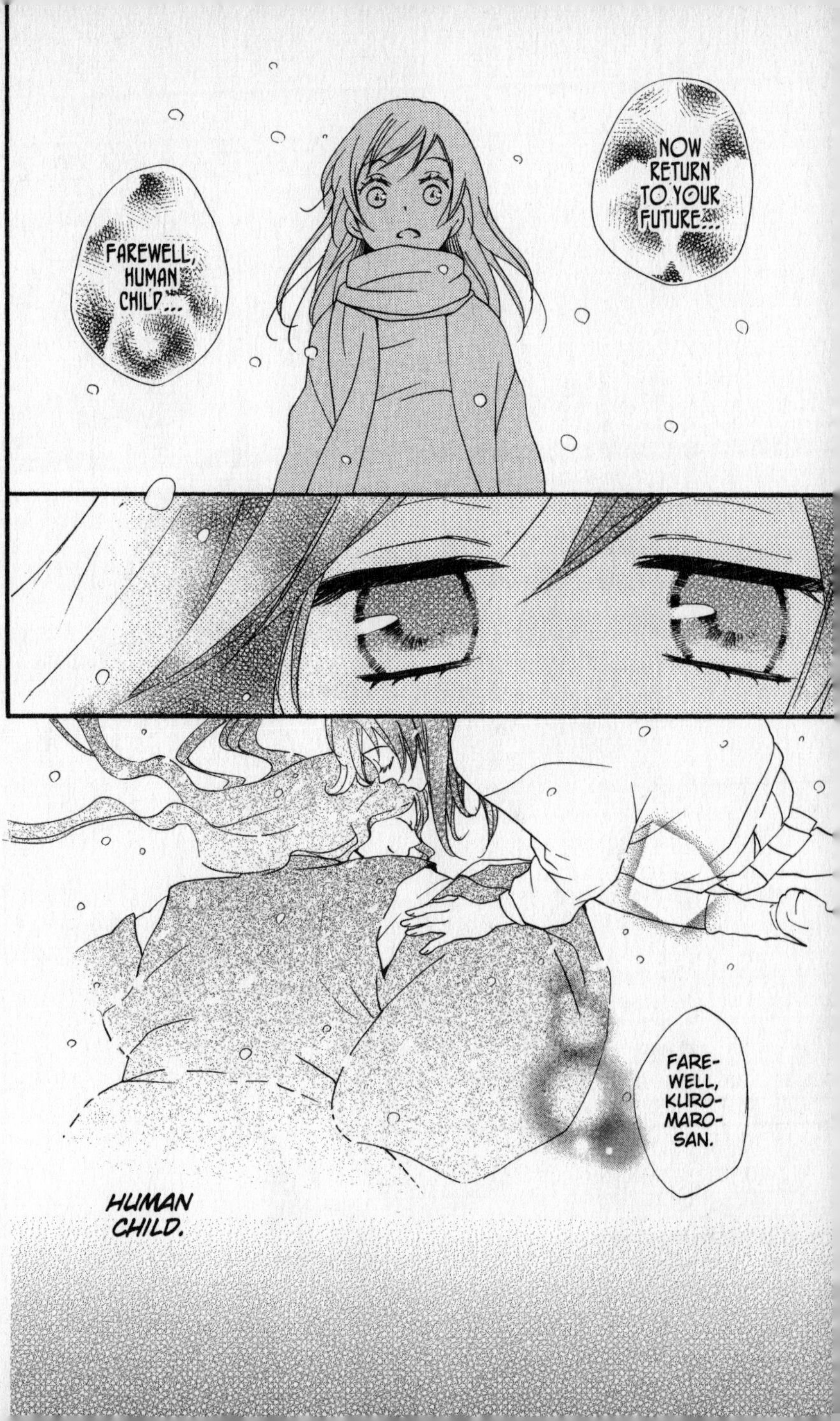
NOW RETURN TO YOUR FUTURE...
FAREWELL, HUMAN CHILD...
FARE-WELL, KURO-MARO-SAN.
HUMAN CHILD.

RETURN TO WHERE THE LIGHT IS SHINING.
YOU MUST LEAVE THIS TIME AND PLACE...
YOU'RE STILL CELEBRATING YOUR LIFE.
IT IS ONLY SOULS THAT HAVE REACHED THE END OF THEIR LIVES ARRIVING AT THEIR FINAL DESTINATIONS.
THERE'S NO NEED TO LOOK INTO THE PAST ANYMORE...

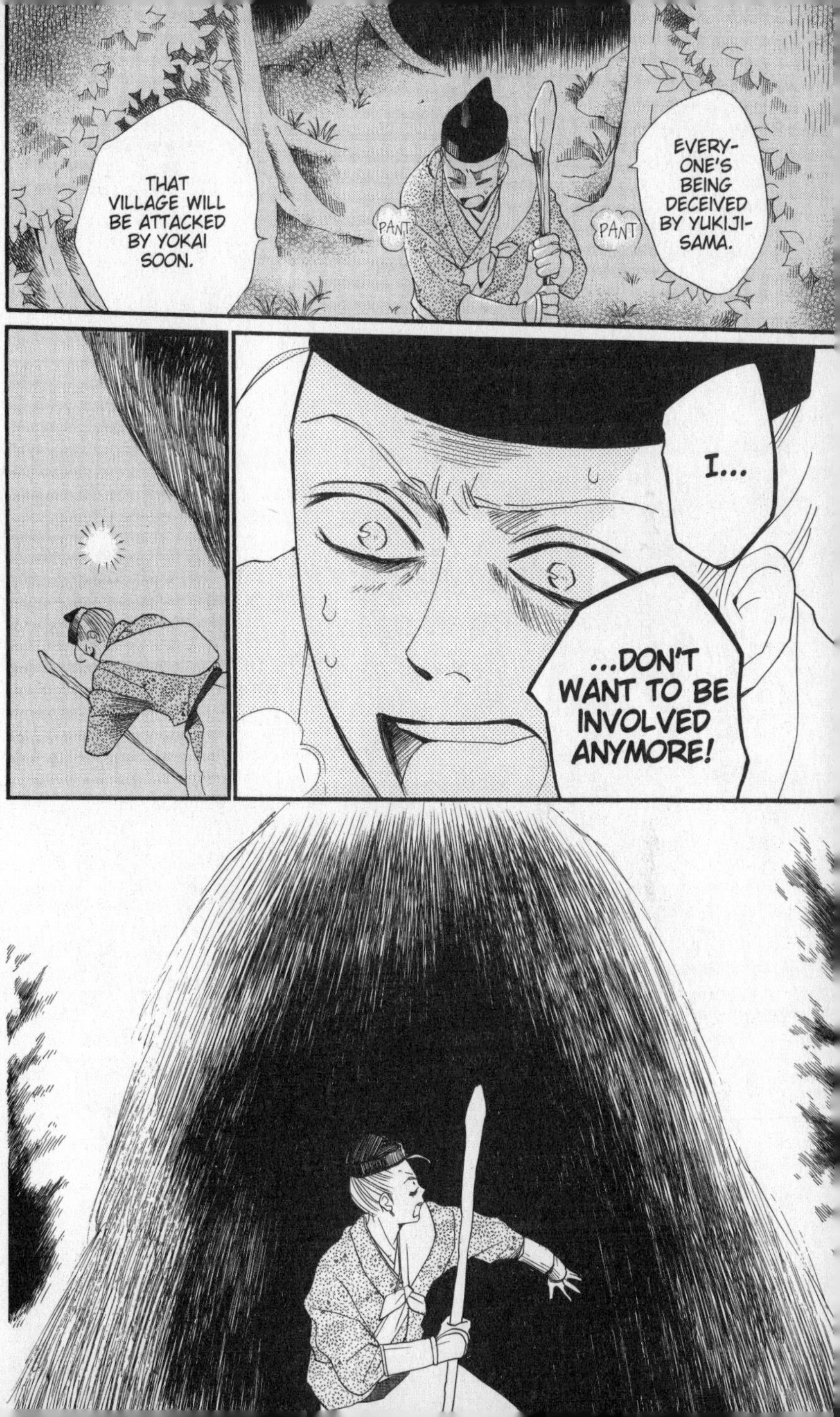
EVERYONE'S BEING DECEIVED BY YUKIJI-SAMA.
PANT
PANT
THAT VILLAGE WILL BE ATTACKED BY YOKAI SOON.
I...
...DON'T WANT TO BE INVOLVED ANYMORE!

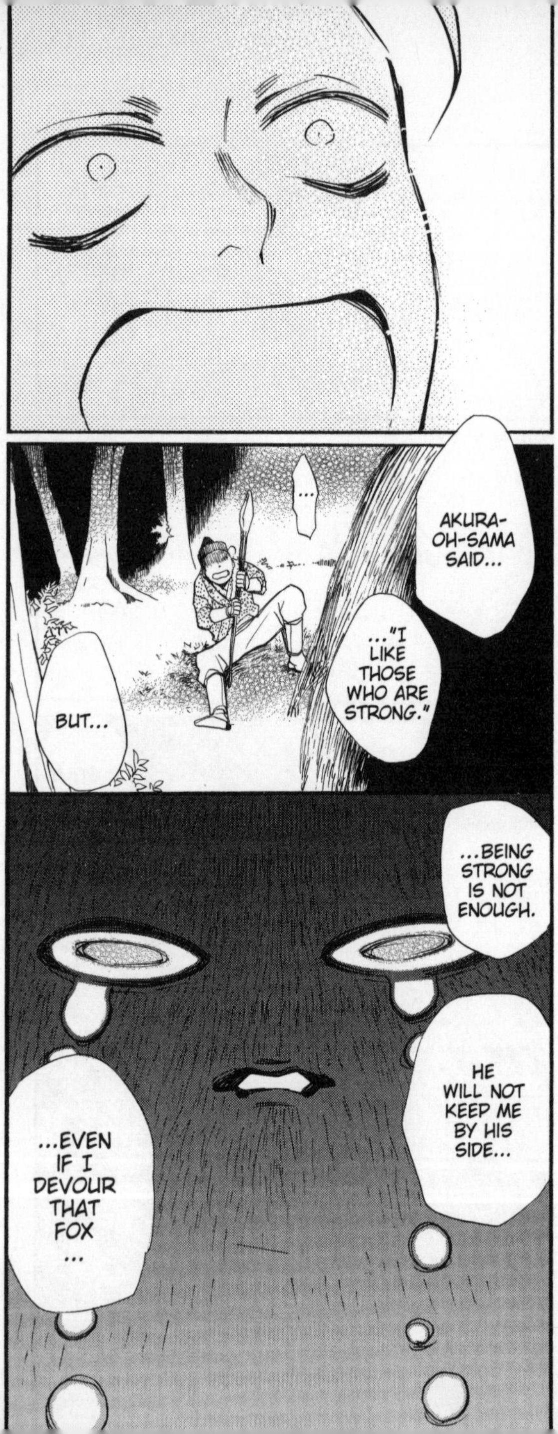
AKURA-OH-SAMA SAID...
...
..."I LIKE THOSE WHO ARE STRONG."
BUT...
...BEING STRONG IS NOT ENOUGH.
HE WILL NOT KEEP ME BY HIS SIDE...
...EVEN IF I DEVOUR THAT FOX...

When I keep writing these sidebars without thinking too much, I get worried that "I've written something like this before..."

There's a bakery I drop by every time I come back from the dentist.

Their pastries are very delicious, and I always end up buying too much!

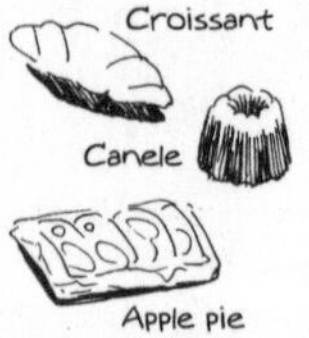
Croissant
Canele
Apple pie

I want to eat them now that I'm drawing them!

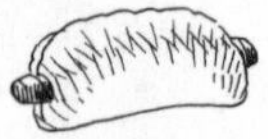
Hot dog

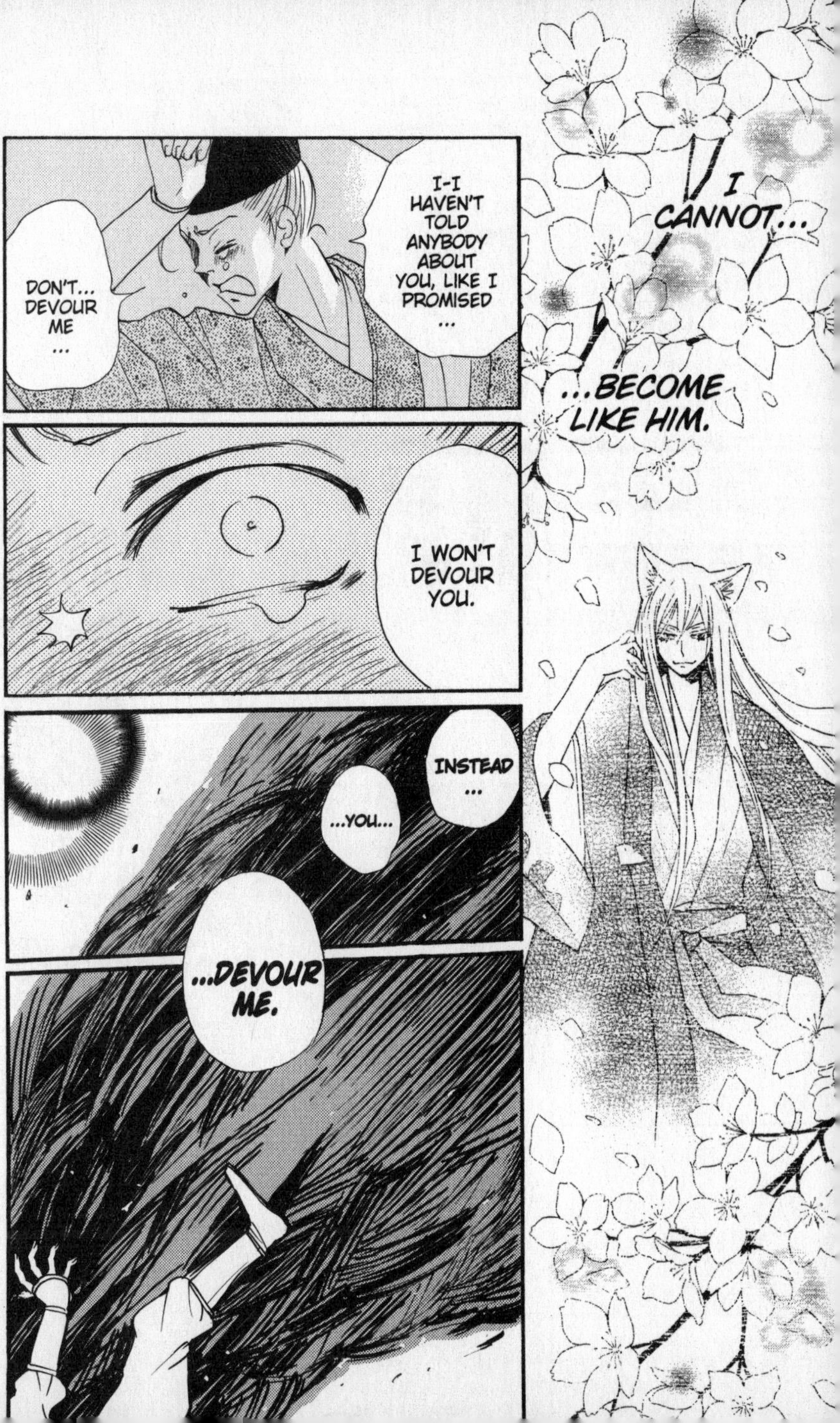
I CANNOT...
...BECOME LIKE HIM.
I-I HAVEN'T TOLD ANYBODY ABOUT YOU, LIKE I PROMISED...
DON'T... DEVOUR ME...
I WON'T DEVOUR YOU.
INSTEAD...
...YOU...
...DEVOUR ME.

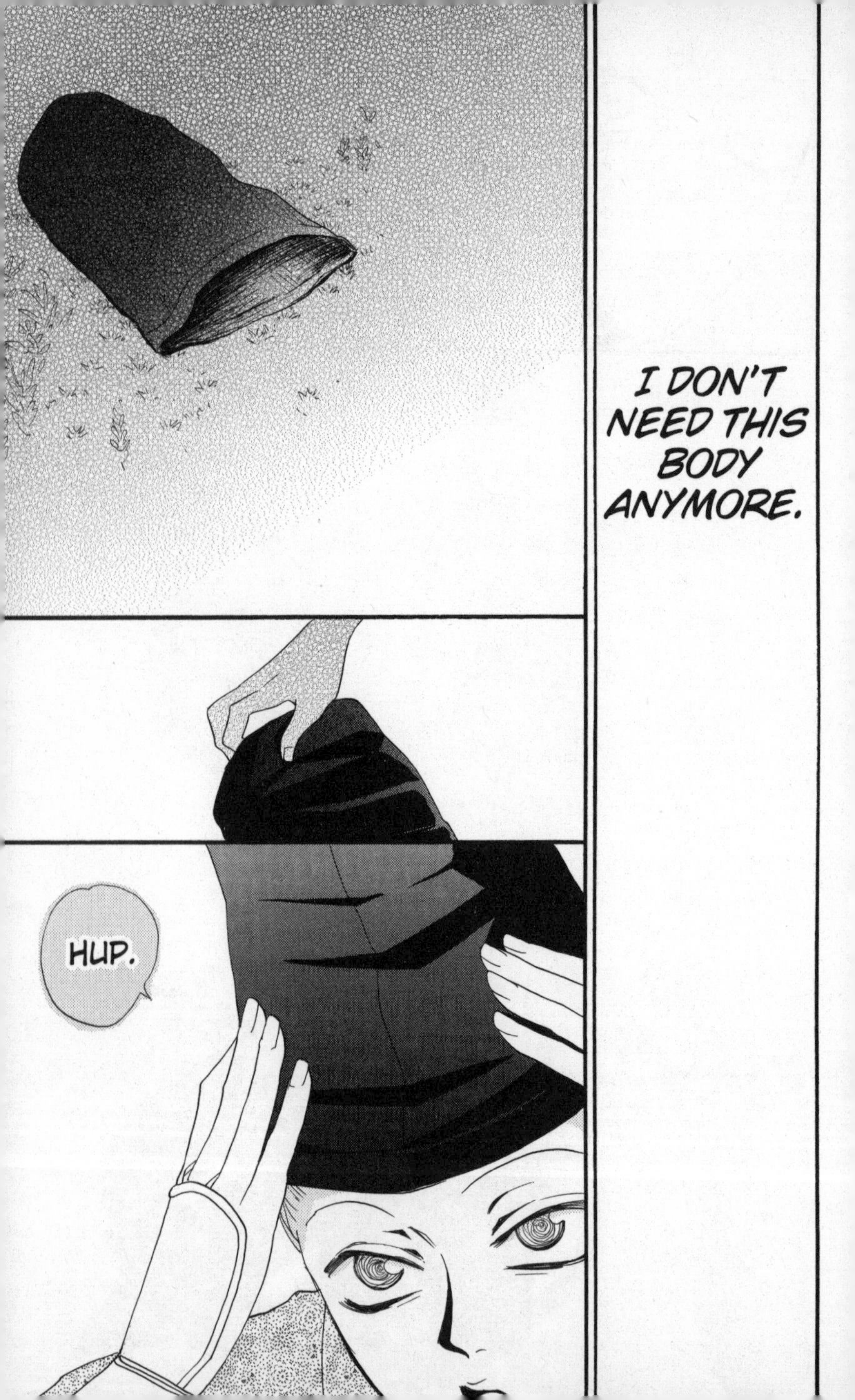
I DON'T NEED THIS BODY ANYMORE.
HUP.

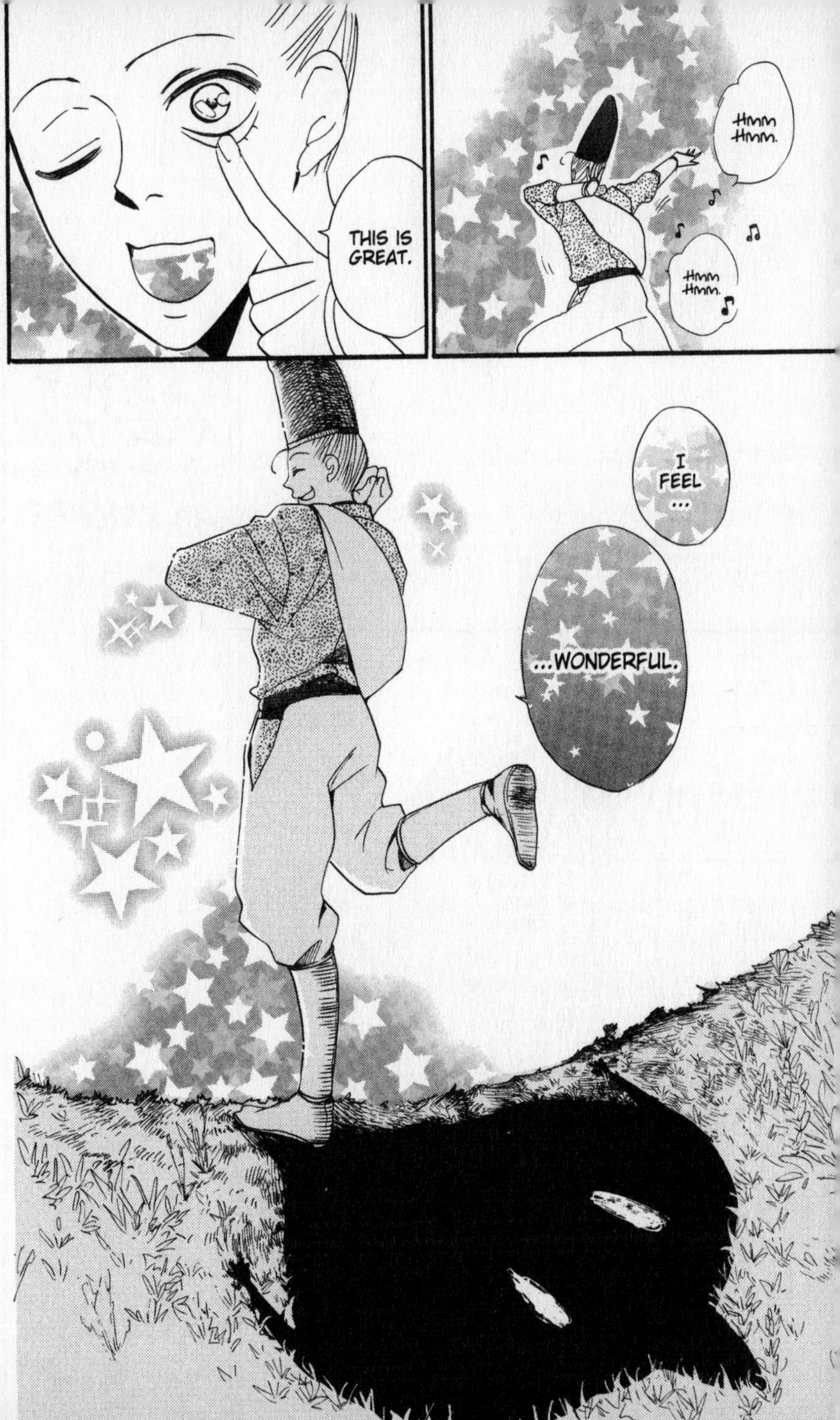
Hmm Hmm.
Hmm Hmm.
THIS IS GREAT.
I FEEL ...
...WONDERFUL.

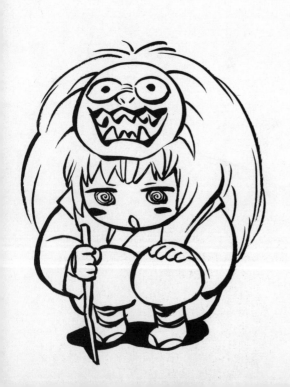

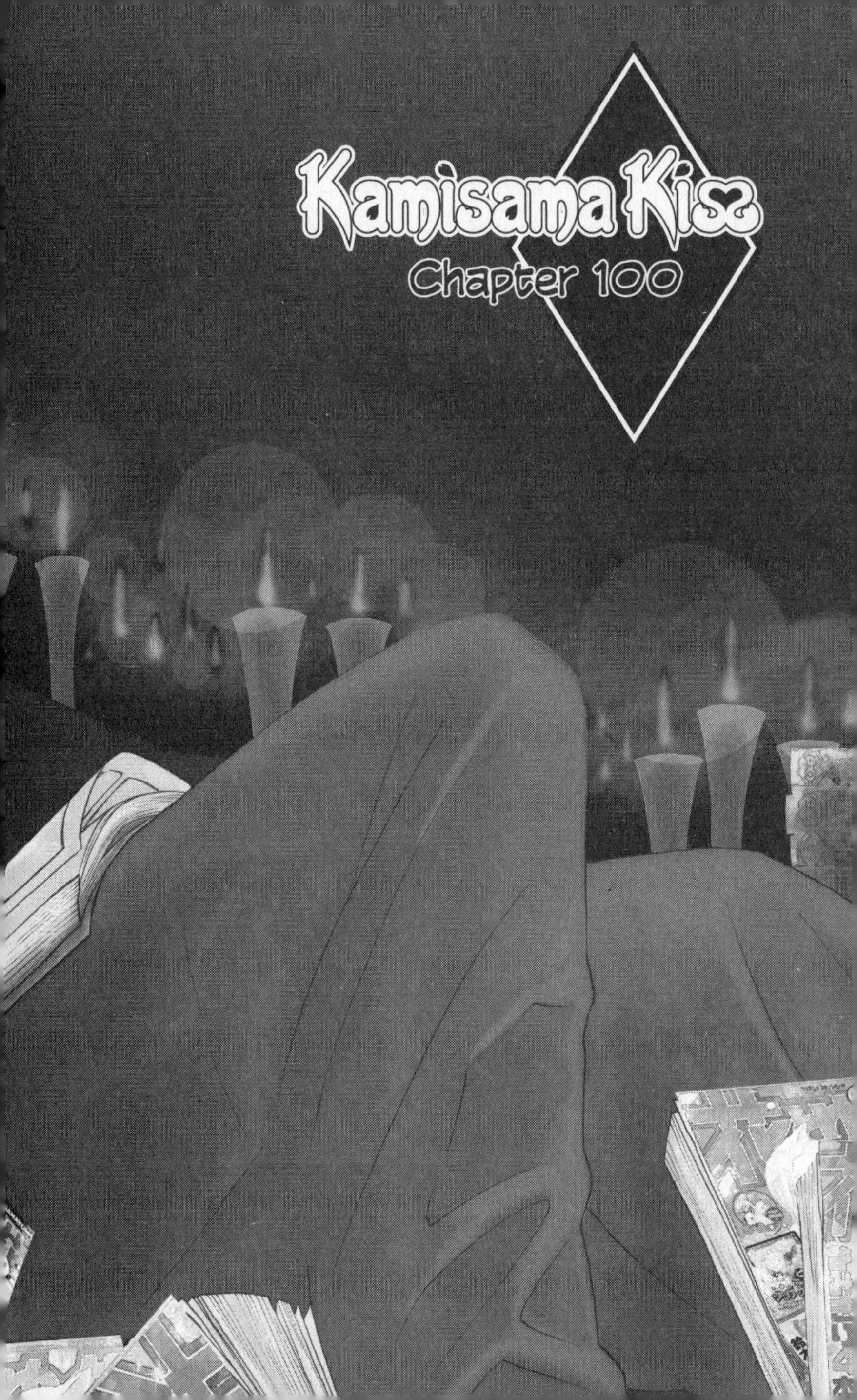
Kamisama Kiss
Chapter 100

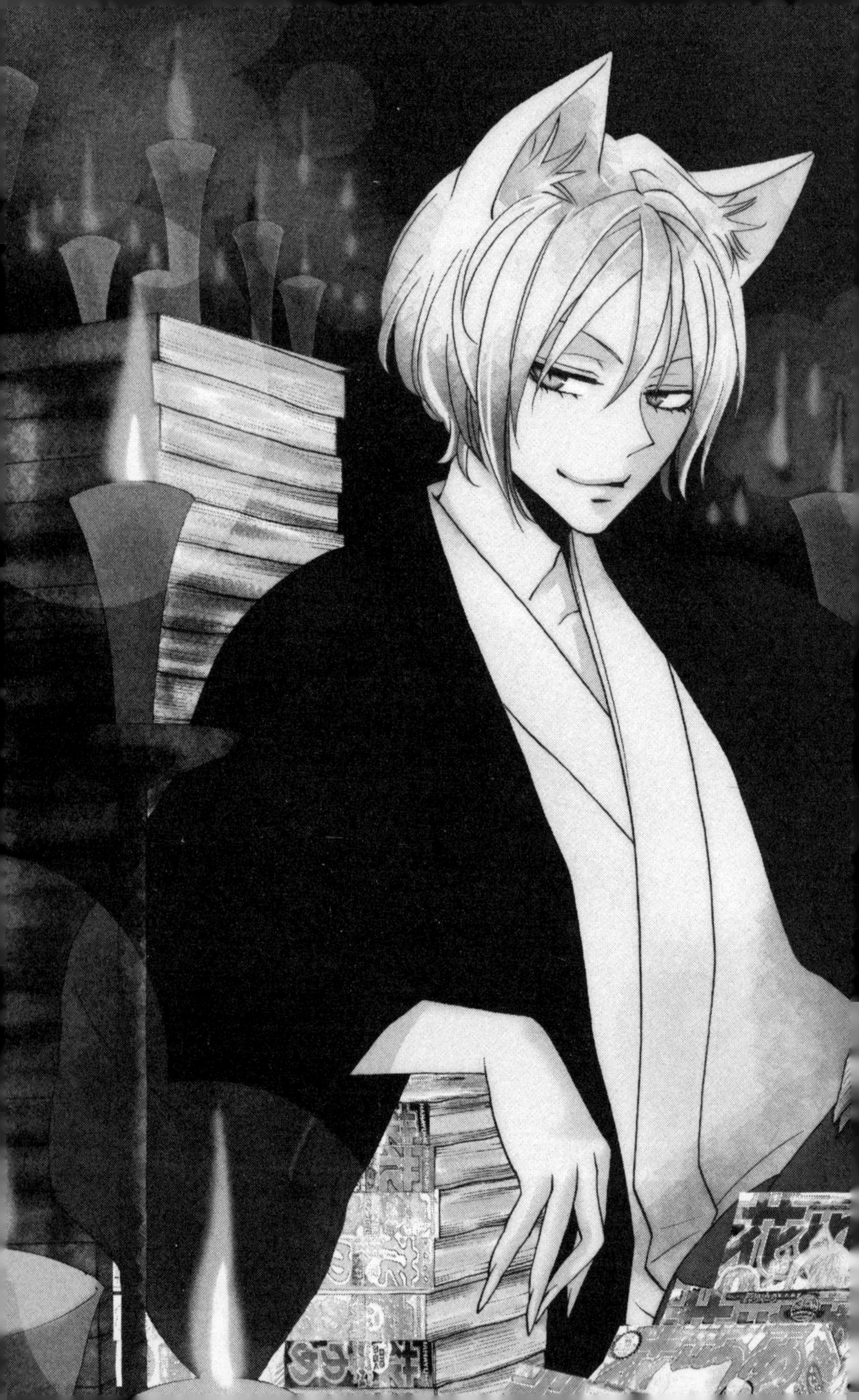

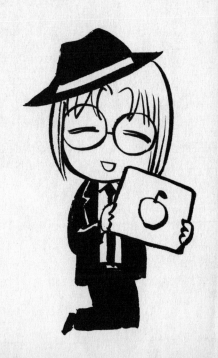

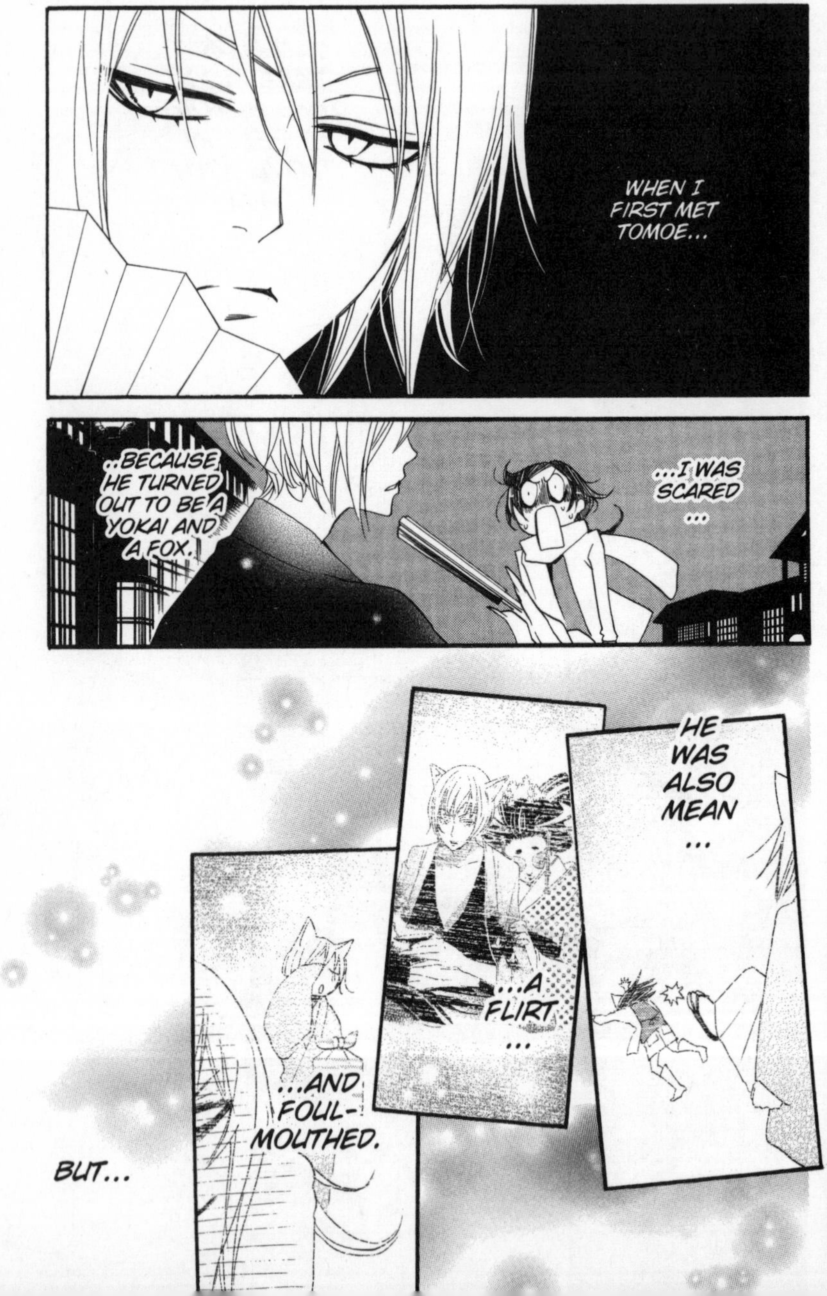
WHEN I FIRST MET TOMOE...
...I WAS SCARED ...
..BECAUSE HE TURNED OUT TO BE A YOKAI AND A FOX.
HE WAS ALSO MEAN ...
...A FLIRT ...
...AND FOUL-MOUTHED.
BUT...

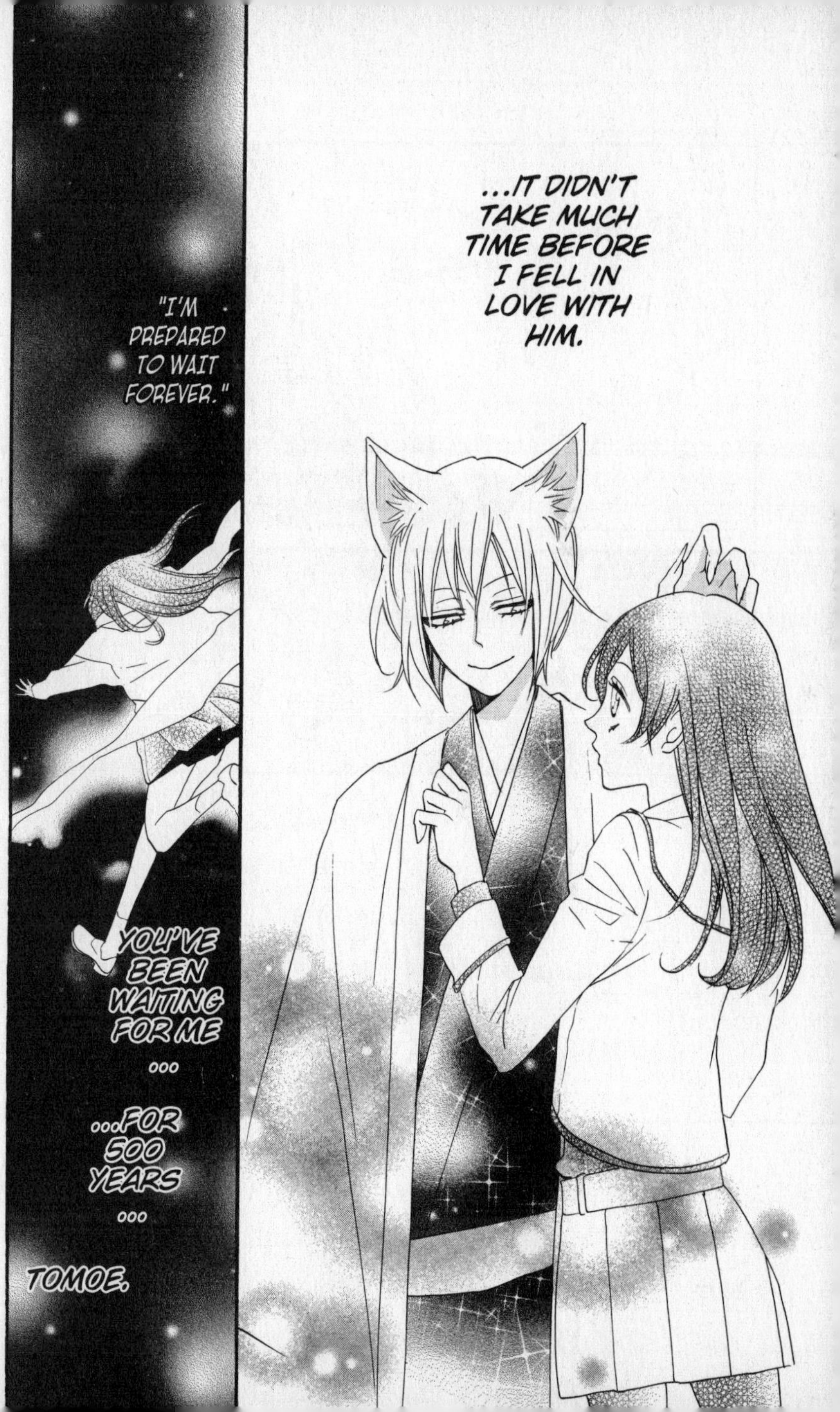
...IT DIDN'T TAKE MUCH TIME BEFORE I FELL IN LOVE WITH HIM.
"I'M PREPARED TO WAIT FOREVER."
YOU'VE BEEN WAITING FOR ME...
...FOR 500 YEARS...
TOMOE.

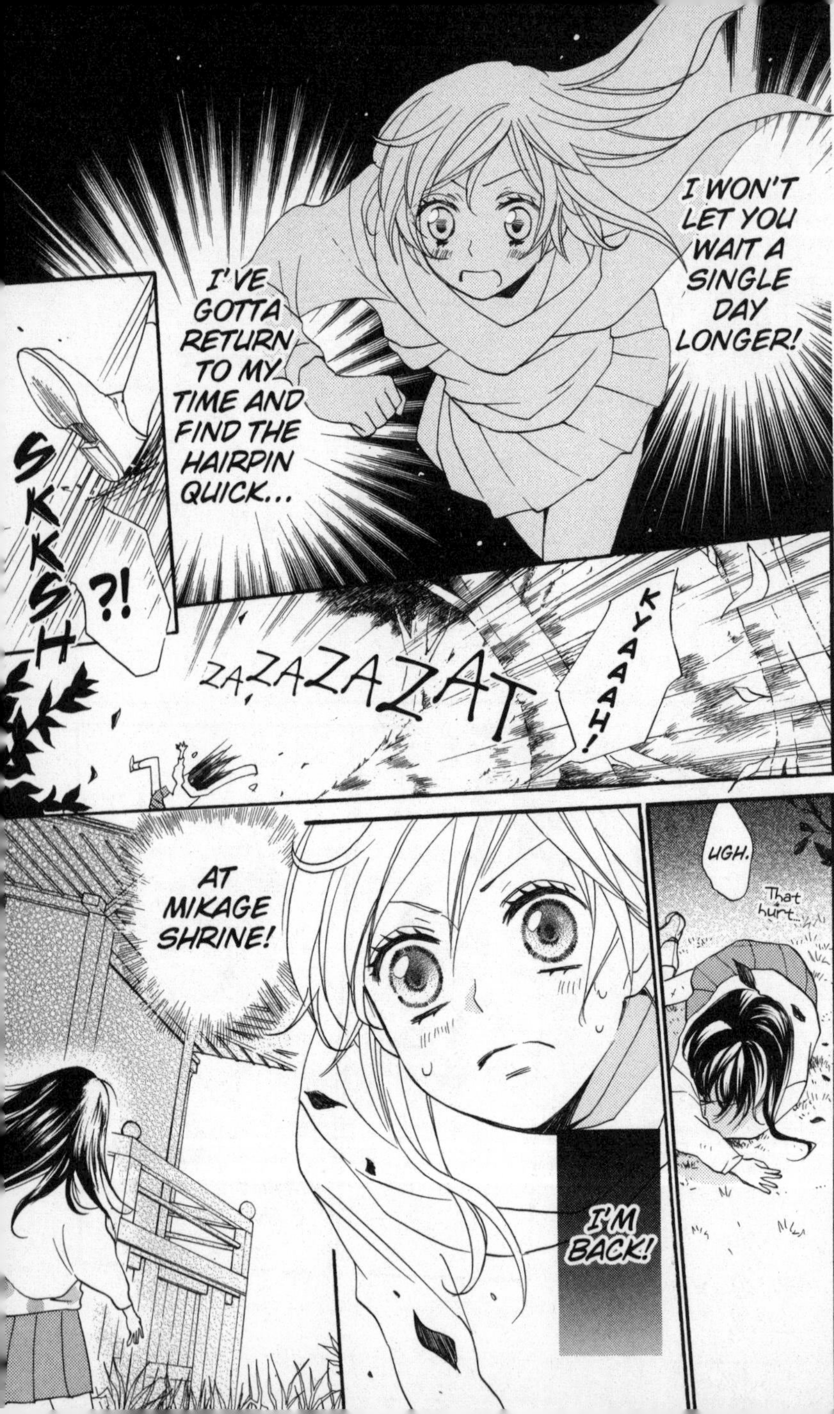
I WON'T LET YOU WAIT A SINGLE DAY LONGER!
I'VE GOTTA RETURN TO MY TIME AND FIND THE HAIRPIN QUICK...
SKKSH
?!
KYAAAAH!
ZA, ZAZAZAT
UGH.
That hurt...
AT MIKAGE SHRINE!
I'M BACK!

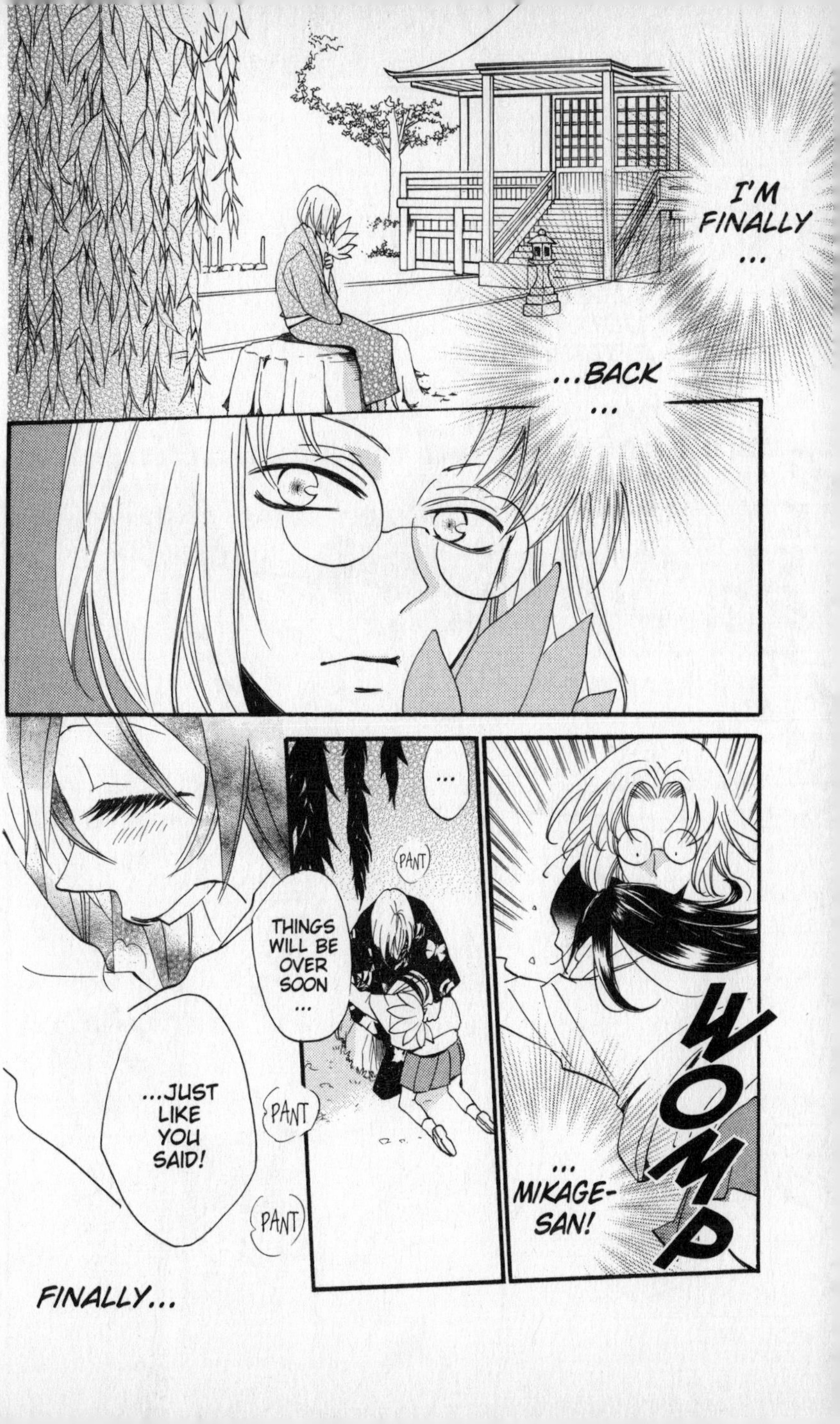
I'M FINALLY ...
...BACK ...
WOMP
... MIKAGE-SAN!
...
PANT
THINGS WILL BE OVER SOON ...
PANT
PANT
...JUST LIKE YOU SAID!
FINALLY...

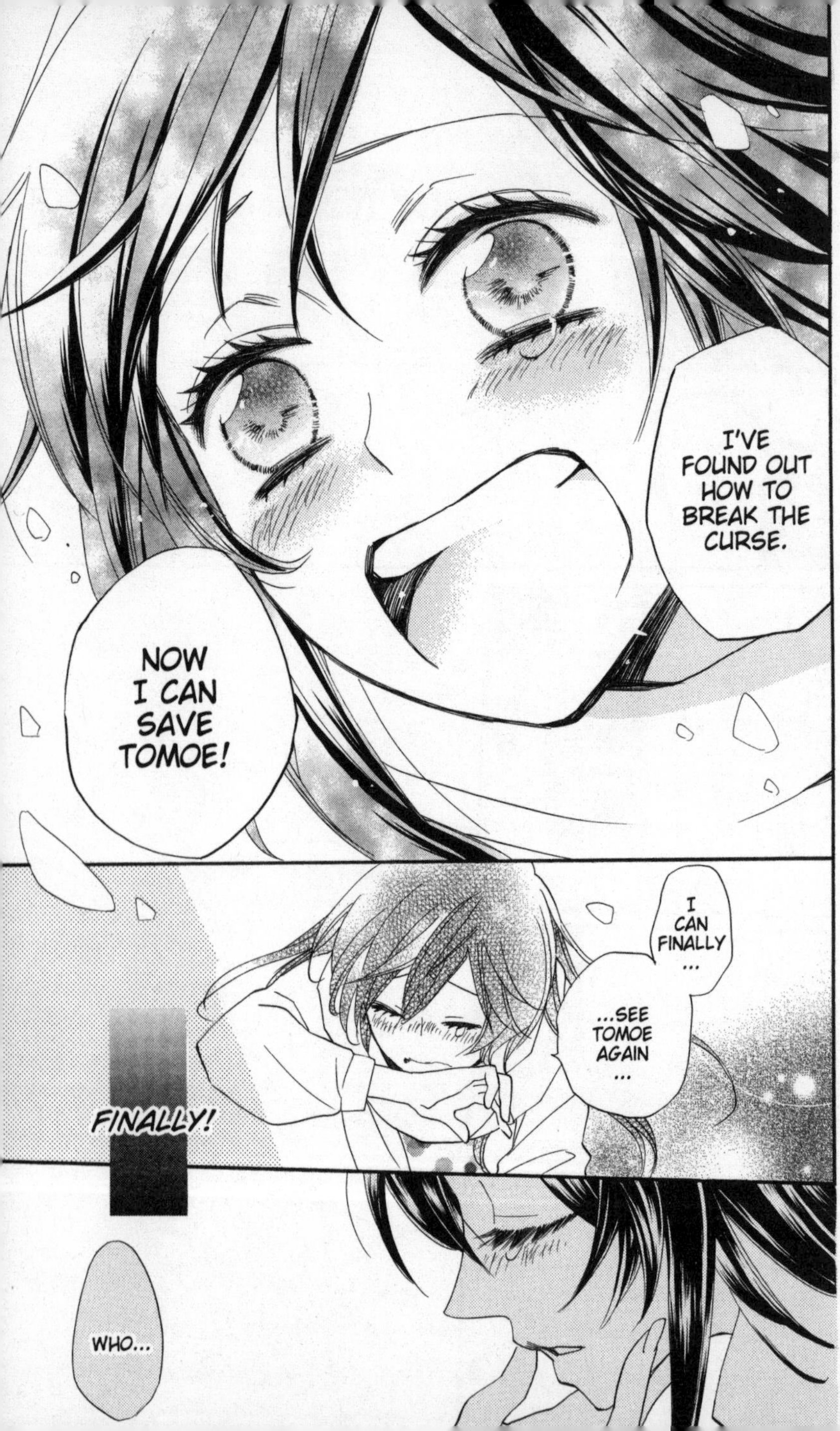
I'VE FOUND OUT HOW TO BREAK THE CURSE.
NOW I CAN SAVE TOMOE!
I CAN FINALLY...
...SEE TOMOE AGAIN...
FINALLY!
WHO...

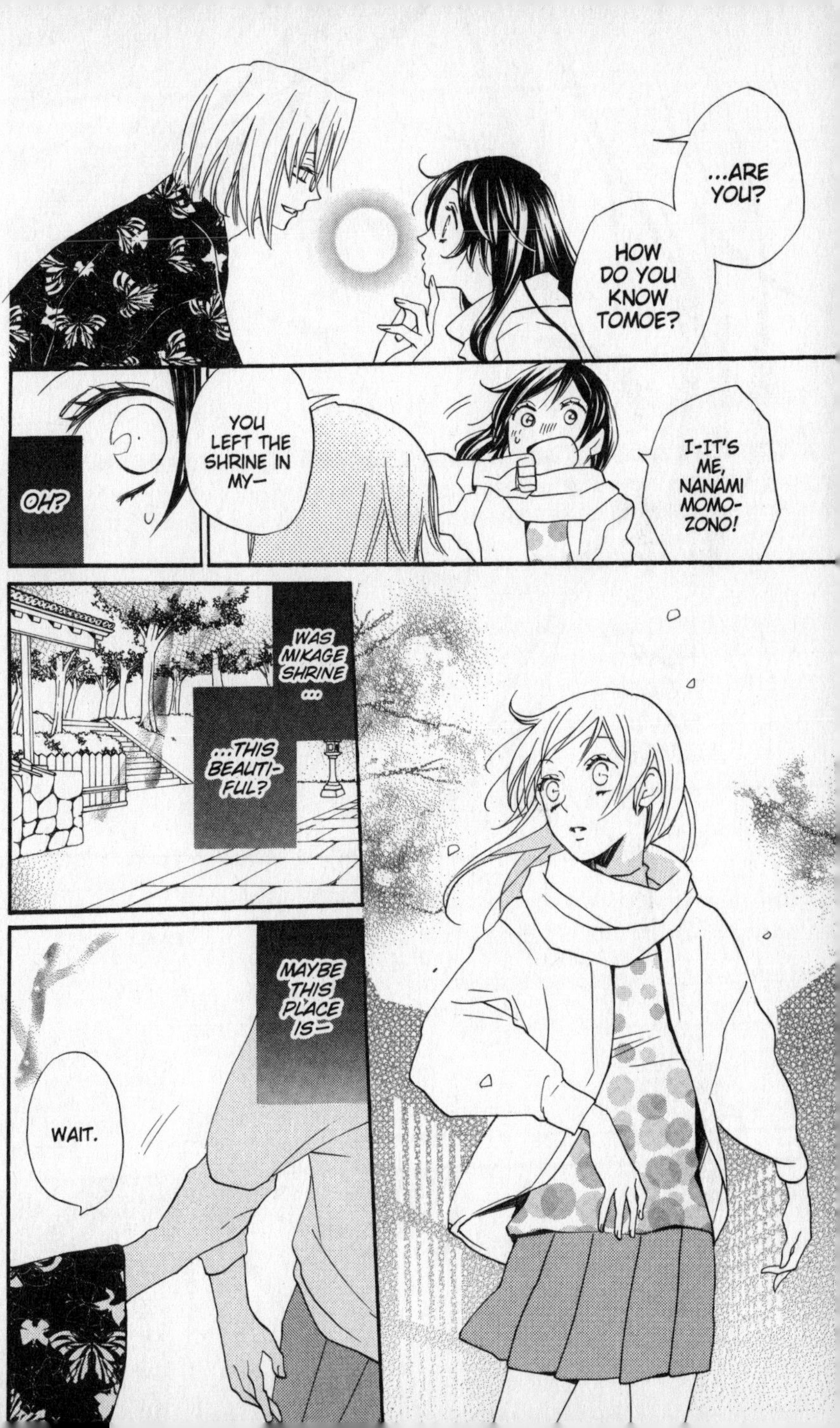
...ARE YOU?
HOW DO YOU KNOW TOMOE?
I-IT'S ME, NANAMI MOMO-ZONO!
YOU LEFT THE SHRINE IN MY—
OH?
WAS MIKAGE SHRINE ...
...THIS BEAUTI-FUL?
MAYBE THIS PLACE IS—
WAIT.

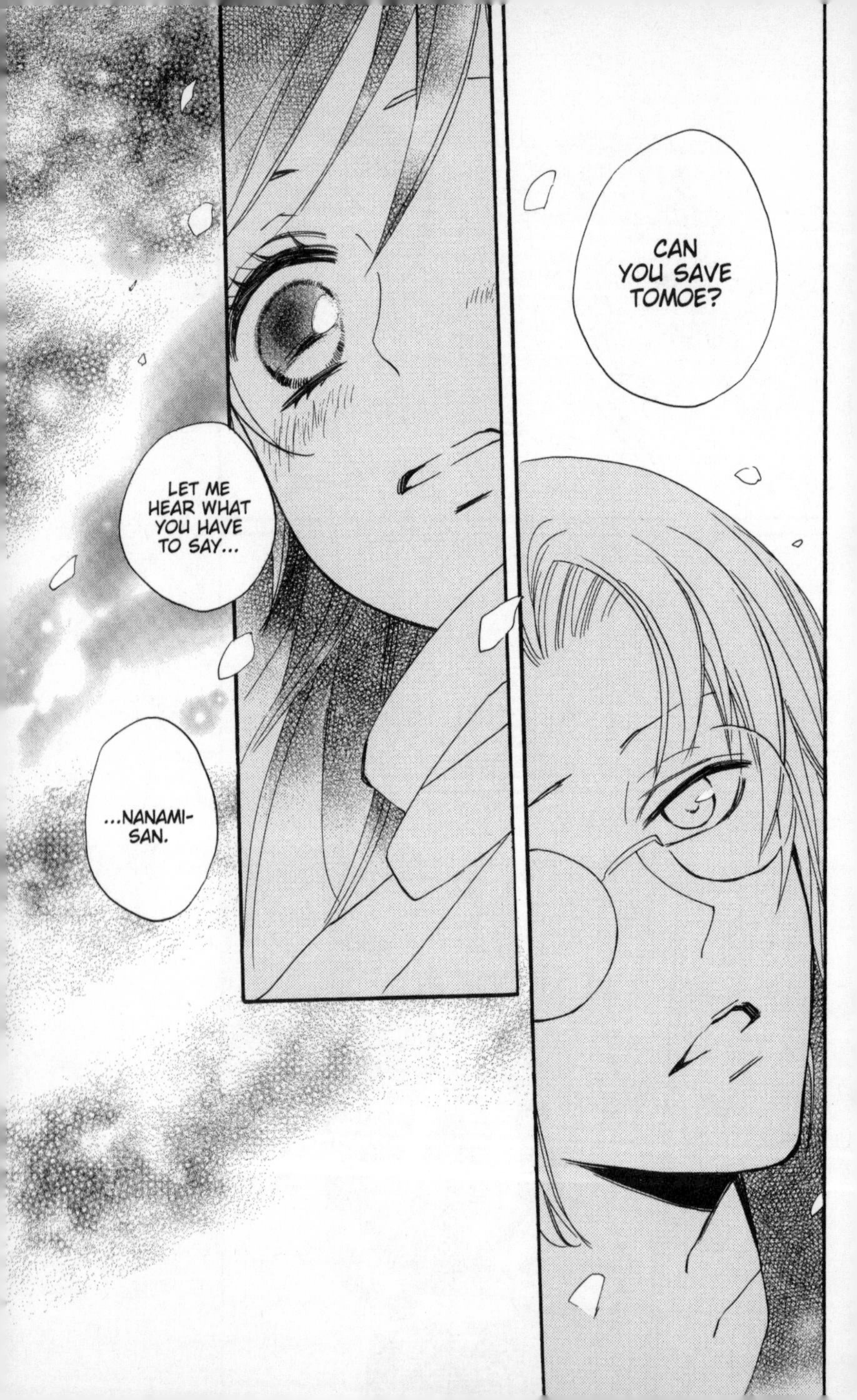
CAN YOU SAVE TOMOE?
LET ME HEAR WHAT YOU HAVE TO SAY...
...NANAMI-SAN.

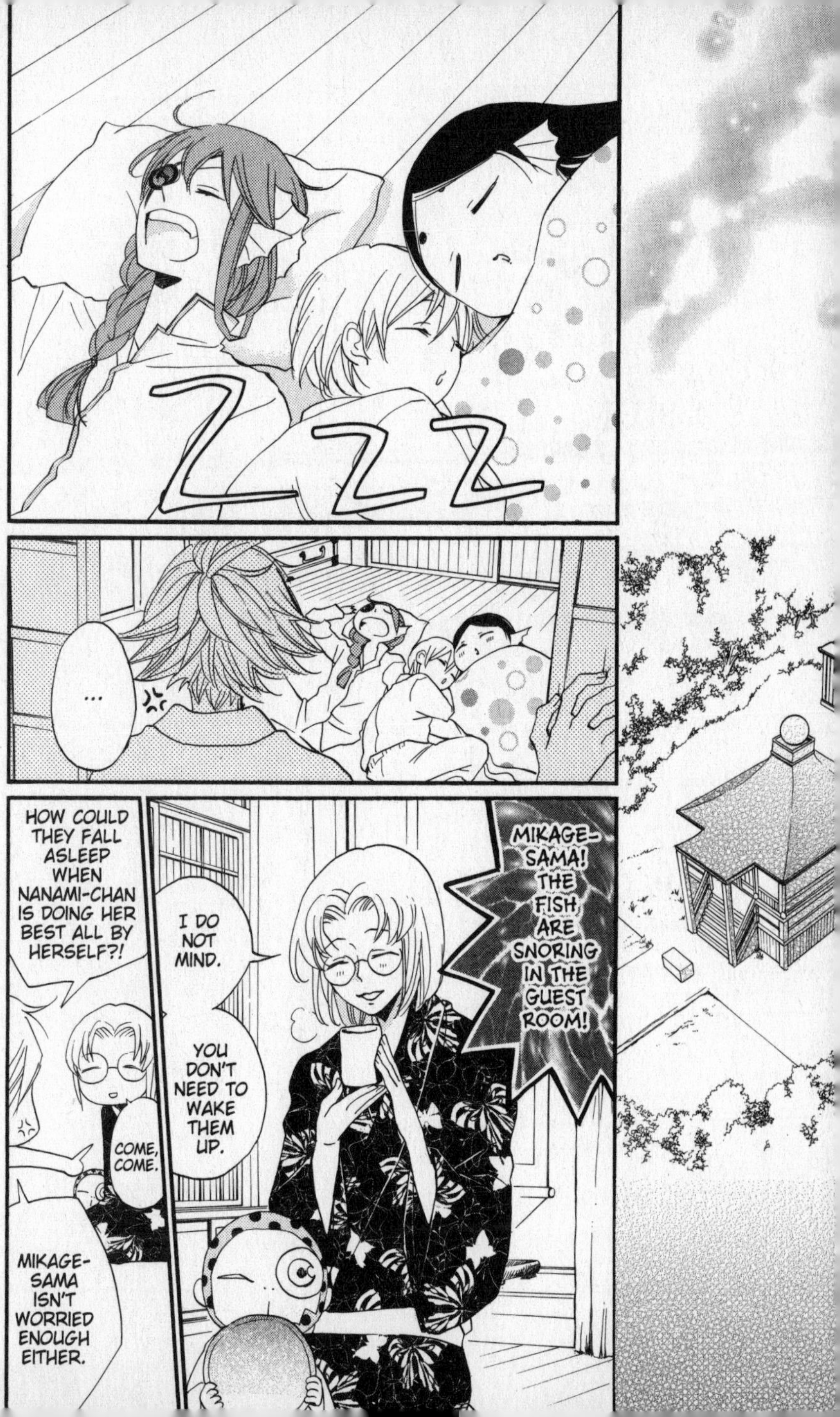
ZZZ
...
MIKAGE-SAMA! THE FISH ARE SNORING IN THE GUEST ROOM!
I DO NOT MIND.
YOU DON'T NEED TO WAKE THEM UP.
HOW COULD THEY FALL ASLEEP WHEN NANAMI-CHAN IS DOING HER BEST ALL BY HERSELF?!
COME, COME.
MIKAGE-SAMA ISN'T WORRIED ENOUGH EITHER.

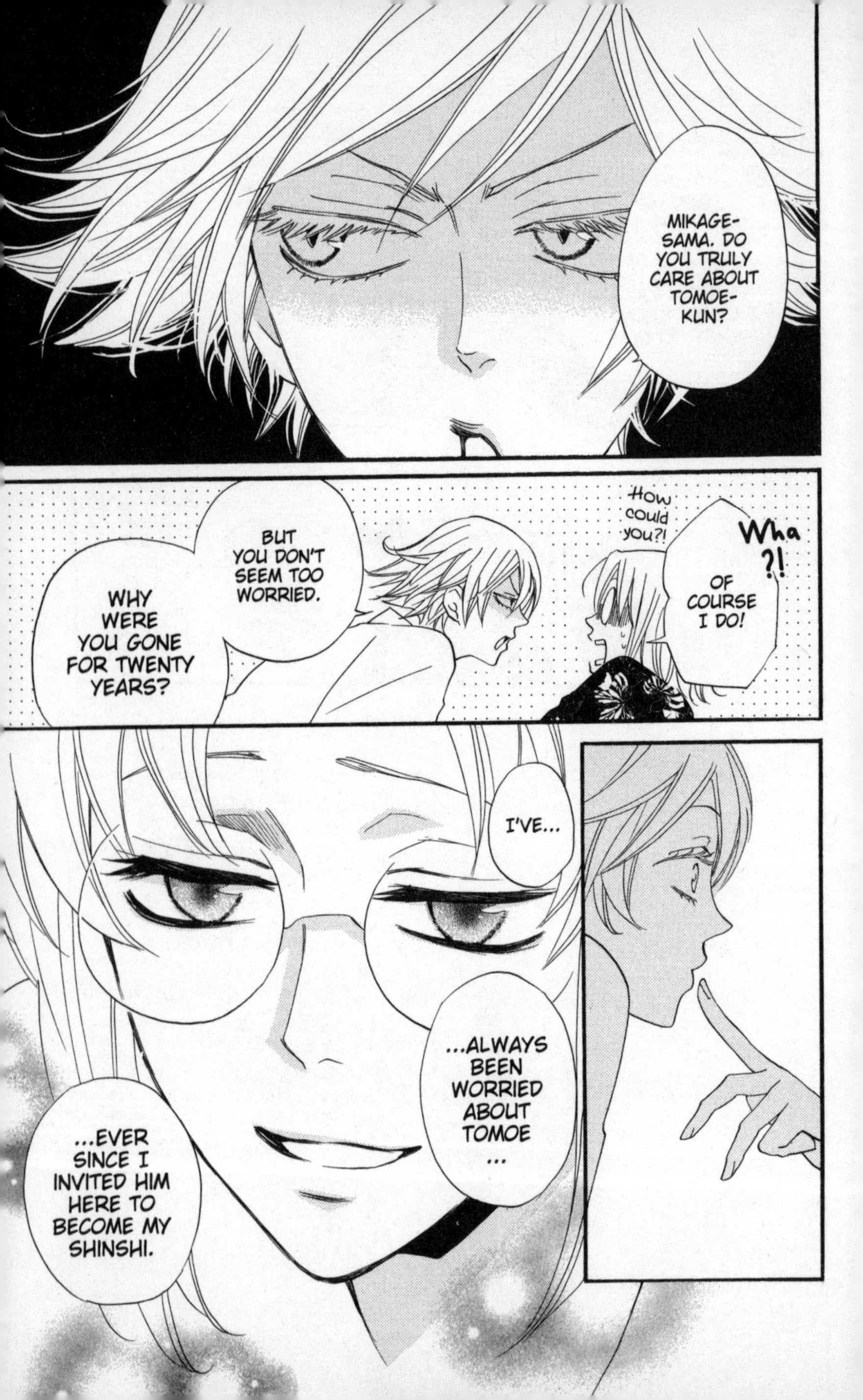
MIKAGE-SAMA. DO YOU TRULY CARE ABOUT TOMOE-KUN?
Wha ?!
OF COURSE I DO!
How could you?!
BUT YOU DON'T SEEM TOO WORRIED.
WHY WERE YOU GONE FOR TWENTY YEARS?
I'VE...
...ALWAYS BEEN WORRIED ABOUT TOMOE ...
...EVER SINCE I INVITED HIM HERE TO BECOME MY SHINSHI.

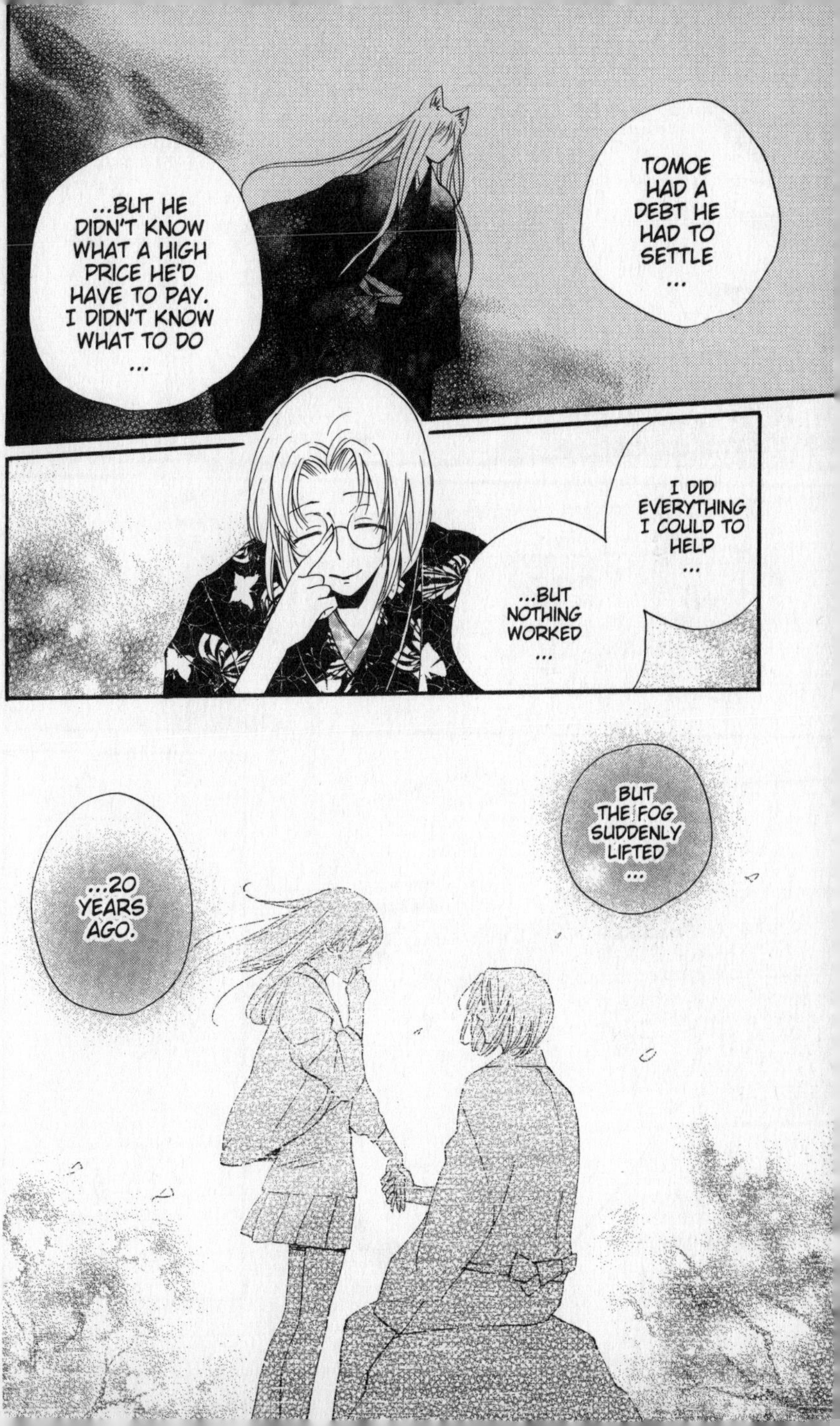
TOMOE HAD A DEBT HE HAD TO SETTLE ...
...BUT HE DIDN'T KNOW WHAT A HIGH PRICE HE'D HAVE TO PAY. I DIDN'T KNOW WHAT TO DO ...
I DID EVERYTHING I COULD TO HELP ...
...BUT NOTHING WORKED ...
BUT THE FOG SUDDENLY LIFTED ...
...20 YEARS AGO.

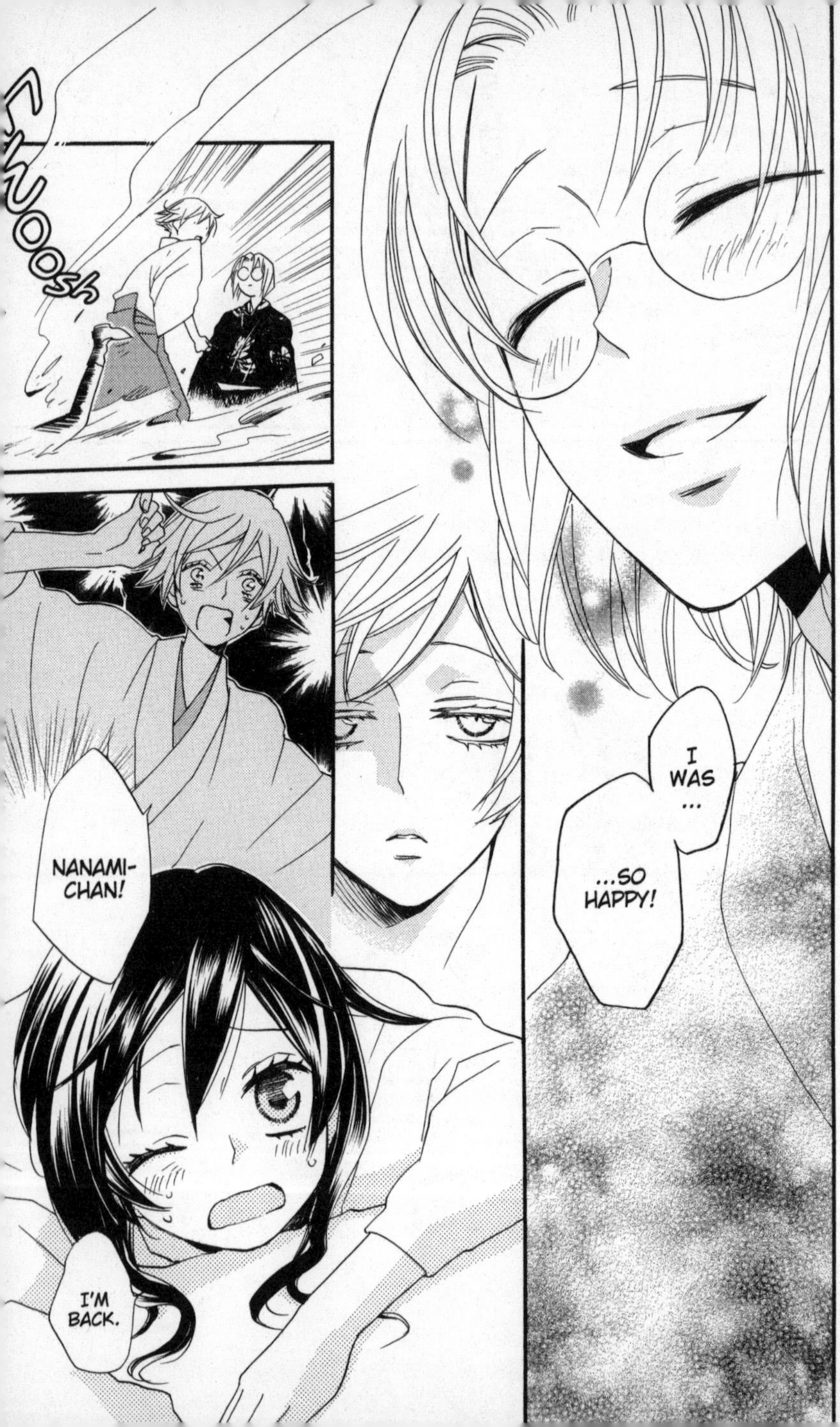

I WAS...
...SO HAPPY!
WHOOSH
NANAMI-CHAN!
I'M BACK.

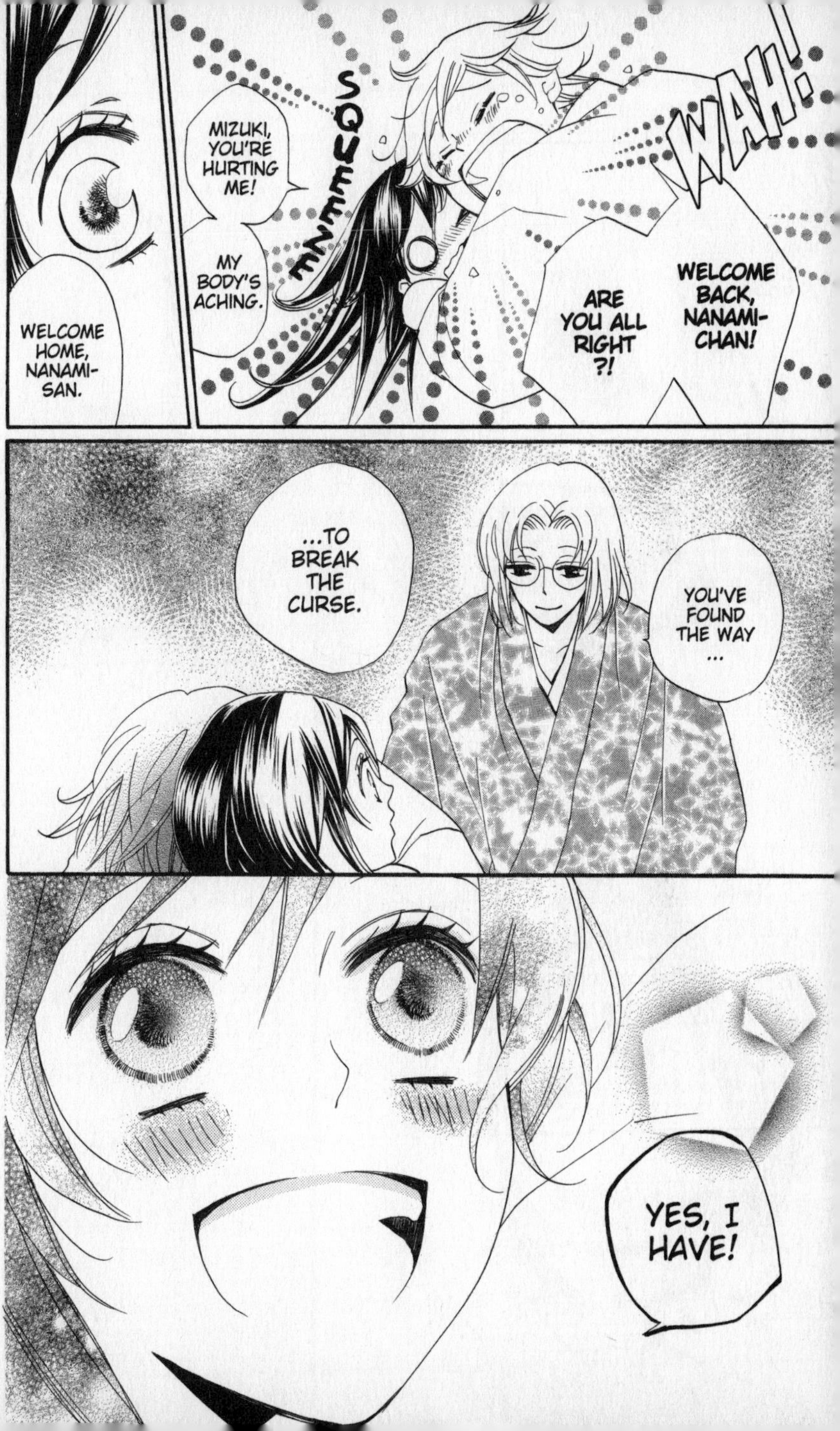
WAH!
WELCOME BACK, NANAMI-CHAN!
ARE YOU ALL RIGHT?!
SQUEEZE
MIZUKI, YOU'RE HURTING ME!
MY BODY'S ACHING.
WELCOME HOME, NANAMI-SAN.
YOU'VE FOUND THE WAY ...
...TO BREAK THE CURSE.
YES, I HAVE!

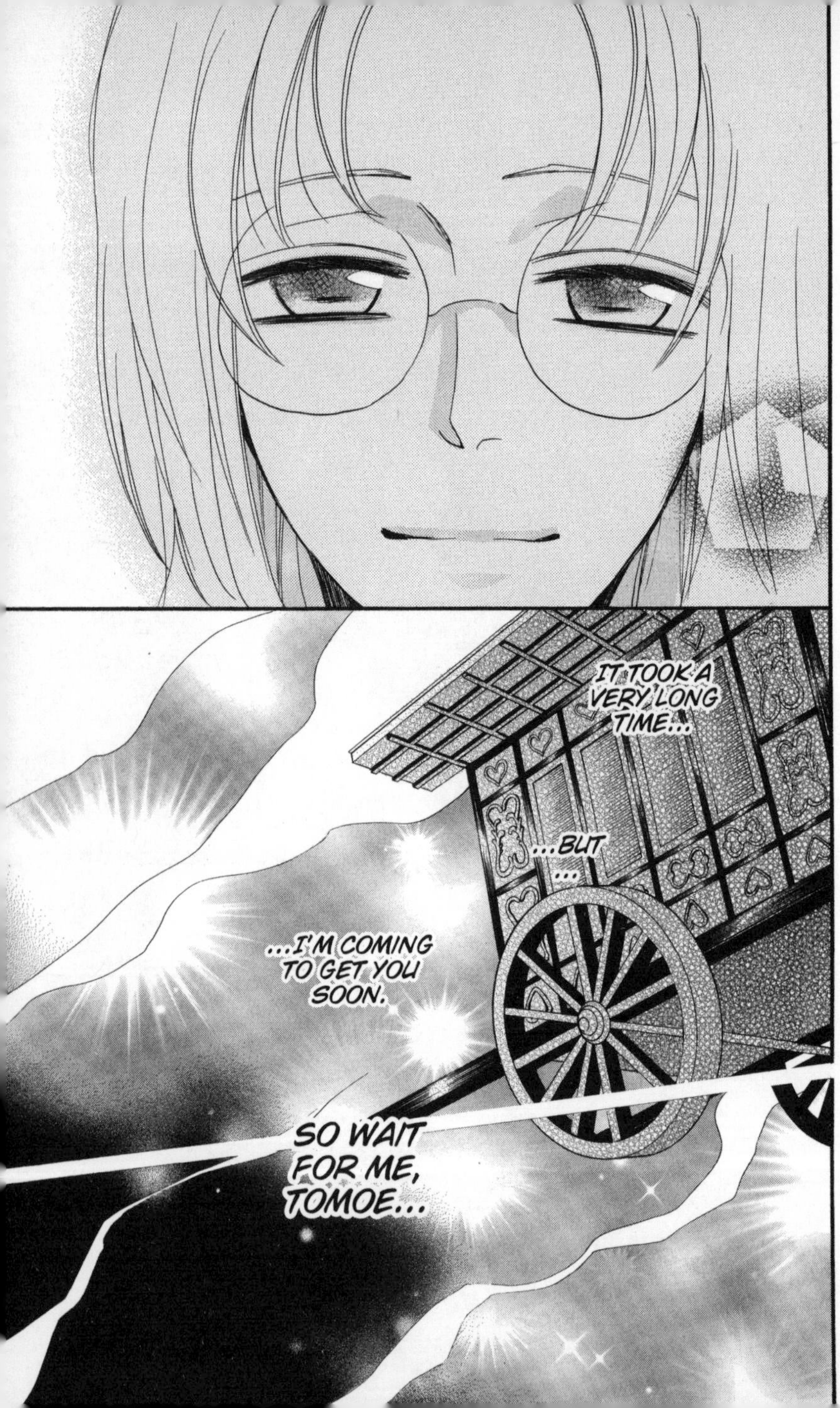
IT TOOK A VERY LONG TIME...
...BUT ...
...I'M COMING TO GET YOU SOON.
SO WAIT FOR ME, TOMOE...

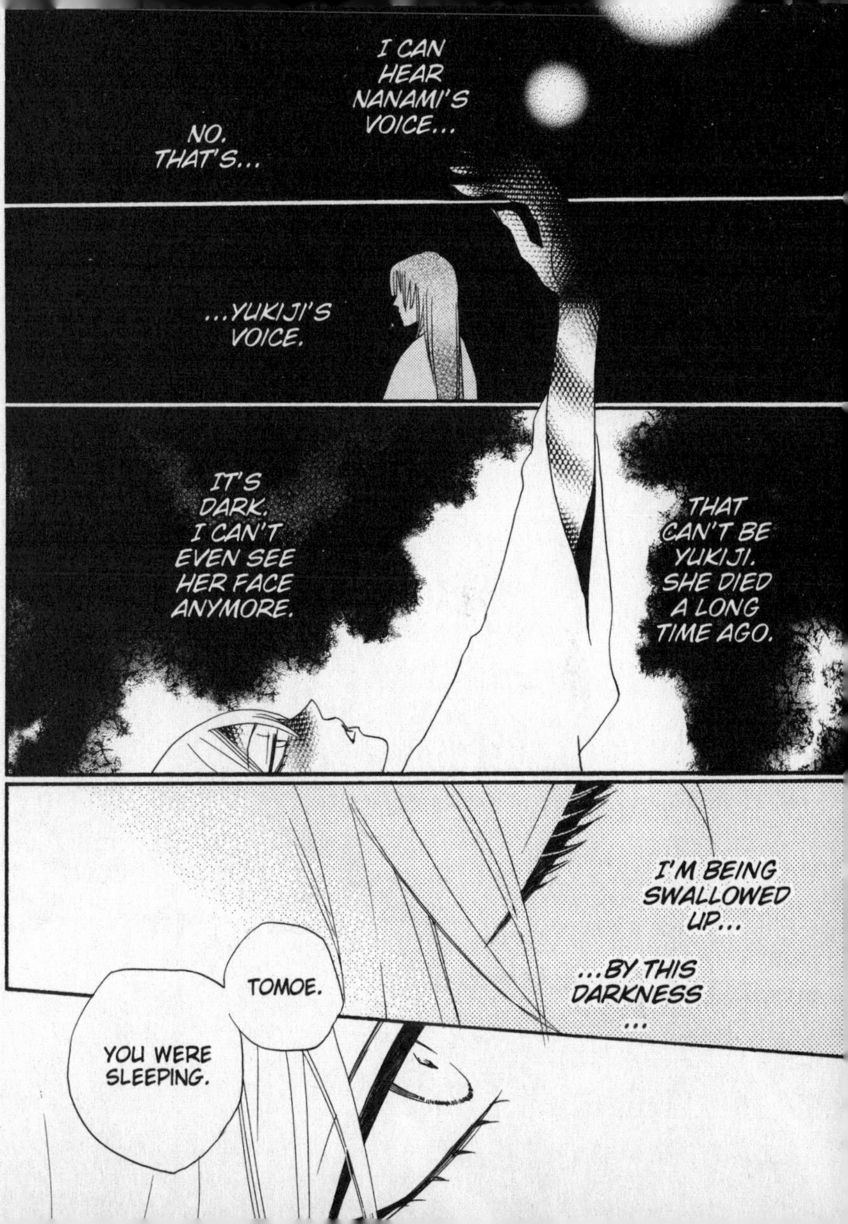
I CAN HEAR NANAMI'S VOICE...
NO. THAT'S...
...YUKIJI'S VOICE.
THAT CAN'T BE YUKIJI. SHE DIED A LONG TIME AGO.
IT'S DARK. I CAN'T EVEN SEE HER FACE ANYMORE.
I'M BEING SWALLOWED UP...
...BY THIS DARKNESS...
TOMOE.
YOU WERE SLEEPING.

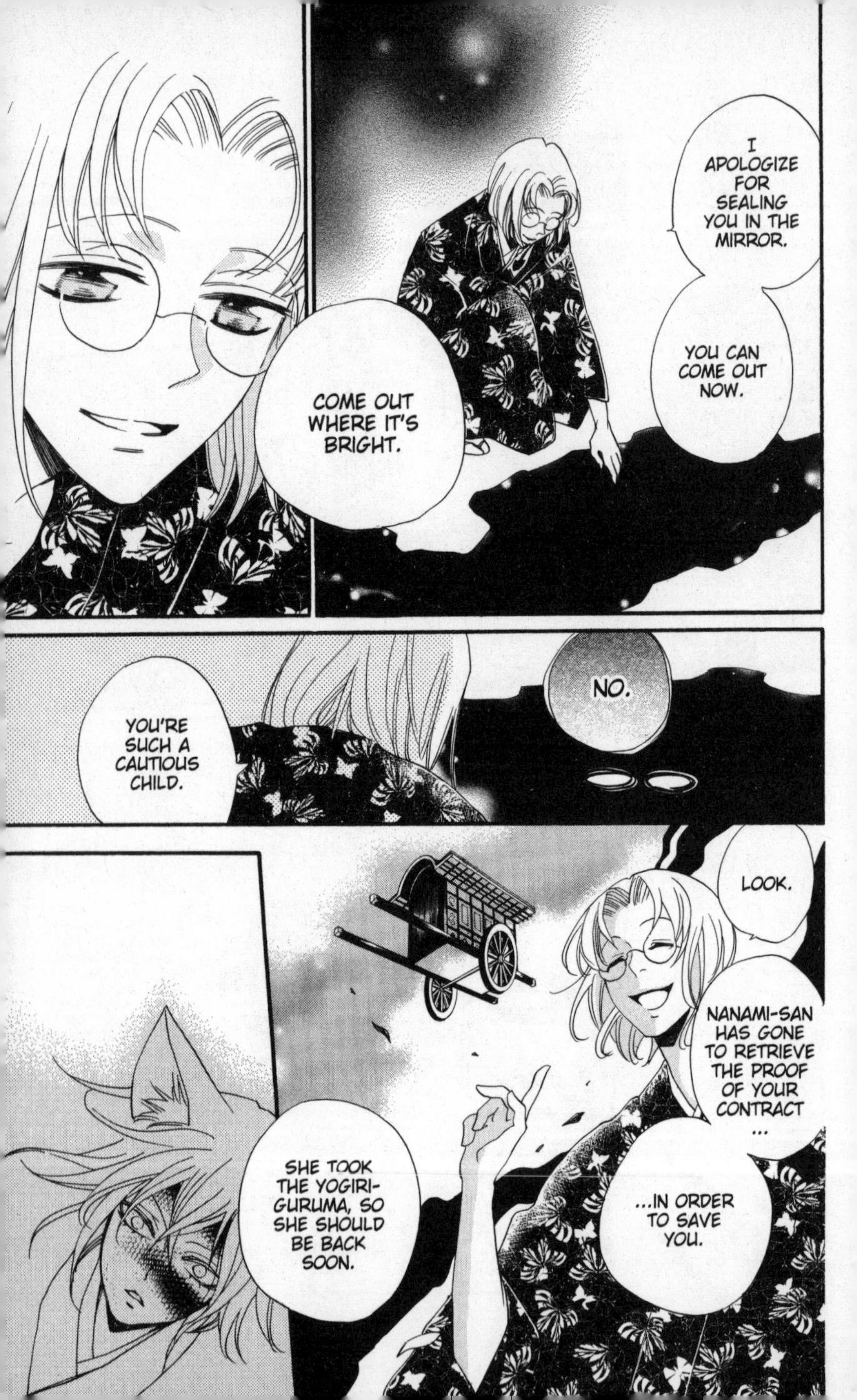
I APOLOGIZE FOR SEALING YOU IN THE MIRROR.
YOU CAN COME OUT NOW.
COME OUT WHERE IT'S BRIGHT.
NO.
YOU'RE SUCH A CAUTIOUS CHILD.
LOOK.
NANAMI-SAN HAS GONE TO RETRIEVE THE PROOF OF YOUR CONTRACT ...
...IN ORDER TO SAVE YOU.
SHE TOOK THE YOGIRI-GURUMA, SO SHE SHOULD BE BACK SOON.

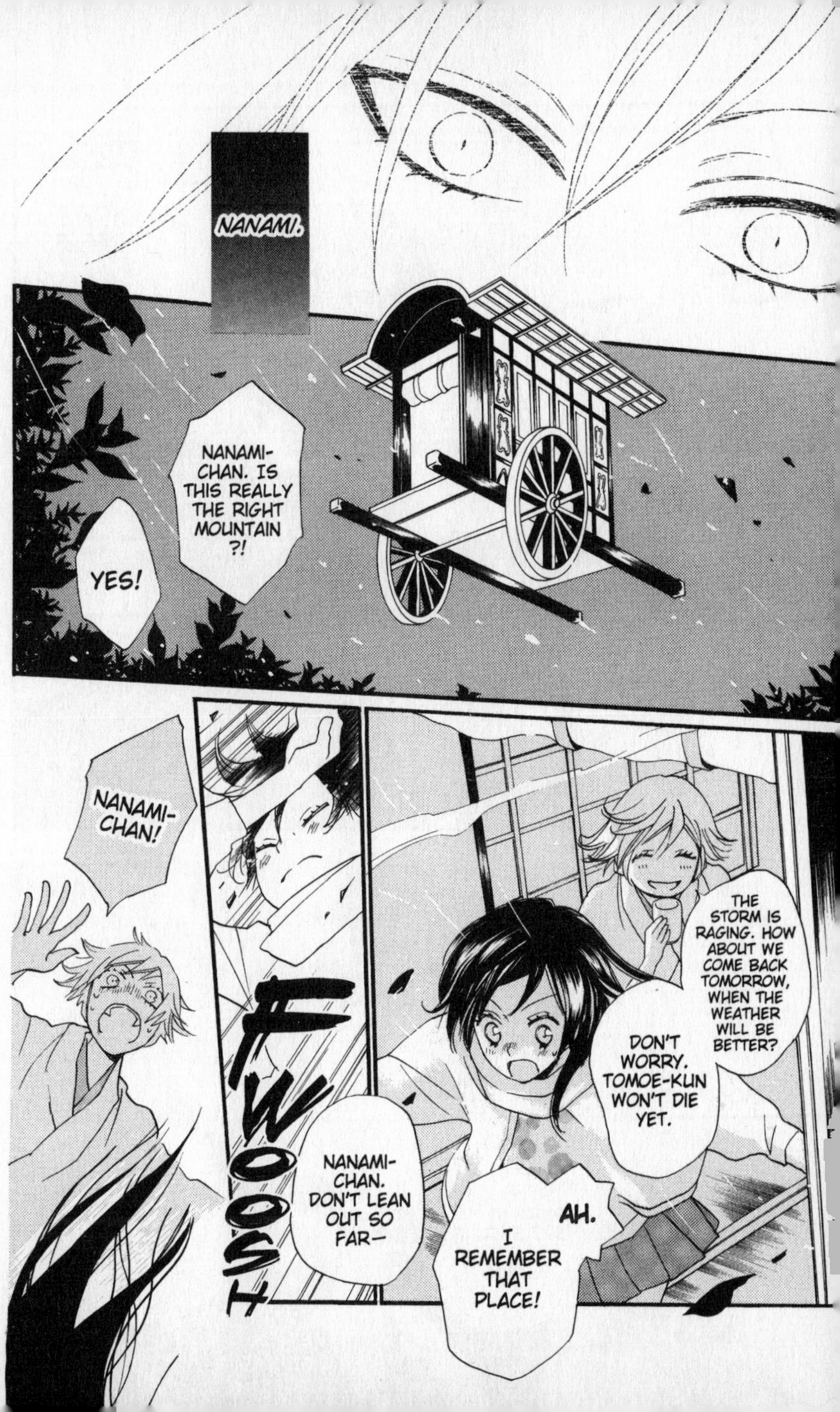
NANAMI.
NANAMI-CHAN. IS THIS REALLY THE RIGHT MOUNTAIN?!
YES!
THE STORM IS RAGING. HOW ABOUT WE COME BACK TOMORROW, WHEN THE WEATHER WILL BE BETTER?
DON'T WORRY. TOMOE-KUN WON'T DIE YET.
NANAMI-CHAN. DON'T LEAN OUT SO FAR—
AH.
I REMEMBER THAT PLACE!
FWOOSH
NANAMI-CHAN!

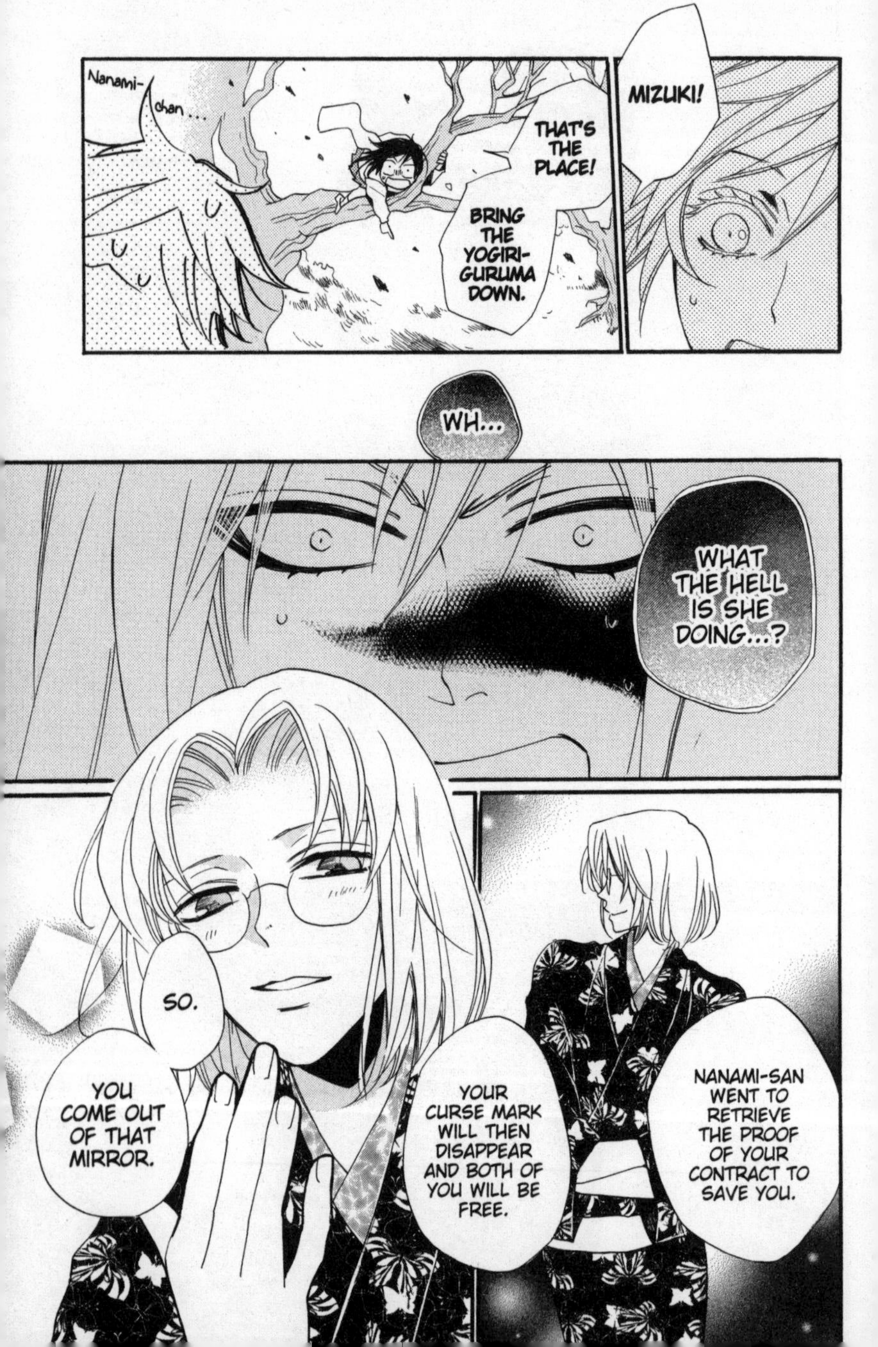
MIZUKI!
THAT'S THE PLACE!
BRING THE YOGIRI-GURUMA DOWN.
Nanami-chan...
WH...
WHAT THE HELL IS SHE DOING...?
NANAMI-SAN WENT TO RETRIEVE THE PROOF OF YOUR CONTRACT TO SAVE YOU.
YOUR CURSE MARK WILL THEN DISAPPEAR AND BOTH OF YOU WILL BE FREE.
SO.
YOU COME OUT OF THAT MIRROR.

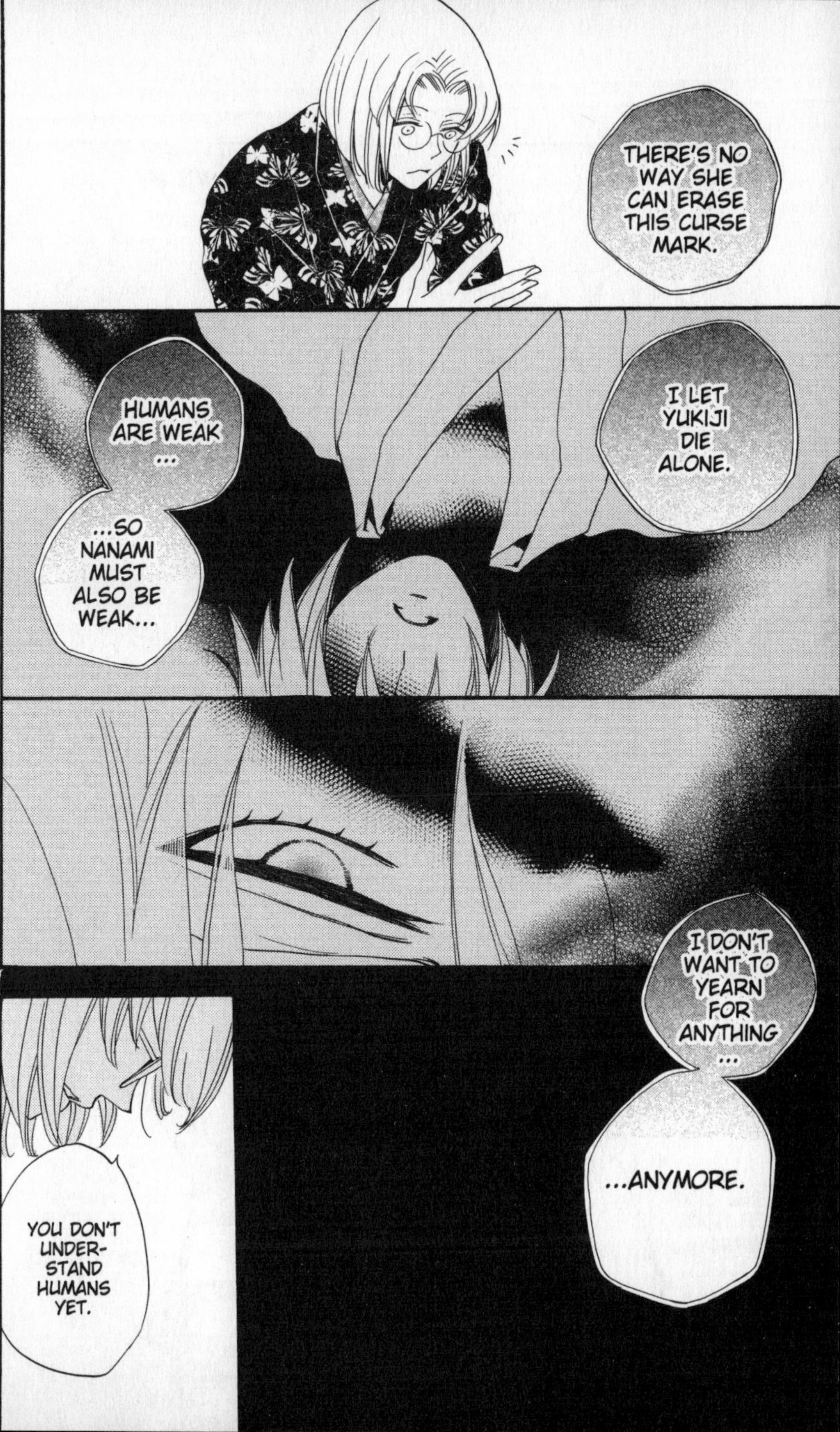
THERE'S NO WAY SHE CAN ERASE THIS CURSE MARK.
I LET YUKIJI DIE ALONE.
HUMANS ARE WEAK...
...SO NANAMI MUST ALSO BE WEAK...
I DON'T WANT TO YEARN FOR ANYTHING...
...ANYMORE.
YOU DON'T UNDER-STAND HUMANS YET.

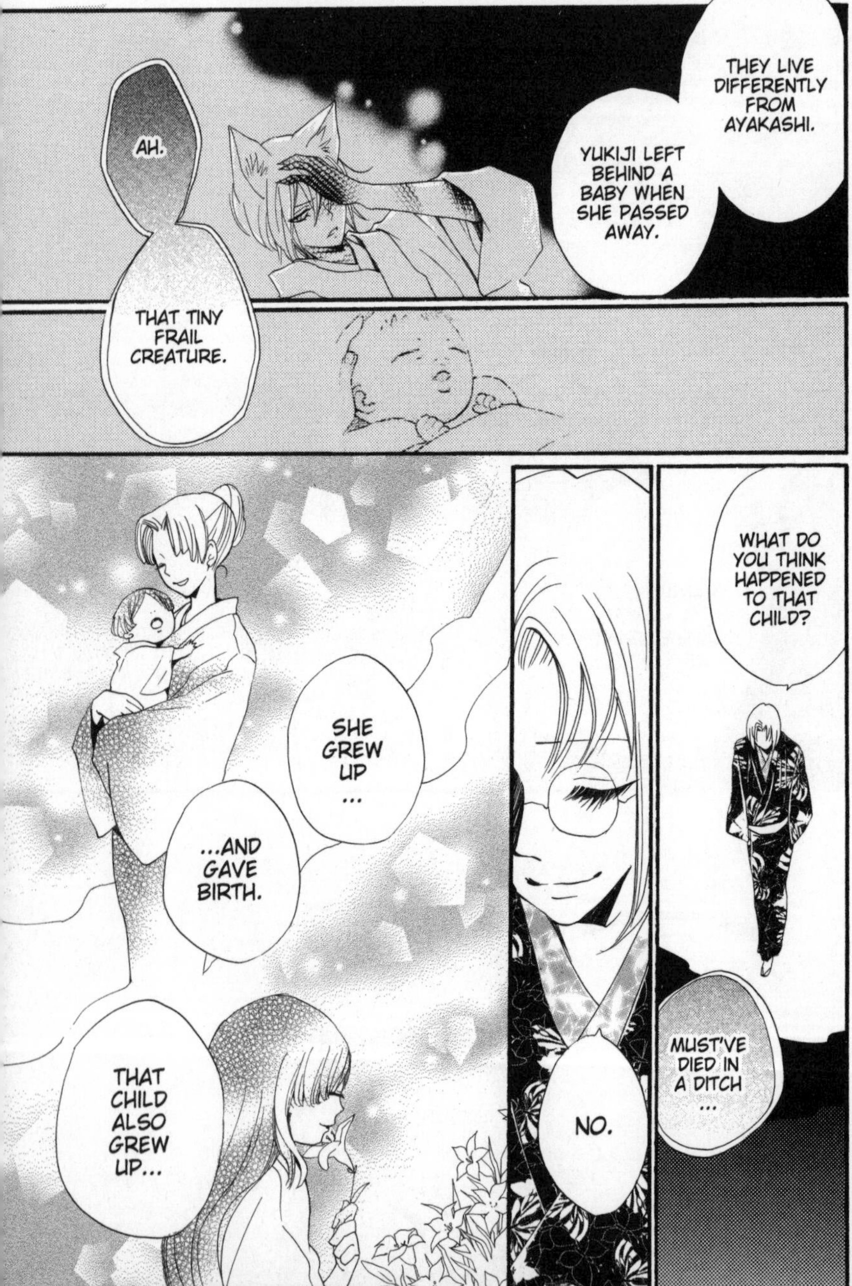
THEY LIVE DIFFERENTLY FROM AYAKASHI.
YUKIJI LEFT BEHIND A BABY WHEN SHE PASSED AWAY.
AH.
THAT TINY FRAIL CREATURE.
WHAT DO YOU THINK HAPPENED TO THAT CHILD?
MUST'VE DIED IN A DITCH ...
NO.
SHE GREW UP ...
...AND GAVE BIRTH.
THAT CHILD ALSO GREW UP...

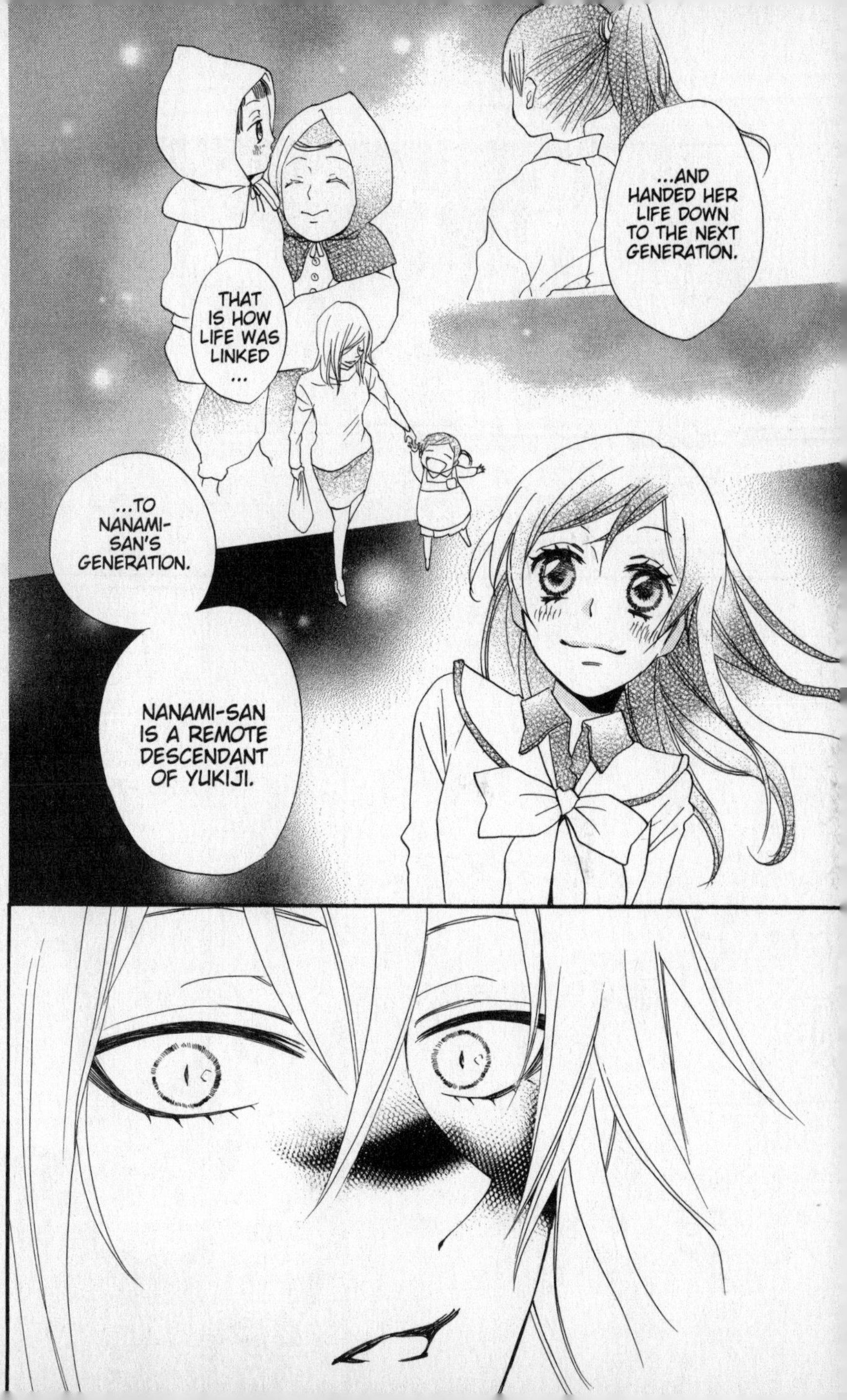
...AND HANDED HER LIFE DOWN TO THE NEXT GENERATION.
THAT IS HOW LIFE WAS LINKED ...
...TO NANAMI-SAN'S GENERATION.
NANAMI-SAN IS A REMOTE DESCENDANT OF YUKIJI.

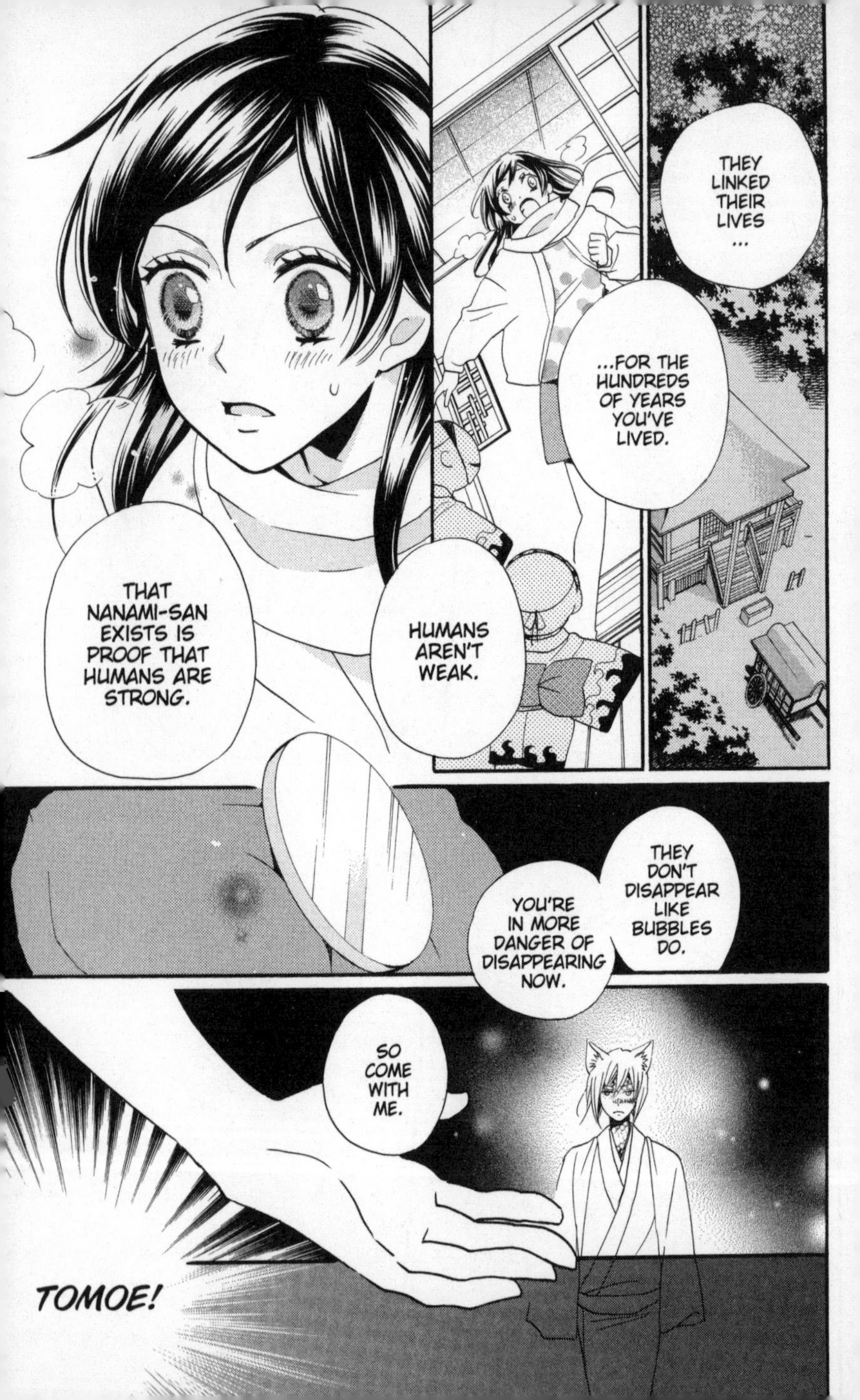
THEY LINKED THEIR LIVES...
...FOR THE HUNDREDS OF YEARS YOU'VE LIVED.
HUMANS AREN'T WEAK.
THAT NANAMI-SAN EXISTS IS PROOF THAT HUMANS ARE STRONG.
THEY DON'T DISAPPEAR LIKE BUBBLES DO.
YOU'RE IN MORE DANGER OF DISAPPEARING NOW.
SO COME WITH ME.
TOMOE!

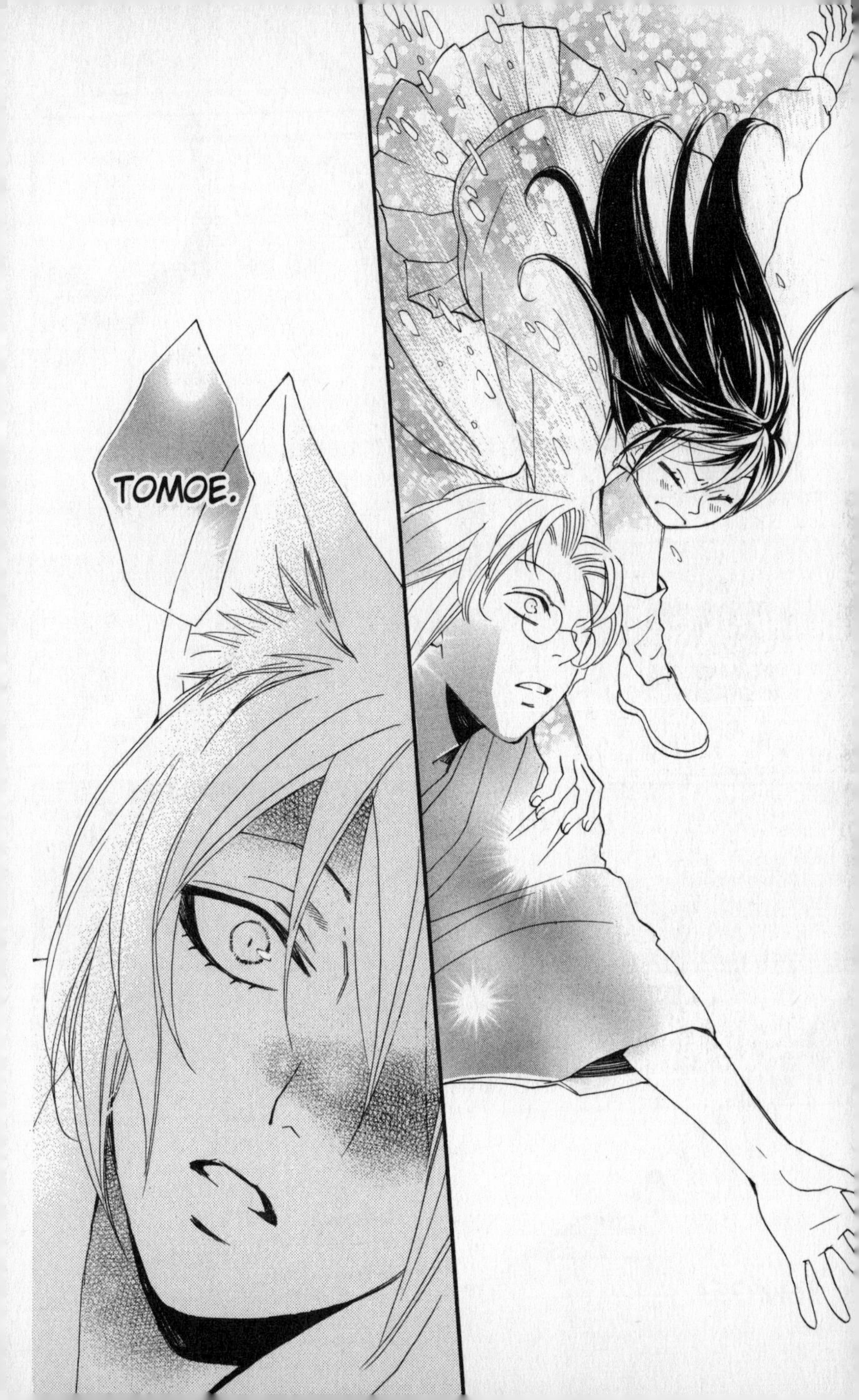
TOMOE.

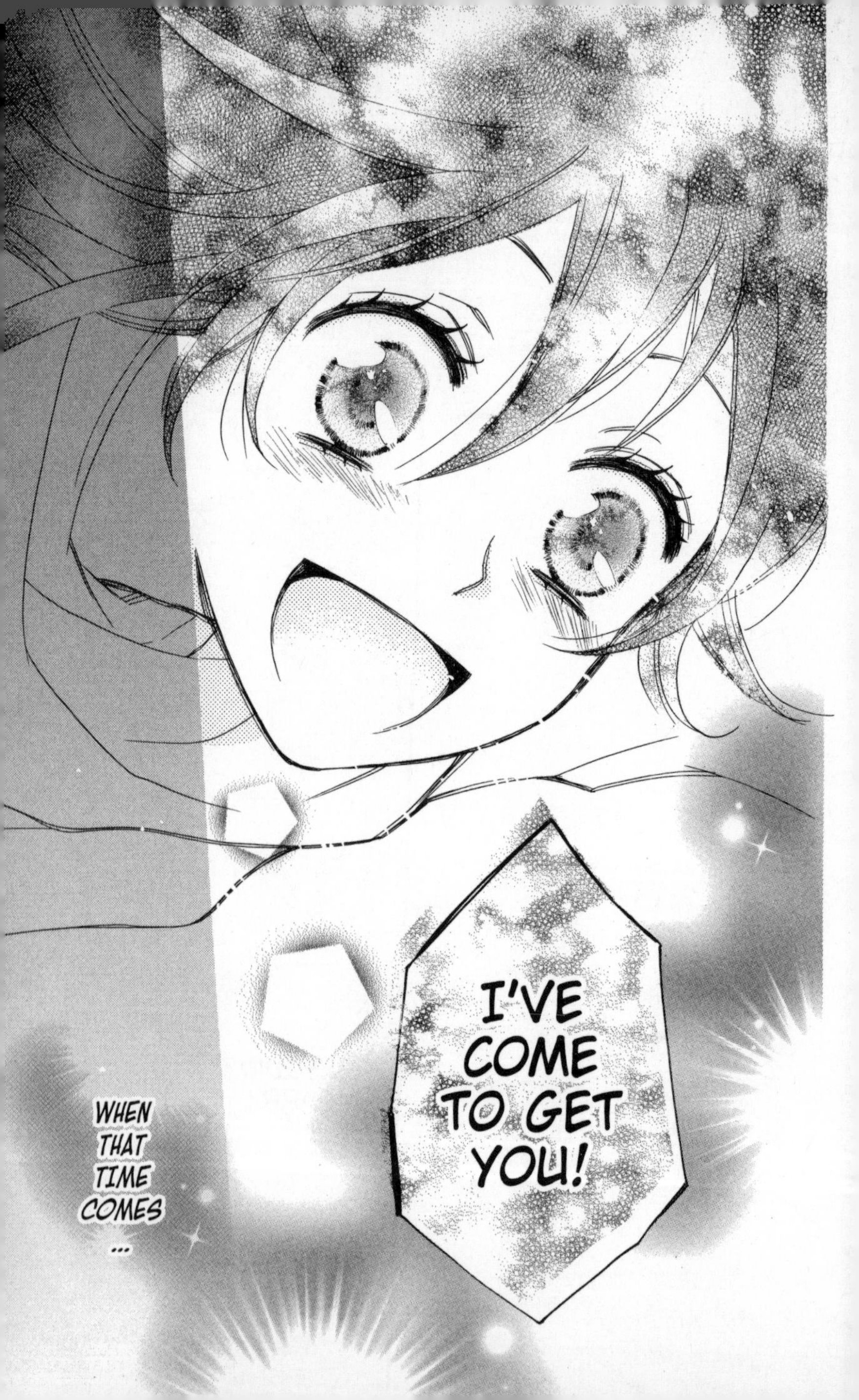
I'VE COME TO GET YOU!
WHEN THAT TIME COMES...

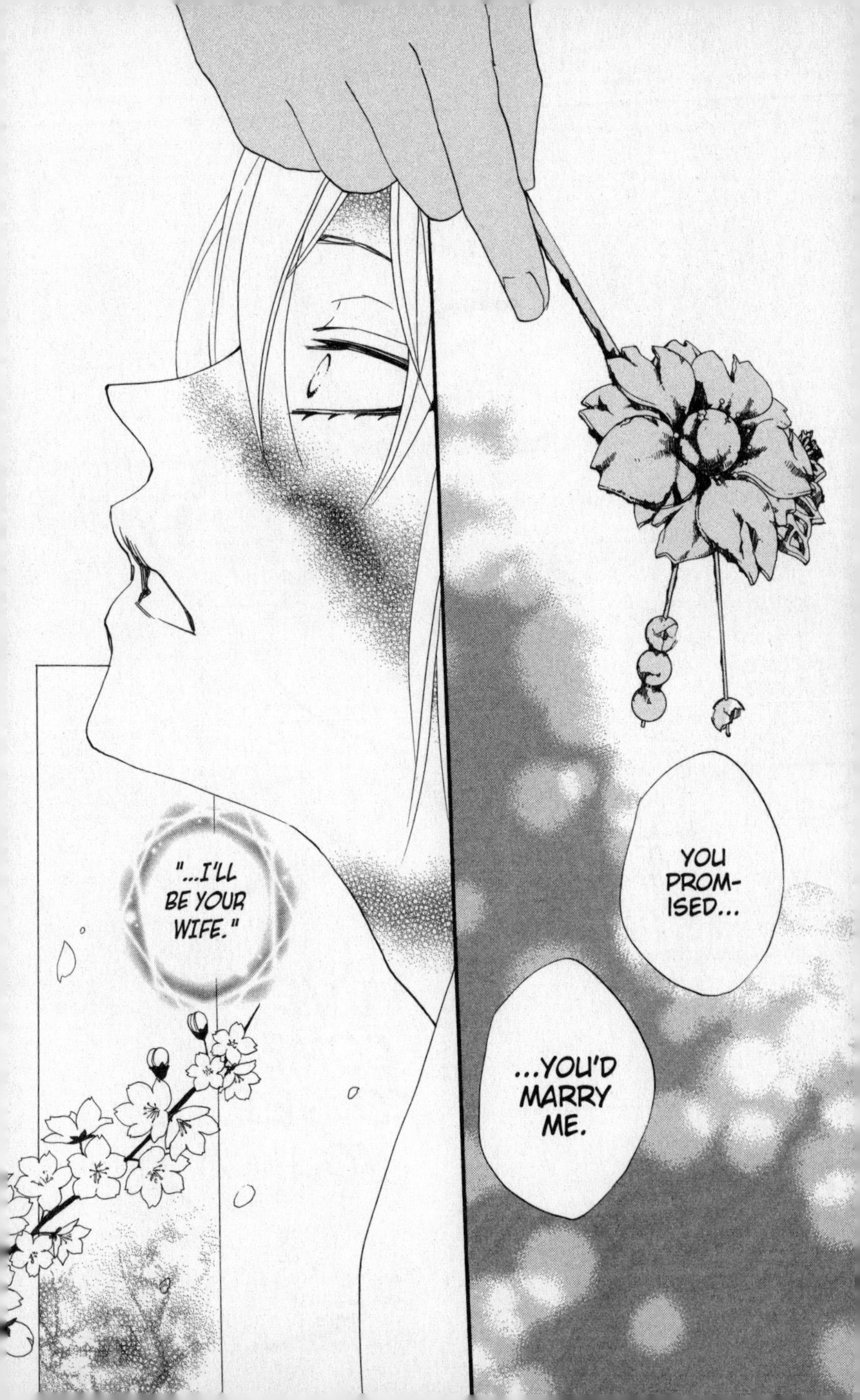
YOU PROM-ISED...
...YOU'D MARRY ME.
"...I'LL BE YOUR WIFE."

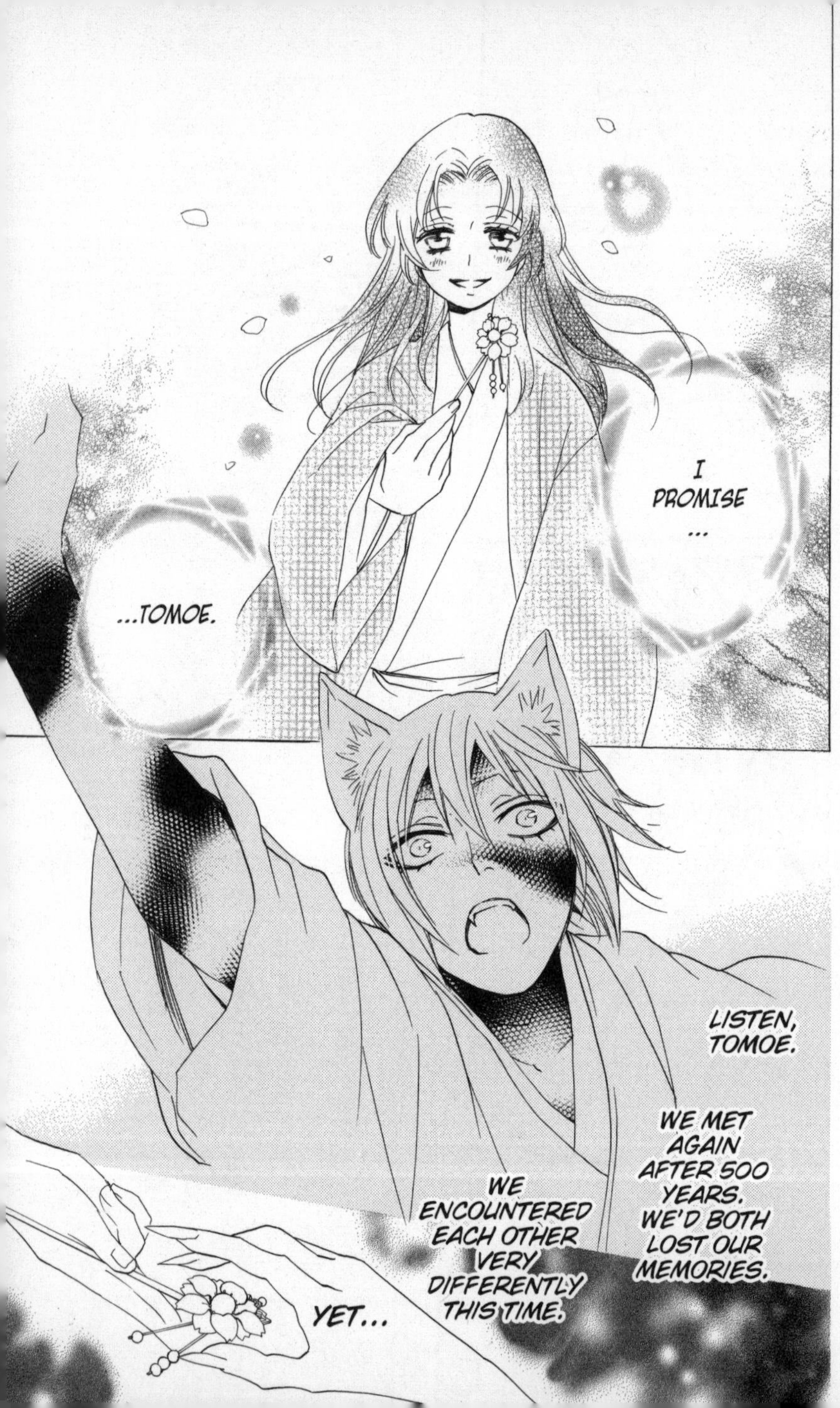
I PROMISE...
...TOMOE.
LISTEN, TOMOE.
WE MET AGAIN AFTER 500 YEARS. WE'D BOTH LOST OUR MEMORIES.
WE ENCOUNTERED EACH OTHER VERY DIFFERENTLY THIS TIME.
YET...

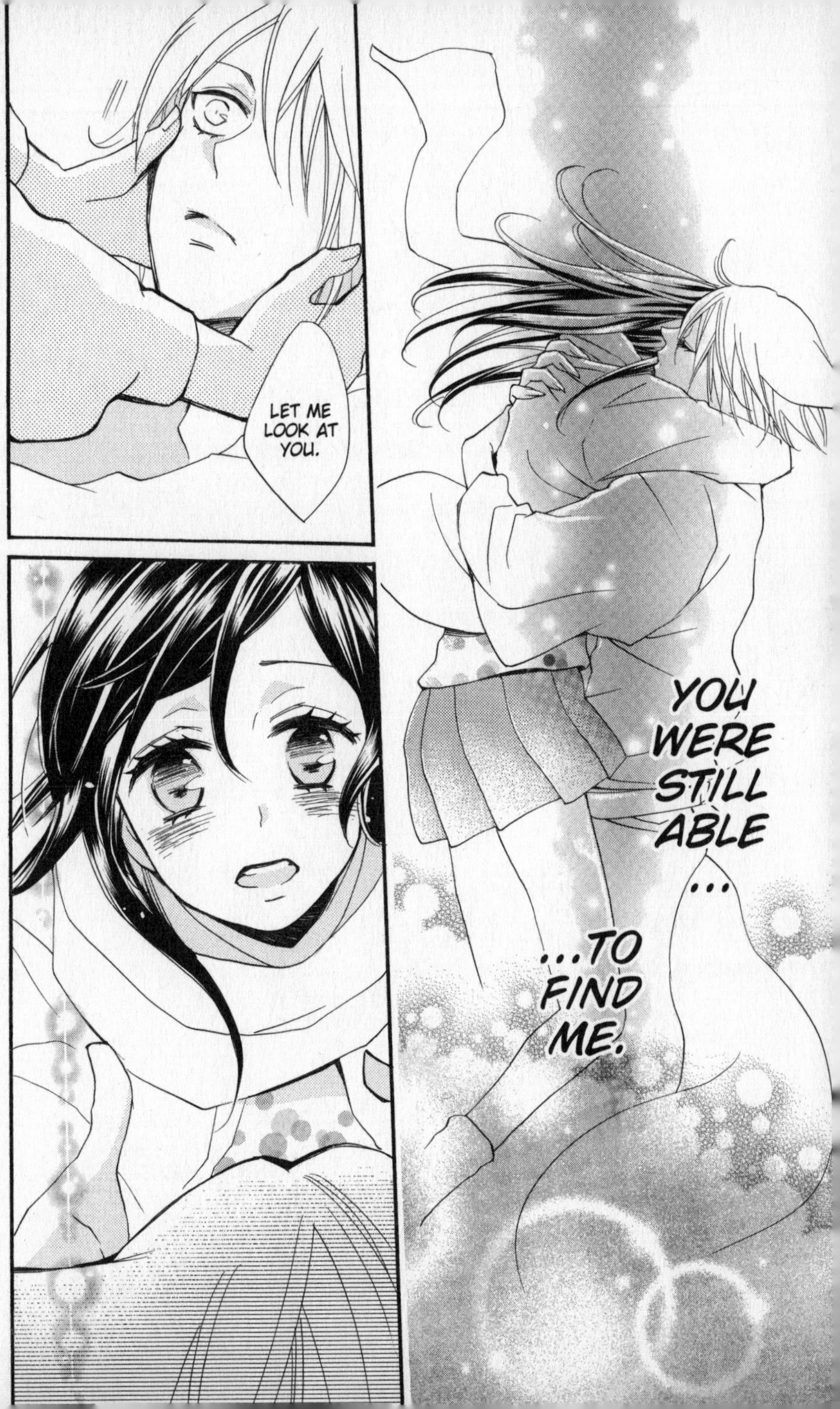
YOU WERE STILL ABLE...
...TO FIND ME.
LET ME LOOK AT YOU.

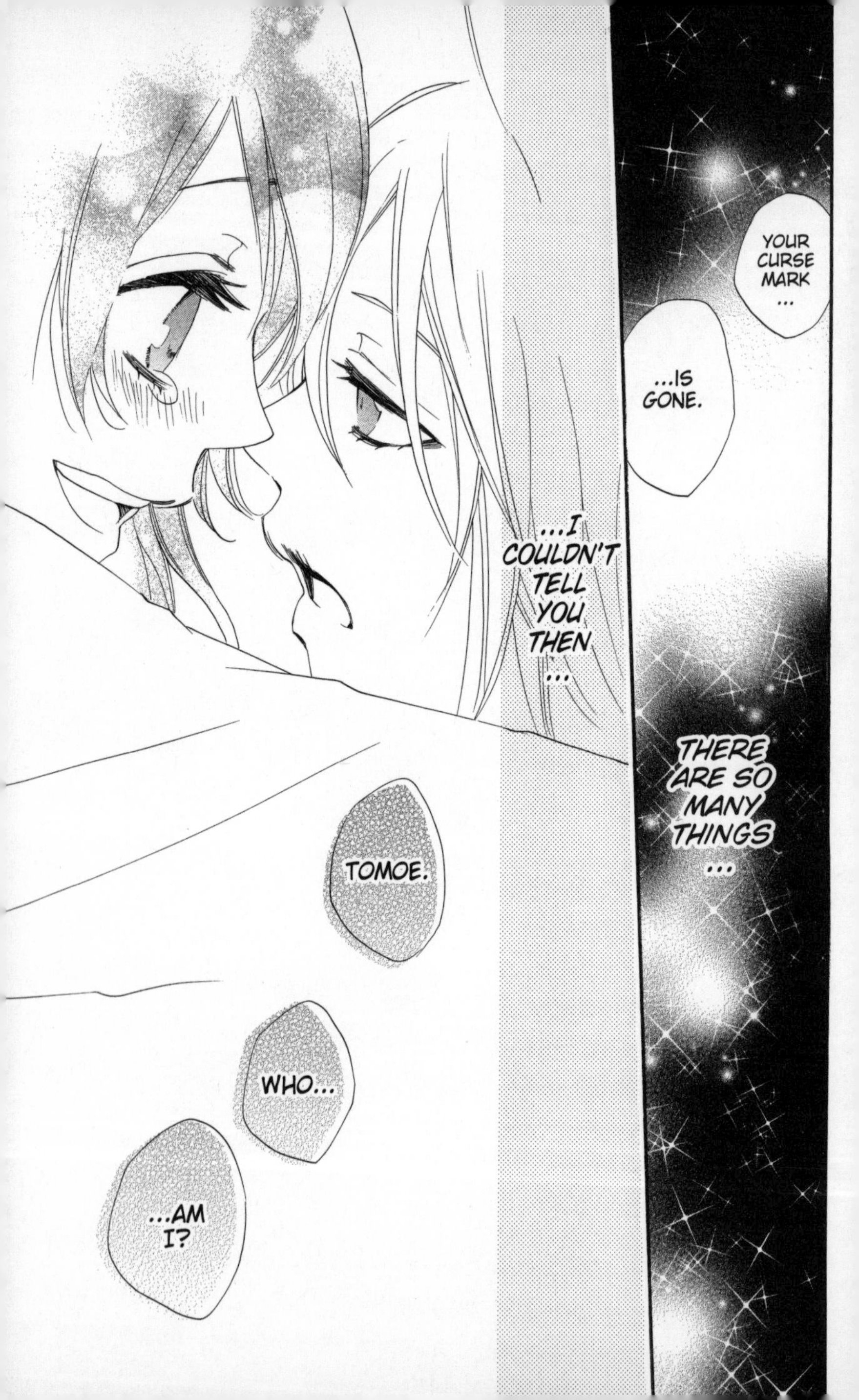
YOUR CURSE MARK ...
...IS GONE.
THERE ARE SO MANY THINGS ...
...I COULDN'T TELL YOU THEN ...
TOMOE.
WHO...
...AM I?

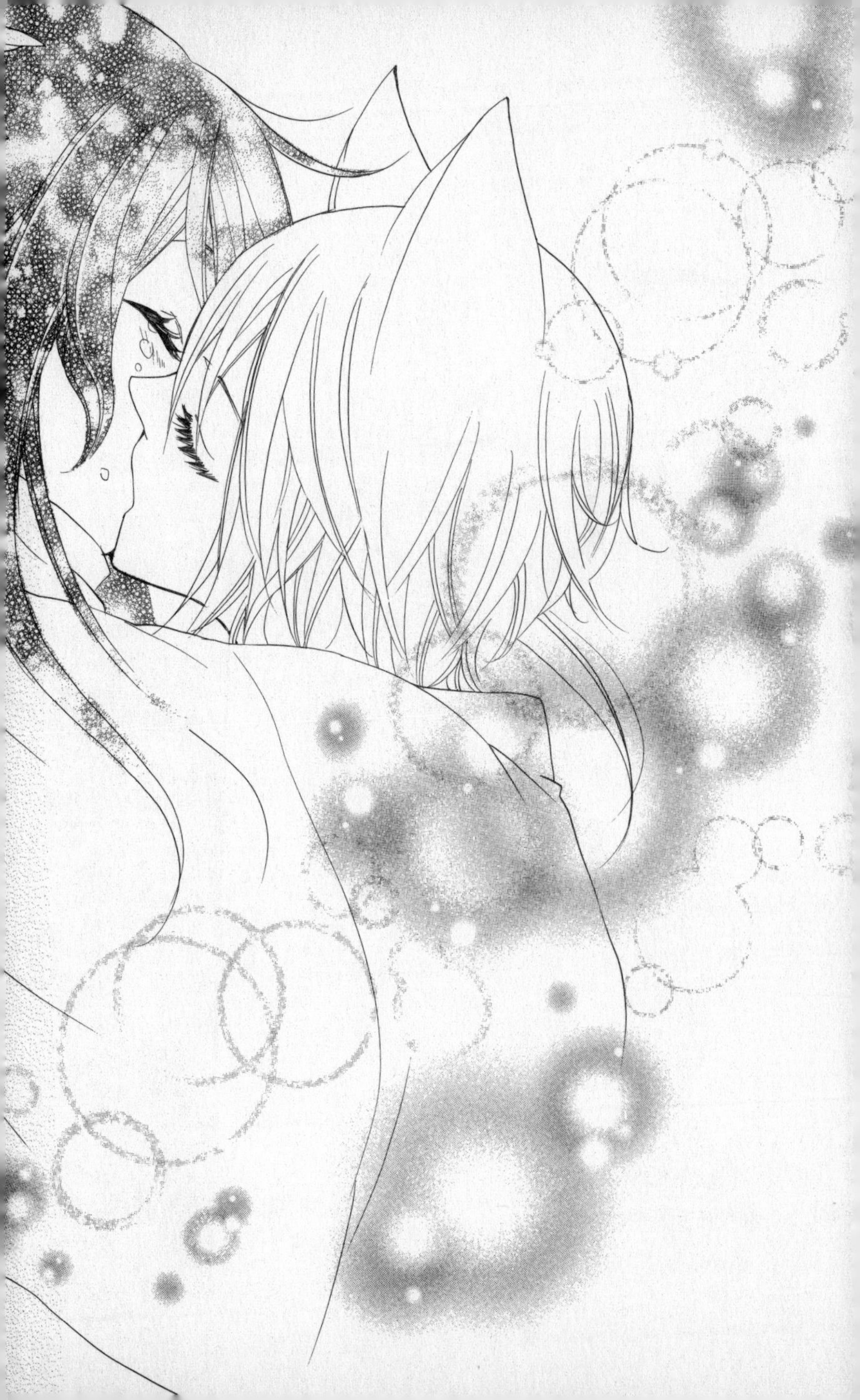

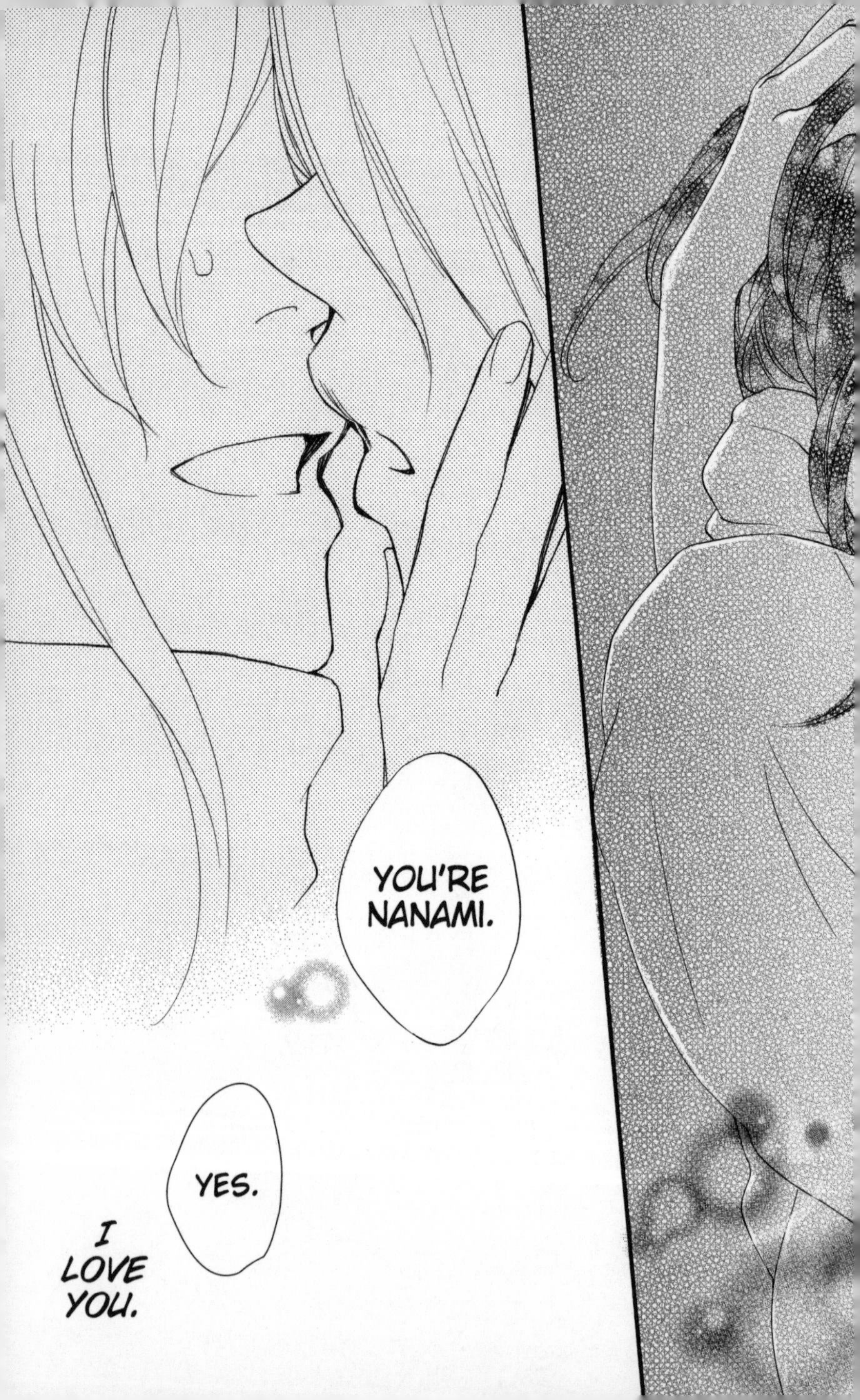
YOU'RE NANAMI.
YES.
I LOVE YOU.

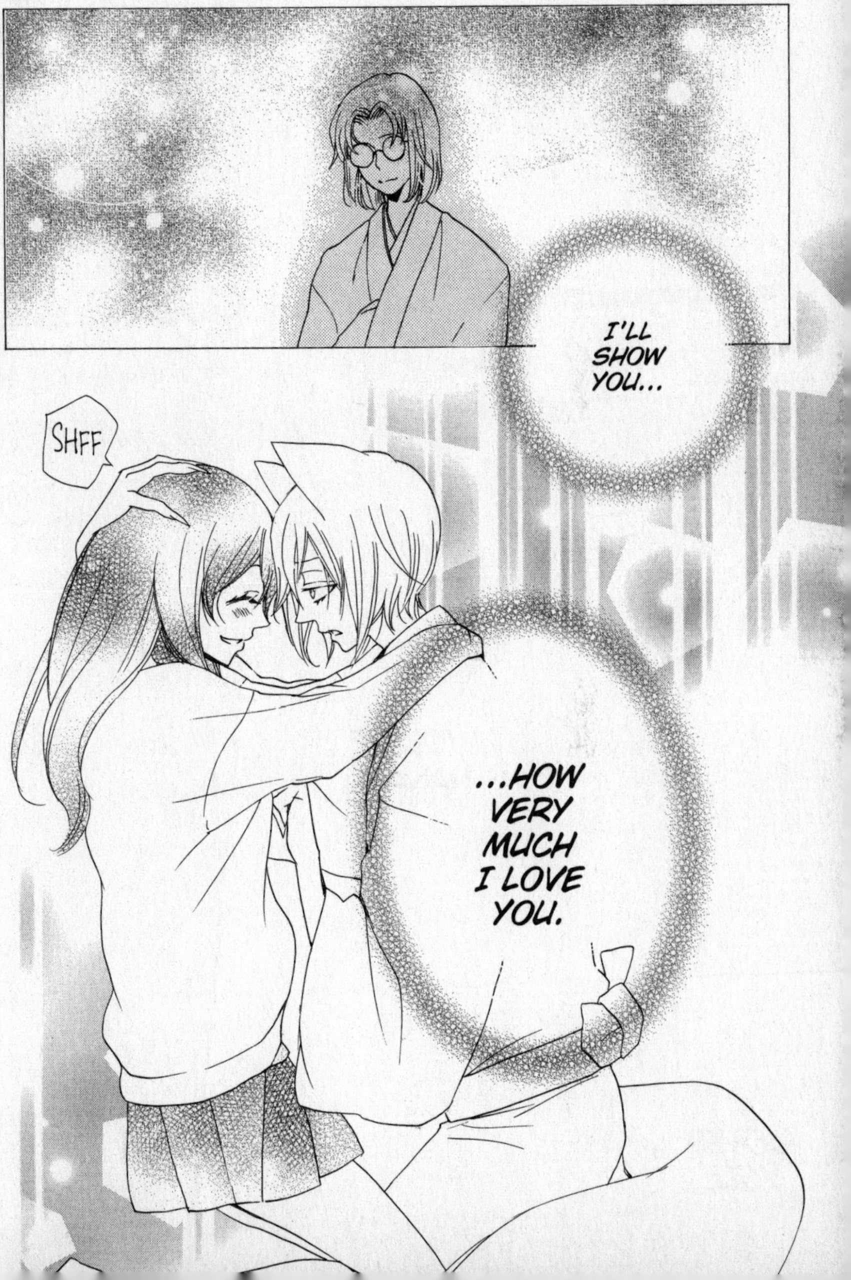
I'LL SHOW YOU...
SHFF
...HOW VERY MUCH I LOVE YOU.

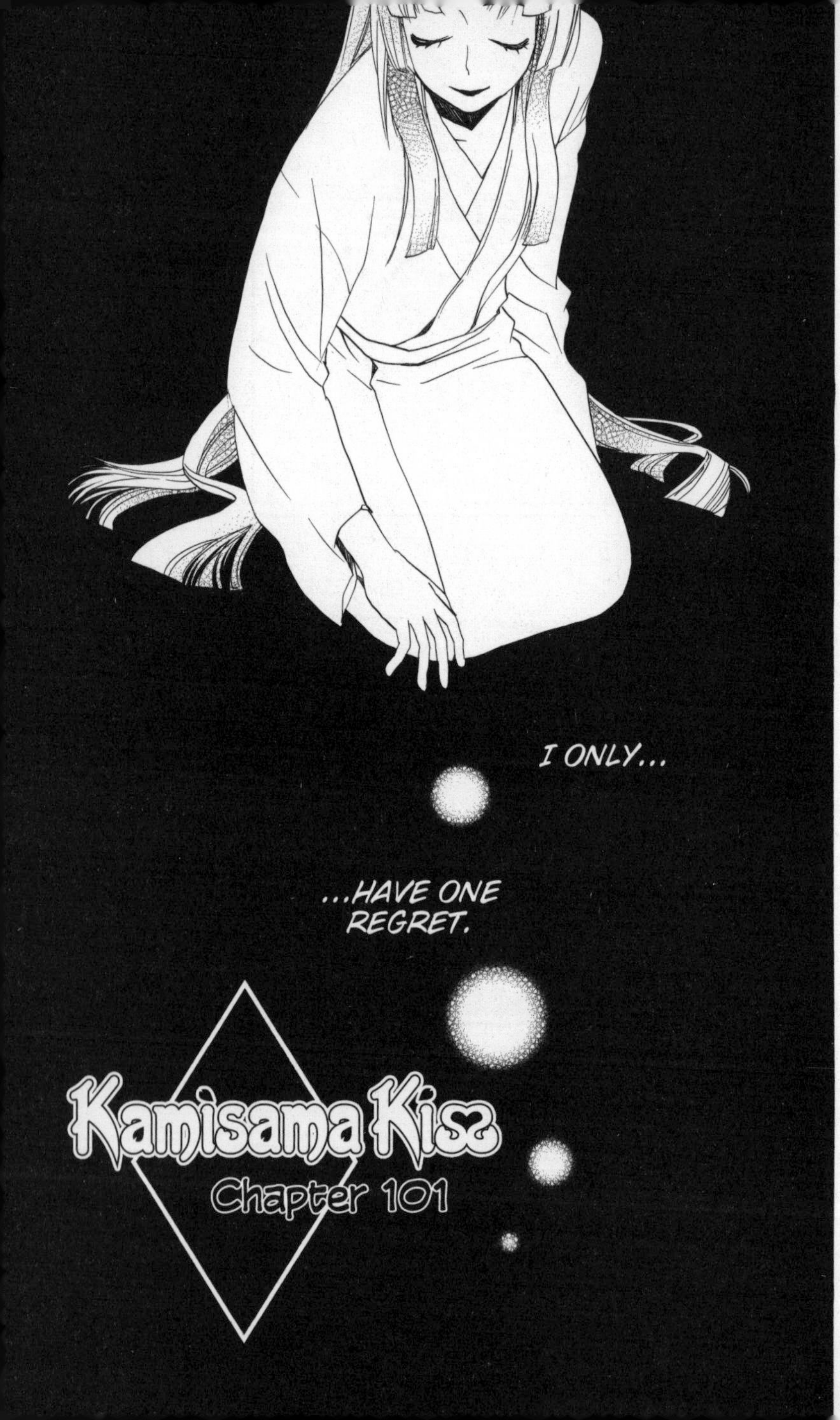
I ONLY...
...HAVE ONE REGRET.
Kamisama Kiss
Chapter 101

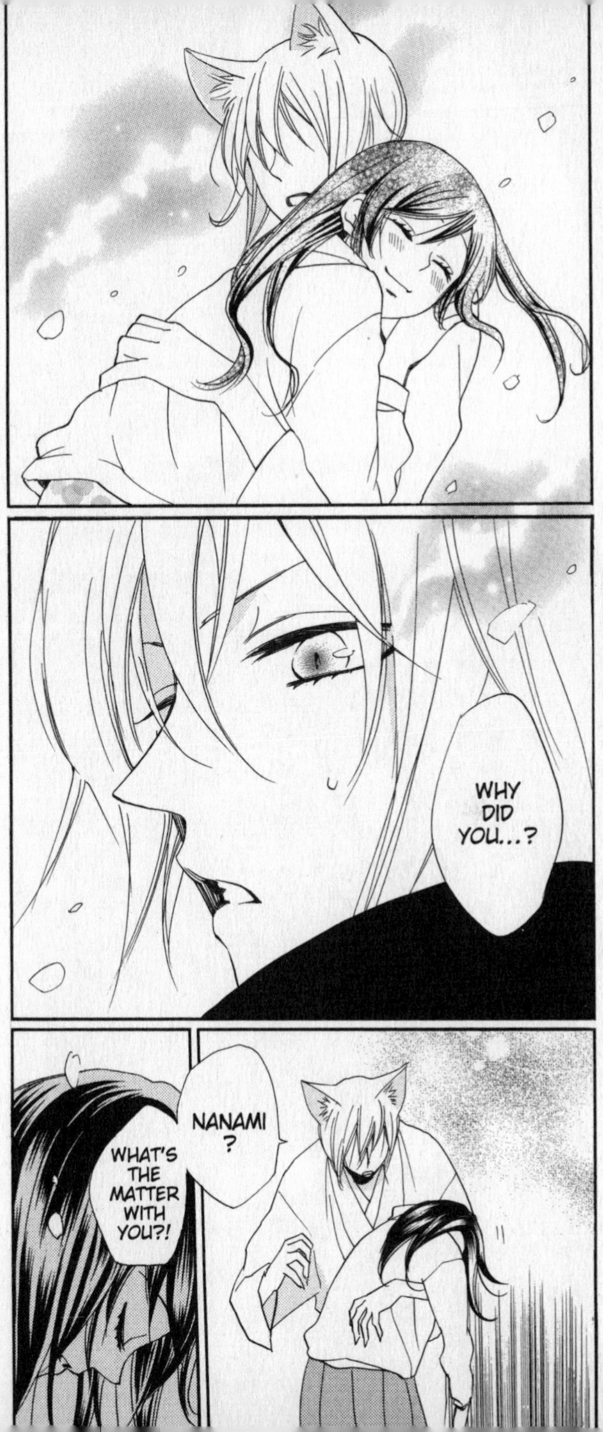
WHY DID YOU...?
NANAMI?
WHAT'S THE MATTER WITH YOU?!

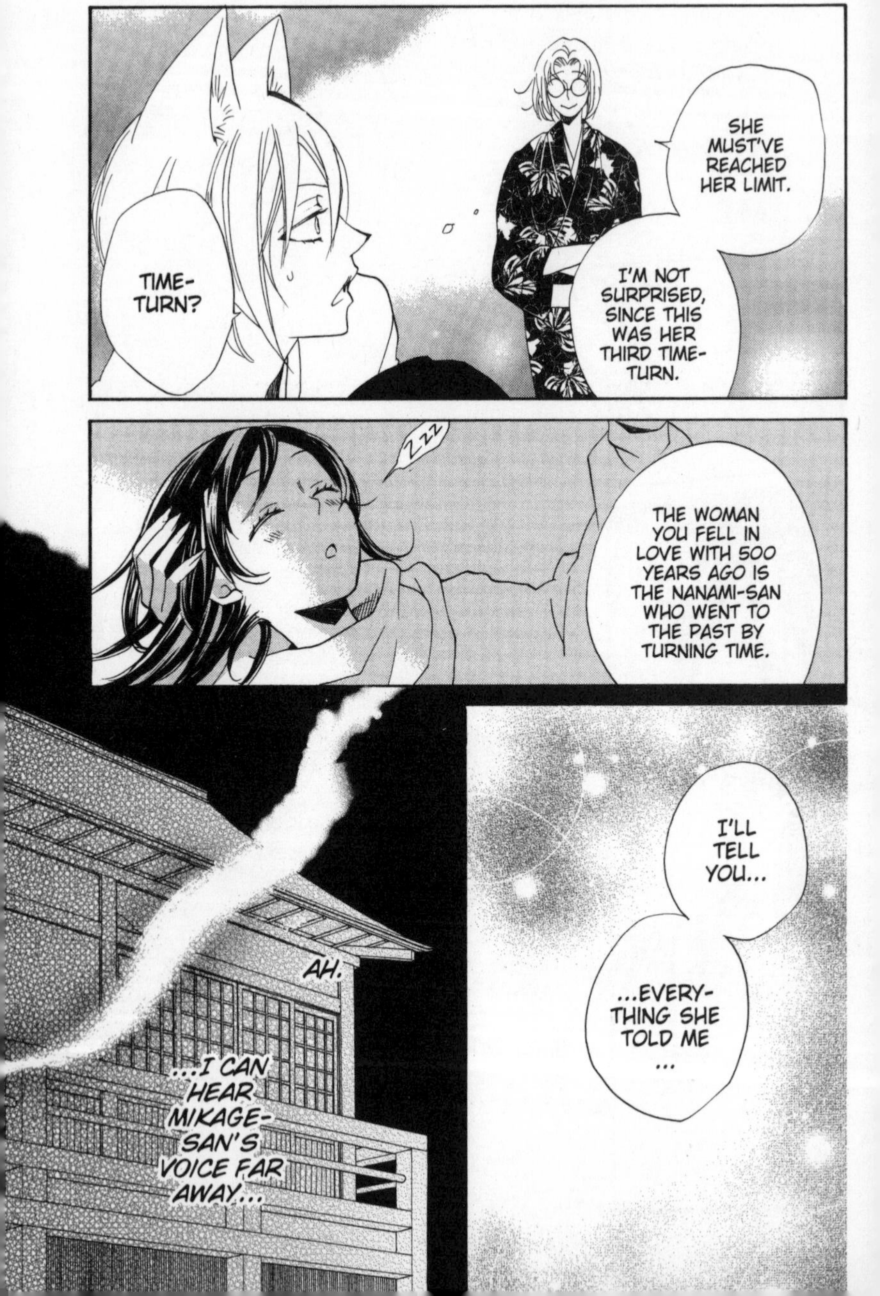
SHE MUST'VE REACHED HER LIMIT.
I'M NOT SURPRISED, SINCE THIS WAS HER THIRD TIME-TURN.
TIME-TURN?
ZZZ
THE WOMAN YOU FELL IN LOVE WITH 500 YEARS AGO IS THE NANAMI-SAN WHO WENT TO THE PAST BY TURNING TIME.
I'LL TELL YOU...
...EVERY-THING SHE TOLD ME ...
AH.
...I CAN HEAR MIKAGE-SAN'S VOICE FAR AWAY...

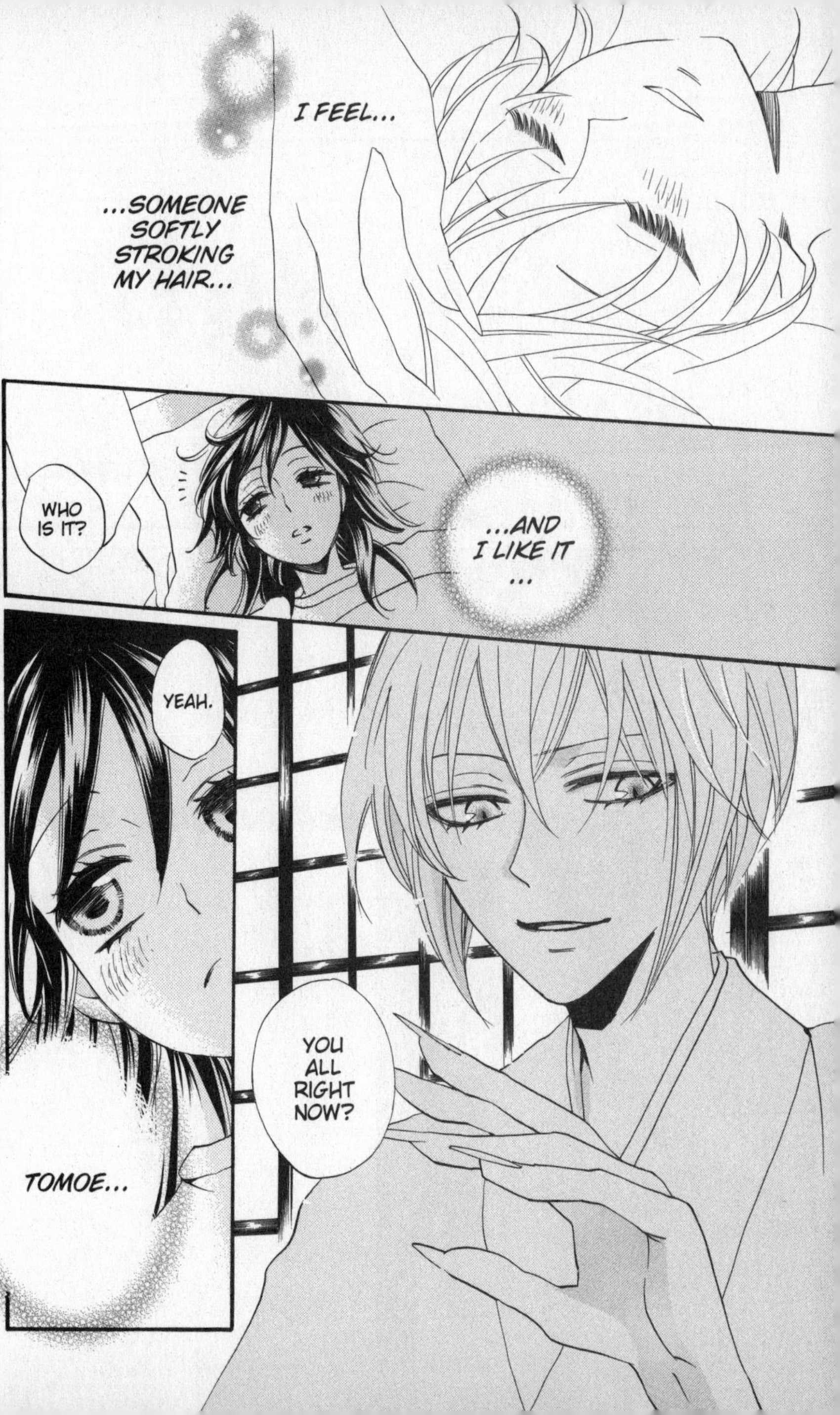
I FEEL...
...SOMEONE SOFTLY STROKING MY HAIR...
...AND I LIKE IT ...
WHO IS IT?
YEAH.
YOU ALL RIGHT NOW?
TOMOE...

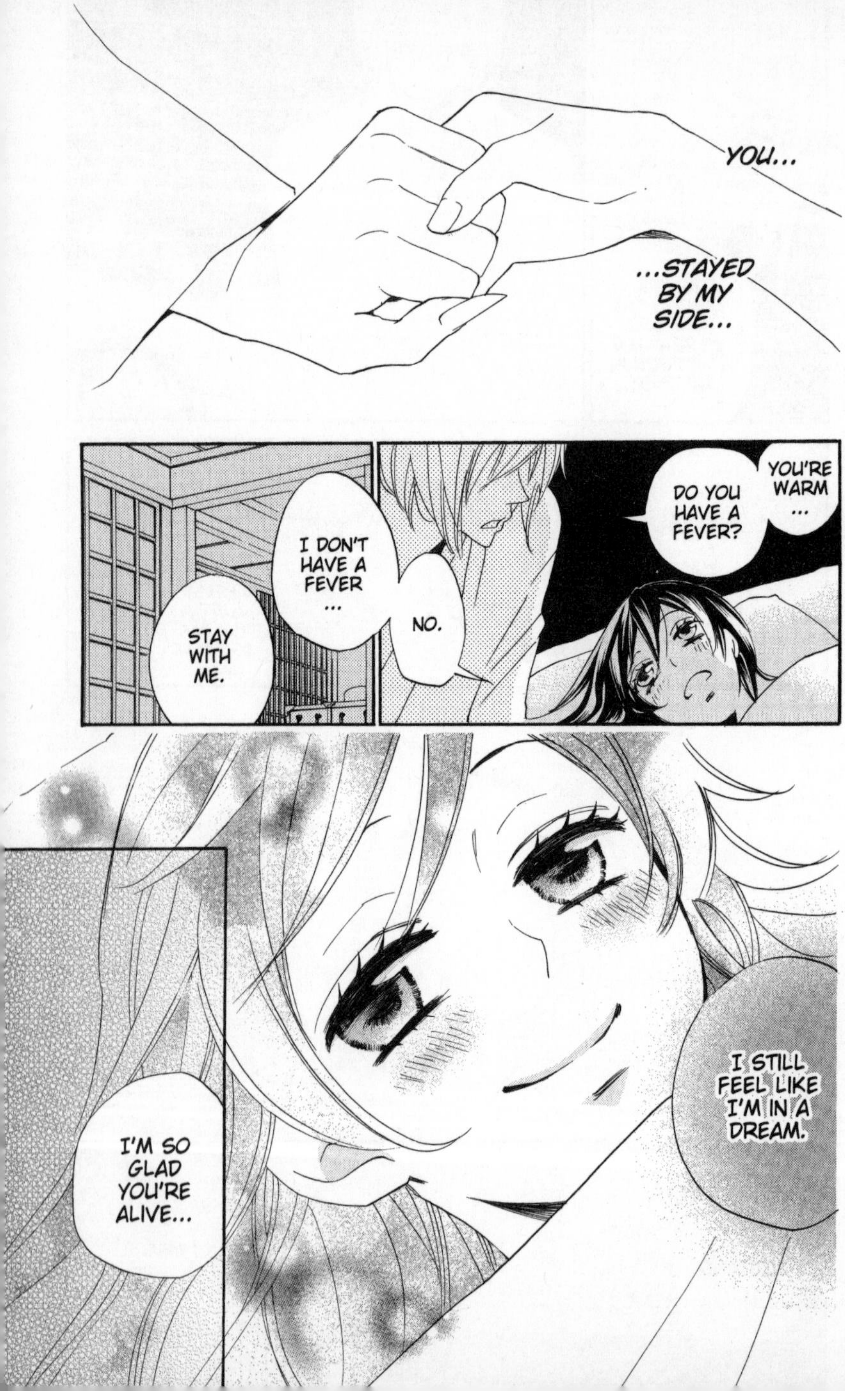
YOU...
...STAYED BY MY SIDE...
YOU'RE WARM ...
DO YOU HAVE A FEVER?
NO.
I DON'T HAVE A FEVER ...
STAY WITH ME.
I STILL FEEL LIKE I'M IN A DREAM.
I'M SO GLAD YOU'RE ALIVE...

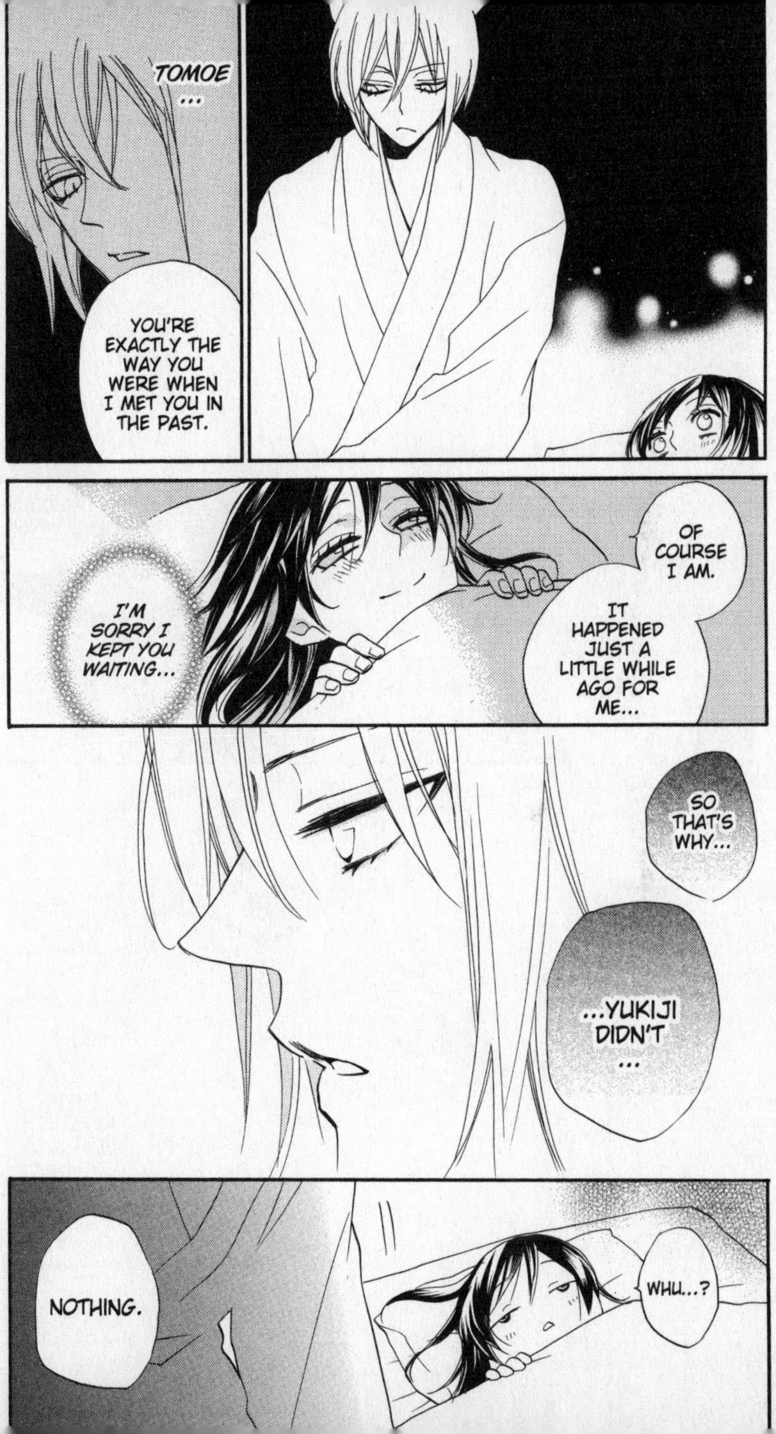
TOMOE ...
YOU'RE EXACTLY THE WAY YOU WERE WHEN I MET YOU IN THE PAST.
OF COURSE I AM.
IT HAPPENED JUST A LITTLE WHILE AGO FOR ME...
I'M SORRY I KEPT YOU WAITING...
SO THAT'S WHY...
...YUKIJI DIDN'T ...
WHU...?
NOTHING.

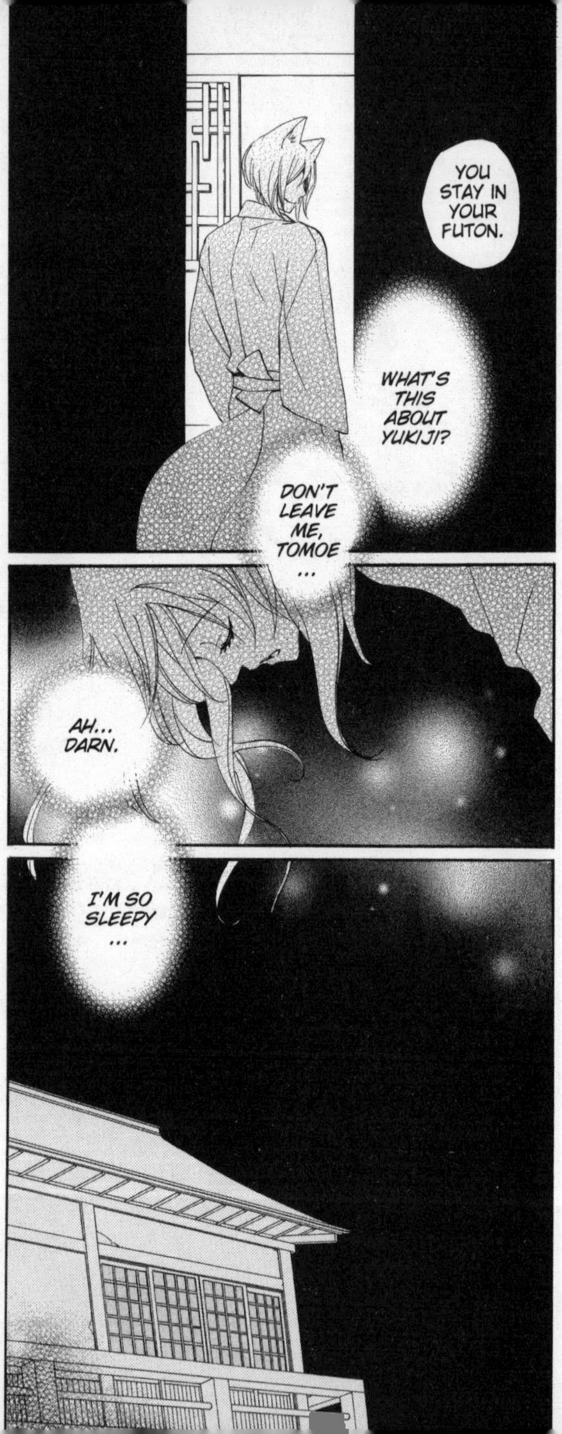
YOU STAY IN YOUR FUTON.
WHAT'S THIS ABOUT YUKIJI?
DON'T LEAVE ME, TOMOE ...
AH... DARN.
I'M SO SLEEPY ...

Thanks for reading this far!

I hope we'll be able to meet again in volume 18, the next volume!

If you have any comments and thoughts about volume 16, do let me hear you!

The address is...

Julietta Suzuki
c/o Shojo Beat
VIZ Media, LLC
P.O. Box 77010
San Francisco
CA 94107

I'll be waiting.

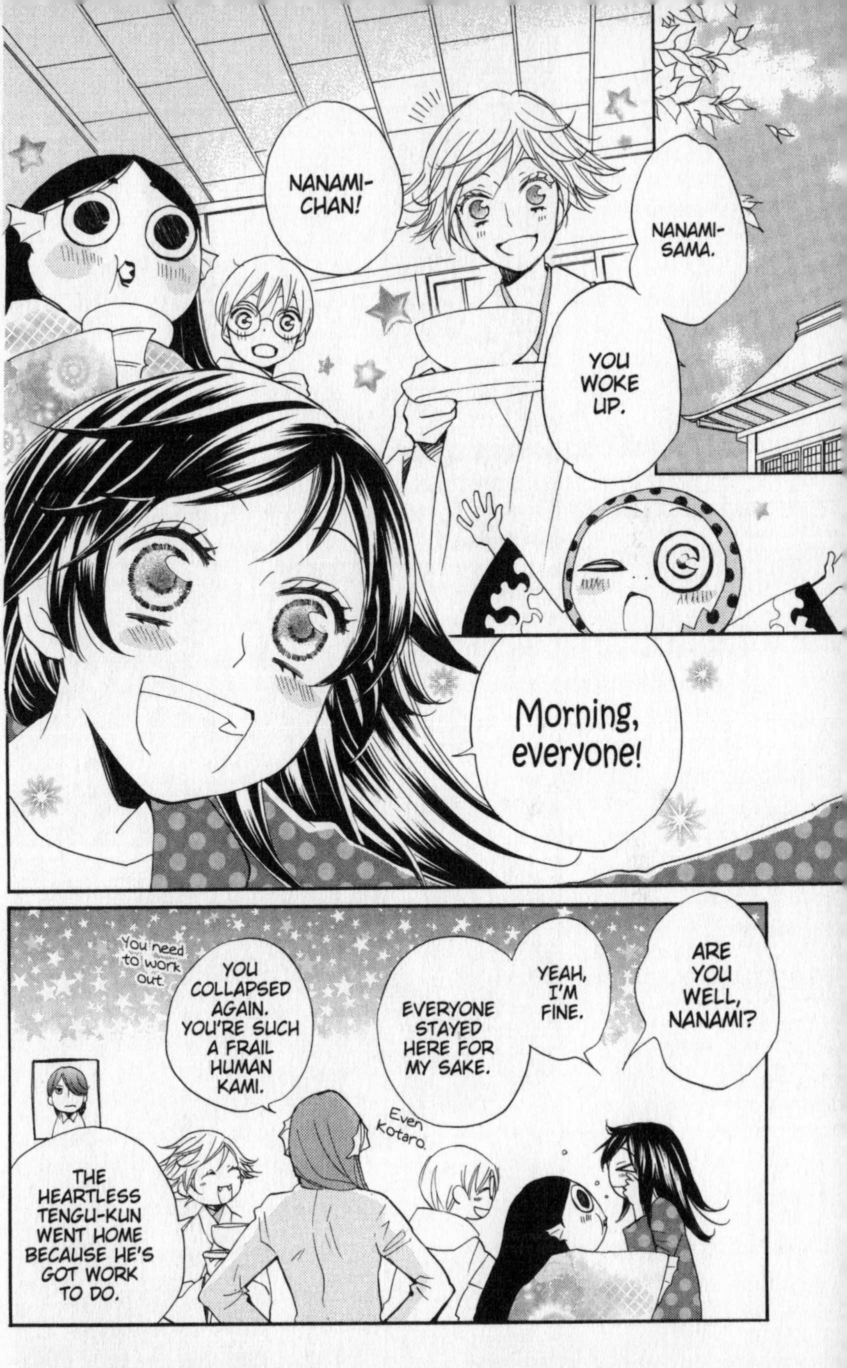
NANAMI-SAMA.
YOU WOKE UP.
NANAMI-CHAN!
Morning, everyone!
ARE YOU WELL, NANAMI?
YEAH, I'M FINE.
EVERYONE STAYED HERE FOR MY SAKE.
YOU COLLAPSED AGAIN. YOU'RE SUCH A FRAIL HUMAN KAMI.
You need to work out.
Even Kotaro.
THE HEARTLESS TENGU-KUN WENT HOME BECAUSE HE'S GOT WORK TO DO.

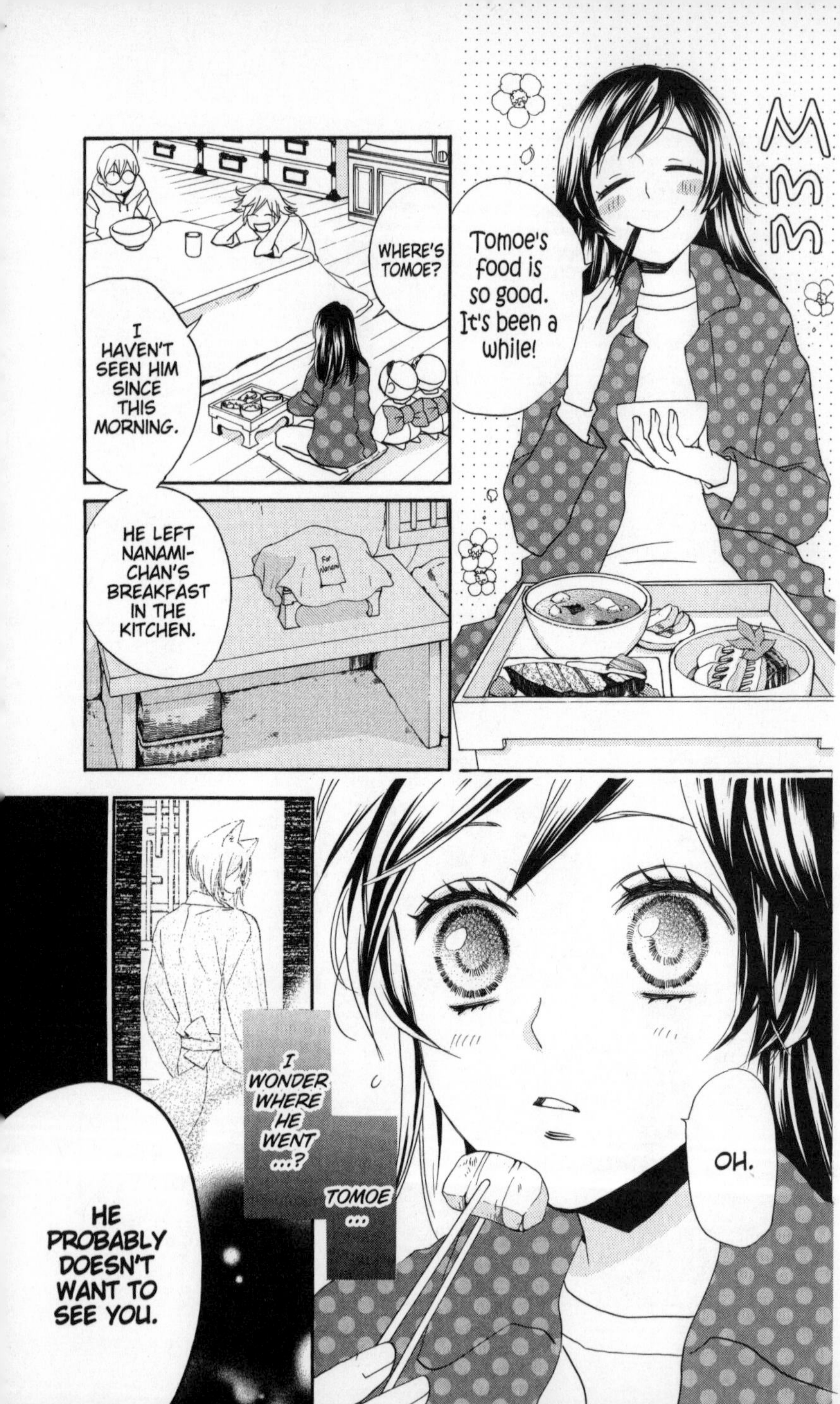
MMM
Tomoe's food is so good. It's been a while!
WHERE'S TOMOE?
I HAVEN'T SEEN HIM SINCE THIS MORNING.
HE LEFT NANAMI-CHAN'S BREAKFAST IN THE KITCHEN.
OH.
I WONDER WHERE HE WENT ...?
TOMOE ...
HE PROBABLY DOESN'T WANT TO SEE YOU.

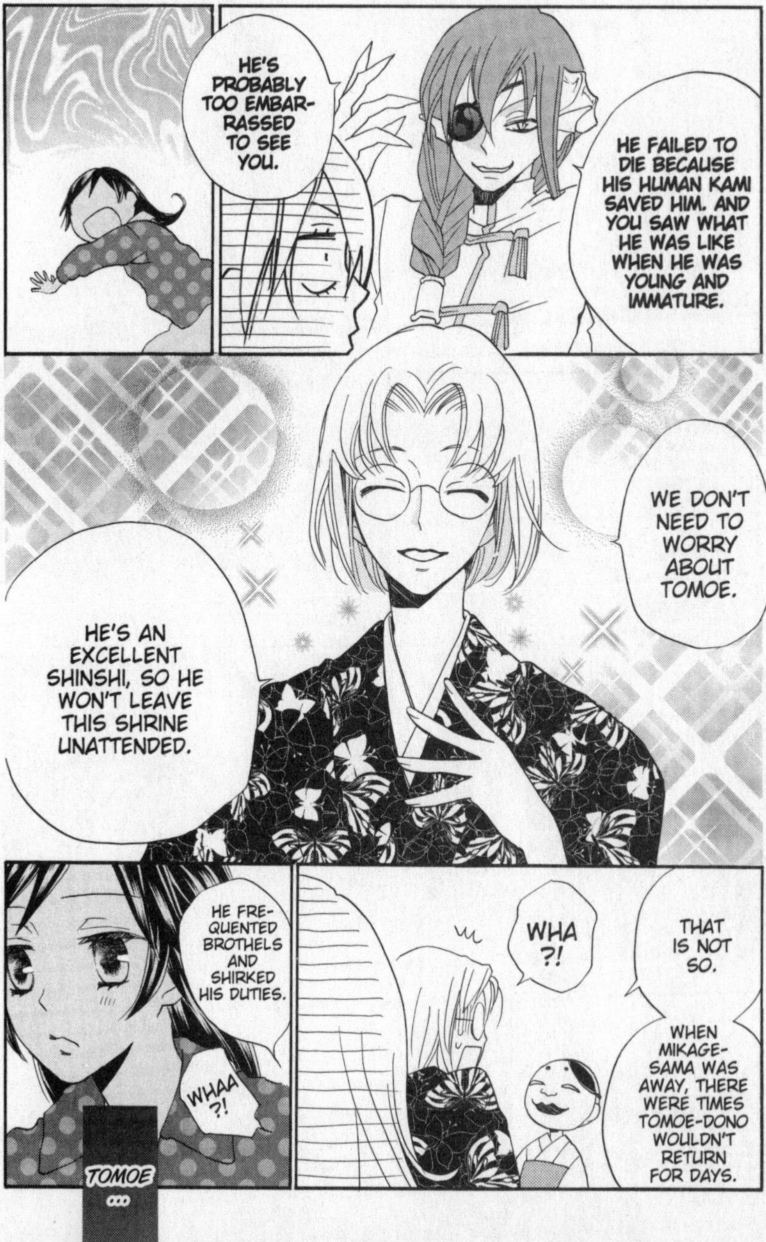
HE FAILED TO DIE BECAUSE HIS HUMAN KAMI SAVED HIM. AND YOU SAW WHAT HE WAS LIKE WHEN HE WAS YOUNG AND IMMATURE.
HE'S PROBABLY TOO EMBARRASSED TO SEE YOU.
WE DON'T NEED TO WORRY ABOUT TOMOE.
HE'S AN EXCELLENT SHINSHI, SO HE WON'T LEAVE THIS SHRINE UNATTENDED.
THAT IS NOT SO.
WHEN MIKAGE-SAMA WAS AWAY, THERE WERE TIMES TOMOE-DONO WOULDN'T RETURN FOR DAYS.
WHA ?!
HE FREQUENTED BROTHELS AND SHIRKED HIS DUTIES.
WHAA ?!
TOMOE ...

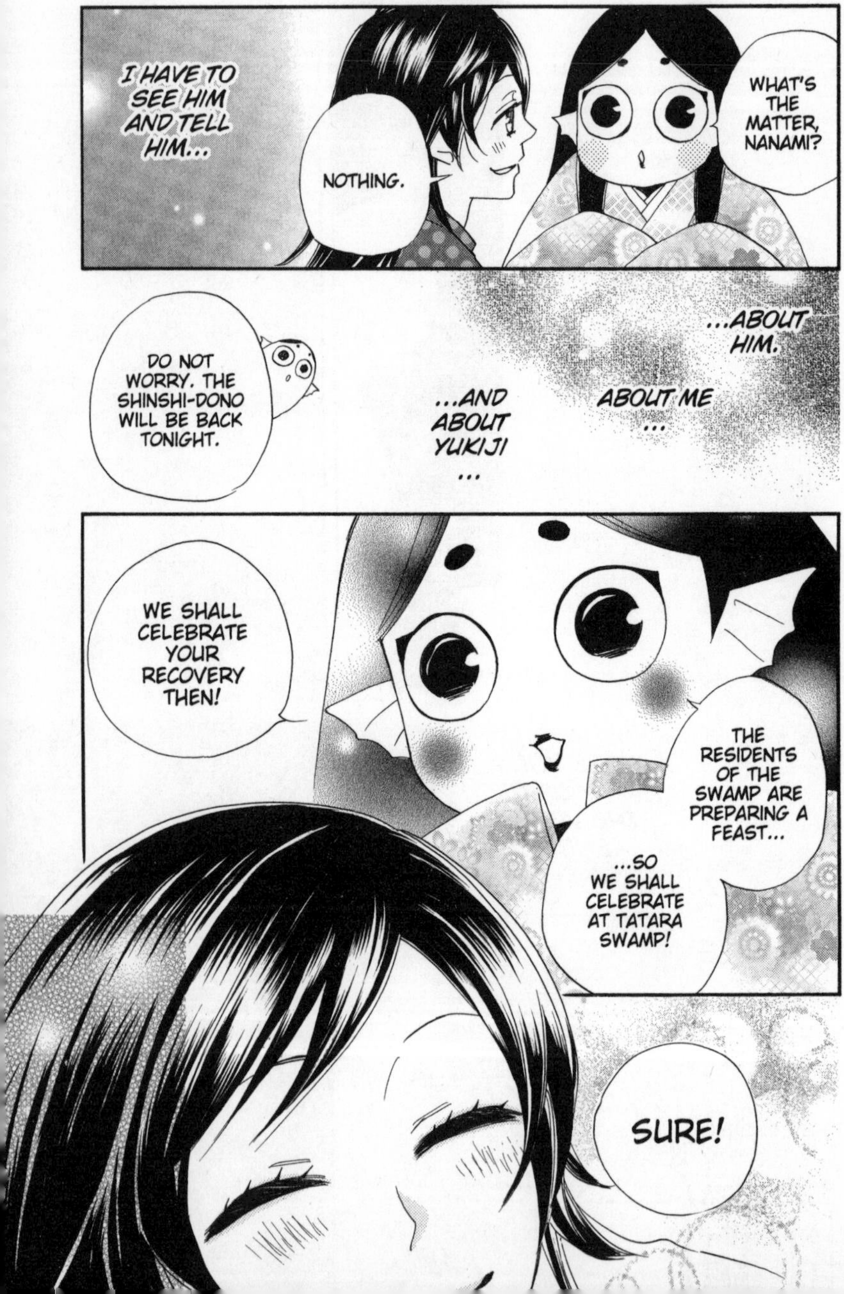
WHAT'S THE MATTER, NANAMI?
NOTHING.
I HAVE TO SEE HIM AND TELL HIM...
...ABOUT HIM.
ABOUT ME ...
...AND ABOUT YUKIJI ...
DO NOT WORRY. THE SHINSHI-DONO WILL BE BACK TONIGHT.
WE SHALL CELEBRATE YOUR RECOVERY THEN!
THE RESIDENTS OF THE SWAMP ARE PREPARING A FEAST...
...SO WE SHALL CELEBRATE AT TATARA SWAMP!
SURE!

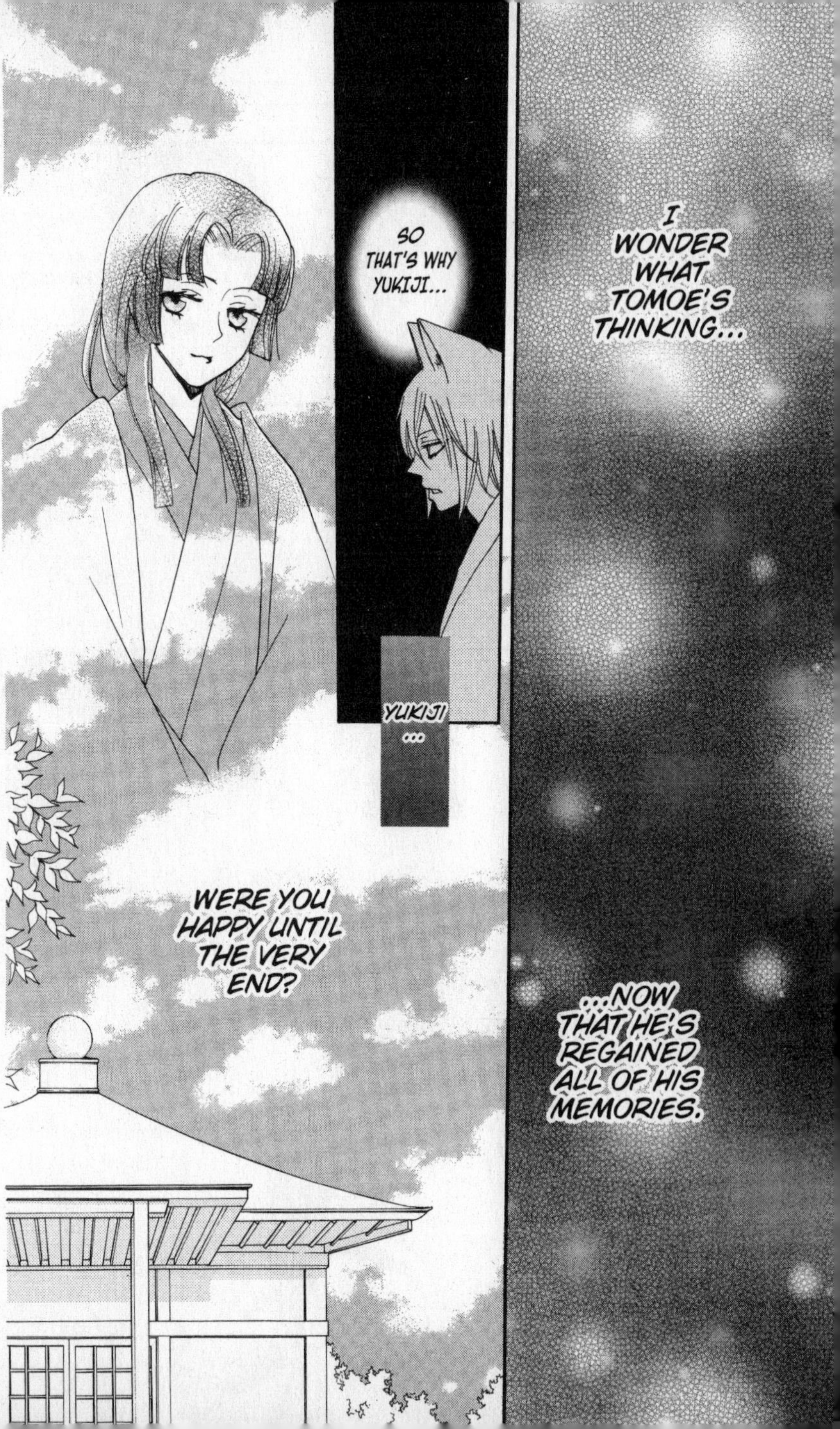
I WONDER WHAT TOMOE'S THINKING...
...NOW THAT HE'S REGAINED ALL OF HIS MEMORIES.
SO THAT'S WHY YUKIJI...
YUKIJI...
WERE YOU HAPPY UNTIL THE VERY END?

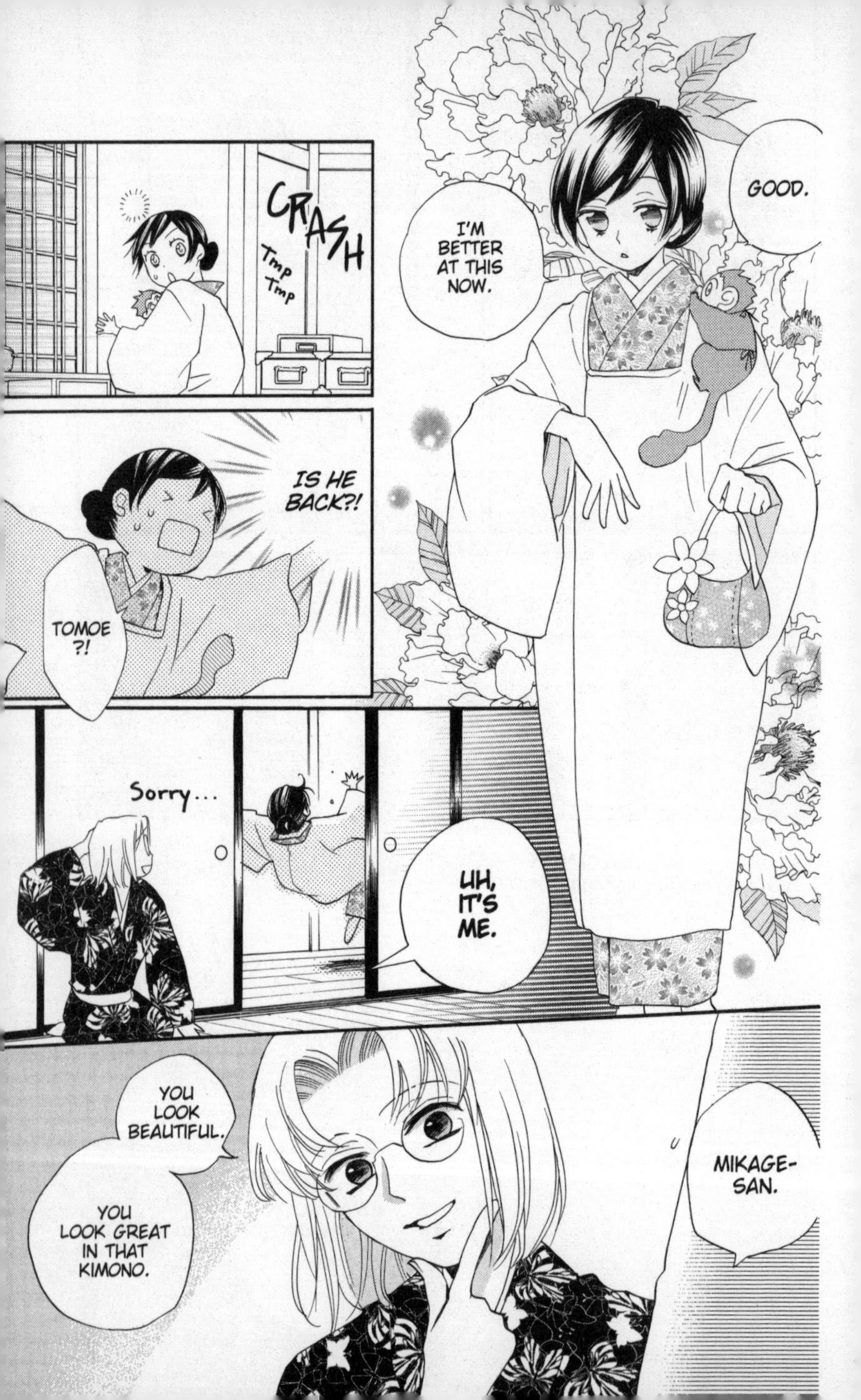
CRASH
Tmp Tmp
IS HE BACK?!
TOMOE ?!
Sorry...
UH, IT'S ME.
GOOD.
I'M BETTER AT THIS NOW.
MIKAGE-SAN.
YOU LOOK BEAUTIFUL.
YOU LOOK GREAT IN THAT KIMONO.

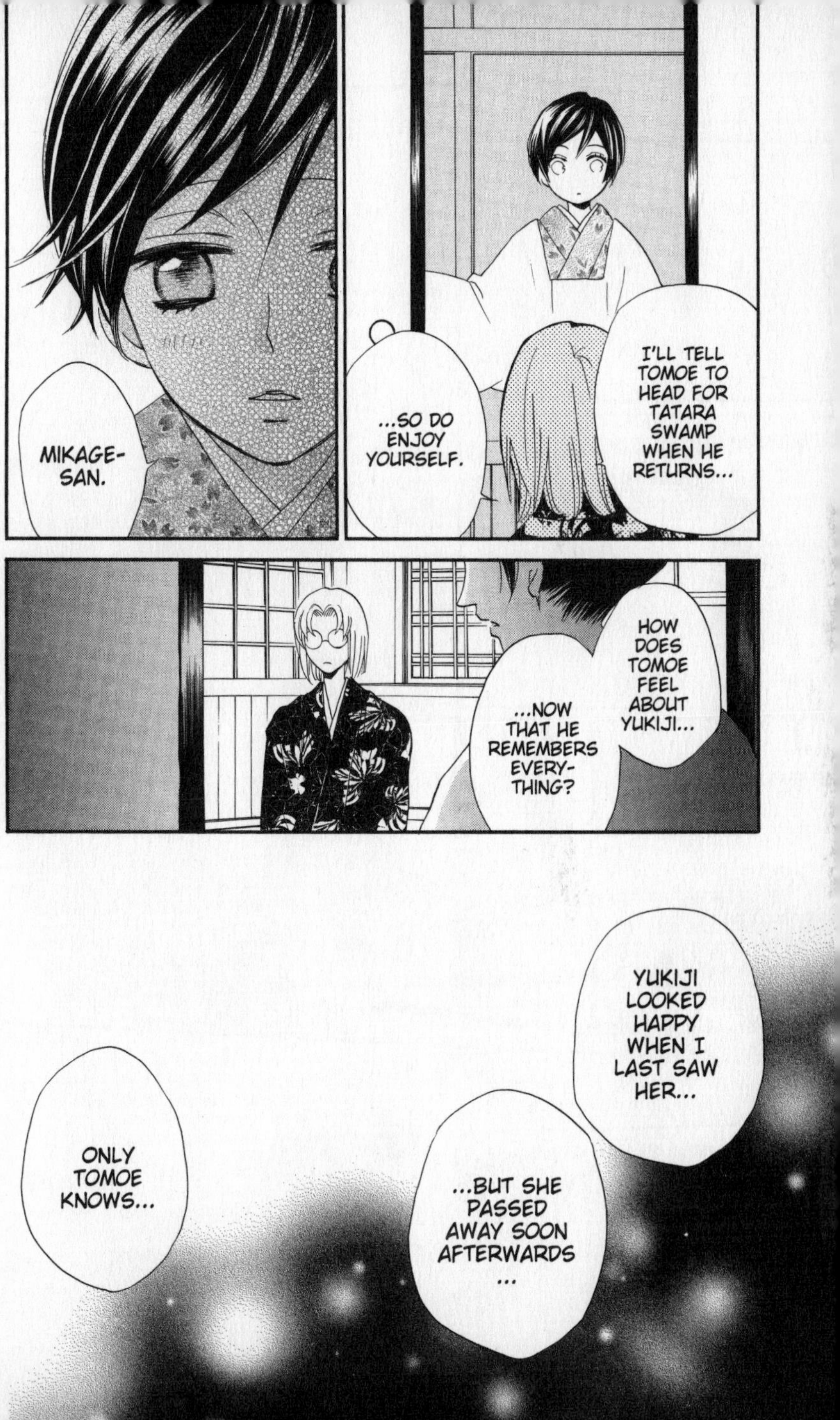
I'LL TELL TOMOE TO HEAD FOR TATARA SWAMP WHEN HE RETURNS...
...SO DO ENJOY YOURSELF.
MIKAGE-SAN.
HOW DOES TOMOE FEEL ABOUT YUKIJI...
...NOW THAT HE REMEMBERS EVERYTHING?
YUKIJI LOOKED HAPPY WHEN I LAST SAW HER...
...BUT SHE PASSED AWAY SOON AFTERWARDS...
ONLY TOMOE KNOWS...

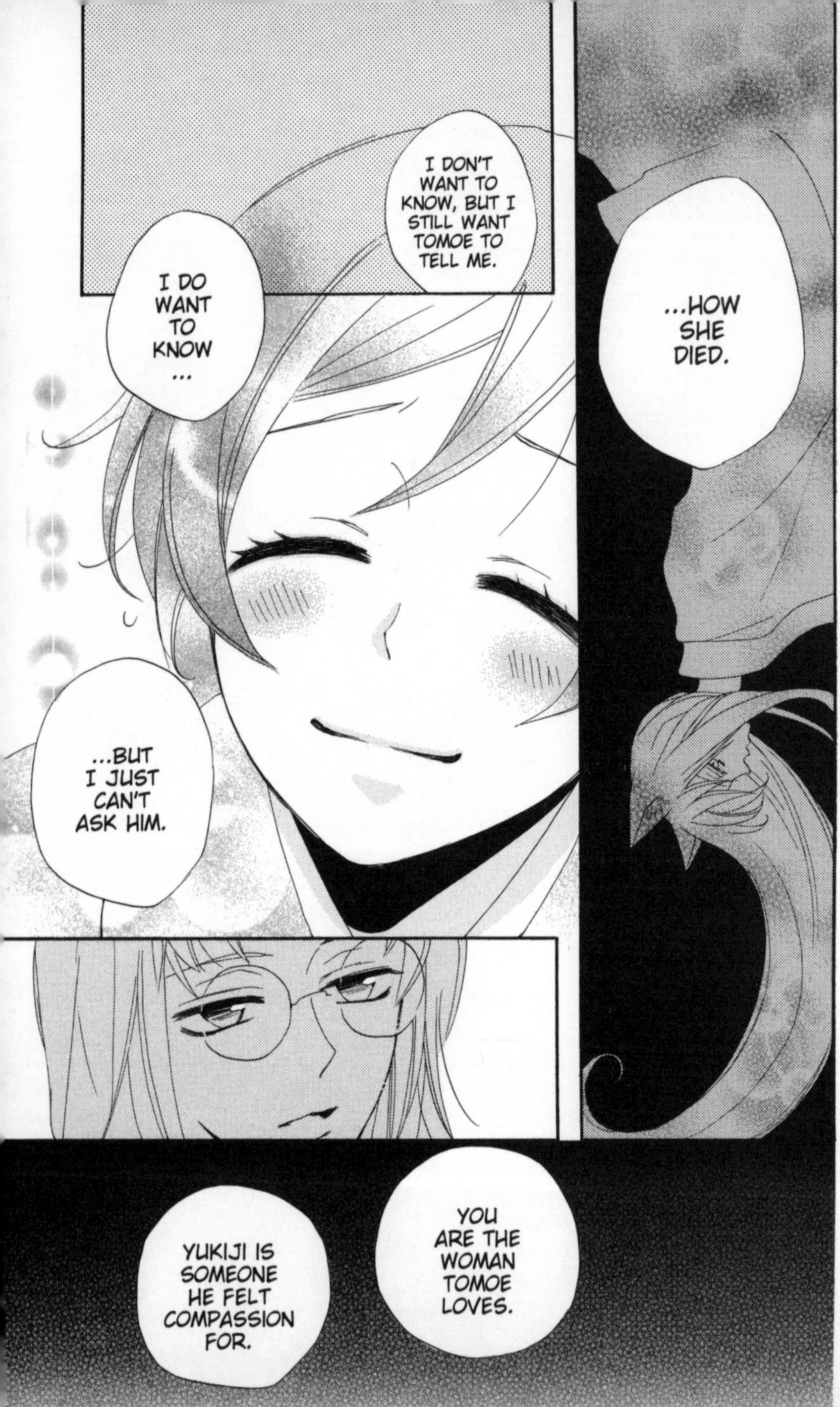
...HOW SHE DIED.
I DON'T WANT TO KNOW, BUT I STILL WANT TOMOE TO TELL ME.
I DO WANT TO KNOW...
...BUT I JUST CAN'T ASK HIM.
YOU ARE THE WOMAN TOMOE LOVES.
YUKIJI IS SOMEONE HE FELT COMPASSION FOR.

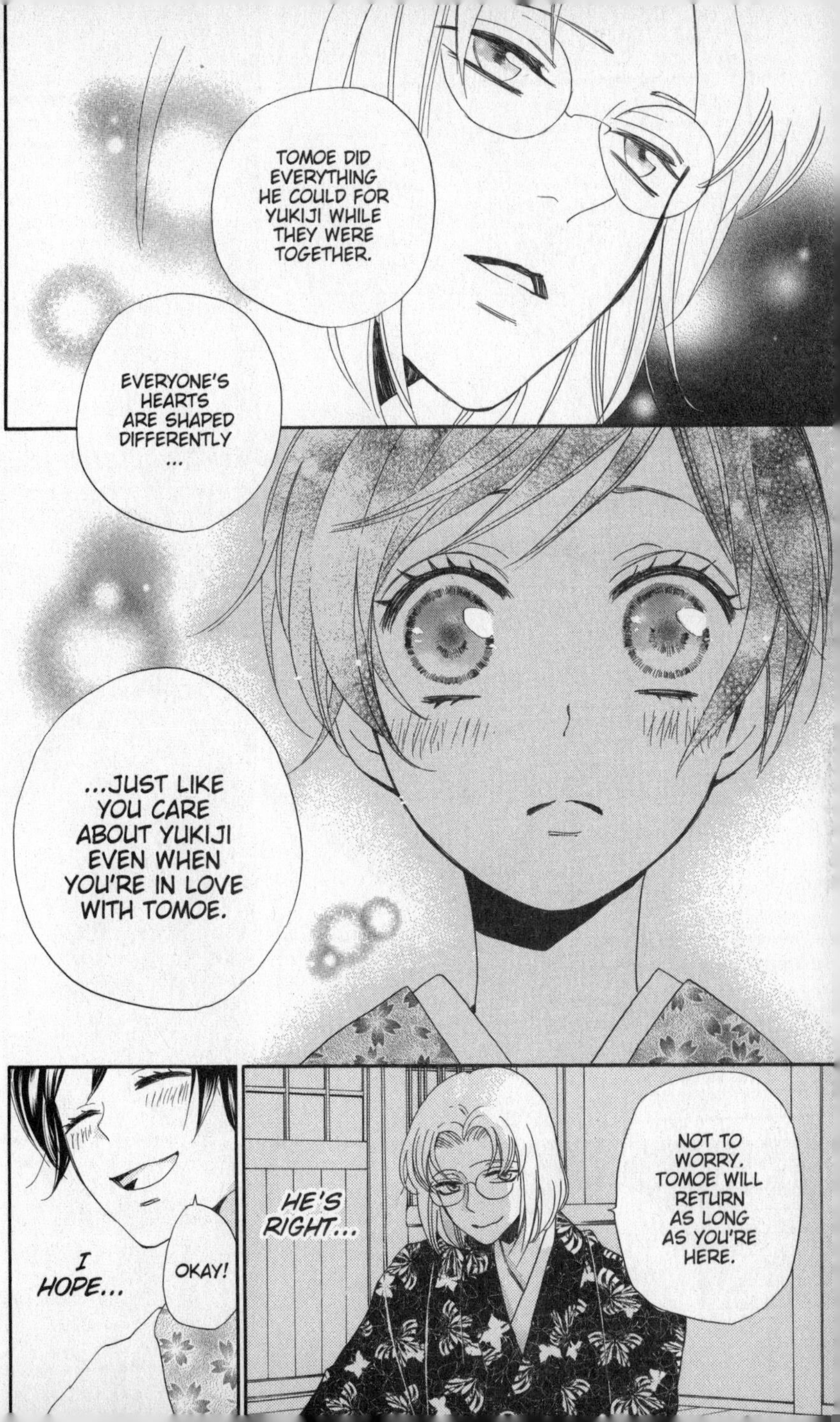
TOMOE DID EVERYTHING HE COULD FOR YUKIJI WHILE THEY WERE TOGETHER.
EVERYONE'S HEARTS ARE SHAPED DIFFERENTLY ...
...JUST LIKE YOU CARE ABOUT YUKIJI EVEN WHEN YOU'RE IN LOVE WITH TOMOE.
NOT TO WORRY. TOMOE WILL RETURN AS LONG AS YOU'RE HERE.
HE'S RIGHT...
OKAY!
I HOPE...

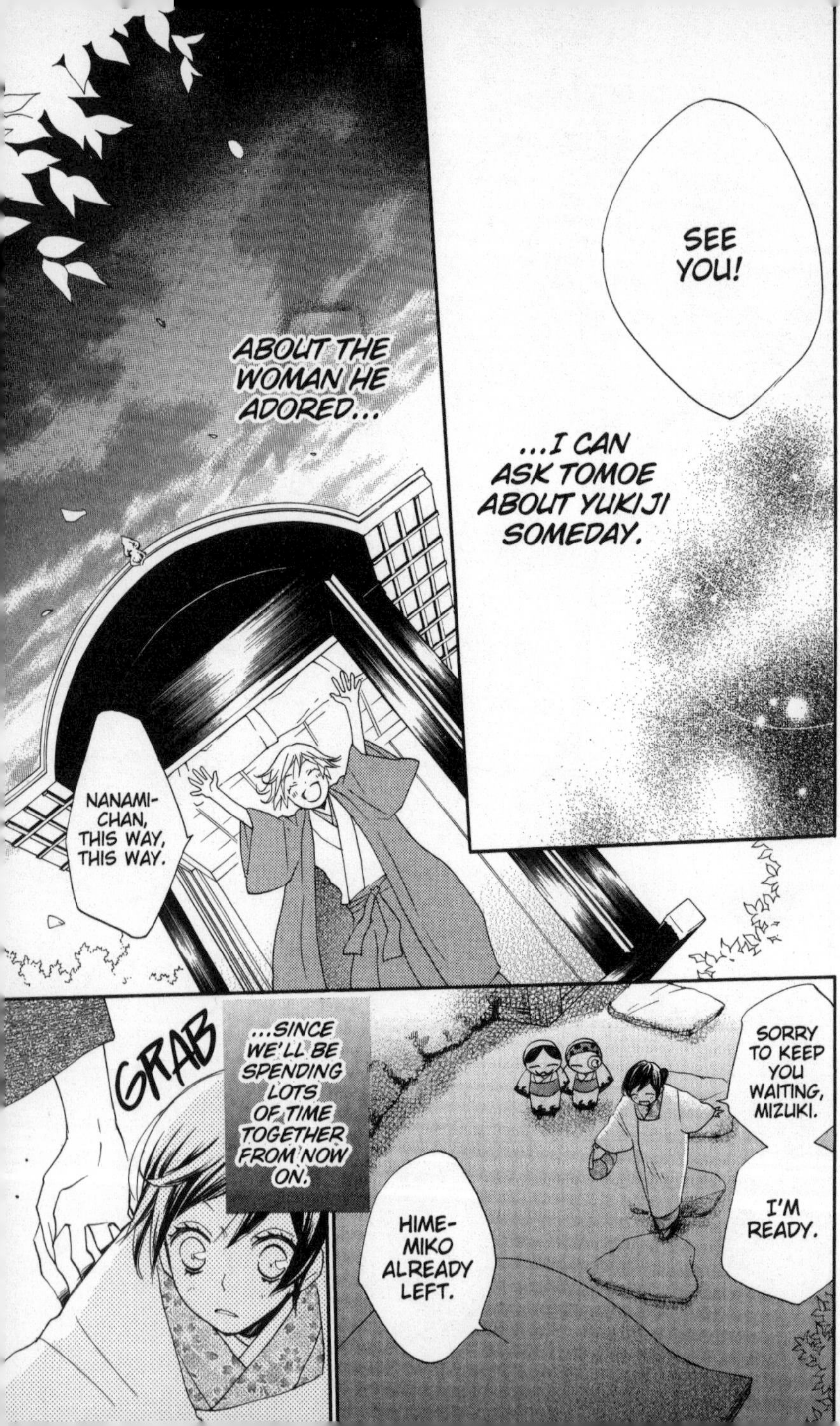
SEE YOU!
...I CAN ASK TOMOE ABOUT YUKIJI SOMEDAY.
ABOUT THE WOMAN HE ADORED...
NANAMI-CHAN, THIS WAY, THIS WAY.
SORRY TO KEEP YOU WAITING, MIZUKI.
I'M READY.
HIME-MIKO ALREADY LEFT.
...SINCE WE'LL BE SPENDING LOTS OF TIME TOGETHER FROM NOW ON.
GRAB

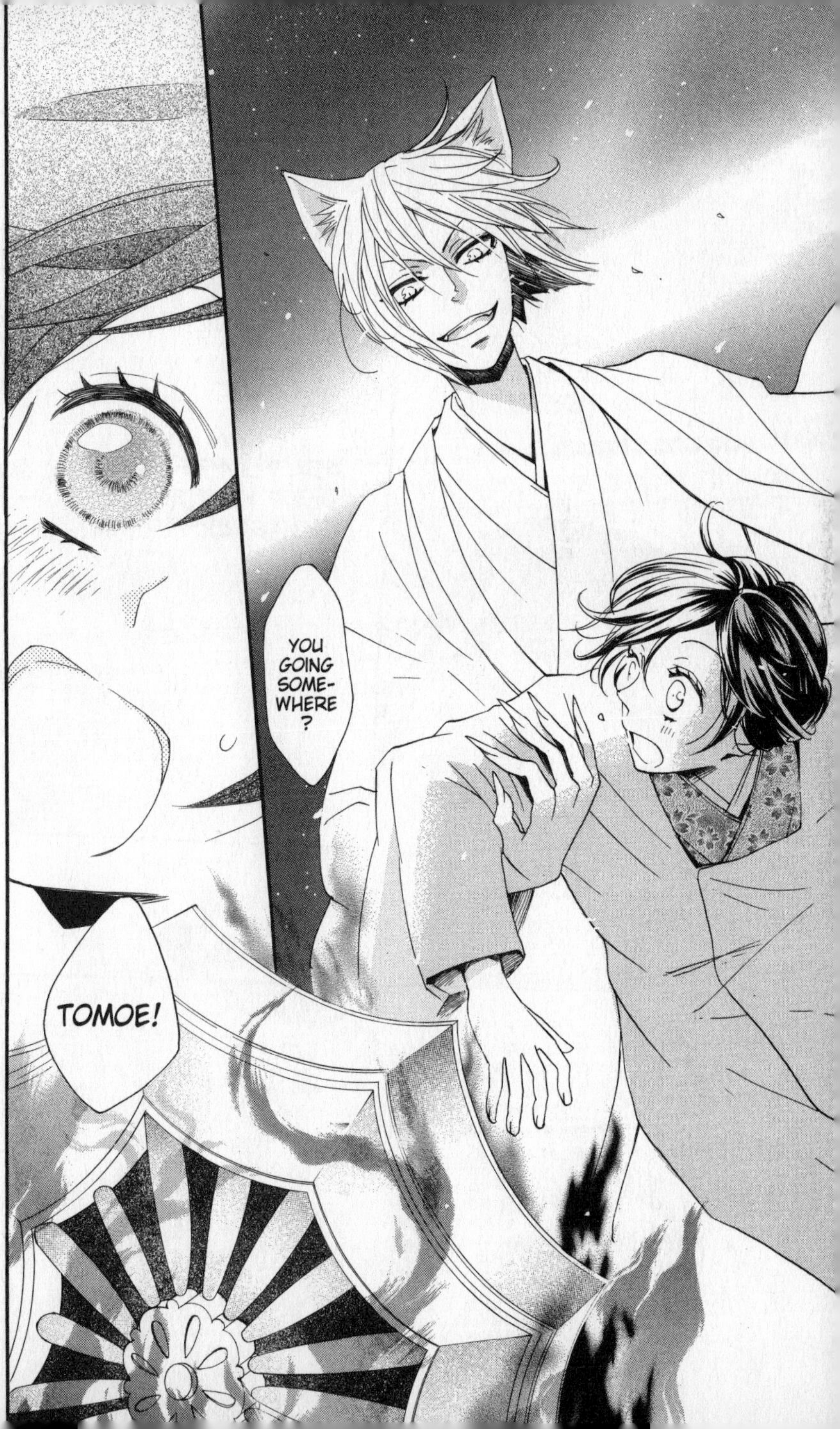
YOU GOING SOME-WHERE?
TOMOE!

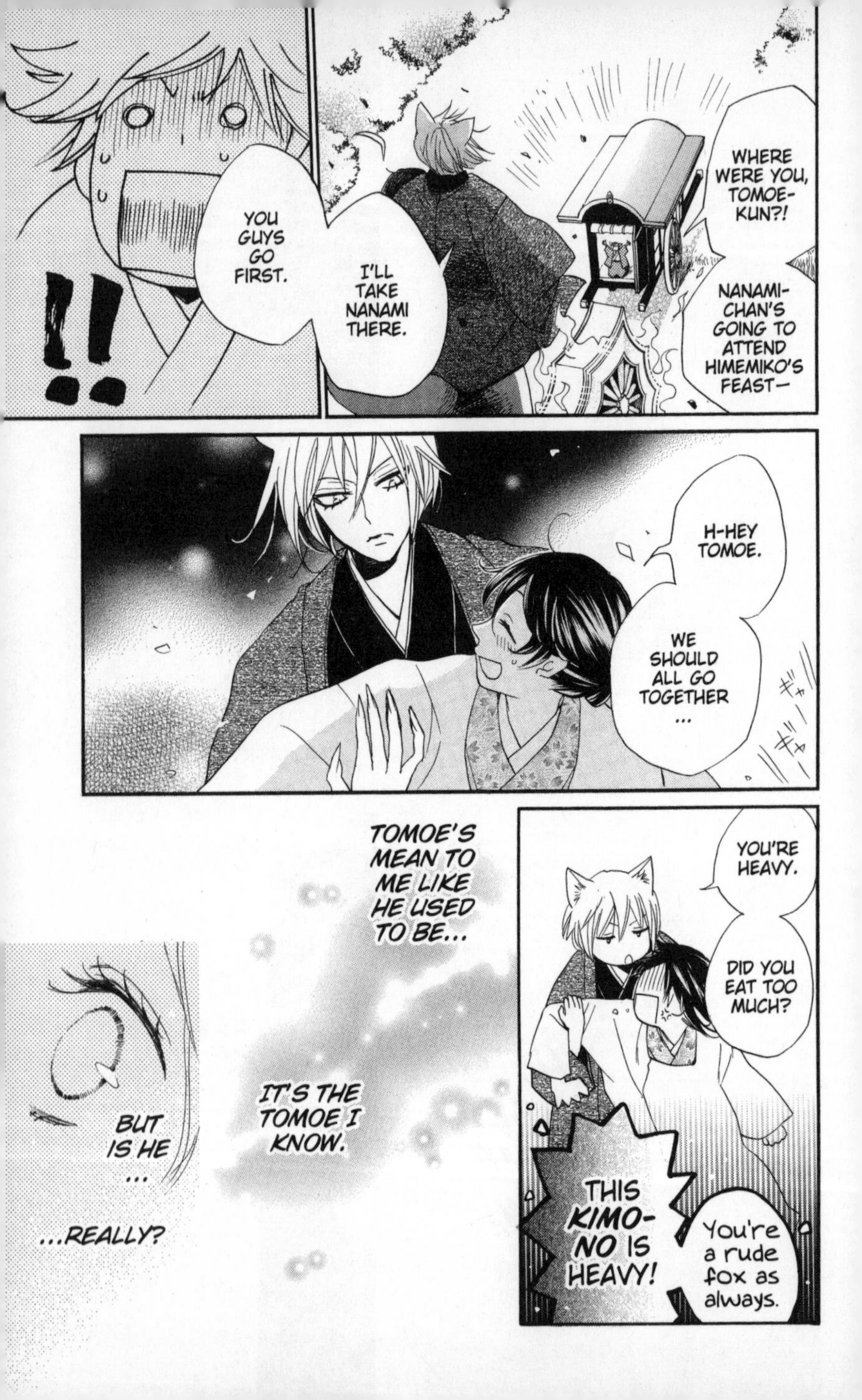
WHERE WERE YOU, TOMOE-KUN?!
NANAMI-CHAN'S GOING TO ATTEND HIMEMIKO'S FEAST—
YOU GUYS GO FIRST.
I'LL TAKE NANAMI THERE.
!!
H-HEY TOMOE.
WE SHOULD ALL GO TOGETHER ...
ギャー ギャー
YOU'RE HEAVY.
DID YOU EAT TOO MUCH?
You're a rude fox as always.
THIS KIMONO IS HEAVY!
TOMOE'S MEAN TO ME LIKE HE USED TO BE...
IT'S THE TOMOE I KNOW.
BUT IS HE ...
...REALLY?

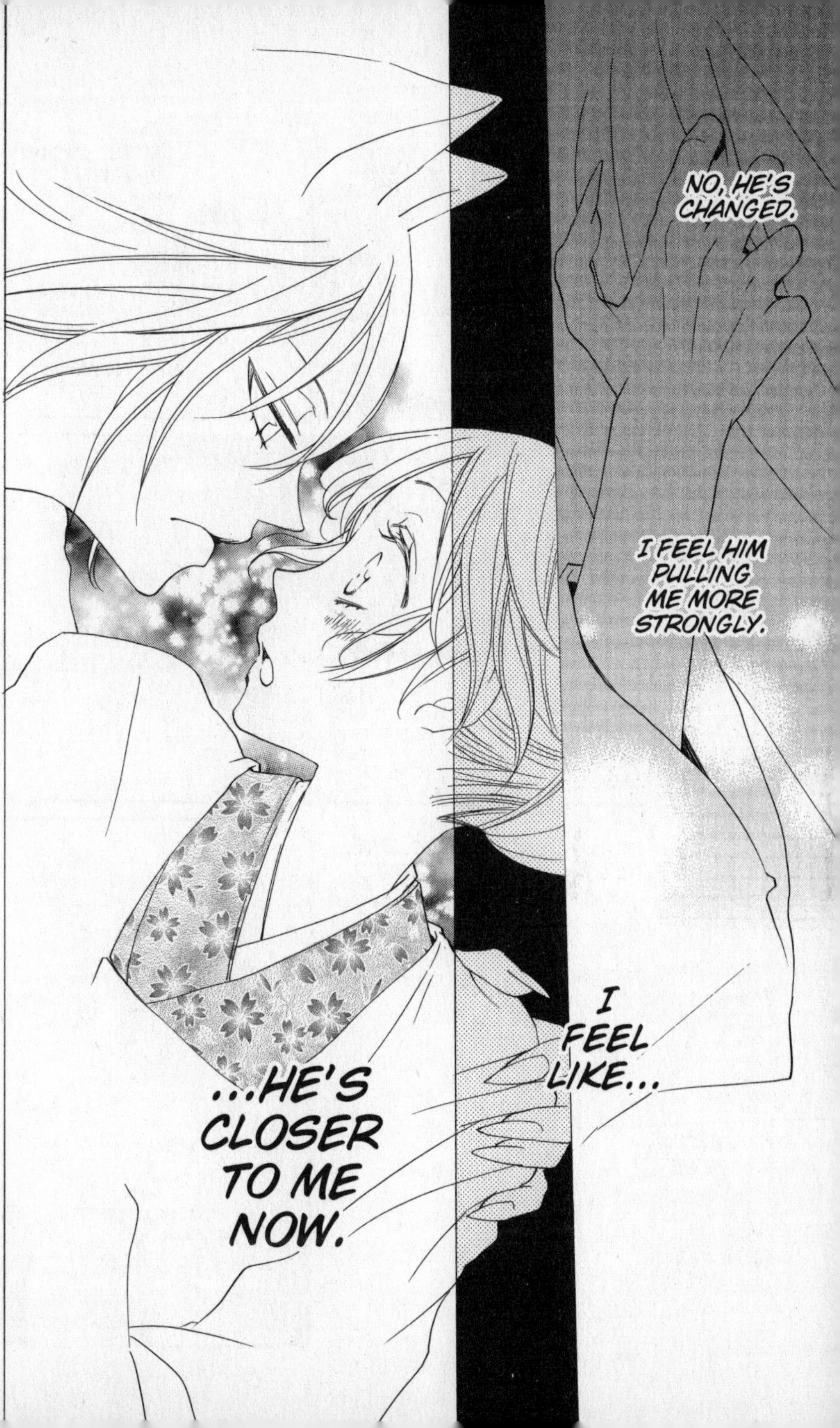
NO, HE'S CHANGED.
I FEEL HIM PULLING ME MORE STRONGLY.
I FEEL LIKE...
...HE'S CLOSER TO ME NOW.

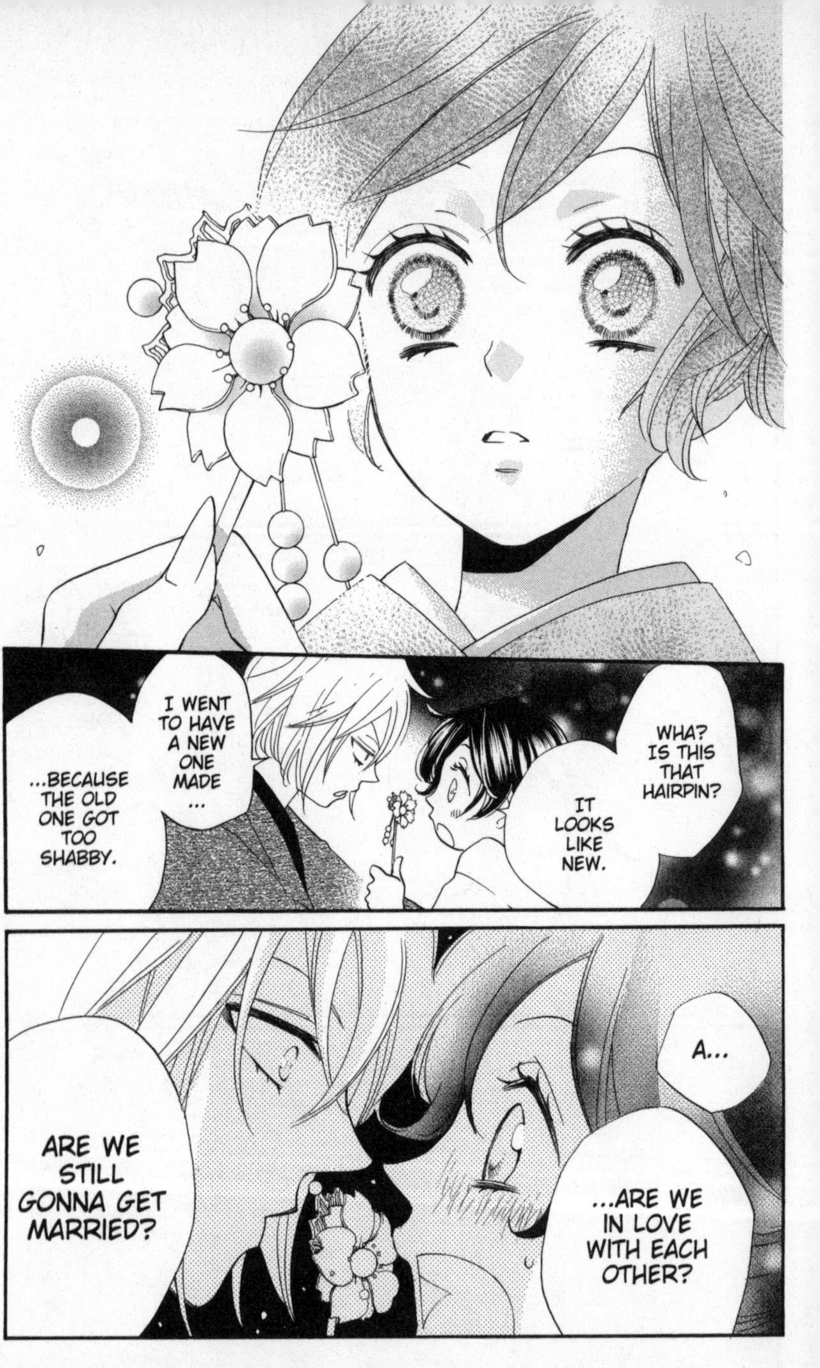
WHA? IS THIS THAT HAIRPIN?
IT LOOKS LIKE NEW.
I WENT TO HAVE A NEW ONE MADE ...
...BECAUSE THE OLD ONE GOT TOO SHABBY.
A...
...ARE WE IN LOVE WITH EACH OTHER?
ARE WE STILL GONNA GET MARRIED?

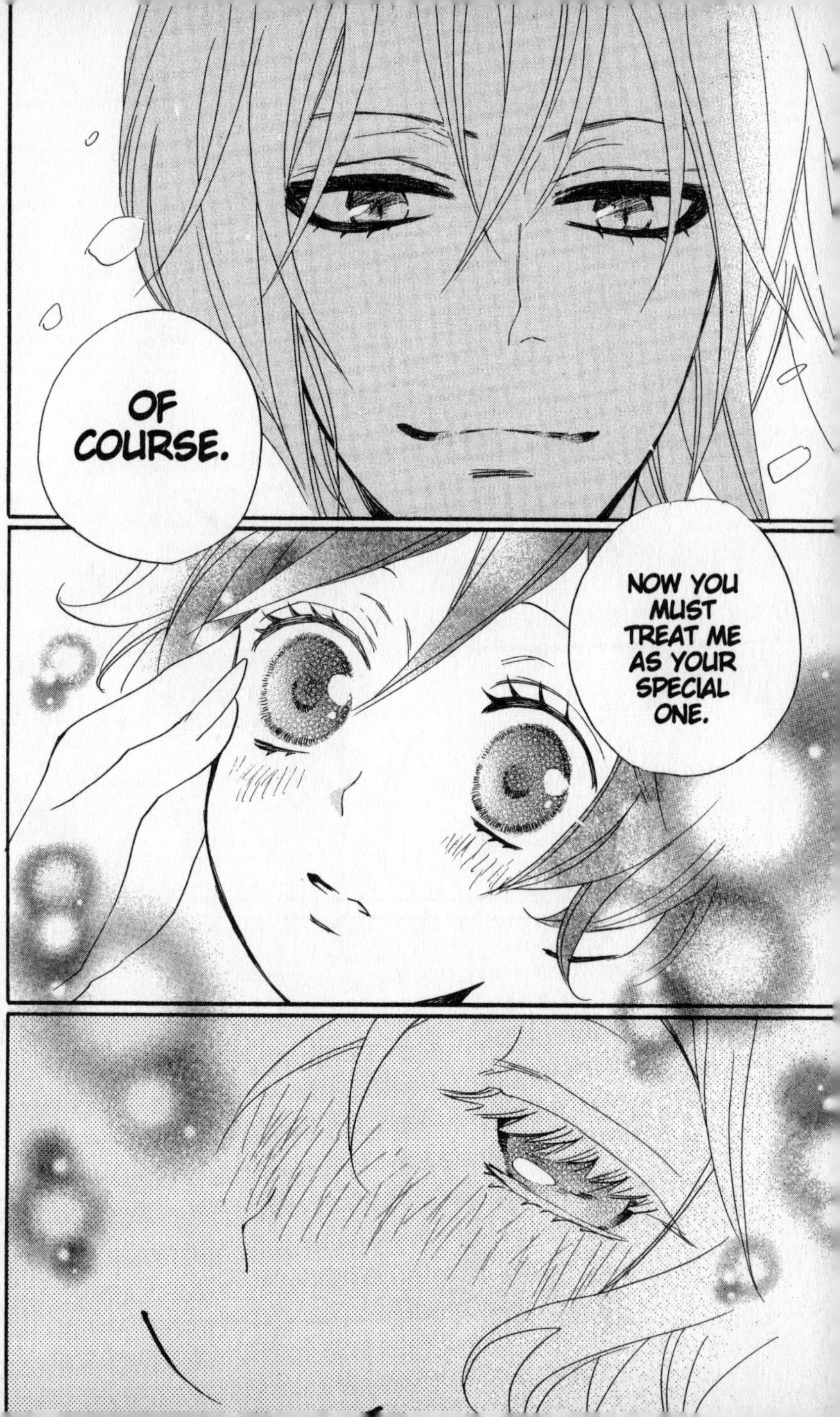
OF COURSE.
NOW YOU MUST TREAT ME AS YOUR SPECIAL ONE.

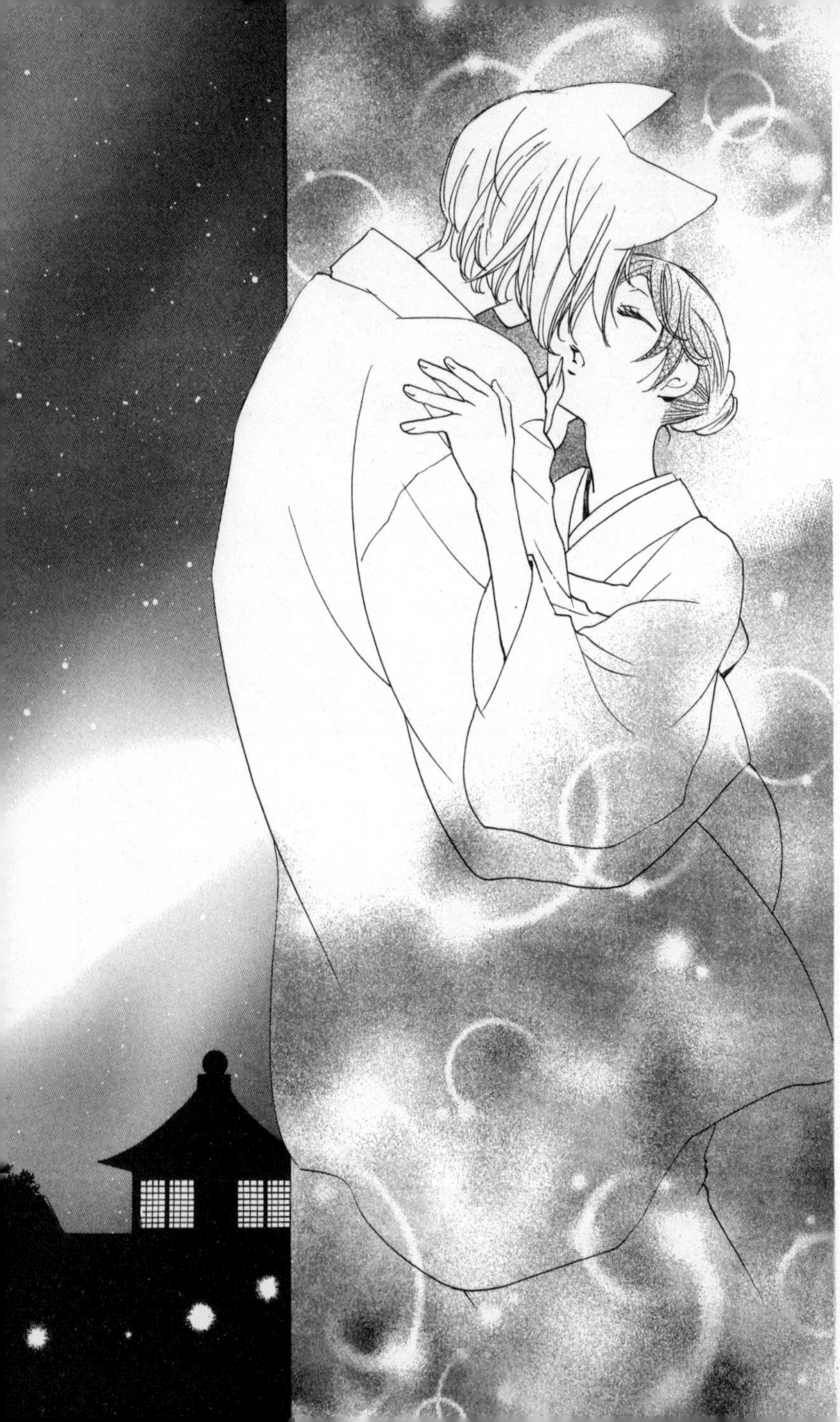

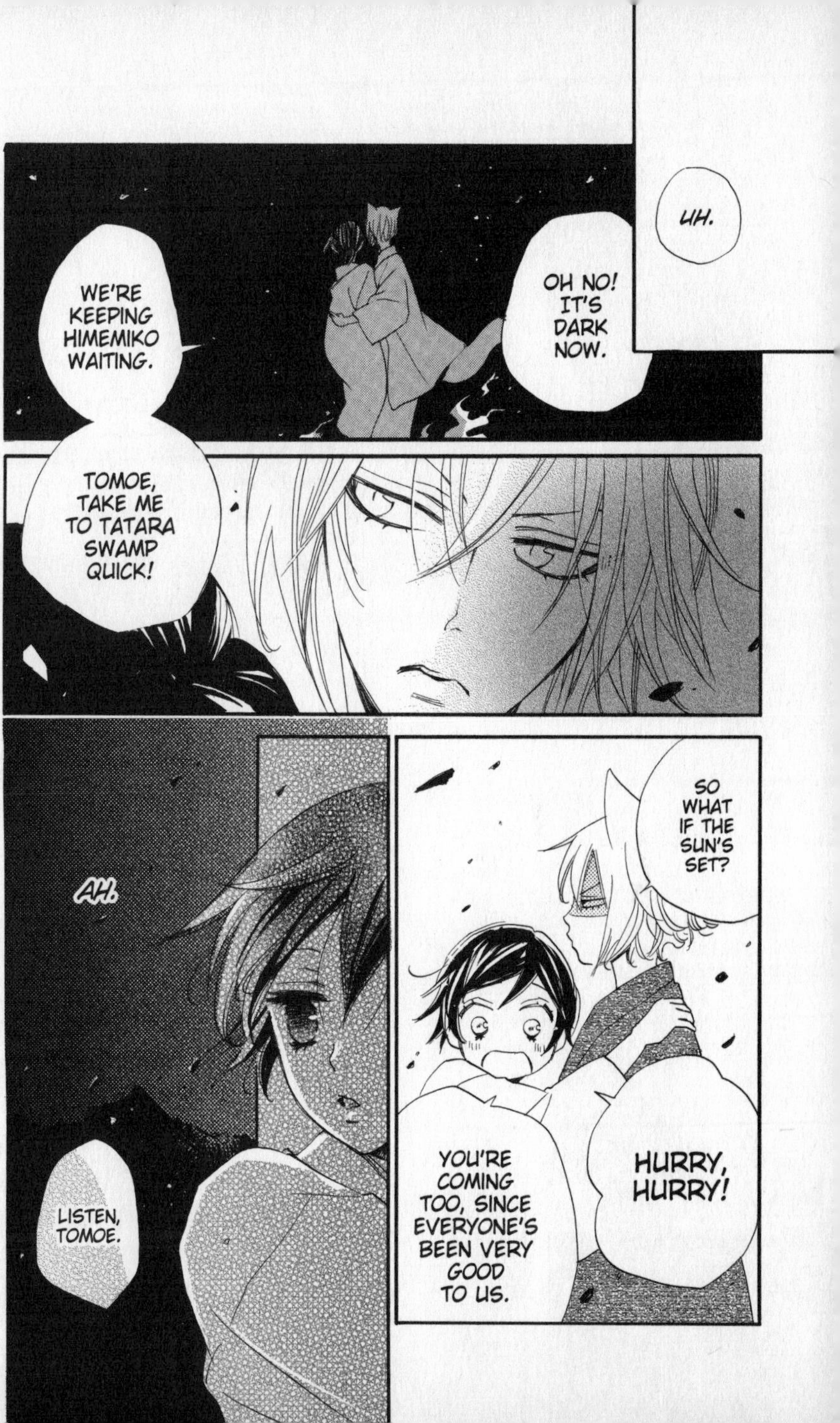
UH.
OH NO! IT'S DARK NOW.
WE'RE KEEPING HIMEMIKO WAITING.
TOMOE, TAKE ME TO TATARA SWAMP QUICK!
SO WHAT IF THE SUN'S SET?
HURRY, HURRY!
YOU'RE COMING TOO, SINCE EVERYONE'S BEEN VERY GOOD TO US.
AH.
LISTEN, TOMOE.

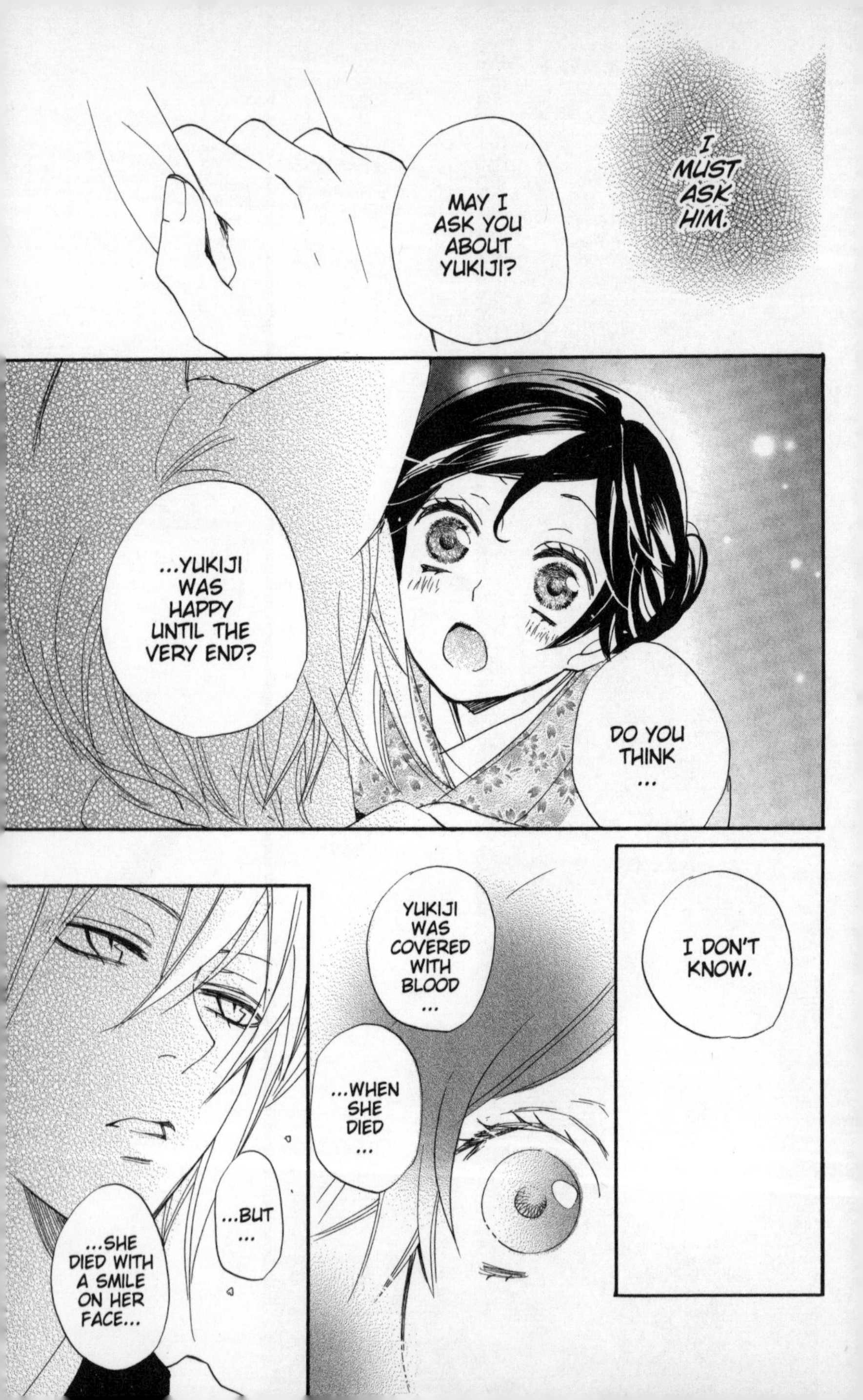
I MUST ASK HIM.
MAY I ASK YOU ABOUT YUKIJI?
DO YOU THINK ...
...YUKIJI WAS HAPPY UNTIL THE VERY END?
I DON'T KNOW.
YUKIJI WAS COVERED WITH BLOOD ...
...WHEN SHE DIED ...
...BUT ...
...SHE DIED WITH A SMILE ON HER FACE...

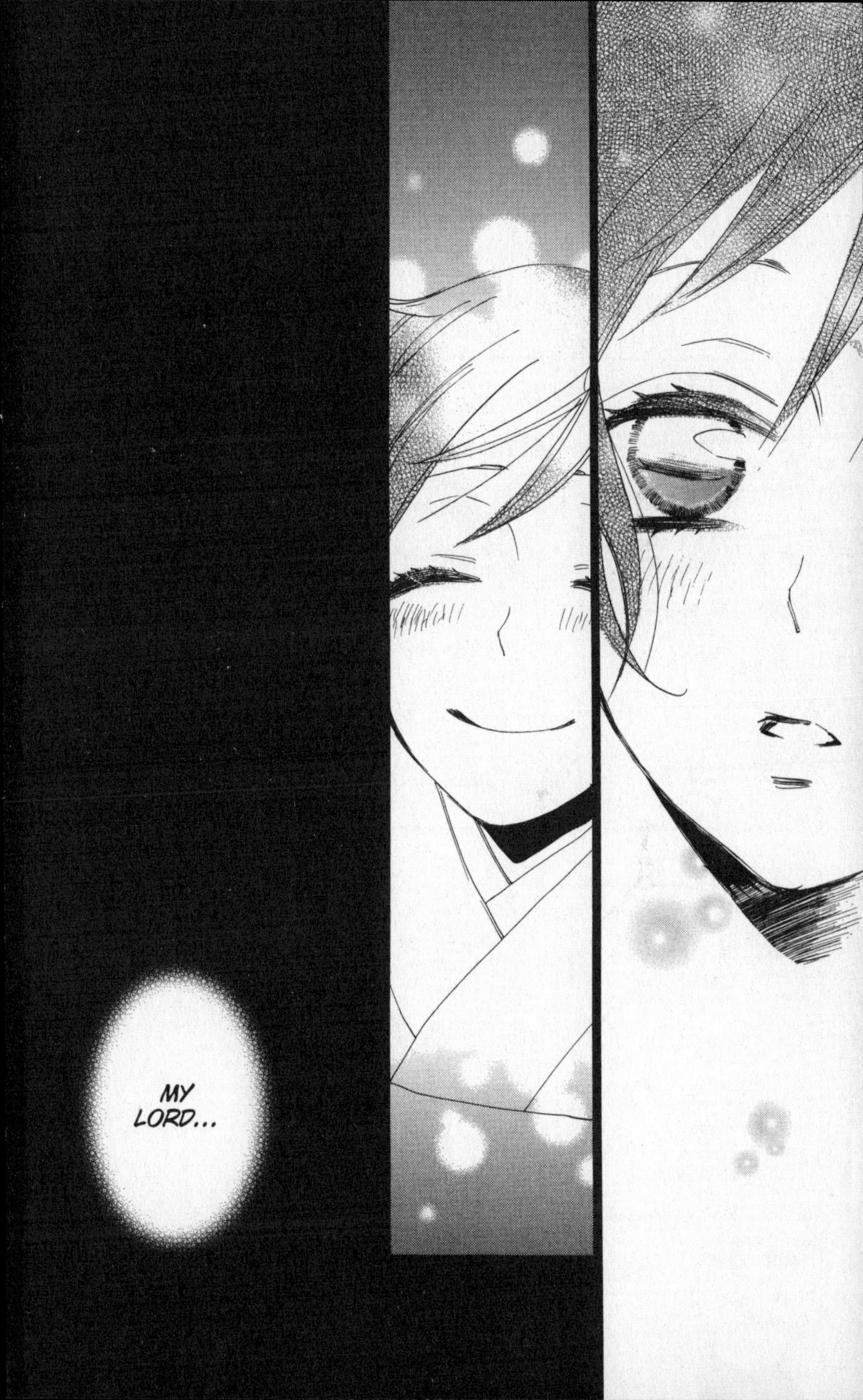
MY LORD...

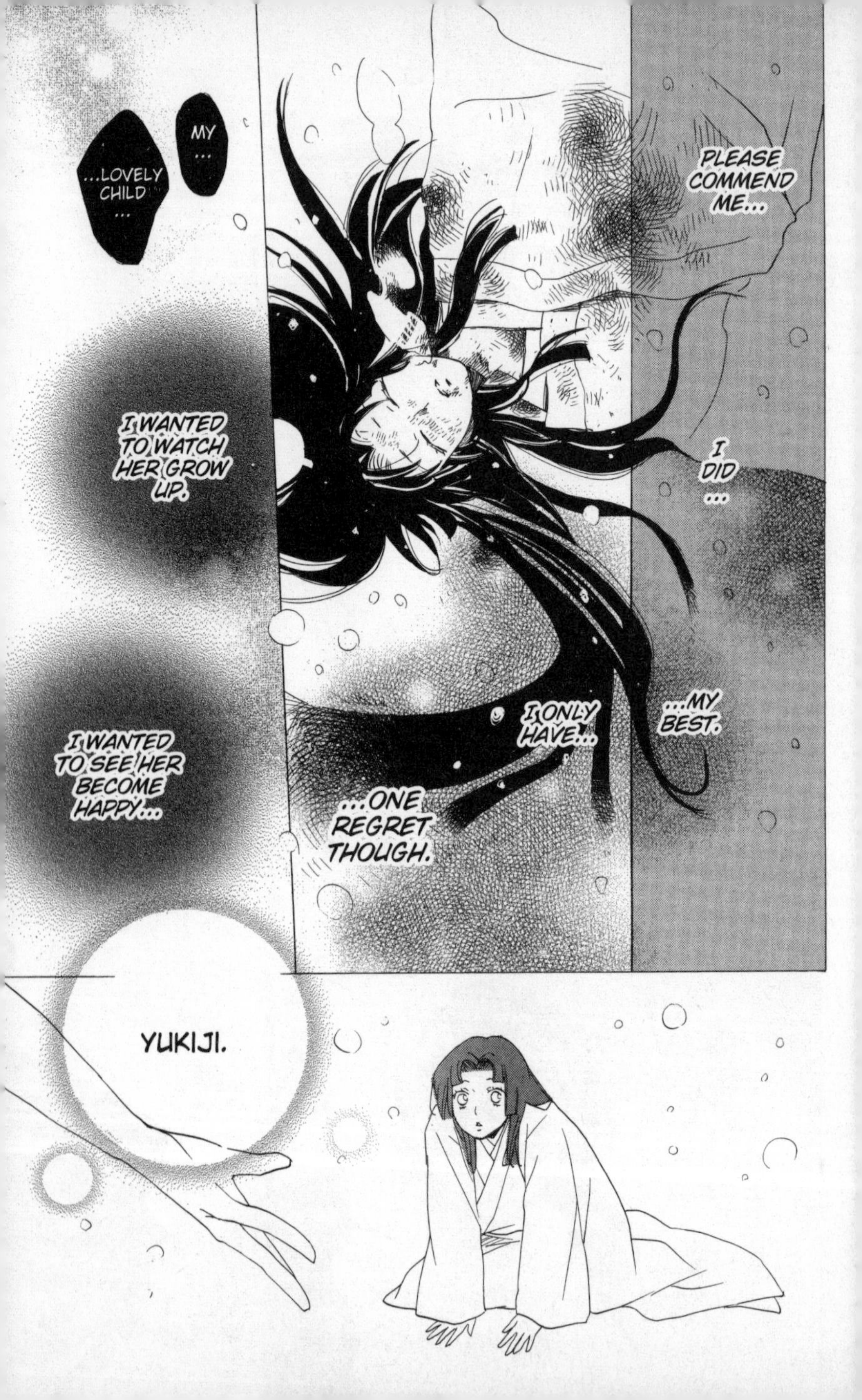
PLEASE COMMEND ME...
I DID...
...MY BEST.
I ONLY HAVE...
...ONE REGRET THOUGH.
MY...
...LOVELY CHILD...
I WANTED TO WATCH HER GROW UP.
I WANTED TO SEE HER BECOME HAPPY...
YUKIJI.

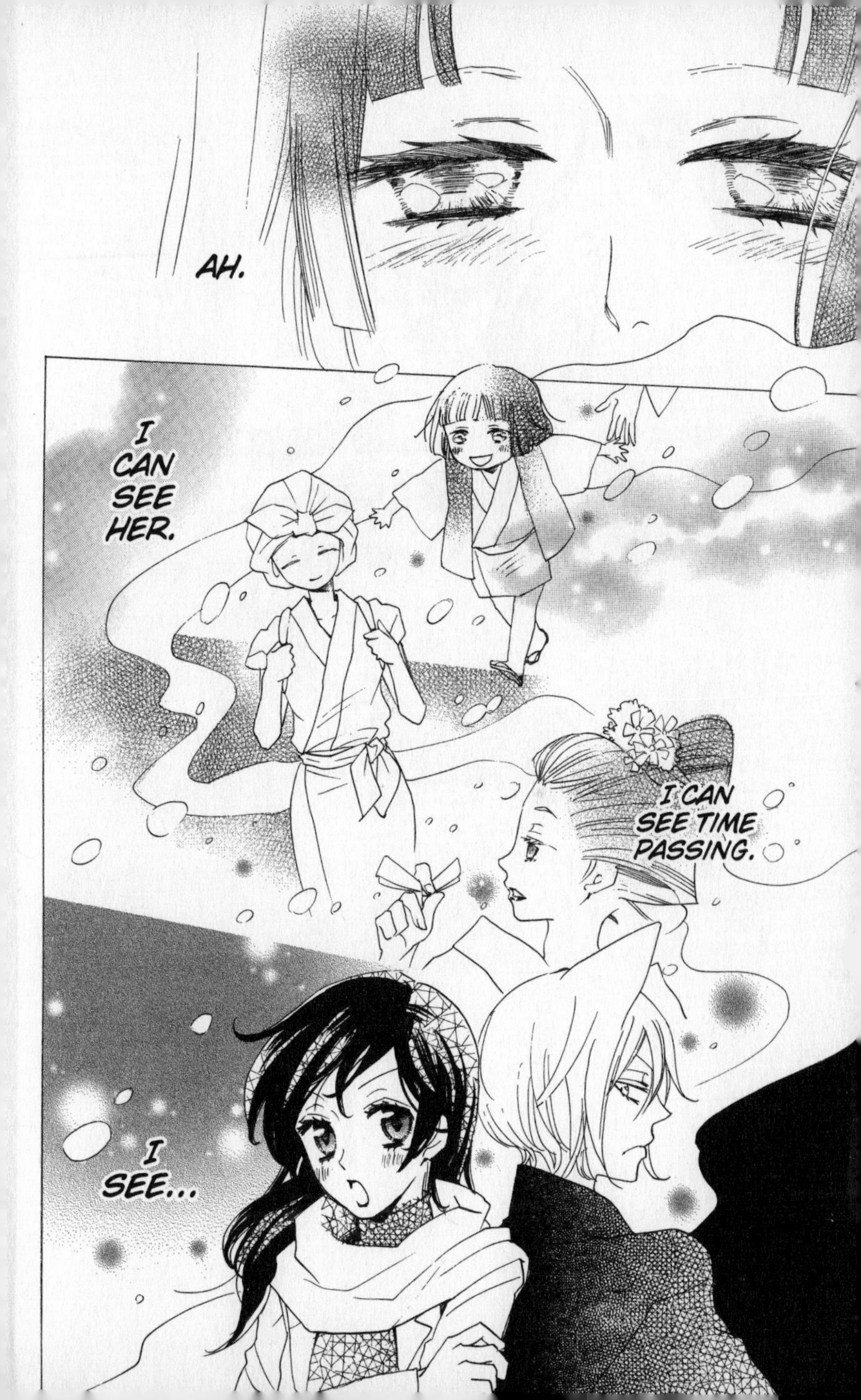
AH.
I CAN SEE HER.
I CAN SEE TIME PASSING.
I SEE...

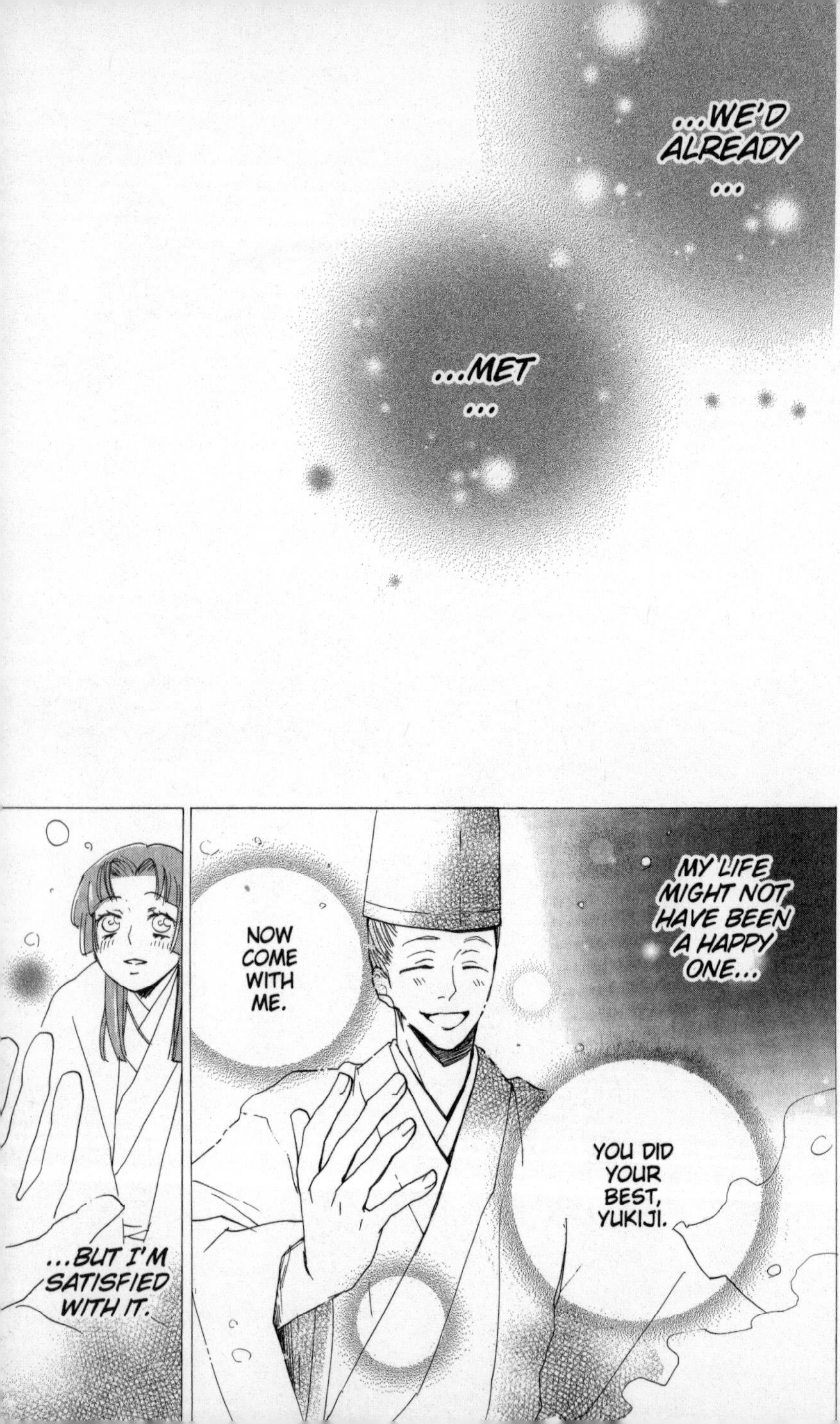
...WE'D ALREADY ...
...MET ...
MY LIFE MIGHT NOT HAVE BEEN A HAPPY ONE...
NOW COME WITH ME.
YOU DID YOUR BEST, YUKIJI.
...BUT I'M SATISFIED WITH IT.

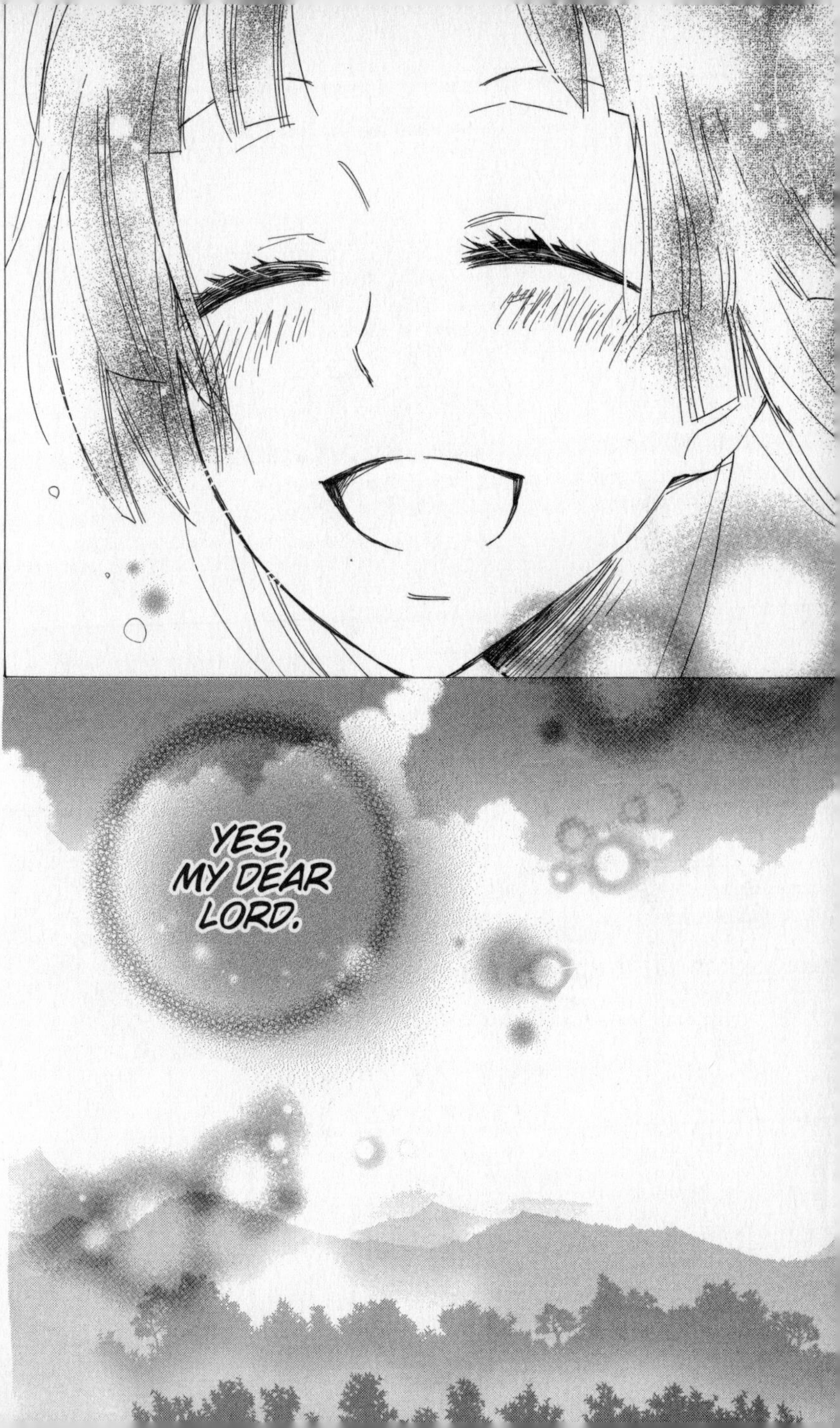
YES, MY DEAR LORD.

The Otherworld

Ayakashi is an archaic term for yokai.

Kami are Shinto deities or spirits. The word can be used for a range of creatures, from nature spirits to strong and dangerous gods.

Onibi-warashi are like will-o'-the-wisps.

Shinshi are birds, beasts, insects or fish that have a special relationship with a kami.

Tengu are a type of yokai. They are sometimes associated with excess pride.

Tochigami (or *jinushigami*) are deities of a specific area of land.

Yokai are demons, monsters or goblins.

Honorifics

-chan is a diminutive most often used with babies, children or teenage girls.

-dono roughly means "my lord," although not in the aristocratic sense.

-kun is used by persons of superior rank to their juniors. It can sometimes have a familiar connotation.

-san is a standard honorific similar to Mr., Mrs., Miss, or Ms.

-sama is used with people of much higher rank.

Notes

Page 53, sidebar: Yoriyori
Yoriyori are fried bread twists and are based on a Chinese pastry called *mahua*.

Page 99, panel 5: Hiiragi
Hiiragi trees (*Osmanthus heterophyllus*) are thought to ward off evil. Planting hiiragi in the northeast of your garden and *nanten* (*Nandina domestica*) in the southwest is believed to protect the house from misfortune.

Page 101, panel 2: Ryu-oh
Literally "dragon king."

Julietta Suzuki's debut manga *Hoshi ni Naru Hi* (The Day One Becomes a Star) appeared in the 2004 *Hana to Yume Plus*. Her other books include *Akuma to Dolce* (The Devil and Sweets) and *Karakuri Odette*. Born in December in Fukuoka Prefecture, she enjoys having movies play in the background while she works on her manga.

KAMISAMA KISS
VOL. 17
Shojo Beat Edition

STORY AND ART BY
Julietta Suzuki

English Translation & Adaptation/Tomo Kimura
Touch-up Art & Lettering/Joanna Estep
Design/Yukiko Whitley
Editor/Pancha Diaz

KAMISAMA HAJIMEMASHITA by Julietta Suzuki
© Julietta Suzuki 2014
All rights reserved.
First published in Japan in 2014 by HAKUSENSHA, Inc., Tokyo.
English language translation rights arranged with
HAKUSENSHA, Inc., Tokyo.

Printed in the U.S.A.

Published by VIZ Media, LLC
P.O. Box 77010
San Francisco, CA 94107

10 9 8 7 6 5 4 3 2
First printing, March 2015
Second printing, December 2015

www.viz.com   www.shojobeat.com

PARENTAL ADVISORY
KAMISAMA KISS is rated T for Teen and
is recommended for ages 13 and up. This
volume contains fantasy violence.
ratings.viz.com

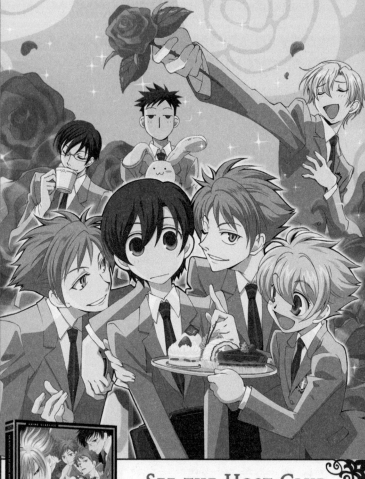

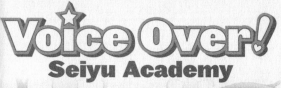

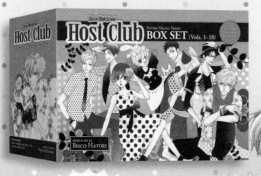

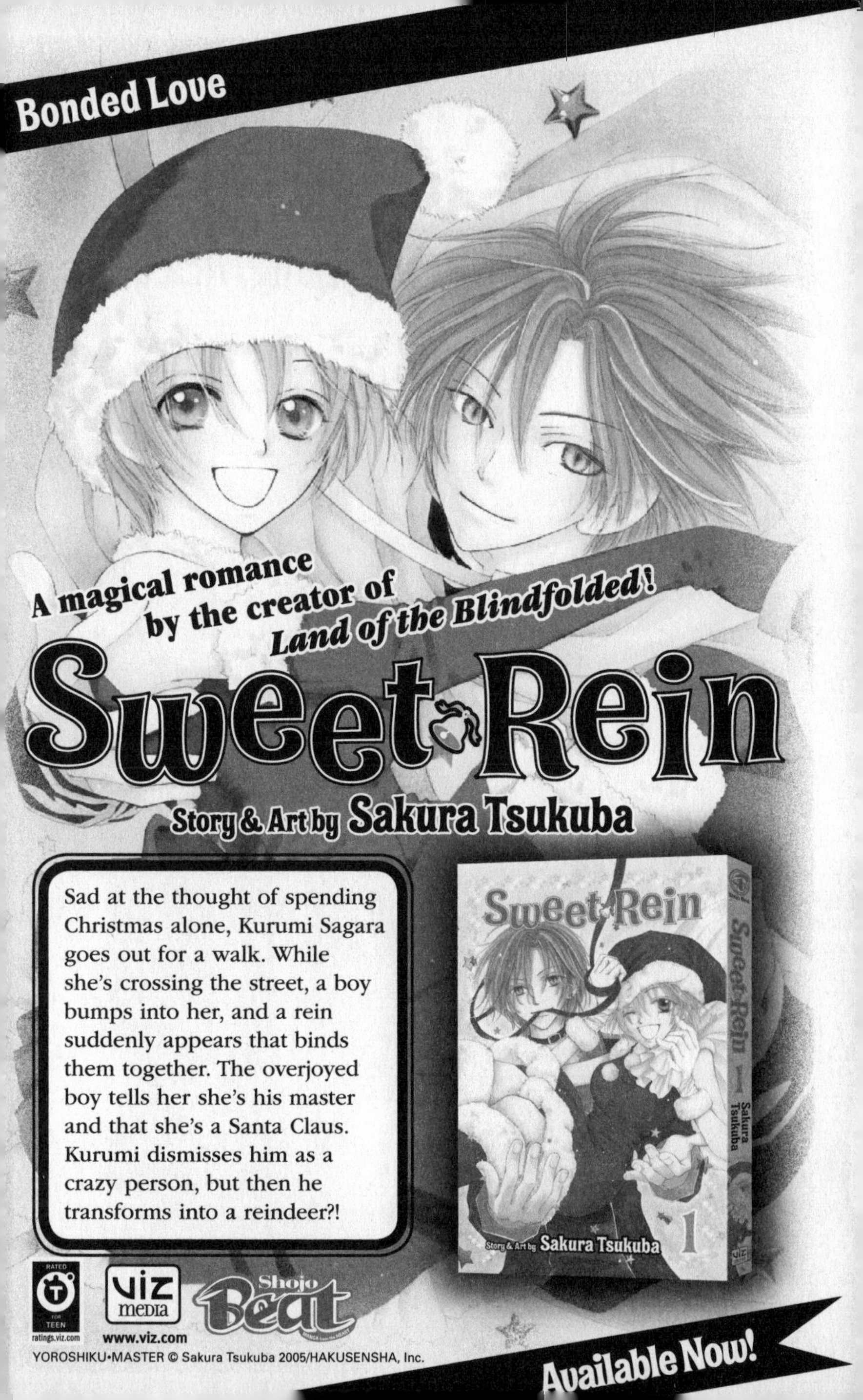

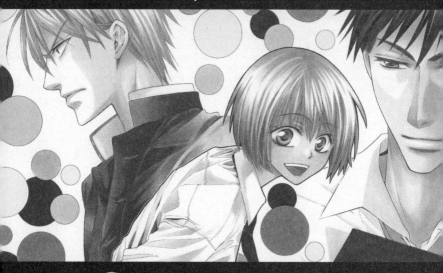
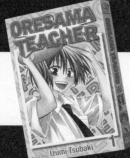

This is the last page.

In keeping with the original Japanese comic format, this book reads from right to left—so action, sound effects, and word balloons are completely reversed. This preserves the orientation of the original artwork—plus, it's fun! Check out the diagram shown here to get the hang of things, and then turn to the other side of the book to get started!